ARTHURIAN ARCHIVES

XXIII

Italian Literature
Volume IV

Il Tristano Riccardiano
MS 1729 (Parodi's siglum 'F')

Biblioteca Riccardiana, Firenze, Ricc. 1729, fol. 93r (old fol. 91r) *Tristano*, example of hand, *su concessione del Ministero della Cultura* (by permission of the Ministry of Culture).

Italian Literature

Volume IV

Il Tristano Riccardiano
MS 1729 (Parodi's siglum 'F')

Edited and Translated by
Gloria Allaire

D. S. BREWER

Editorial matter © Gloria Allaire 2024

All Rights Reserved. Except as permitted under current legislation no part of this work may be photocopied, stored in a retrieval system, published, performed in public, adapted, broadcast, transmitted, recorded or reproduced in any form or by any means, without the prior permission of the copyright owner

First published 2024
D. S. Brewer, Cambridge

ISBN 978-1-84384-716-8

D. S. Brewer is an imprint of Boydell & Brewer Ltd
PO Box 9, Woodbridge, Suffolk IP12 3DF, UK
and of Boydell & Brewer Inc.
668 Mt Hope Avenue, Rochester, NY 14620–2731, USA
website: www.boydellandbrewer.com

A catalogue record of this publication is available
from the British Library

The publisher has no responsibility for the continued existence or accuracy of URLs for external or third-party internet websites referred to in this book, and does not guarantee that any content on such websites is, or will remain, accurate or appropriate

This publication is printed on acid-free paper

With gratitude to all my teachers

CONTENTS

Preface	ix
Acknowledgements	xi
List of Abbreviations	xiii
Introduction	xv
Note on Transcription and Translation	xxxvii
Il Tristano Riccardiano (Parodi's siglum 'F')	1
Bibliography	165
Index	171

PREFACE

The Arthurian hero Tristan enjoyed great popularity in medieval Italy as attested by various translations from the French prose *Roman de Tristan*. Two of these adaptations are preserved in the Biblioteca Riccardiana in Florence. The better known *Tristano Riccardiano*, MS 2543, has been edited, re-edited and translated. However, the fourteenth-century MS 1729 has suffered almost complete critical neglect, perhaps due to its complex amalgam of regional dialects and its idiosyncratic script.

Shorter than its sister, this other Riccardian *Tristan* demonstrates important links among extant *Tristan*s in Italy. Most of the material (Tristan's birth, early adventures and love affair with Yseut) follows that of MS 2543, with certain noteworthy variants. The famous three-day tournament conserved in the *Tristano Panciatichiano* and that constitutes the bulk of the *Tristano Corsiniano* does not appear, probably due to a faulty model. From a different model, MS 1729 contains the final episodes (Tristan's fatal wounding, the lovers' deaths, lamentation at Arthur's court) that do not appear in MS 2543.

This volume includes the previously unedited original text accompanied by a facing-page English translation, bibliography and index.

ACKNOWLEDGEMENTS

I wish to thank Norris J. Lacy, General Editor of the Arthurian Archives series published by D. S. Brewer, for his interest and approval of this project. With deep appreciation I acknowledge Christopher Kleinhenz, my long-term mentor who many years ago invited my participation in the Italian Literature branch of this series in order to produce the *Tristano Panciatichiano* edition. Once again, his valuable suggestions and useful comments have helped to improve and enhance the present volume. For assistance in preparing the linguistic analysis of Ricc. MS 1729, I am indebted to Leslie Zarker Morgan for sharing her extensive knowledge of Franco-Italian and medieval Italian dialectology. The personnel of the William T. Young Library's Circulation and Interlibrary Loan Departments at the University of Kentucky were most helpful in obtaining numerous reference sources. For printing and technical services, I thank the Lexington Public Library, North Side Branch. I owe an enormous debt of gratitude to Dott. Fulvio Silvano Stacchetti, then director of the Biblioteca Riccardiana, and his staff for once again allowing me access to their collection and extending me every courtesy while I was transcribing and verifying the 'other' *Tristano Riccardiano*. Finally, special thanks to Caroline Palmer and her capable staff at Boydell and Brewer for their patience, generosity and expertise in bringing forth yet another Italian *Tristan*.

ABBREVIATIONS

Modern critical editions are cited with their page numbers (not paragraph numbers).

Briquet   Briquet, C. M. *Les filigranes: Dictionnaire historique des marques du papier des leur apparition vèrs 1292 jusqu'en 1600: A Facsimile of the 1907 Edition* [...]. Ed. Allan Stevenson. 4 vols. Amsterdam, 1968.

Corti   Corti, Maria. 'Emiliano e Veneto nella tradizione manoscritta del *Fiore di virtù*'. *Studi di filologia italiana* 18 (1960), 29–68.

Infurna   *La Inchiesta del San Gradale. Volgarizzamento toscano della 'Queste del Saint Graal'*. Ed. Marco Infurna. Biblioteca della Rivista di Storia e Letteratura Religiosa, Testi e documenti 14. Florence, 1993.

Lös.   Löseth, Elhert. *Le roman en prose de Tristan, le roman de Palamède et la compilation de Rusticien de Pise: Analyse critique d'après les manuscrits de Paris*. Bibliothèque de l'École des Hautes Études, Sciences Historiques et Philologiques 82. Paris, 1891; rpt. Burt Franklin: Research & Source Works Series 426, Essays in Literature & Criticism 49. New York, 1970.

Rohlfs   Rohlfs, Gerhard. *Grammatica storica della lingua italiana e dei suoi dialetti: Fonetica*. Trans. Salvatore Persichino. Piccola Biblioteca Einaudi 148. Vol. 1. Turin, 1966; and *Grammatica storica della lingua italiana e dei suoi dialetti: Morfologia*. Trans. Temistocle Franceschi. Piccola Biblioteca Einaudi 149. Vol. 2. Turin, 1968.

TP   *Italian Literature I. Il Tristano Panciatichiano*. Ed. and trans. Gloria Allaire. Arthurian Archives 8. Cambridge, 2002.

TR   *Italian Literature II. Il Tristano Riccardiano*. Rev. ed. and trans. F. Regina Psaki. Arthurian Archives 12. Cambridge, 2006.

TR-Parodi	*Il Tristano Riccardiano*. Ed. E. G. Parodi. Collezione di opere inedite o rare di scrittori italiani dal XIII al XVI secolo, R. Commissione pe' testi di lingua nelle provincie dell'Emilia 74. Bologna, 1896.
TV	*Il libro di messer Tristano ('Tristano Veneto')*. Ed. Aulo Donadello. Medioevo Veneto. Venice, 1994.
Tav. Rit.	*La Tavola Ritonda o l'Istoria di Tristano: Testo di lingua.* Ed. Filippo-Luigi Polidori. Collezione di opere inedite o rare dei primi tre secoli della lingua [8–9]. 2 vols. Bologna, 1864–6.
West	West, G. D. *French Arthurian Prose Romances: An Index of Proper Names*. University of Toronto Romance Series 35. Toronto, 1978.

INTRODUCTION

THE MANUSCRIPT

This volume presents the first complete transcription of a unique redaction of the prose *Tristan* found in a fourteenth-century miscellany that was copied in a single hand. Like the more famous *Tristano Riccardiano* edited by E. G. Parodi in 1896, this manuscript is preserved in the Biblioteca Riccardiana in Florence. Its modern shelf mark is Ricc. MS 1729. Its former shelf mark N.IV.40 was assigned by Giovanni Lami, the librarian who was responsible for cataloguing the Riccardian collection in the early eighteenth century. An additional unidentified number – '63' – is written in red pencil on the first original front guard leaf. The manuscript contains no notes of possession, dates or marginalia, but on the first of the two original guard leaves, there is an accurate table of contents written in a late fourteenth- or early fifteenth-century Tuscan *mercantesca*.[1] On a front guard leaf that was attached to the codex much later, the contents of the manuscript are printed in a clear book hand. The copyist's name 'Johannes' appears in a rubricated colophon at the end of the *Fior di virtù* section (fol. 63r).[2] His is the text hand for the entire manuscript.

According to library records,[3] on 10 January 1972 the manuscript was restored, disinfected and rebound in white parchment over stiff cardboard to resemble the original Riccardian books; however, there is no title or lettering on the spine or on the new cover. A small, printed paper label with the words 'Biblioteca Riccardiana' and the machine-stamped shelf mark '1729' is glued onto the base of the spine. Another such label appears on the inside front cover, at the top left corner. A late fifteenth-century (?) page was added at the front only, to cover the original two flyleaves. At the time of its modern rebinding, three pages of paper were inserted as additional flyleaves at the front, thus: iii (modern restoration) + i (c. 1500?) + ii (original). At the end are two original pages, left blank, which serve as end papers, followed by another three modern restoration ones, thus: ii + iii. None of the front flyleaves are numbered; the two blank original folios at the end are numbered 189 and 190 in the same *mercantesca* hand as the index on one front guard leaf.

The condition of the manuscript is fairly good, with light staining and foxing throughout. There are no torn pages or patches, no worm holes, no vermin damage or candle wax drippings. For the most part, there is no loss of text.

---

[1] An example of this hand in a commercial letter dated 1383 is reproduced in Anna Chiostrini Mannini, *I Davanzati: mercanti, banchieri, mecenati* (Florence, 1989), p. 32. Another such list – an inventory of books owned by Giovanni di Carlo Strozzi, written in a similar hand and dated 1424 – appears in Florence, Biblioteca Nazionale Centrale, MS Nuovi Acquisti 509.

[2] As identified by Rebecca Balatresi in her thesis, 'I codici 1729–1756 della Biblioteca Riccardiana di Firenze: Descrizione e storia', Tesi di laurea in codicologia, Università degli Studi di Firenze, Facoltà di Lettere e Filosofia, 1996–97, 38, 192.

[3] See Balatresi, 'I codici', 37.

THE CONTENTS OF THE MANUSCRIPT

This manuscript anthology contains five separate textual sections, the first four primarily of a didactic or morally edifying nature. According to the medieval table of contents on the first original flyleaf, these are described as follows:

I)   *Fior di Virtù* (fols 1–66v). This text was a widely-circulated *florilegum* of which seventy-seven manuscripts survive, in various languages. It was probably composed in 'northern or north-central Italy [...] between 1300 and 1323',[4] perhaps by Friar Tommaso who has been identified with Tommaso Gozzadini, a Bolognese notary. The text consists of thirty-six chapters dedicated to the alternating depictions of virtues and vices, allegorically represented by various animals.

II) *Insengniamenti de' savi dottori e di Santo Paolo Apostolo* (Teachings of the Learned Men and of Saint Paul the Apostle) (fols 67r–72v).

III) *Insengniamenti naturali per via da senpri* (moral *exempla* from the world of nature) (fols 73r–80v).

IV) *Il Savio Romano* (The Wise Roman), a sort of conduct book for educating a young boy (fols 81r–85v).[5] Following this text, folios 86–90 were left blank.

V)   The final section is listed simply as *di Tristano* ('about Tristan') (fols 91r–188r).[6]

DATING AND WATERMARKS

In the Introduction to his edition of the *Tristano Riccardiano*, which was based on Ricc. MS 2543, E. G. Parodi unequivocally declared that MS 1729 was copied 'alla fine del sec. XV' (at the end of the fifteenth century).[7] This late date has been echoed by numerous scholars.[8] Radaelli's mid-fifteenth century date is earlier

---

[4]   Paul F. Grendler, *Schooling in Renaissance Italy: Literacy and Learning, 1300–1600*, The Johns Hopkins University, Studies in Historical and Political Science, 107th Series 1 (Baltimore, 1989), p. 278.

[5]   No particular ancient philosopher is referred to, but the rubric's opening 'Entendj filglio' makes it clear that this is for the education of a boy. Text consists of little verses, with initials (at margin, flush left) trimmed with red slashes. This pedagogical text was a 'classic', appearing in print as late as 1481.

[6]   It may seem incongruous to find texts that taught 'good morality' copied alongside 'the adventures of knights and ladies who lusted, fought, and killed', but 'chivalric romances entered the classroom as reading texts in vernacular schools' (Grendler, 'Form and Function in Italian Renaissance Popular Books', *Renaissance Quarterly* 46 (1993), 451–85, on 484, 472).

[7]   *Il Tristano Riccardiano*, ed. E. G. Parodi, Collezione di opere inedite o rare di scrittori italiani dal XIII al XVI secolo, R. Commissione pe' testi di lingua nelle provincie dell'Emilia [74] (Bologna, 1896), p. xi; hereafter cited as 'TR-Parodi'.

[8]   *La leggenda di Tristano*, ed. Luigi Di Benedetto, Scrittori d'Italia 189 (Bari, 1942), p. 372; Daniela Delcorno Branca, *I romanzi italiani di Tristano e la 'Tavola Ritonda'*, Università di Padova, Pubblicazioni della Facoltà di Lettere e Filosofia 45 (Florence, 1968), p. 24; Giancarlo Savino, 'Ignoti frammenti di un Tristano dugentesco', *Studi di filologia italiana*

Introduction

than Parodi's, but others say simply fifteenth century.[9] On the other hand, Maria Corti describes the hand as similar to the fourteenth-century notarial tradition, but not a fifteenth-century type.[10] Fabrizio Cigni asserts positively that the date is fourteenth century.[11] I concur with these earlier suggestions, but would narrow the manuscript's dating still more. As we shall see, the preponderance of evidence (watermarks, hand, style of pen cut, addenda written in a later hand) points to the third quarter of the fourteenth century. This corresponds exactly to the contemporary cultural interest in the *Tristan* romance. Its extreme popularity and wide transmission is shown by numerous extant manuscripts and fragments that were produced in Italy in the late thirteenth and fourteenth centuries, the heyday of Arthuriana in Italy.[12]

The paper used for this manuscript bears two basic watermark designs: one *fleur de lis* and two variants of a *camel*. The *fleur de lis*, with its symmetrical, cross-like base, is identical in shape to Briquet's item 7259 (Grenoble, 1344), but slightly smaller. A variant group of lilies mostly dates to the 1360s and 1370s.[13]

---

37 (1979), 13; reprinted in *Dante e dintorni*, ed. Marisa Boschi Rotiroti, Quaderni degli 'Studi Danteschi' 14 (Florence, 2003), 59; *Il romanzo di Tristano*, ed. Antonio Scolari, Testi della cultura italiana 17 (Genoa, 1990), p. 22; Marco Villoresi, *La letteratura cavalleresca: Dai cicli medievali all'Ariosto*, Università 219, Lingua e letteratura italiana (Rome, 2000), p. 32; and Roberta Morosini, '"Prose di romanzi" ... o novelle? A Note on the Adaptations of "franceschi romanzi". The Case of the *Tristano Riccardiano* and the *Novellino*', *Tristania* 22 (2003), 42.

[9] Anna Radaelli, 'Il testo del frammento Vb² del *Roman de Tristan en prose* (Biblioteca Apostolica Vaticana, Vat. lat. 14740)', *Studi mediolatini e volgari* 50 (2004), 220; Marie-José Heijkant, 'La tradizione del *Tristan* in prosa in Italia e proposte di studio sul "Tristano Riccardiano"', Catholic University, Nijmegen, 1989, 38; Grendler, 'Il libro popolare nel Cinquecento', in *La Stampa in Italia nel Cinquecento: Atti del Convegno, Roma, 17–21 ottobre 1989*, ed. Marco Santoro (Rome, 1992), p. 216; and *Il Tristano Corsiniano: Edizione critica*, ed. Roberto Tagliani, Atti della Accademia Nazionale dei Lincei, Classe di scienze morali, storiche e filologiche, anno CDVII (2010); Memorie, ser. 9, vol. 28/1 (Rome, 2011), p. 20. In a later study, Heijkant revises her opinion to 'first half of the fifteenth century' ('From France to Italy: The Tristan Texts', in *The Arthur of the Italians: The Arthurian Legend in Medieval Italian Literature and Culture*, eds Gloria Allaire and F. Regina Psaki, Arthurian Literature in the Middle Ages 7 [Cardiff, 2014], p. 53).

[10] Maria Corti, 'Emiliano e Veneto nella tradizione manoscritta del *Fiore di virtù*', *Studi di filologia italiana* 18 (1960), 29–68, on 60; hereafter, 'Corti'.

[11] Fabrizio Cigni, review of *Il romanzo di Tristano*, ed. A. Scolari; and *Tristano Riccardiano*, ed. E. G. Parodi, introduction and notes M.-J. Heijkant, *Rivista di letteratura italiana* 11.1–2 (1993), 329.

[12] See Heijkant, 'From France to Italy', pp. 43–4. Several of these were produced in northern Italian regions. Parchment *bifolia* from dismembered Arthurian romances, including one *Tristan* in French, were used to bind notarial documents in Udine (Cesare Scanlon, *Libri, scuole e cultura nel Friuli medioevale: 'Membra disiecta' dell'Archivio di Stato di Udine*, Medioevo e umanesimo 65 (Padua, 1987), pp. 6, 176–8, and plate XLI). For additional evidence on the transmission of *Tristan* to northeastern Italy, see my *Italian Literature III. Il Tristano Corsiniano*, Arthurian Archives 20 (Cambridge, 2015), pp. xiii–xiv.

[13] C. M. Briquet, *Les filigranes: Dictionnaire historique des marques du papier des leur apparition vèrs 1292 jusqu'en 1600. A Facsimile of the 1907 Edition [...]*, ed. Allan Stevenson, 4 vols (Amsterdam, 1968), hereafter cited as 'Briquet'. Item 7263 has a differently shaped base; its variants are localizable and datable as follows: Siena (?), 1370; Spain, 1340–51; Provence, 1352; Grenoble, 1362–73; Pistoia, 1363; Genova, 1364–73; Udine and Venice, 1366; Lucca,

The first camel watermark seems to be a modification of a contemporary horse watermark which featured a prominently rounded head, bear-like ears, a smoothly arched neck, a little circle for the eye, and so on.[14] This 'camel' maintains the horse's pasterns (area between hoof and fetlock) and flowing tail (!), the bridle and rein have been removed, and slight swellings on the now-curved back hint at two humps. In addition, the horse's feet have been reshaped somewhat to resemble cloven hooves. The second camel variant in Ricc. MS 1729 is a deformed version of the first, which may have occurred as the wire pattern was reused and lost its original shape. The camel watermarks in this codex are not like Briquet's three published examples; our Camel 'A' is most similar to one used in Lucca in 1370.[15] Another example similar to our manuscript's Camel 'B' is 'found in paper used by the Chancellery of the old Kingdom of Aragon from 1379 to 1387. Like most figures of animals, this one is of Italian origin.'[16] According to Briquet, the camel with one or two humps was an exclusively Italian watermark which was used for about twenty years.[17] If Camel 'B' was created in Italy prior to 1379 as seems likely, this supports other evidence that Ricc. MS 1729 was copied in the third quarter of the fourteenth century. In the Gravell Watermark Archive, eleven 'camel' examples span the twenty-seven years from 1361 to 1388.[18] In addition, Piccard provides several examples of camels (items 481–501), most of which are Tuscan and date to the 1360s–70s.[19] Although his tracings are very shaky which makes accurate identification difficult, Piccard's item 496 (Lucca, 1377) is the closest to Camel 'A' in Ricc. MS 1729. Most similar to the manuscript's Camel 'B' are Piccard 484 (Pisa, 1370) and 490 (Lucca, 1374). Watermark evidence is vitally important for establishing the date of the manuscript as much earlier than Parodi had hypothesized. Although then, as now, paper may not have been used immediately, it seems unlikely that it would have been purchased, stored and used over a century later. Furthermore, the 1360s or 70s as a copying date parallels that of another northeastern Italian production: the *Tristano Corsiniano*. Its single watermark is 'datable to 1370–80 from either Pistoia or the Verona-Vicenza region'.[20]

1367/69; Pisa, 1368; Fano, 1373; Palermo, 1376. See also Briquet's comments in vol. II, p. 399. His tracings are found in vol. III, unpaginated.

[14] Somewhat similar to traits in *cheval*: Briquet 3565 (Pisa, 1369) and 3566 (var. Venice, 1373), described in Briquet, vol. I, p. 230.

[15] One of the additional tracings now online as part of the Thomas L. Gravell Watermark Archive. See 'Camel.004.1, Briquet no. 193056' at *https://memoryofpaper.eu/gravell*. Accessed 23 August 2023.

[16] F. de Bofarull y Sans, *Animals in Watermarks* (Hilversum, 1959), p. 23 and fig. 301.

[17] '[U]n filigrane exclusivement italien qui n'a été en usage que durant une vingtaine d'ànnées' (Briquet, vol. I, p. 222).

[18] Italian examples are from Venice, 1364; Florence, 1366 and 1371; Lucca, 1370; and Pisa, 1388.

[19] Gerhard Piccard, *Wasserzeichen verschiedene Vierfüssler* (Stuttgart, 1987), vol. 3, pp. 20, 103–106 '*Dromedar*'.

[20] *Tristano Corsiniano*, ed. and trans. Allaire, p. xv. See Briquet items 3219 and 3221.

Introduction

HAND AND INK

The entire manuscript was copied in a single, northern Italian script. The highly idiosyncratic style could perhaps be termed a late Gothic book hand, although this description is being generous.[21] The text was written with a Gothic style pen cut which did not allow for cursive elements; this too indicates pre-fifteenth century production. Graphic traits include angular letters with 'flags' on ascenders, three types of *r* and tiny bowls on the lower case *b*. The copyist Johannes was anything but a professional.[22] In fact, given the earlier didactic texts in the anthology and the amateur sketches that decorate them, in all probability he was a juvenile. His inexpertise in sharpening the pen, in orthography and – in all likelihood – in reading ability suggest an aficionado of Arthurian romance, an 'amateur' in every sense, doggedly determined to copy the lengthy prose narrative of Tristan's adventures that fills half the codex.

For the most part, the text ink is dark brown, but at times is extremely light brown – suggesting uneven mixing or poor-quality ink. Also, Johannes did not prepare his pen well because every few words the ink fades as its supply runs low (especially around fols 129v, 130r–v, 131r). One finds stunning examples of the pen needing to be sharpened (fols 141v–142r) or being badly cut (fol. 182v). Red ink was used for *capitulum* symbols, for a few completed rubrics, and to trim capital letters and proper names. In the *Tristano* portion, there are large red initials at the heads of narrative divisions, accompanied by tiny guide letters in brown ink in the margins, both done in the scribal hand.[23]

PAGE PREPARATION AND NUMERATION

Page preparation was done in dry point. Rulings mark off all four margins and all internal lines. The number of lines per page ranges unevenly from twenty-one to twenty-six throughout the course of the book. Prickings (tiny holes) are visible along the extreme right edges; these were never trimmed off. There is one wide column of text per page. The *octavo* page size is fairly consistent, measuring approximately 219–220 mm x 146–148 mm. The writing space throughout the codex, not just in the *Tristano* portion, varies: 140–150 mm x 95–102 mm.

The later Tuscan book owner numbered the pages in the upper right corner on the *recto* of folios, in Arabic numerals. After folio 132 he skipped a folio; I refer to this unnumbered folio as 132*bis*. A series of modern, machine-stamped numbers appears in the lower right corner of every *recto*, with a duplication of 168. Since neither series is perfect, in this volume I have opted to refer to the medieval pen numberings.

---

[21] Parodi (TR-Parodi, p. xi) terms it 'brutta scrittura, non toscana' (an ugly, non-Tuscan hand).

[22] Corti (62) refers to the 'confusione grafica, ben riferibile a un copista indotto, rozzo e per di più portato alla mescolanza [...] di tradizioni grafiche differenti quali la pisano-lucchese, [...] la veneta e la franco-veneta' (confusion of graphic forms, easily assignable to an unskilled copyist, crude and for the most part given to mixing [...] of different orthographic traditions such as Pisan-Lucchese [...] Veneto and Franco-Veneto).

[23] On fols 94v, 95r, 97v, 100r, 109v, 110v, 111v, 115v, 119v, 120v, 121r, 122r, 127v, 128r, 128v, 129r, 133v, 134v, 136r, 138v, 140r, 143r, 144r, 145r, 156r (twice), 156v, 157r, 157v, 158v, 161v, 162r, 162v, 163r, 164r, 165r, 168r, 169v, 170r, 171r, 172r, 173r, 174r, 174v, 175r, 177r, 177v, 178v, 179r, 181r, 184v, 185r, 185v, 186r, 186v, 187v.

FASCICLES

Quires (gatherings of folded sheets of paper) are irregular. There are fifteen such gatherings. These contain varying numbers of pages, although become more regular in size in the second half of the codex. The *fleur de lis* watermark was used for quires I, II and the end of IV; Camel 'A' for quires III–VI, fol. 115, and quire XI; and Camel 'B' for quires VII–XIII. The paper in quires IX, X, XII–XV comprises of a mixture of the two camel watermarks.

Catchwords appear on the *versos* of folios 20, 36, 52, 82, 100, 112, 124, 133, 145, 157, 169, 181. Blank pages at the ends of the first and fourth textual sections (fols 66v, 90v) are without text or catchwords. I provide the catchwords in the footnotes of my transcription of the *Tristano* section.

I	[Part I]	10 folios sewn at middle	Catchword fol. 20v
II		8 folios (*otterni*)	Catchword fol. 36v
III		8 folios (*otterni*)	Catchword fol. 52v
IV	[Part I ends]	7 folios (*setterno*)	No catchword, fol. 66v blank
V	[Part II begins; entire Part III; Part IV begins]	8 folios (*otterno*)	Catchword fol. 82v
VI	[Part IV ends]	4 folios (*quaderno*), then 8 blank pages	No catchword, fol. 90v blank
VII	[Part V *Tristano* begins]	5 folios (*quinion*)	Catchword fol. 100v
VIII		6 folios (*senion*)	Catchword fol. 112v
IX		6 folios (*senion*)	Catchword fol. 124v
X		5 folios (*quinion*)	Catchword fol. 133v
XI		6 folios (*senion*)	Catchword fol. 145v
XII		6 folios (*senion*)	Catchword fol. 157v
XIII		6 folios (*senion*)	Catchword fol. 169v
XIV		6 folios (*senion*)	Catchword fol. 181v
XV		6 folios (*senion*) originally, but lost the last three pages of this quire (arranged as follows: 6 'pages' + threads at the fold + 3 remaining pages)	

Introduction xxi

DECORATION

Inconsistent and idiosyncratic attempts at decoration demonstrate the copyist's amateur status, alluded to above, and suggest that he was producing this book for his own use. As with all elements of the manuscript, one finds great inconsistency and many anomalies. Folio 1r has the only professionally-done piece of ornamentation ('industrial grade,' Northern Italian style): a very large capital letter 'U' done mostly in blue ink with touches of red. In the *Fior di virtù* segment (fols 1–66v), strokes of red ink were used to ornament capital letters at the beginning of sentences. At the heads of major sections spaces two lines high were left for larger initials, which were never completed; these are indicated by tiny brown guide letters visible in the margins. Throughout the manuscript, Johannes often left spaces for rubrics, but these were executed only sporadically (fols 57r, 58r, 60r, 61r, 62v, 63r, 67r, 68v). Throughout the *Tristano*, rubrics were never executed; however, approximately one hundred blank spaces, ample enough for illuminations, were left. The explicit to *Tristano* was done in red ink (fol. 188r). Chapter beginnings are marked logically with red *capitulum* symbols, at times rather crudely executed. In places the same red symbols were used to indicate new paragraphs, excessively so for each item in Part II and less often (forty-one times) in the *Tristano*. In the moral instruction sections (Parts III and IV), each first word at the left margin has a red slash on its capital letter (fols 73r–80v, 81r–85v). In the lengthy narrative *Tristano*, the scribe uses red slashes on normal-sized capital letters at beginning of lines and for proper names.

Larger red capital letters are scattered throughout textual sections Parts III, IV and V. While these are decorative, many seem unnecessary, such as the unique instance of a red capital *R* on the *Re* in *Tristano* (fol. 137r). At the beginning of IV (fol. 81r), the scribe has drawn a very crude 'A', three lines high, in dark brown ink framed in red. At the beginning of the *Tristano* (fol. 91r), space was left for a large initial which was never illuminated. Other decorative letters in the *Tristano* are three large red initials used to signal lengthy episodes; thirteen smaller red initials to open new paragraphs, three of which follow a blank space left for illumination. The copyist also uses a red capital 'C' five times, four of which follow unilluminated spaces (fols 91r, 92r, 99r, 101r) and another mid-sentence at the top of fol. 106r.

In places, the do-it-yourself artist attempts to decorate his pages in emulation of professionally produced books for merchant class readers. In discussing the *Fior di virtù* section, Rebecca Balatresi hypothesizes that the illustrator must have had a model before him or a good knowledge of the text and of the iconographic tradition.[24] In Part II (fols 67r–72v), the copyist introduces a new decorative element: on the bottom lines of pages, for letters with descenders (*p, f, q*), he has added horizontal dashes alternating with vertical lines to create 'tails' on the letters in the brown text ink (fols 67r, 67v, 68r, 69v, 70r, 71r); these 'tails' extend into the lower margin. On fol. 73r, in the third textual section, he has sketched

---

[24] 'L'illustratore deve aver avuto davanti a sé un modello o essere ben a conoscenza del testo e della codificata iconografia' (Balatresi, 'I codici', 37).

hideous red squiggles across the top margin, in imitation of the ubiquitous viny, leafy decorations of contemporary manuscripts.

Mise-en-page indicates the desire for illuminations, but this was hardly the work of a professional programmer. In conformity with other elements, the fact that only one very large initial was painted by a professional (fol. 1r) proves that this book was not owned or commissioned by a well-to-do patron. Throughout the book, the copyist left spaces of varying sizes, shapes and dimensions. A few examples from the beginning of the book amply demonstrate the lack of planning and symmetry: spaces five lines high, half column wide (fols 6v and 9v at gutter; fol. 12v at left margin); other spaces six lines high, half column wide at gutter (fols 7v, 8v); five full lines blank (fol. 10v); seven lines high, two-thirds column wide at left margin (fol. 11v); three lines high, two-thirds column wide at the gutter (fol. 12r); seven full lines across the bottom (fol. 14r); and so on. For Parts III and IV (axioms and didactic verse), no spaces were left. In the *Tristano* section, designs were clearly intended to illustrate dramatic moments in the story. Throughout this volume, I indicate these spaces meant for images with the symbol |||.

The didactic nature of the first four texts, as well as the brevity of the *exempla* included, indicate this book's usefulness in educating children. The notion that children would have had access to it is borne out by five crude sketches which can only be examples of art by children of three different skill levels. Four of these appear in the *Fior di virtù* which used animal allegories to convey its allegorical lessons. The thematic concerns and details (bugs, a hunter, a running dog) plus the difference in style suggest that children of different ages were the artists.[25] On folio 20v, where the text treats *Prudentia* and *Intelligencia*, brown stick-figure insects with three legs per side and antennae on their heads (i.e., ants) busy themselves among three mounds; one is carrying (or attacking?) a larger bug. Given the text on fol. 21v *La Providençia si esta en provedirse dinançi enançi ale soe bissongne*, the sketch of industrious ants makes perfect sense. On folio 22v, a bearded hunter on foot, outlined in brown ink with a colored-in red hat and garment, is about to stab a very male quadruped (i.e., wild ox). The animal's horns and penis are done in red. A brown tree sketched in front of the hunter perfectly portrays the text's description of a wild ox that becomes enraged at the color red and how to entrap such an animal.[26] This is a complex pictorial

---

[25] For analogous children's drawings, see the fly caught in a spider's web in Venice, Biblioteca Marciana, MS Cl. IX, 175, datable to ca. 1336 (reproduced in Ernesto Monaci, *Facsimili di antichi manoscritti per uso delle scuole di filologia neolatina* (Rome, 1881–92), plate 55). See also Florence, Biblioteca Nazionale Centrale, MS Cl. VIII, 1272, fol. 79v, for a bearded hunter with a bird and a running dog.

[26] Fol. 22v lists various types of *passía* (madness): *passi lunatiçi, passia de malenchonia* and four subcategories of *passia en aver pocho senno*. The passage that begins just above the hunter drawing reads: 'E posi à [...] la pascía al bo salvaçio che natural mente àe en odio tute le cosse rosse siché quando la chassatore lo volonno pilliare, Elli si vestono de Rosso e vanno lae onde lo bue E lo buoe vedendo lo, encontenente li chore adosso E cha[fol. 23r]çatore fuge da po uno arbore ch'ello àe aportato. El buoe credendo dare al chaçadore dà ende l'arbore E davi sì forte che non si po partire. alora lo chassadore si l'auçide' (fols 22v–23r). The 'wild ox' is a simplification of the very old *autalops* motif from moralized bestiaries: '[J]ust as the antelope

Introduction xxiii

design, but the handling of the pen is shaky and outlines are not firmly drawn. On folio 23v, the textual section concerns *Justiçio* (Justice) and speaks of the 'King of Bees'. Here another stick-figure design – all in brown ink – shows a different species of insect: six of them, this time with eyes, ovoid bodies and eight stubby legs. The bees 'flying' in a swarm are arranged at different angles to indicate movement; they 'fly' above simple graphic representations of plants and adjacent to what appear to be boxes with drawers on legs (i.e., beehives). Again, despite the economy of details and paucity of technique, the very young child who drew this conveys the activity of the bees. The handling of the pen in forming ovals and squares is quite sure. On fol. 30v, in brown ink with light strokes of red, a running canine is portrayed, apparently chasing balls: ten round objects surround the animal. Here the drawing seems inappropriate because the text is concerned with telling the truth and enumerates types of lies and liars. The animal allegory is *la talpa che non àe ochi* (the mole which has no eyes). The moral is that lies are like a blind mole, always underground.[27] The dog-like creature in the sketch clearly has an eye. Perhaps the young artist simply did not know what a mole looked like or inserted an image from the model into the wrong space. Finally, on folio 113r (in the *Tristano* section) a very shaky brown outline shows a human head on an incomplete torso, this time done by a much younger child, perhaps just learning to hold the pen.

THE CONTENTS OF THE *TRISTANO* EXEMPLAR

'The story of Tristan is decidedly the most popular thread of the Arthurian matter in Italy,' as F. Regina Psaki declares, and in Italian redactions 'Tristan is conceived and represented as easily the best knight in the world'.[28] Like the Riccardian MS 2543 (Parodi's base text), our exemplar belongs to the so-called 'Version I' of the French prose *Tristan*, an abbreviated version of the 'Vulgate' or Version II. The French redactor had reworked materials from the verse tradition, elevating the eponymous hero to a level of knightly prowess that rivalled that of Lancelot and Galahad and darkening King Mark into a dangerous and inept despot.[29] The

---

snags its horns in a bush and is slain by the hunter, so the Christian, trusting in the two horns of the Old and New Testaments, must avoid the snares' of sin. This was an 'often repeated visual motif' from the *Physiologus*, 'a popular source of exempla and a favorite school-text in the Middle Ages' (*Beasts and Birds of the Middle Ages: The Bestiary and Its Legacy*, eds Willene B. Clark and Meradith T. McMunn, University of Pennsylvania Press, Middle Ages Series (Philadelphia, 1989), pp. 2, 9 n. 5). For manuscript illuminations of the antelope, see Ron Baxter, *Bestiaries and their Users in the Middle Ages* (London, 1998), pp. 65, 86, 101.

[27] According to bestiaries, the mole was one of only four animals that lived in a single element.
[28] *Italian Literature II. Il Tristano Riccardiano*, ed. A. Scolari, trans. F. Regina Psaki, Arthurian Archives 12 (Cambridge, 2006), pp. ix–x; hereafter TR.
[29] For a summary of innovations, see Emmanuèle Baumgartner, 'The Prose *Tristan*', trans. Sarah Singer, in *The Arthur of the French: The Arthurian Legend in Medieval French and Occitan Literature*, eds Glyn S. Burgess and Karen Pratt, Arthurian Literature in the Middle Ages 4 (Cardiff, 2006), pp. 326–9.

narrative content of Ricc. MS 1729 follows that of Ricc. MS 2543 very closely, albeit with some slightly different readings. Near its end, after certain ellipses, probably due to lacunae in a faulty model, the narrative leaps to the final episode of Mark wounding Tristan, the deaths of the lovers and the general mourning that follows.[30] Given the condition of MS 2543, illegible at its end, there is no way to tell if it had ever contained this episode.[31] Thus, for comparative purposes, we must look to other analogues in Italian dialects: the *Tristano Panciatichiano* (TP) and the *Tristano Veneto* (TV), both of which do contain the final episode. TV also features Lancelot's revenge for Tristan against Mark and Tintagel. Longer still is the amplified redaction known as the *Tavola Ritonda* (*Tav. Rit.*), which contains the deaths of the lovers episode as well as an expanded account of the vengeance taken on Mark.

The 'R' redaction – represented by the two Riccardian manuscripts – focuses even more tightly on Tristan's life than did the *Roman de Tristan*. As with MS 2543, MS 1729 omits information about the hero's ancestors and begins with his father's disappearance while hunting, an event that motivates his mother's excursion into the wilderness, where she gives birth to her son and names him. Merlin rescues the newborn, appoints Governal as his guardian and prophesies the boy's greatness (Löseth §20).[32] After Tristan's father remarries, his stepmother repeatedly tries to poison him (Lös. §22). Governal flees with Tristan to Faramont's court where the king's daughter – smitten with Tristan – nearly causes his execution. When Tristan departs for Cornwall, the desperate maiden sends gifts and a letter to Tristan, then commits suicide (Lös. §§24, 26, 27).

In Gaul, a court fool had warned the Morholt to beware of Tristan (Lös. §25). This prophecy comes true when Tristan engages the Morholt in individual combat to prevent collection of a tribute; Tristan fatally wounds the Morholt, but is in turn wounded with a poisoned arrow (Lös. §§28–9). Seeking a cure, Tristan and Governal sail for months, eventually landing in Ireland where Yseut heals him (Lös. §29).

While in Ireland, Tristan attends a tournament with Yseut's father, King Anguin; encounters Palamides, his rival for Yseut's love; and participates in a second tournament in which he defeats Palamides, who leaves lamenting (Lös. §§30–2). MS 1729 contains all these events, but due to an earlier error in the transmission process its paragraphs are out of order.[33] After the tournament, Yseut prepares a bath for Tristan; her mother, the queen, discovers the splintered

---

[30] These are the concluding events in Bibliothèque nationale de France, MS fr. 757, the best exemplar of the short version (Ibid., p. 329).

[31] TR, pp. xi–xii.

[32] This comparative plot analysis is very useful for scholars of *Tristan* and related manuscripts: Elhert Löseth, *Le Roman en prose de Tristan, le Roman de Palamède et la Compilation de Rusticien de Pise: Analyse critique d'après les manuscrits de Paris*, Bibliothèque de l'École des Hautes Études, Sciences Historiques et Philologiques 82 (Paris, 1891); rpt. Burt Franklin: Research and Source Works Series 426, Essays in Literature and Criticism 49 (New York, 1970), hereafter cited as 'Lös.'.

[33] The same misordering had already appeared in Ricc. MS 2543.

Introduction xxv

sword he used to kill the Morholt, but the king spares Tristan who returns to Cornwall with Governal (Lös. §33).

In Cornwall, a dwarf tells Mark that Tristan will bring him dishonor; in MS 1729, this prophecy occurs much later than in the French textual tradition (Lös. §23). Mark assembles his court, intending to have an assignation with the wife of one of his knights; instead, she becomes enamored of Tristan and sends her dwarf to summon him. Mark attacks Tristan as he rides to the lady; his wound bleeds into her bed; and her husband threatens her and then fights with Tristan. Later, another knight asks Mark for a boon and carries the lady away, while being chased by her husband. Since Tristan came to save her too late, she rejects him and stays with her abductor (Lös. §34).

Fearing Tristan's prowess, Mark sends him on a dangerous mission to Ireland to obtain Yseut as Mark's wife. Blown off course in a storm, Tristan again encounters Anguin and agrees to be his champion (Lös. §36). Tristan meets a damsel with a split shield and defeats Breus (Lös. §37). In a trial by combat, Tristan defeats Anguin's accuser. As a reward, Tristan receives Yseut to be Mark's wife; they sail for Cornwall with Governal and Brangain (Lös. §38). During the voyage, the servants mistakenly give the love potion to Tristan and Yseut, binding them in a lifelong, passionate affair (Lös. §39). A sea storm carries them to the Island of Giants where Tristan complies with an evil custom established at the time of Joseph of Arimathaea: he must kill Brunor and his lady in order to free his entourage (Lös. §40). Brunor's daughter goes seeking her brother Galehot, who sails to the Island with reinforcements to avenge his parents. After making peace with Tristan, he writes a letter to Guenevere announcing that he has abolished the evil custom (Lös. §41).

Once Tristan's entourage returns to Cornwall, Mark weds Yseut and crowns her queen. On their wedding night, Brangain lies with the king to conceal Yseut's infidelity (Lös. §42). Later, fearing that Brangain might inform the king, Yseut orders two servants to murder her. They fake her death, and she is rescued by Palamides and taken to a convent. Yseut repents her deed. Palamides asks for a boon if he is able to recover Brangain (Lös. §43). Following a sizeable lacuna, the narrative resumes as in the second half of Löseth §44, with Tristan fighting Palamides beneath Yseut's tower. MS 1729 conserves material outlined in Löseth §§45–9, including the enchanted drinking horn scene, but somewhat reordered. The Wicked Damsel (Lös. §49) arrives at court, is spurned by Tristan and then schemes with 'Ghedis' to betray him. Their two attempts to trap Tristan in Yseut's chamber are reversed: according to MS 1729, in their first attempt they place scythes around Yseut's bed; however, in the larger tradition this happens the second time (Lös. §48). According to MS 1729, in the second attempt there are no scythes, Mark forbids entry to Yseut's room, Brangain warns Tristan to flee, Tristan turns highwayman and kills two knights; finally, Mark sends a letter of pardon. This series of events happens first in the French textual tradition.

At this point the narration breaks off and no longer follows that of Ricc. MS 2543. There is a huge ellipsis before the deaths of the lovers episode. Within the final episode, MS 1729 is considerably abbreviated and contains some minor differences, some unique, but it recounts events also found in the *Panciatichiano*

and the *Tristano Veneto* as well as in *La Tavola Ritonda*. Tristan and Yseut are guests at the Castle of Dinas (beginning of Lös. §545). Mark stabs Tristan with a poisoned spear; Tristan flees; Mark gloats about Tristan's fatal wound, and Yseut wants to die with him (Lös. §546). The dying hero asks to see Mark and Yseut (Lös. §547); as Tristan and Yseut talk, his arms are very weak and his eyesight is failing (Lös. §548). The next morning Sagremor brings his sword and shield. While bidding farewell to his arms, Tristan admits defeat; he pardons Mark, then embraces Yseut, and they die together (Lös. §549). Mark and all Cornwall mourn; Mark has a rich sepulcher constructed for the two lovers (Lös. §550). Sagremor carries Tristan's arms to Logres (Lös. §551).[34] En route, Sagremor encounters a knight, and they exchange sad news (Lös. §568). At court Arthur summons his remaining knights, and Sagremor recounts Tristan's end (Lös. §569) whereupon Arthur, Lancelot and Guenevere write commemorative *lais*. Black clothing is worn in mourning for the first time to honor Tristan's demise (Lös. §570).

COMPARISON OF ITALIAN REDACTIONS

While this is not the place for a complete examination of the manuscript's position in the overall textual tradition,[35] it will be useful to offer some observations on the relationship of the account preserved in Ricc. MS 1729 ('F') with the better-known Riccardian MS 2543 ('R'), edited by E. G. Parodi. With lengthy passages that are nearly verbatim to MS 2543, our manuscript clearly belongs to the same branch as his base text yet certain differences signal the uniqueness of this redaction. Daniela Delcorno Branca echoes Parodi in asserting that conservative readings in MS 1729 harken back to the 'stadio primitivo del romanzo' (early phrase of the *roman*).[36] As evidence, she points to two unusual names: 'Chieso' (Kay), also found in *Tav. Rit.*; and Brunoro, a knight of the *Tavola Vecchia* (Old Table).[37] Marie-José Heijkant suggests that MS 1729 was 'a key manuscript witness' for transmission from Tuscany to the Veneto, a piece of evidence that allows Italy 'to document a very early stage of elaboration of the prose *Tristan*, possibly close to that of Luce's *Estoire*'.[38]

As with any medieval text, a given redaction will contain variants created as a result of the transmission process. In general, when compared to MS 2543, MS 1729 is abbreviated. For example, on folio 115r the manuscript omits details of

---

[34] At this point the French prose *Tristan* recounts a long series of the Round Table knights' adventures and deaths (Lös. §§552–67), but this was uniformly omitted in Italian redactions.
[35] See Heijkant's pioneering comparison of Italian *Tristan*s: 'La tradizione', 136–251. See also Psaki's succinct summary in TR, p. xi.
[36] Delcorno Branca, *Tristano e Lancillotto in Italia: Studi di letteratura arturiana*, Memoria del tempo 11 (Ravenna, 1998), p. 110 n. 28.
[37] Ibid., pp. 108 n. 23, 112 n. 35, 235 n. 36. Also found in TP and Florence, Biblioteca Nazionale Centrale, MS Palatino 556.
[38] Heijkant, 'From France to Italy', pp. 53, 59.

Introduction

fighting in a tournament (cf. TR, p. 52).[39] On fol. 117v it elides a short conversation between Gawain and a damsel (TR, p. 56). A notable excision occurs around fol. 118r where MS 1729 omits Gareth's appearance and completely elides Brangain's conversation with Anguin about the winner of the tournament (TR, pp. 58–60). Two other passages on fols 139r–140v (the split shield episode) and fol. 152v are shorter than in TR (pp. 94–6, 114). Despite its abbreviations, in some places MS 1729 conserves more difficult readings than TR. Concerning Meliadus' imprisonment, TR reads 'là ove tue ieri. E incontanente lo ree sì volle [...]' (p. 10). However, fol. 95r conserves a more difficult wording: 'onde tu eri encantato. E lo Re vuolle [...]'.[40] An especially telling instance concerns the verb *delongnare* (fol. 134r); it had clearly belonged to the model for MS 2543 as shown by that scribe's self-correction: *distruggere o dilungare* (TR, p. 90). In the same episode, where the barons scheme with Mark on how to remove Tristan, MS 1729 preserves the harder reading *dissengno* (fol. 134v), which was simplified as *disserono* in MS 2543 (TR, p. 90).

Conversely, even though MS 1729 is often condensed, in some places it contains amplifications. On fols 128r and 136v–137r, the manuscript adds dialogue not found in TR, pp. 78 and 90. Fol. 153v provides a good example of the redaction process: shorter overall, with slight wording differences, it nonetheless inserts an authorial intrusion not found in TR, p. 118.

Slight differences in wording are to be expected, such as fol. 95v *vis-à-vis* TR, p. 12, but at times MS 1729 and its Italian brethren feature different details compared to their French ancestors. After Tristan and Yseut drink the love potion, a little dog licks a spilled drop (fol. 145r). This link to the Middle English *Sir Tristrem* is not found in TP or TV, but does appear in TR, p. 104 and *Tav. Rit.* p. 120. Another animal serves as a point of reference for manuscript relations: on fol. 105v, Bellice sends a squire to deliver a letter to Tristan along with gifts of a sword, a hound and a warhorse. The horse was added in Italian redactions,[41] but is not mentioned in French manuscripts according to Löseth's *Analyse*. In French manuscripts, the *dama de Landes* proclaims a tournament (Lös. §§29–30) whereas in MS 1729, fol. 112v, and other Italian redactions it is the King of Scotland who announces the event.[42] In the French tradition, King Mark's *amie* is unnamed and her husband is Segurades (Lös. §34), but in MS 1729 and other Italian texts she is called the Lady (or Damsel) of Thornwater and her 'knight' is Lambegues. In the French, 'Blioberis' wins the damsel as a boon (Lös. §34); by contrast, in MS 1729, fol. 133r, 'Bordo' rides off with her. In the final episode, French manuscripts depict Tristan playing his harp (Lös. §546), but in MS 1729, Yseut is singing when Mark wounds Tristan. 'This unusual inversion of gender

---

[39] In this discussion, I refer to our manuscript by its folio numbers, but give page numbers for the corresponding passages in other edited Italian texts. For convenience, I refer to these with the abbreviations, shown above. Throughout my transcription, footnotes will alert the reader to specific similarities or differences between and among these texts.

[40] TR, p. 10: 'there where you were. And immediately the king wanted [...]'. MS 1729, fol. 95r: 'where you were enchanted. And the king wanted [...]'. Emphasis added.

[41] TR, p. 28; TP, p. 148; *Tav. Rit.*, p. 61. TV is lacunose in this episode.

[42] TR, p. 46; TP, p. 158; *Tav. Rit.*, p. 76.

roles occurs only in manuscripts [...] copied and translated in Italy'.[43] Another innovation concerns Galehot's letter declaring that he had eliminated the evil custom. In the French prose *Tristan*, Galehot writes only to Guenevere.[44] The addition of Arthur's name as co-recipient appears in TR, p. 122; in TP, p. 204; as well as in Ricc. MS 1729, fol. 156r.

Certain tantalizing bits of evidence indicate the wide circulation of *Tristan* redactions in northern Italy. One lexical puzzle *pur ales tuto* (fol. 143v) turned out to be a rare instance of conflated readings from two different Italian versions.[45] In the final episode, there is a stunning moment in which the redactor refers to different versions. In the French *roman* and other Italian texts, Tristan and Yseut sojourn at the Castle of Dinas. In MS 1729 after Tristan is wounded, he flees to the *castello de Pinogres* (fol. 179r), a place named in the Vulgate version.[46] The final episode (fol. 186v) also contains a group of knights not mentioned in any of the Italian analogues: Taulas *le grand*, Damas, Damadas, Senelas and Harpin took part in the later *Quest* adventures and their deaths are recounted in a single narrative segment (Lös. §510).

Finally, MS 1729 includes some names and narrative details worth pointing out with respect to the larger tradition. In French manuscripts, Tristan's enemy in Cornwall is 'Andret' (Lös. §§34, 45, 48–9); but in MS 1729 he is called 'Bendin' (fol. 129v), 'Beldin' (fol. 132r) or 'Ghedis' (fol. 167v), similar to 'Gedis' in TR, p. 398; or TP, p. 172. However, in the final episode where Mark wounds Tristan (not preserved in TR), he is called 'Durin' (fol. 178v).[47] During the lamentations for the dead hero, there is a reference to 'King Gioni', said to be a dear friend of Mark's (fol. 184v).[48] After the lovers' entombment, Sagremor dwells in Cornwall a long time before carrying Tristan's arms to Arthur's court (fol. 186r) whereas in other texts he leaves on his mission immediately. To summon the surviving Round Table knights to hear Sagremor's announcement, Arthur has a

---

[43]   Heijkant, 'From France to Italy', p. 52. See also TV, p. 540; and TP, p. 712. Episode not preserved in TR.

[44]   *Le Roman de Tristan en prose*, ed. Renée L. Curtis (Leiden, 1976), vol. II, p. 90; Lös. §41; and TV, p. 209. For the significance of Galehot's correspondence with Guenevere, see Sylvia Huot's analysis in *Outsiders: The Humanity and Inhumanity of Giants in Medieval French Prose Romance*, The Conway Lectures in Medieval Studies 2012 (Notre Dame, Indiana, 2016), pp. 200–209.

[45]   *Io la voglio pur per lo ree* (TR, p. 102); *Io la voglio al postutto per lo re* (TP, p. 186), emphasis added.

[46]   Variants: *Pynogre, Pinogres*. See G. D. West, *French Arthurian Prose Romances: An Index of Proper Names*, University of Toronto Romance Series 35 (Toronto, 1978), p. 258; hereafter cited as 'West'.

[47]   See Delcorno Branca, 'I cantari di *Tristano*', *Lettere Italiane* 23 (1971), 296 n. 30.

[48]   West (p. 137) records 'Geon' or its variant 'Jeon' (as found in Lös. §540 n. 1). Perhaps an allusion to the legendary hero King Giano of Padua who defended Padua, Rimini and Venice against the invading Huns. See *Attila flagellum Dei: poemetto in ottava rima riprodotto sulle antiche stampe*, ed. Alessandro D'Ancona, Collezione di antiche scritture italiane inedito o rare 3 (Pisa, 1864), composed by the Bolognese notary Niccolò da Casola between 1358 and 1367/8. The hero's name in the original Franco-Italian version was "le rois Gilius de Pahue".

special horn sounded (fol. 187r) as in Lös. §569, not a little bell as in TV p. 555 '*campaniel*'; or *Tav. Rit.* p. 510 '*una squilletta*'.[49]

THE LANGUAGE OF THE MANUSCRIPT

The editor of the better-known *Tristano* at the Biblioteca Riccardiana, E. G. Parodi, signaled the language of Ricc. MS 1729 (his exemplar *F*) as remarkable and worthy of study. He hypothesized its language was somewhere between the Veneto and Emilia regional dialects, as Ferrarese would be, but very mixed.[50] In the decades after his seminal edition appeared, scholars accepted the 'veneto-emiliano' conjecture as fact.[51] However, in 1960, Maria Corti made a more careful examination of this 'curioso impasto dialettale' (curious dialectal pastiche), finding that very little is purely Emilian.[52] For example, the typical Ferrarese initial *h-* on the verb *avere* appears only twice in the *Tristano* portion of the manuscript: *havia* (fol. 102r) and second person plural *have'* (fol. 108r). Another Ferrarese trait employed is the third person singular preterit verb ending *-i*, principally for *vidi*,[53] with scattered examples for other verbs: *diedi*,[54] *laysi* (fols 108r, 111r); and *missi* (fols 109v, 115v). Corti asserted that whereas many traits are indeed found in northeastern Italy, several are also characteristics of Tuscany. In fact, many forms are specific to the dialects of Pisa and Lucca: *amboro*[55] (*ambedue*, 'both'); *populo* ('people' fols 93r, 115v);[56] and the single or doubled *s* instead of *z* in noun endings.[57] One also finds singular nouns ending

---

49   The final lines of TP are damaged so these details cannot be verified.

50   '[T]ra veneto ed emiliano, come sarebbe il ferrarese, ma fortemente mescolato' (TR-Parodi, p. xii).

51   Parodi's Veneto-Emilian hypothesis was repeated by Armando Balduino, *Manuale di filologia italiana*, Biblioteca Universale Sansoni (Florence, 1979), p. 97; Vittore Branca (cited by Scolari in his *Il romanzo di Tristano*, p. 23); Savino, 'Ignoti frammenti', 13, and its reprint, 59; Delcorno [Branca], *I romanzi italiani di Tristano*, p. 24.

52   Corti, 55. Her focus was on *Fior di virtù*, the first portion of this manuscript anthology, but all of its texts were copied contiguously in the same hand.

53   *vidi*: fols 99r, 106r, 112r, 112v, 113r, 117r, 121v, 122r, 123r, 124v, 126v, 128v, 131r, 132v, 138v, 152v, 153v, 154r, 157r, 157v, 165v, 166r, 170r, 171v, 176r, 177r, 178v, 180r, 182v. See Corti, 41.

54   *diedi*: fols 109v, 116r, 126r, 127v, 139v, 146v.

55   *amboro*: fols 91v, 103v, 109v, 119r, 125r, 128v, 132*bis*-v, 148r; *ambori* 102v, *anboro*: 109v, 132*bis*-v, 145r, 148r, 166v, 169v, 184r, 185r. See Corti, 56. See also *La Inchiesta del San Gradale: Volgarizzamento toscano della 'Queste del Saint Graal'*, ed. Marco Infurna, Biblioteca della Rivista di Storia e Letteratura Religiosa, Testi e documenti 14 (Florence, 1993), pp. 71, 81; hereafter cited as 'Infurna'.

56   See Corti, 57. One also finds the Tuscan form *povolo* (fols 115v, 146v) used by Boccaccio (Salvatore Battaglia, *Grande dizionario della lingua italiana*, 21 vols (Turin, 1961–2002), vol. IV, p. 527); and also documented in medieval Verona (Franco Riva, 'Storia dell'antico dialetto di Verona secondo i testi in versi: Morfologia e sintassi', *Atti e memorie della Accademia di Agricoltura, Scienze e Lettere di Verona* 4 [1952–53], 71, 72; and Giambattista Carlo Giuliari, 'Proposta di una bibliografia de' dialetti italiani con un documento aneddoto in antico veronese', *Il Propugnatore* 5 [1872], 328, 332, 333, 335, 336).

57   *al(l)egressa*: fols 95v, 101v, 102r, 107v, 110r, 118r, 119v, 125r, passim; *bellessa*: fols 101v, 112v, 117v, 134v, passim; *le bellesse*: fols 95v, 99r, 101v, 106v, 112v; *costumansa*: fol. 147r;

in -*ieri*, a constant presence in texts from Prato, Pistoia, Lucca, Pisa, Arezzo and Cortona;[58] and the spelling *c(h)avallaria*.[59] A noticeable Pisan-Lucchese trait is the diphthong -*au*- as in *autro*, *taula*; and in verb forms *repausare* (fols 95v, 117v, 132v, 141v); *sauperon* (fol. 101r); *saupesse* (fols 91r, 111v, 116r); *sauputo* (fols 97r, 126v, 133v).[60]

Other grammatical forms and spellings are specific to Lucca, such as the possessive adjective forms, rare in this exemplar: *nossa* (fols 147r, 154r), *nosse* (fol. 183v); *vosse* (fols 151v, 175r).[61] Certain spellings prevalent in Pisan-Lucchese texts also appear in Ricc. MS 1729:[62] *ancho* ('also') (fols 120r, 129v, 132*bis*-r, 145v, 146v, 170r, 180v) as opposed to *anche* (four times); and the group comprising *afina* (fols 135v, 145v); *enfina* (fols 100v, 109v, 110v, 111r, 138r); *fina* (fols 108v, 124r, 137r, 140v, 149r, 155v); *infina* (fol. 100r). In this *Tristano*, as in other Pisan-Lucchese texts, endings with -*qua* are predominant over -*que*:[63] *adonqua* (fol. 134v); *donqua* (fols 106r, 109r, 122v, 138r, 172r, 173r); *unqua* (fols 101r, 106v, 107v, 108v, 109v, 117v); but there are rare occurrences of *adonque* (fol. 133r) and *donque* (fols 96v, 117r).

Verb forms traceable to a remote Pisan-Lucchese redaction include the first personal singular present indicative of *avere* with -*b*-: *abo*, but also *io abi* (fol. 133r);[64] conditional or future stems of *avere* lacking a -*v*- common in Prato, Pistoia, Pisa, Lucca: *arebe* (fols 104r, 133v); *arebenno* (fol. 107v); *aresti* (fol.

---

prodessa: fols 94r, 94v, 100r, 115r, 115v, 117v, 120r, 123r, passim; *prodesse*: fols 134r, 135v, 136r, 146r, 150v, passim; *ussansa*: fols 132v, 147v, 151v, 155r, passim; and the rare *nosze*: fol. 158r. Following Corti's findings (56–8), scholars began to discard Parodi's Veneto-Emilian hypothesis in favor of a Pisan-Lucchese substrate with Veneto elements: Delcorno Branca, 'Sette anni di studi sulla letteratura arturiana in Italia: Rassegna (1985–92)', *Lettere Italiane* 4 (1992), 480 n. 52: 'zona pisana-lucchese'; Heijkant, 'La tradizione', 38: 'area linguistica pisano-lucchese con elementi veneti'.

[58]   Singular noun ending -*ieri*: fols 91v, 104v, 105v, 106r, 112v, 113r, 114v, 118v, 120v, 124r, passim; also *lo destrieri*: fols 106r, 106v, 115v, 123v, passim. See Infurna, p. 75.

[59]   *c(h)avallaria*: fols 104v, 116r, 120r, 133r, 134r, 155v, 159r, 162v; and the plural *chavallarie* on fol. 136r. See Infurna, p. 72.

[60]   *autro*: fols 93r, 96r, 99r, 101r, 104r, 109v, passim; *autri*: fols 97r, 102v, 107r, 111r, 112v, passim; *taula*: fols 114v, 115r, 115v, 128r, 132r, 138r, 182v, 183r, 186v, 187r; *taule*: fols 100v, 101v, 114v, 120v, 128r. See Corti, 56; and Infurna, p. 71. This spelling can also be due to French influence in the Veneto as we shall discuss below.

[61]   Gerhard Rohlfs, *Grammatica storica della lingua italiana e dei suoi dialetti: Fonetica*, trans. Salvatore Persichino, Piccola Biblioteca Einaudi 148, vol. 1 (Turin, 1966); and vol. 2 *Morphologia*, trans. Temistocle Franceschi, Piccola Biblioteca Einaudi 149 (Turin, 1968), §266: 'in alcune zone della Toscana [...] antico lucchese'. This form was still being used in Garfagnana (north of Lucca) and Isola d'Elba in 1949, the date of Rohlfs' study (hereafter cited as Rohlfs).

[62]   Infurna, pp. 73, 80.

[63]   Infurna, pp. 80–1.

[64]   *abo*: fols 92v, 105r, 105v, 109r, 126v, 127r, 134v, 161r, 162r, 182v. See Infurna, p. 77; and Bruno Migliorini, *The Italian Language*, rev. ed. T. Gwynfor Griffith (New York, 1966), p. 105. The single occurrence of *abe* (fol. 164r) may be due to graphic confusion of *e* / *o*, but it is used here as second person singular.

Introduction xxxi

104r);⁶⁵ and the western Tuscan past participle *ditto, ditte*.⁶⁶ Third person singular preterit endings *-ette, -itte* found in this manuscript are also common in Pisan and Lucchese.⁶⁷

By the time this *Tristano* was copied, the orthographical *k* found throughout the older Ricc. MS 2543, had entirely disappeared.⁶⁸ The manuscript preserves numerous typically Tuscan noun forms such as *cuore* (fol. 104v) or *chuore* (fols 104v, 106r, 106v); *fuocho* (fol. 96v); *luogo* (fols 94v, 146v, 152r); the adjective *buono* (fol. 188r); *buoni* (fol. 123v); and possessives *tua* ('your') (fols 97v, 106r, 107v, 112v, passim); *tuo* (fols 94v, 104v, 105r, passim); *sua* ('hers', 'its') (fols 92v, 95r, 95v, 109r, 110r, 135v, passim); *suo* ('his', 'its') (fols 95v, 100v, 106v, passim); *suoy* (fol. 111r); and *fuora* ('outside') (fols 104r, 112r, 123r, 132v, 159v, 182r). This phenomenon furnishes additional information for dating the manuscript because the diphthong *-uo-* did not appear outside of Tuscany until after the mid-1300s.⁶⁹ Some interesting forms were created due to hypercorrection or on analogy with Tuscan, such as *alberguo* (fols 113r, 121v, 123v); *asberguo* (fol. 124r) or *esberguo* (fol. 124v); *luoguo* (fols 92v, 123r, 156r, 161v, 182v); *longuo* (fol. 97v); *verguonça* (fol. 115v); *vuolta* (fol. 112r). This also happens with verbs: *preguo* (fols 103v, 105r, 109v, 110v, 117r); *veguo* (fols 92v, 109r, 130r, 135r); and in an entire series from *volere* ('to want') in the present – *vuolio, vuolli, vuolie* – as well as the preterit of the verb *volgere: vuolse*.

Despite the wealth of evidence that points to a western Tuscan ancestor for the model, this *Tristano* contains numerous non-Tuscan elements such as the voiced *d* instead of *t* produced by lenition. Where Tuscan would normally use unvoiced consonants, the manuscript has substituted voicings characteristic of the upper Veneto region. For example, *podere* (vs. Tuscan *potere*) (fols 127r, 134v, 135r, 137r, 152r, passim).⁷⁰ The voiceless occlusives *t* and *c* vary with their voiced representations *d* and *g*, independent of context and even in the same passage: *grido* and *cridato* (fols 102v, 103r); *manti* (Tuscan *mandi*) (fol. 140r); and *saludete* (fol. 151v), *saludò* (fols 92r, 106v, 139v). Forms of *dire* ('to say') spelled with *g* (*dig[u]a, digue*) are shared by Veneto and Veronese dialects.⁷¹

---

⁶⁵   Infurna, pp. 73, 80.
⁶⁶   *ditto / ditte*: fols 92r, 92v, 103v, 115v, 125v. See Infurna, p. 80.
⁶⁷   *abatette*: fols 115v, 127v, 170v; *guaritte* fol. 127v, *partitte*: fols 93v, 95r, 115r, 120r, 137r, 156v; *prendette* fol. 108r, *sentitte* fol. 110r, *ussitte* fol. 99v. See Infurna, pp. 79, 81. Emilian uses *-itte* in perfect tenses as well (Corti, 56–7).
⁶⁸   In Florentine *k* was still frequent as late as 1294. Its use diminished in the course of the fourteenth century, but one must allow for regional differences (Migliorini, *Italian Language*, pp. 102, 144).
⁶⁹   Corti, 34–6.
⁷⁰   Rohlfs §201.
⁷¹   *digua, digue*: fols 122r, 127r, 179r, 182r; and the subjunctive *diga* fol. 140v. For documented medieval Veronese occurrences, including *digo*, see Riva, 'Storia dell'antico dialetto' (1952–53), 9, 15, 73, 79; and TV, p. 549. For the gerund *digando*, see TV, pp. 53, 57, 58, 127, 128, 546. For *digando* in Veronese texts, see Giuliari, 'Proposta', 332, 337; and Anna Cornagliotti, 'Un volgarizzamento del "Transitus Pseudo-Josephi de Arimathea" in dialetto veronese', *Atti della Accademia delle scienze di Torino, Classe di scienze fisiche, matematiche e naturali*, tome I, vol. 113 (1979), 197–217, on 213.

Such evidence indicates that the copyist's model was a distant descendent of a *Tristano* redaction in Tuscan; as it circulated in the northeast, native tendencies would have interfered into the written product.[72]

In addition to the dialectal impact on spellings, there is indisputable graphic confusion among *g*, *ç* and the latter lacking its tail. In the Veneto *ç* is very frequent, although it can be found to a lesser degree in Pisa and Lucca.[73] Its excessive use here demonstrates Franco-Italian influence and points to the Veneto as the general area of production.[74] Similarly, second person singular verbs ending in *-s* (*sias*, *debias*, *estias*) are found only in the Veneto.[75] Non-normative doubled consonants, *benne* (fols 95r, 100r, 102r, 118r); *buonno* (fol. 116r); *montonno*, *cavalcharonno* (fol. 101r); *pommo* (fol. 104v); *prreguo* (fol. 102r); *purro bonno* (fol. 98r); *unno* (fol. 94r) are also common in the Veneto.[76] A sprinkling of other Veneto elements appear, such as nouns with an initial *h-*: *hamore* (fol. 103r); *hofensa* (fol. 155r); *homo* (fols 92r, 93v, 95r, 96r, 97v, passim); *honor(e)* (fols 94v, 103r, 114v, 120r, 155r, 162r, passim); *hora* (fols 94r, 95v, 102v, 116r, 121v, 124v, passim); *hoste* (fol. 147r)[77] or the unusual verb *sgumentate* (fol. 136r)[78] as well as *autro* which can also be Pisan-Lucchese, as noted above. The spelling *pl-* instead of *pi-* was typical Veneto usage in Dante's day: *plante* (fol. 105v) or *planto* (fols 106v, 109r); the adjective *plieno* (fol. 183r); verb forms *plaçe* (fols 103v, 114r, 143v) or *plaçia* (fols 106v, 108v, 141v); *plaçera(e)* (fols 121v, 166v); *plançere* (fol. 92r) or *plangere* (fols 93r, 96v, 98v); and the gerund *plangendo* (fols 92r, 92v).[79]

Through her examination of northeastern linguistic traits in the *Fior di Virtù* segment, Maria Corti was able to localize precisely this exemplar's production to the Treviso-Belluno area.[80] The almost exclusive use of *onde* ('where') instead of Tuscan *dove* points to Belluno and Treviso, where the adverb was widely diffused in medieval texts and was still observed at the time of Corti's mid-twentieth century study.[81] Additional evidence for Treviso-Belluno production is the use of

---

[72]   Corti, 63.
[73]   In his *Tristano Corsiniano*, Roberto Tagliani comments on the same mixing of traits: 'con patina veneta ma recante vistosi debiti linguistici di un antigrafo toscano, probabilmente da assegnare all'area pisano-lucchese' (with a Veneto patina, but possessing visible linguistic debts to a Tuscan model, probably assignable to the Pisa-Lucca area) (p. 20, translation mine.)
[74]   Among the choices of graphic forms, the scribe favors the *ç* (Corti, 57, 61–2).
[75]   *debias*: fols 96r, 101v, 106v, 110r. See Corti, 58; and TV, pp. 37, 44, 51.
[76]   For additional geminations, see TV, p. 39.
[77]   See TV, p. 41; and Jole M. Ruggeri, 'Versioni italiani della "Queste del Saint Graal"', *Archivum Romanicum* 21 (1937), 476, 477, 480. The initial *h-* may be attributed to hypercorrection from Latin influence. It is also recorded in fourteenth-century Veronese texts (Riva, 'Storia dell'antico dialetto' [1951–52], 323; and Giuliari, 'Proposta', 328, 331, 332, 337, 338);
[78]   *Il Canzoniere di Nicolò de' Rossi*, ed. Furio Brugnolo, Medioevo e umanesimo 16 (Padua, 1974), vol. I, p. 339.
[79]   See *De vulgari eloquentia*, ed. and trans. Steven Botterill, Cambridge Medieval Classics 5 (Cambridge, 1996), §XIV, p. 9. See also Ruggeri, 'Versioni italiani', 478, 479; and Rohlfs §186.
[80]   Cigni supports Corti's conclusions: 'trevisano-bellunese con un fondo più antico pisano-lucchese ('*Roman de Tristan* in prosa e "compilazione" di Rustichello da Pisa in area veneta: A proposito di una recente edizione', *Lettere Italiane* 47 [1995], 602).
[81]   Lichtenhahn observed the modern use of *onde* in Belluno, Vicenza, Agnedo and Pirano (quoted by Corti, 60). Rare appearances of *dove* in MS 1729 (fols 97r, 99v, 104v, 108r, 112v, 125r) survive from this redaction's Tuscan ancestor.

Introduction

the grapheme *gu* to signify *g* (*Guovernale*) and the loss of *-u-* after *q-*, even in secondary developments: *chello, chesto* instead of Tuscan *quello, questo*.[82] The exclusive use of the verb *parere* instead of *sembrare* is another clue that points to Treviso.[83] There are rare instances of a singular definite article with plural nouns ending in *-esse* in our *Tristano*, a Pisan-Lucchese trait also used in Treviso and Belluno: *l'alegresse* (fol. 143v) and *la prodesse* (fol. 154r).[84] Spellings with *-ay-* indicate Franco-Italian influence and were used in the area of Belluno.[85] Future and conditional stems of *-are* verbs with *-ar-* are found throughout the exemplar.[86] Significantly, the same forms appear in the verses of Niccolò de' Rossi, a native of Treviso.[87] In addition, the *Tristano Corsiniano*, likely copied by a Veronese, is rife with these forms. Another common Veronese element found in Ricc. MS 1729 is the adjective *grande* with endings *-o / -a*, also used extensively in the *Corsiniano*.[88]

A further level of complexity concerns the presence of Gallicisms, suggesting that the copyist or one of his predecessors had a comfortable degree of familiarity with French or Franco-Italian, a linguistic hybrid used for many of the romances and secular narratives that circulated in northeastern Italy. Such an awareness is hardly surprising when one considers that the production of Franco-Italian chivalric texts in that area was at its zenith during the mid-fourteenth century.[89] Indeed, the entire second half of the fourteenth century was a time of great diffusion of texts in French and, as a result, an intense period of hybridization.[90] Old French or Franco-Italian influence on the language of this Riccardian *Tristano* include *plus*,[91] *quanto* (O.F. *quant*) with the meaning '*quando*', *sobra*,[92] and *salut, perdut, chonossut* lacking a final vowel.[93] Franco-Italian pronouns employed are

---

[82] For Treviso and Belluno traits, see Corti, 58–60. On /k/ written *qu-*, see Rohlfs §163.
[83] *Il Canzoniere*, ed. Brugnolo, vol. I, p. 338.
[84] Corti, 57, 61.
[85] Corti, 61. See also TV, p. 41.
[86] *mutaray* fol. 94v, *camparanno* fol. 94v, *gardarà* fol. 95r, *jurarò* fol. 103v, *jurarete* fol. 139r, *tallaray* fol. 104r, *demandarà*: fols 107r, 111r; *demandaro(e)*: fols 104r, 122r; *dimandaroe* fol. 134v, *parlarae* fol. 120r, *espeytaroe* fol. 122v, *comprareste* fol. 125v, *apellarò* fol. 132v, *metarò* fol. 135r, *trovarete* fol. 136r, *trovarae* fol. 175r, *salutarete* fol. 183v. These are also found in Verona (Riva, 'Storia' [1951–52], 326, 328) and Siena (Rohlfs §140).
[87] *Il Canzoniere*, ed. Brugnolo, vol. II, pp. 3, 237.
[88] '[G]li antichi testi settentrionali ci offrono non di rado [...] *granda* [...] *grando*' (Rohlfs §396). Ruggeri considers these traits as 'veneti, o, ancor meglio, veneziani' ('Versioni italiane', 472). They were also used in Verona: see Riva, 'Storia' (1952–53), 70, 71; and Corti, 54.
[89] Carlo Dionisotti, '*Entrèe d'Espagne, Spagna, Rotta di Roncisvalle*', in *Studi in onore di Angelo Monteverdi*, ed. G. G. Marcuzzo, 3 vols (Modena, 1959), vol. I, pp. 207–41.
[90] 'Il secondo Trecento è certamente il periodo della più grande diffusione del libro francese' (Lorenzo Renzi, 'Il francese come lingua letteraria e il franco-lombardo: L'epica carolingia nel Veneto', in *Storia della cultura veneta, I: Dalle origini al Trecento*, ed. Girolamo Arnaldi [Vicenza, 1976], 568); 'un'epoca di maggior ibridismo' (Corti, 33).
[91] *plus*: fols 104r, 104v, 105v. For Gallicisms and Franco-Italian influence in Trevisano-Bellunesi texts, see Corti, 61–3.
[92] *sobra*: fols 109v, 124r, 131v, 132bis-v, 136r, 144v, 153r, 172r; *sobbra* fol. 126r.
[93] *salut*: fols 106v, 111v, 152v, 156r; *perdut* fol. 92r; *chonossut* fol. 105r. These were also Old French or Venetian forms.

the second personal plural *vos*[94] and the ubiquitous third person plural possessive *lur*.[95] Rare untranslated examples from French include the adverb *non* (fol. 142r) as well as the borrowed negative expression *non ... gare* (*guère*, fol. 126v). One finds numerous spellings with *au-*;[96] *-y-* (*laysar, may, damaysella, preysone, raysone, coysi*);[97] and the prosthetic *e-* before *s* + consonant beginning nouns and verbs (*esbergo, eschudo, espada, estare*). The verb spelling *saveremo* (fol. 102r), *ssavere* (fol. 103r) is French influenced; and a single appearance of *donare* (fol. 167r) stems from Old French *doner*.[98]

A final group of lexemes would have been common to many regions of Italy, but again link the probable dating of Ricc. MS 1729 to the fourteenth century. During this period, hundreds of Latinisms entered the Italian vernacular.[99] The Latinizing form *fenestra* ('window') (fols 96r, 110v, 165v, 166r, 167v, 175v, 176v) was used by Petrarch. The manuscript contains scattered examples of Latinate subject pronouns: *illo* (fols 97r, 111v, 112v, 114r, 117r, 127r, 130r, 139v, 152v, 154v); *illa* (fols 97r, 162v, 173r); *illi* (fols 108r, 108v, 111v, 141r, 149r, 184v) as well as the infinitive *ire* (fols 150v, 158v); future tense *irà* (fol. 144v); and past participle *ito* (fol. 126v). Infrequent, semi-learned spellings with *np* or *pn* apparently derive from medieval ecclesiastical Latin relating to the verb *damner*.[100] In the manuscript this occurs on nouns that indicate harm or doubt: *danpno* (fol. 156v); *dapno* (fol. 147r); *dapnaçio* (fol. 149v); *dapnagio* (fols 120r, 154r, 181v); *dapnage* (fol. 150r); *donptare* (fol. 183r). Due to hypercorrection or analogy, the scribe also inserted the *p* into two semantically unrelated words: *(e)npbaysatori* (fols 107v, 108r) and *compbatere* (fol. 117r). There are also a few conservative Latinate consonant groupings: *facto* (fols 92v, 93r, 93v, passim); *decto* (fols 95r, 102r, 102v, 110v, passim); *sancti* (fols 91r, 93r, 103v, 139r, 145r); *ciptate* (fol. 140r); and *omni* (fol. 188r).

In conclusion, when we consider the linguistic traces from different idioms – western Tuscan, Veneto, French, Franco-Italian, even erudite Latinisms – together with the many corrupt readings and textual variants attributable not merely to monogenetic copying errors, we have an inkling of the huge number of prose *Tristan* manuscripts that must have circulated in Italy in the fourteenth century, and the many copyists through whose hands this particular redaction passed. The mixed spellings and hybridization of graphic forms suggest that, as readers of diverse documents and books, these copyists had good acquaintance not only with various spoken languages and dialects, but with written forms. Furthermore, Ricc. MS 1729 adds to the growing body of evidence regarding the transmission history of Arthurian romances in Italy. Its Pisan-Lucchese linguistic substrate reinforces the

---

94   Fol. 113r, a unique occurrence. See *La Geste Francor: Edition of the 'Chansons de geste' of MS. Marc. Fr. XIII (=256)*, ed. Leslie Zarker Morgan, Medieval and Renaissance Texts and Studies 348, 2 vols (Tempe, 2009), vol. 2, p. 1435; William F. Kibler, *An Introduction to Old French*, Introductions to Older Languages 3 (New York, 1984), pp. 87–8.
95   *lur*: fols 101r, 121r, 123v, 127v, 129v, 130r, 132v, passim. See also Corti, 63.
96   As discussed above, this can be Pisan-Lucchese or Veneto (Corti, 56, 61, 62).
97   Corti, 61. One also finds the related Franco-Italian *choisi*.
98   *Il Canzoniere*, ed. Brugnolo, vol. I, p. 281.
99   Migliorini, *Italian Language*, pp. 135, 152.
100   *Dictionnaire du Moyen Français (1330–1500)* online at: zeus.atilf.fr/dmf/ Accessed 23 August 2023. *Dapno* was used by Machiavelli (Battaglia, *Grande dizionario*, vol. 15, p. 482).

notion that western Tuscany was an important production center for the originally French Arthurian romances.[101] One narrative detail, not found in the French prose *Tristan* or the *Tristano Veneto*, again points to western Tuscany: Tristan avenges his father's murder by destroying the city of 'Prescia', i.e., Brescia (fol. 100r). The inclusion of an Italian toponym within the Arthurian literary landscape is striking. Historically, the Guelf city Brescia was besieged and captured by Henry VII in 1311 thereby reigniting old, subalpine political conflicts. It seems likely that early in the transmission process this city's name was inserted by a redactor or copyist who found it an apt metaphor for Tristan's cruel vendetta. The real-world intrusion could have stemmed from either Guelph Lucca or politically-divided Pisa.[102] Other Arthurian literary examples produced in Tuscany are the hybrid Tuscan *La Inchiesta del San Gradale*, the beginning of which forms part of the compilation known as the *Tristano Panciatichiano*, and the recently discovered 56-folio Florentine fragment of the prose *Lancelot*.[103] The linguistic evidence of our *Tristano* exactly mirrors the geographical evidence furnished by the watermarks clearly traceable to Pisa and Lucca, and possibly to Florence or Venice. The commercial lines of transmission for paper stocks would have offered routes for cultural transmission as well. Thus, the trajectory of Ricc. MS 1729 – copied in northeastern Italy, but demonstrating western Tuscan characteristics – parallels that of another *Tristano* which is geographically and chronologically close: the *Tristano Corsiniano*. Its language similarly indicates a Tuscan antecedent for a text that migrated north-eastward, where it passed through Veronese and Venetian hands and, in the case of MS 1729, ultimately to a copyist in the Treviso-Belluno area.[104]

CONCLUSION

The twin aims of this project were to make another exemplar of the prose *Tristan* in Italy available to scholars of Italian as well as to Arthurian literature afficionados and Anglophones. Despite the infelicities in this manuscript's production and the

---

[101] See for example, Cigni, 'La ricezione medievale della letteratura francese nella Toscana nord-occidentale', in *Fra toscanità e italianità: Lingua e letteratura dagli inizi al Novecento*, eds Edeltraud Werner and Sabine Schwarze, Kultur und Erkenntnis 22 (Tübingen and Basel, 2000), pp. 78–9; and Adriana Di Domenico, 'Un cavaliere sotto l'insegna del leone rampante: Una nuova ipotesi di committenza', in *La Tavola Ritonda: Manoscritto Palatino 556, Firenze Biblioteca Nazionale Centrale*, ed. Roberto Cardini, I codici miniati, 2 vols (Rome, 2009), vol. I, p. 117: 'il codice Riccardiano 1729 [...] testimonierebbe il passaggio in area padano-veneto di materiali della redazione R [...] che ha un suo sviluppo indipendente in Toscana'; and *Lancellotto: Versione italiana inedita del 'Lancelot en prose'*, ed. Luca Cadioli, Archivio Romanzo 32 (Florence, 2016), p. 101.

[102] This datum furnishes a *terminus post quem* for our manuscript's ancestor, Ricc. MS 2543, in which 'Bresia' is named (TR, p. 18). The accurate spelling 'Brescia' is in TP, p. 138.

[103] Florence, Biblioteca della Fondazione Ezio Franceschini, MS 1. See Cadioli, 'A New Arthurian Text: the Tuscan translation of the Lancelot en prose', *Journal of the International Arthurian Society* 2.1 (2014): 63–9.

[104] *Tristano Corsiniano*, ed. Allaire, pp. xxii–xxiii. See also my 'Literary Evidence for Multilingualism: The *Roman de Tristan* in its Italian Incarnations', in *Medieval Multilingualism: The Francophone World and its Neighbours*, eds Christopher Kleinhenz and Keith Busby, Medieval Texts and Cultures of Northern Europe 20 (Turnhout, 2010), pp. 145–53.

apparently 'degraded' form of the text when compared to its distant ancestors, this redaction conserves valuable evidence in several areas: 1) With respect to medieval multilingualism, its mixed traits present a rich linguistic loam that should be examined in detail. Although such a study is beyond the scope of this volume and outside the principal expertise of this author, I have sought to preserve all such evidence in my transcription. 2) By bringing this neglected witness to light, more work can be done on comparing its narrative content to the other extant *Tristans* that were copied in Italy. 3) Riccardian manuscript 1729 provides more evidence for the transmission of Arthuriana into the northeastern part of the peninsula, another lengthy written exemplar that takes its place beside *Tristano Veneto* and *Tristano Corsiniano*. These redactions must be considered alongside numerous visual depictions of Arthurian material in wall murals, frescoes, ceiling panels and luxury objects in that region.[105] Mario Salmi once hypothesized 'that there were contacts between the authors of certain chivalric codices and the school of painting which flourished between the thirteenth and the fourteenth century, *particularly in Treviso*, where the Loggia dei Cavalieri was elaborately decorated with paintings derived from miniatures'.[106] An inventory from Treviso dated 1335 mentions an ivory chess set acquired in Venice that apparently included a King Arthur chess piece.[107] Meliadus' image was included among illustrious Greek, Roman and biblical rulers in a cycle of decorative wooden ceiling panels created for the late medieval Palazzo Ghiringhelli in Bellinzona, once part of the Visconti territory.[108] 4) Finally, this edition celebrates a manuscript that was long since identified, but discarded by Parodi, as an important witness to the pan-European popularity of the Tristan legend.

Gloria Allaire
Lexington, Kentucky
8 September 2023

[105] Allaire, 'Arthurian Art in Italy', in *Arthur of the Italians*, pp. 209–12, 216–18, 220, 223–4.
[106] Mario Salmi, *Italian Miniatures*, trans. Elisabeth Borgese-Mann (New York, 1954), p. 40, emphasis mine.
[107] Allaire, 'Arthurian Art in Italy', p. 224.
[108] Vera Segre, 'Illustrazioni cavalleresche fra manoscritti e carte dipinte nella Lombardia del Tre e Quattrocento', in *Narrazioni e strategie dell'illustrazione: Codici e romanzi cavallereschi nell'Italia del Nord (secc. XIV–XVI)*, eds Annalisa Izzo and Ilaria Molteni, I libri di Viella: Arte. Études lausannoises d'histoire de l'art 19; Studi lombardi 6 (Rome, 2014), pp. 35, 38, 42, and plate 16. Tristan's father had himself been the protagonist of a lost *Roman de Meliadus*, echoes of which survive in *Guiron le Courtois* and Rustichello's *Compilation*.

NOTE ON TRANSCRIPTION AND TRANSLATION

PREVIOUSLY PUBLISHED EXCERPTS

Tristano Riccardiano, ed. Parodi, pp. xii–xix (portions of [modern numbered] fols 93r, 180r, 182r, 183r, 188r–v, 189r–v, 190r.)

TRANSCRIPTION NORMS

As is true for many medieval manuscripts, the scribe often confuses *s* / *l* or *s* / *f*. At times it is hard to discern the difference between *e* or *o*. I have included remarks on these orthographic difficulties in my footnotes. This *Tristano* contains a dazzling array of spelling variants beyond even medieval norms, for example, the pronoun 'each one': *chiascuno* (fols 99v, 154r, 159v); *chiadascuno* (fol. 153r); *chiaschaduno* (fols 132*bis*-v, 141v, 165v, 172r); the noun 'pavilion(s)': *pavalione* (singular or plural, fols 130r, 130v, 136v, 137v, 140v, 168v); *pavaligni* (fol. 130v); *pavaliogne, -i* (fols 130r, 130v, 137v, 142v, 163v); *pavallogni* (fol. 129r); *pavalloni* (fol. 128r); forms of the verb 'to begin': *chomençia* (fol. 115r); *chomençò* (fols 92r, 130r); *chominçano* (fol. 126v); *chominçho(no)* (fols 92v, 96r, 99v, 125r, 132r); *enchomenchiò* (fol. 100v); *enchomençiò* (fols 114r, 115v); *enchomenço(no)* (fols 92v, 95v, 96v, 99r, 118v, 120v, 125r, 125v); *enchominçiano* (fol. 100r); *enchominçio(no)* (fols 96r, 107r); *enchominçò* (fols 107r, 111r); and the infinitive 'to kill': *ançidere* (fols 101r, 155r); *honcidere* (fol. 96v); *oncidere* (fols 96v, 104v, 120r); *ucidere* (fols 93r, 95v, 98r, 136v, 145v); *uncidere* (fol. 93v). For linguistic reasons, I preserve all spellings and variants, but use < > to indicate letters or words that appear superfluous.

The manuscript contains certain spellings with '*j*'. In the initial position a capitalized *J* has a bar across it with the letter sometimes descending below the line. Within words and in the final position, I have converted -*j* to -*i* according to modern Italian norms.

The protagonist's name is spelled *Trisstaino* only once (in the passage where his mother names her newborn); thereafter, when written *in extenso* it is consistently *Tristano*. In the manuscript, most occurrences of his name are abbreviated as .*T*. The heroine's name, most often shown with the abbreviation *Y*., is written *in extenso* both as *Yssota* (fols 112r, 135r, 143v) and less often as *Ysota* (fols 111v, 114v). Following the linguistic norms of the redaction, such as the analogous spellings *yssola*, var. *issola* ('island') (fols 149v, 150r, 150v, 151r, 152v, 156v, 185r) or *Jossepo / Josseppe / Giossepe* (fols 146v–147r), I have expanded the *Y*. abbreviation with two -ss-, but I conserve *Ysota* where it appears *in extenso*. All *Y* spellings have been retained. The scribe frequently writes a

dot above a final -*y* – for example, *dey* ('God') – as well as for other words. *Governale*, the spelling normally found in Tuscan redactions, is used frequently here, sometimes with the regional use of a doubled *l*. In the rare cases of a *G.* abbreviation, I have expanded it with the normative *Governale* spelling. One also finds many instances of *Guovernale*, the *gu-* being a grapheme that simply signals *g*, i.e., /g/ the velar, not the palatal. However, since this is specific to the Treviso-Belluno area, I have retained all forms as found in the manuscript when written *in extenso*. For minor characters' names and toponyms, I retain all spellings as found in the manuscript. For example, *Scorçia* ('Scotland'), most often written with -*r*-, is shown as found without comment. Where spellings are clearly erroneous with respect to the larger textual tradition, I indicate this in footnotes. Such errors could be due to lack of familiarity with the material, misreading the model or a faulty model, or due to incorrect expansion of single initials used to abbreviate characters' names.

The inexpert scribe did not seem to understand the function of certain basic abbreviations and often failed to copy or expand them; of course, some errors could be due to flaws in his model. The scribe often omits the titulus, yet elsewhere writes *nn* with an extraneous titulus. Sometimes he uses a titulus or long horizontal pen stroke to represent a letter other than *n* / *m*. He never used the '*9*'-shaped abbreviation for '*con*' and often omits the '*n*' from *con* spellings. To correct such omissions, I show the missing letters in square brackets. For the word *co(m)pagnia*, when written with a titulus, I expanded it with an -*m-* following manuscript norms where it was written *in extenso*. The unusual use of a final -*y* to represent -*us* occurs in the name *Meliadus* nine times (fols 91r, 92r, 93r, 94v, 95v, 99v, 100r) as well as in the colophon blessing *Referamus* (fol. 188r).[1] At times the scribe writes two dots above a letter that seem to indicate *r*, especially at the ends of infinitives, but this is not consistent. The scribe does use the abbreviation for *quando*, written as *qu* with a tilde-like stroke above it. He also uses the normal abbreviation – *aut* followed by a superscripted *o* or *a* – for *autro* or *autra* (fols 144v, 145r). I have expanded these and other standard abbreviations (such as *per*, *pr*) without comment in my transcription.

In all aspects of the copying, irregularities abound. Punctuation and accents have been added according to modern norms. For Roman numerals, the scribe normally writes a *punctus* to each side; where missing, I have added them. The scribe infrequently uses a *punctus* with the value of a comma to show internal phrasing or pauses. This practice can indicate that a manuscript was intended for reading aloud.[2] I have added or adjusted capital letters to reflect modern practice. However, I maintain the capital letter on titles (*Re, Redina, Madonna, Mes[s]er*) as found in the manuscript. For nouns written with a Gothic capital

---

[1] This may be a misreading of the final -*x* abbreviation found in medieval texts. See Françoise Veillard and Olivier Guyotjeannin (eds), *Conseils pour l'édition des textes mediévaux. Fascicule I: conseils généraux*, École nationale des chartes, Groupe de recherches 'La civilisation de l'écrit au Moyen Âge' (Paris, 2001), p. 28 §12.

[2] Jacqueline Wessel, '"Quirks and Twists": Looking over the Shoulder of the Middle Dutch *Ferguut* Scribe', paper read at the XXV Congress of the International Arthurian Society, Universität Würzburg, 25 July 2017.

Note on Transcription and Translation

R especially '*Realme*', I have used lower case. The title indicating 'sir' (from French, *monsieur*) appears *in extenso* with either a single -*s*- (*Meser*: fols 113r, 141r, 141v, 143r, 155v, 186r, 186v, 188r) or double -*ss*- (*Messer*: fols 113v, 167v, 186r, 186v, 187r). One also finds *Mes(ser)* written with a single -*s*- plus the *ser* abbreviation (fols 122r, 144v, 186v). For consistency, I have capitalized this title where the scribe did not.

Since this is an irregularly formed, non-cursive hand, the use of spacing varies greatly. There are often spaces within single words, especially in the case of conjunctions. I unite these logically according to modern norms: *dapoyché, encontra/o, ende / onde, enfra, ensieme, entre, enverso; perché, poiché, siché, sichome* including variants with -*que*; *neancho, neanque, neuno; tutavia*. Adverbs in -*mente* (at times -*mentre* or -*mento*) are normally united in the manuscript; if not, I have united them.³ Tonic pronouns are normally written with a space and are only infrequently attached to the verb. In the second person singular challenge to combat *gàrdate*, I have united the verb and pronoun for consistency and added an accent for clarity; elsewhere, *gardate voy* is clearly plural.

When the preposition *a* is followed by a definite article, the scribe overwhelmingly unites them, e.g., *ala, alo*: 124 times attached (94%) against seven times with a space (6%) in my sampling. For the sake of consistency, I have united the remaining few. By contrast, *de* followed by a definite article is more often written with a space, e.g. *de lo, de la*: 100 times (66.3%) versus united fifty-one times (33.7%). Following these norms, in my transcription I have detached *de* from its article wherever these had been written attached. Without exception, *del* is always connected, and I have maintained this contraction. I have also maintained a space when either preposition occurs before the proper name 'L'Amoroldo'.

Throughout the manuscript one notes the lack of a preposition with verbs followed by a masculine singular article and place name, e.g., *remanendo el desserto* (fol. 92r). This follows the Old French practice in which *el* used alone meant the singular *en + le*, and *es* meant the plural *en + les* ('in the').⁴ There are also rare examples of the Tuscan style prepositional contraction: *nel mondo* (fol. 155v), *nel realme* (fol. 178v).

There are no rubrics or chapter indications in this *Tristano* exemplar. Structurally throughout the text, the formula 'Ora disse lo conto' and its variants clearly mark new narrative episodes. Red *capitulum* characters indicate divisions within the longer episodes. For the most part, these are quite logical with reference to the narrative structure, not merely decorative, and may reflect the copyist's model. Based on these scribal indications, I have inserted modern chapter numbers in square brackets. To help the modern reader, I have further broken up large blocks of text by creating internal paragraphs based on content or the appearance of new 'actors', similar to scenes in a theatrical play; however, I did not create a new paragraph for each interlocutor as in modern fiction.

---

3 For numerous Veronese examples, see Riva, 'Storia' (1951–52), 320.
4 Veillard and Guyotjeannin (eds), *Conseils,* p. 45 §28.

SPECIAL SYMBOLS

As noted above, the scribe left numerous blank spaces for intended miniatures that were never executed. These voids are valuable evidence because they likely reflect what was found in the scribe's model and also provide clues about reader reception. I indicate such spaces with three vertical 'pipes' ||| and describe their dimensions relative to the text in my footnotes. From folio 151r on, there are a few instances where the scribe broke up the text, positioning partial lines at the outer margin or gutter, to frame the intended miniature. For these broken sentences, I mark the line breaks with a single vertical line (|). Finally, to properly represent a peculiarity of Italian linguistics, raised dots indicate syntactic doubling: *e·ffar*, *so·nnome*, *mi·ppote*, *la·ssera*, *e·vvegne*.

TRANSLATION NORMS

As is the case with the *Tristano Riccardiano* of Ricc. MS 2543, edited by Parodi, the lexicon of this witness is very limited. Given the fact that Ricc. MS 1729 was a later descendent and had undergone multiple adaptations into non-Tuscan dialects, if anything, its language is still more simplified. I have avoided an 'interpretative' translation and did not enrich the language with synonyms or try to polish its style. For benefit of scholars who may be collating *Tristan* versions, I have tried to echo the rhetorical, semantic and sonic value of the manuscript while eschewing anachronisms. This version of *Tristano* is a far cry from the more erudite rhetorical style of the *Panciatichiano*. As with TP, Ricc. MS 1729 contains an excessive amount of conjunctions *e* and *ma* ('and', 'but'), often used with interchangeable meanings. I have taken the liberty of translating them more logically to assist the modern reader, but in the transcription itself all occurences are retained. As a result of the ubiquitous conjunctions, clauses and sentences tumble out with hardly a pause, giving the story an urgency better suited to oral performance than to silent reading. Yet despite modern criticisms of monotony or repetition in these romances, the breathless tempo builds a kind of suspense that keeps the reader or listener engaged.

I have tried to respect the original syntax to the greatest extent possible, only rarely inverting clauses to avoid convoluted structures. By inserting punctuation to better elucidate passages for the modern reader, I hope to convey the rhythm and cadence of this *Tristano* without adding words or fracturing long descriptive sentences into shorter units. However, in a departure from the medieval narrative strategies of relying on present tense or of mixing tenses within a single sentence or paragraph, I have regularized tenses according to modern English use. In some places, I used parentheses for apparent narratorial asides. Due to differences in word division and syntax, page breaks in the English translation are not always in the same place as in the transcription; I have aligned them as closely as possible to those of the original text.

Although I attempted to translate words consistently with only one English equivalent, in the case of common verbs with idiomatic meanings such as *dare*, *fare* and *menare*, I took some liberties in adjusting these for good sense in English.

Note on Transcription and Translation

For verbs of communication, I rendered *dire* normally as 'to say' or 'to tell', at times 'to ask' or even 'to reply' as logic dictates, but *parlare* as 'to speak'. A striking anomalous verb use is *venire* ('to come') with the significance of *andare* ('to go'). This seems to be a colloquialism connected to the narrator's point-of-view and indicates a redactor's or copyist's close engagement with the material. As always, I have preserved all original words in the Italian transcription without comment and have only adjusted their sense in my translation.

A few nouns and expressions did seem to require synonyms, but I kept the English choices to a minimum. For example, the ubiquitous noun *dolore* can express physical or emotional suffering and is shown variously as 'sorrow' or 'pain'. I translated *donne* as 'ladies' when it pertains to rank or society, but as 'women' when gender is at issue. Wherever possible, the noun *realme* is given as 'realm', but also as 'kingdom' according to context. The expression *in tal maniera* is rendered variously as 'in that way', 'in that manner' or 'in that fashion'. The related forms *che, ché, que, qué*; present a special problem: these may be relative pronouns or shortened forms of the conjunctions *perché* or *siché*. The translator's task is complicated by manuscript variants, dialectal spellings and the lack of accents. Any one of these can yield a plethora of possible meanings: 'that', 'who', 'whom', 'because', 'so that', 'since'.

Another challenge when translating from Romance languages into English concerns possessives: there is no apostrophe and final *-s*. Instead, these are constructed with a noun followed by a clause with *di / de*: 'the nephew of King Mark'. Throughout, I conserved the Romance construction where this carries more rhetorical weight or must smoothly connect to the following clause. If not, I streamlined these with the English *'s*: 'King Mark's nephew'. In addition, the third person possessive adjective (*so, soa,* and variants) are gender-neutral ('his' or 'hers'); I translate these logically according to context. Finally, as in modern Italian, possessive adjectives are not used where the possessor is obvious. Thus '*l'espada*' or '*li cavalli*' do not simply mean 'the sword', 'the horses', but signify '*his* sword', '*their* horses'.

Gallicisms do appear in the manuscript, although not to the extent found in the *Panciatichiano* which was much closer to the French original. Due to cultural connections between France and northern Italy, and the vast circulation of French texts, many common loan words and calques were accepted into local use. In this Ricc. MS 1729 is no exception. Thus wherever possible, I employ cognates to respect the redaction's French ancestor or its newer, borrowed forms: *apresso* (Fr. *après* 'after'); *chamera* (Fr. *chambre* 'chamber'). I translate the common expression *a tanto* variously as 'in that moment', 'just then', 'at that'. Certain words and expressions belonging to the *fin'amors* context are semantically loaded and cannot be easily translated into English: for *folle amore,* I chose 'mad love' to mirror the non-erudite norms of the manuscript's language; but I show *amicho, amis* as *ami, amis*. From *chanson de geste* influence, one finds the multivalenced adjective *prode* or *prodo* (Fr. *preu*), that crucial trait for warriors,

which I rendered as 'valiant'. An anomaly influenced by Old French *quan* or *quanto* is the use of *quanto* ('how much') to mean *quando* ('when').[5]

With regard to proper names and toponyms, in my transcription I preserve all variant spellings and inaccuracies as found in the manuscript, but in the translation I have standardized these names according to the larger textual tradition and in consultation with the various editions of the *Tristano Riccardiano* or the *Tristano Panciatichiano*. I also made frequent recourse to the Old French tradition to discern the most 'authentic' spelling of certain characters' names. Thus I render the heroine's name as *Yseut* to correspond to the form *Ys(s)ota* found in the manuscript as well as its standard abbreviation for that character. This choice also respects the original French rather than the Germanic *Isolde*. The heroine's handmaiden *Branguina* is translated as *Brangain*. *Palamides* is the scribe's preferred spelling which I maintained throughout. I show *Languis* as *Anguin*, *Galioto* as *Galehot* and *Bramor* as *Blanor*. For some knights' names there are oscillations and misreadings: for example, *Lanbique, Lanbis, Lanbuigues, Lanbigues, Lanbigue* which I standardized as *Lambegues*; and the misspelling *Beldin* or *Bendin* has been changed to *Ghedis*, in accordance with other Italian redactions.

As with any unusual proper names, Arthurian place names can present many variants: the common toponym for Ireland is variously spelled *Milanda*, *Verlanda* or most often, *Landa*, which I have regularized throughout as *Ireland*. I have shown the manuscript's *Longres* as *Logres*; and I have standardized variants *Leones*, *Leonis* and the rare *Lionis* as *Leonis*. I preserved inconsistencies of singular or plural toponyms, such as the Faraway Island(s) as they appear in the exemplar.

Due to a vigorous and lengthy textual transmission process, numerous corruptions and/or abbreviations have crept into the narrative. At times these create illogical moments or even contradictions, notably in the final episode of Tristan's wounding and the lovers' deaths. I have translated these difficult passages as literally as possible based on the readings conserved in the manuscript. Problematic moments are signalled in the footnotes to the transcription and will refer the reader to variant readings from analogous editions that are often more complete. Words in square brackets are my own additions offered for clarity, especially where a flurry of pronouns can obscure a particular characters' identity.

---

[5] For example, on fols 179v, 186r. See *Geste Francor*, ed. Zarker Morgan, vol. 2, p. 1365.

Il Tristano Riccardiano
(Parodi's siglum 'F')

[1] [fol. 91r] *[A]l nome sia de Dio e de la Virge Maria e de tuti li soy sancti de Dio. Diròve del naysemento de Tristano, come verrà e[n] esto mondo, chome fenite, e grande trevvalli aversa de la soa aventura.*[1]

[2] *Or*[2] *disse lo conto que lo Re Meliadus andando a chaçiare com altri chavalieri de la soa corte, andoron con luy ala chaçia. E cominçiano la [ca]ccia bella e grande, may niuno non v'era que saupesse de chaçia quanto lo Re Meliadus. E ello persequendo uno servo molto bello* |||[3] *delonguo se da li soy baroni. E andò in <per> uno grando desserto siqué non si guarda là ond'ello va. E laysò li chavalieri soi e <li chavalieri soi> andò en tal manera da l'ora de vespore i[n]fine al'ora de prima.*[4]

E alora lo Re Meliadus perviene a una fontana. Estando per una pocha d'ora, viene una damayssella e disse: 'Re Meliadus, si tu fosse coysì francho chavaliere e sì prode come altry ti tiennono, io ti mostrería più alt<r>e[5] *aventure que may chavaliere trovasse'.*

Alora disse lo Re Meliadus, 'Damaysella, si voy aventura me most[r]ate, e io venrò com vui là unque voy volete'.

[fol. 91v] *E alora la damaysella cavalchò inanti, e lo Re Meliadus apresso, cavalcando for de l'estrada per uno stritto sentieri. E tanto cavalcano que pervenneno ala torre di la damaysella e qui ne smontono amboro. E la damaysella presse lo Re Meliadus per la mano e menelo ende la sala del palayso, e quine si dessarmò lo Re. E poyché fo dessarmato, la damaysella lo presse per la mano e menò lo ende la camera, la quale era encantata. Quando lo Re Meliadus fo dentro, non si recorde de la Redina Eliabella nì de so realme nì de li suo baroni, si none de la damaysella que vede denançi da sé.* |||[6]

Quando le donne de Leones sepeno que lo Re Meliadus era perduto ende la foresta, montono a cavallo e vannolo cercando per tuto lo desserto e non lo trovanno en nulla parte. E venendo la notte, tuti li baroni se ne tornano. Alora la Redina Eliabella, vedendo que non si trovava, ela medesma disse ch'ella vollie andare a ce[r]chare. Allo matino si leva <d>[7] *la redina, s'apareça e monta a cavallo; una damaysella li fae compagnia. Alora si partino dal pa* [fol. 92r] *layso e cavalcano*

---

[1] Parodi published excerpts from the beginning and end of Ricc. MS 1729 to supplement his base text, MS Ricc. 2543. He refers to the folios according to the modern, machine-stamped numbering at lower right corners of *rectos* (TR-Parodi, pp. xii–xix). I indicate these previously published extracts in italics. However, my edition follows the original scribal folio numbers and makes corrections to Parodi's transcription.

[2] Space for large initial, never executed. No guide letter visible. TR-Parodi, p. xii shows 'Et'; however, the usual enterlace formulae begin with *Or / Ora*. See, for example, *Ora laysa lo conto* fol. 102r, *Ora disse lo conto*: fols 103v, 110r, 111r.

[3] Throughout the MS, scribe left spaces for miniatures that were never executed; here, six full lines blank.

[4] This is illogical according to medieval method of telling time. TR, p. 4 conserves the proper order.

[5] See TR, p. 4: *piue alta aventura*.

[6] Five full lines left blank for miniature or rubric.

[7] Stray 'd' is an inexplicable scribal anomaly. See also fols 135r, 136v, 149v, 182r, 185r, 186r.

[1] [fol. 91r] In the name of God and of the Virgin Mary and of all God's saints. I will tell you about the birth of Tristan, how he came into this world, how he left it, and the great travails of his adverse fortune.

[2] Now the tale says that King Meliadus was going hunting with other knights of his court who were going with him to the hunt; and they began a fine, great hunt, but there was no one who knew as much about hunting as King Meliadus. While he was chasing after a very nice stag, he drew apart from his barons and went through a great wilderness since he was not watching where he was going, and he left his knights behind and went on in that manner from the hour of prime until the hour of vespers.

And then King Meliadus came upon a fountain.* After a short while, a damsel came along and said: 'King Meliadus, if you were as brave and valiant a knight as others hold you to be, I would show you more noble adventures than a knight ever found'.

Then King Meliadus said, 'Damsel, if you'll show me adventure, I'll come with you wherever you wish'.

[fol. 91v] And then the damsel rode ahead, and King Meliadus after her, riding off the main road along a narrow path, and they rode so much that they came to the damsel's tower and here both of them dismounted. And the damsel took King Meliadus by the hand and led him into the great hall of the palace, and here the king removed his armor. After he had disarmed, the damsel took him by the hand and led him into her chamber, which was enchanted. When King Meliadus was inside, he didn't remember anything about Queen Eliabel nor about his realm nor about his barons, except for the damsel whom he saw before him.

When the women of Leonis found out that King Meliadus was lost in the forest, they mounted their horses and went searching for him throughout the wilderness, but they didn't find him anywhere. And since nightfall was coming, all the barons returned. Then, upon seeing that they didn't find him, Queen Eliabel said that she herself wanted to go and search. In the morning the queen arose, prepared herself and mounted her horse; a damsel kept her company.

---

*   I translate *fontana* with its cognate, although 'fountain' conjures images of ornate marble structures, illogical in a wilderness. Medieval illuminators were faced with this dilemma as well. Their depictions range from a naturalistic font emerging from rocks (Bibliothèque de l'Arsenal, MS 5073, fol. 139r) to a simple man-made trough built around a spring (BnF, MS fr. 99, fol. 37r) to the more ornate, artificial construction (The Morgan Library and Museum, MS M.41, fol. 81r).

giù per la ciptà. E va [tanto][8] que se ne va alo desserto e cerchalo da onni parte: non lo possono trobare. La Redina dolendi si de lo Re Meliadus, cavalcando per lo desserto, pervenonno a una gra[n]de foresta a una montagna e guarda su per lo monte. E vide venire uno homo a cavallo enverso de lei. Cavalcando son[9] giunti ensieme; e la Redina lo saludò cortessamente; ello li rende soe salute. E la Redina disse, 'Saperiaste [dir] me novelle de lo Re Meliadus qui è perduto el[10] desserto?'

Quelli resposse e disse, 'Dama, le cosse perdute non si trovan may. May lo Re Meliadus <non si trova>[11] non è perdut,[12] may voy non lo vedrete may, e retrovarà si bene'. E dapoyqué ebe ditte quelle parolle, si partìo de la Redina e cavalchò fortamente. ||||[13] (May si alcuno me demanderà chome avea nome aquesto homo a cavallo, io dirò que à·nnome Merlino lo profeta.)

E la Redina remanendo el desserto e pensando, e udì le parolle que Merlino li avia decte, encominçò forte a plançere e de ch[i]amarse 'lassa Redina' e 'dolorsiossa (sic) Redina'. En tal maniera que lo dolore del so ventre li chomençò a perdere sì chome fa a ferire que era gravida. E plangendo, la Redina disse, 'Giovanetta, venuto [è 'l] tempo [fol. 92v] de la mia deliberat[i]o[n]e[14] del mio ventre'. E la damaysella disse, 'Non poteresste voi cavalchare enfine ala villa?' Ella disse che *non*.

Alora enchominçia fortamente a cridare, de chiamare Idio e la sua Matre che si devesseno aytare. Sufrendo gra[n]de dolore e plangendo, repossò[15] uno filliolo mascho en uno foresto luoguo. Dapoyqu'ella ebe facto, disse ala damaysella, 'Dàmi lo figliolo ché io lo vuolio vedere'. Alora la damaysella lo li posse en brachio. 'Ora ti veguo la più bella creatura que may debia essere. Dapoyqué la prima fessta ch'io abo auto per te si è en dolori – e io per te t[r]ista debo essere, dapoyché in dollore d'abo aquistato – vullio que per recordamento de li mie dolore abi nome Trisstaino'. E dapoyché la redina ebe ditto queste parolle, disse, 'Patre celestial, abi merçe de l'anima mia'. E encontenente morirò la Redina.

Dapoyqué la damaysella vide la Redina morta, presse lo fantino e 'nvolope lo ende lo mantello de la Redina. E poy enchominçò a fare lo maor pianto que may fosse udito per una damaysella, e enchomençò a metere grande vosse siché tuto lo desserto facea ressonare. May venendo .ii. cavalieri per lo desserto e utendendo lo rumore que la damaysella facia, ||||[16] [fol. 93r] li chavalieri andaron

---

[8] Omission in MS. Insertion follows Parodi's transcription (TR-Parodi, p. xiii).

[9] In MS, *fon*. Confusion of *s* / *f* is a common problem. See Alfredo Stussi, 'Esse, non effe!', *Italianistica* 23 (1994), 513–14.

[10] In MS adverbial clauses with place names often lack a preposition: the definite article alone comprises 'in'. This follows the Old French practice in which *es* meant *en* + *les*.

[11] Scribe began one phrase with *non*, expunctuated the next two words, and then wrote the phrase correctly, also beginning with *non*.

[12] Lack of final vowel is an Old French or Venetian trait.

[13] Five full lines left blank; miniature never executed. Parodi's first transcribed excerpt ends here (TR-Parodi, pp. xii–xiv).

[14] Cf. TP, p. 130: *diliveragione*.

[15] This verb with a meaning specific to childbirth is not found in TR, TP nor TV. In the broadest sense of ceasing a difficult mental or physical labor, see Battaglia, *Grande dizionario*, vol. 16, p. 697. See also fol. 95v for the infinitive *repausare* and the gerundial form: *repausando*.

[16] Scribe left five full lines blank; miniature never executed.

Il Tristano Riccardiano *(Parodi's siglum 'F')*

Then they left the [fol. 92r] palace and rode down through the city. They went so far that they got to the wilderness and searched for him everywhere; they could not find him. With the queen grieving so for King Meliadus, riding through the wilderness, they came to a large forest on a mountain, and she looked upward at the mountain and saw a mounted man coming toward her. As they continued riding, they met up, and the queen greeted him courteously; he returned her greeting. And the queen said, 'Would you be able to tell me news of King Meliadus who is lost in the wilderness?'

That fellow replied and said, 'Lady, lost things are never found, but King Meliadus is not lost; even though you will never see him, he will indeed be found'. And after he had said those words, he departed from the queen, riding hard. ||| (But if anyone asks me who this mounted man was, I will say that he was called Merlin the prophet.)

And the queen, remaining in the wilderness, thinking over the words that Merlin had told her, began to weep very hard and to call herself 'woeful queen' and 'sorrowful queen', and in such a way the pains of her belly began to seize her hurtfully as happens to pregnant women. And weeping, the queen said, 'Maiden, the time [fol. 92v] for the deliverance of my belly has come'. And the damsel said, 'Couldn't you ride as far as the town?' She said no.

Then she began to cry out loudly, calling upon God and his Mother to help her. While suffering great pain and weeping, she bore a male child in a wild place. After she had had him, she said to the damsel, 'Give me my little son because I want to see him'. Then the maiden placed him in her arms. 'Now I see the most beautiful creature that ever could be. Since the first time I rejoiced about you was in pain because of you – and because of you I must be sad, since in sorrow I have acquired you – in remembrance of my sufferings, I want you to be named "Tristan".' And after the queen had said these words, she said, 'Heavenly Father, have mercy on my soul'; and at once the queen died.

When the damsel saw the queen dead, she took the infant and wrapped him in the queen's mantle. And then she began to make the greatest lament that was ever heard from a damsel, and she began to emit such great sobs that she made the whole wilderness resound. But two knights coming through the wilderness, upon hearing the noise that the damsel was making, ||| [fol. 93r] the knights went

a ley e demandono qui era questa dama qu'era morta. E la damaysela disse, 'Questa è la Redina Eliabella, lo quale èi morta de parto'.

E li chavalieri vedendo que chesta[17] èi la redina e vedendo lo figliolo ch'ella avea facto, disse uno de li chavalieri al'autro,[18] 'Ora possemo noy essere segnore de lo realme de Leones perché èi perduto lo Re Meliadus e non si trova, e la Redina Eliabella è morta, e 'l filgliolo que àe facto è qui.[19] Enperò potemo essere segnore de lo realme de Lionis. Ucidiamo questo garçone c'àe facto, e non desia may più parolle'.

Alora la damaysella [encominçò] fortamente a plangere e a pregare li chavalieri per Dio che non devesseno ucidere lo garçone. 'E io ve jurirò sopra li sancti que io me n'anderò en tale parte che voy non udirete novella de me nì del garçone'. (E si alchuno me demandasse qui eranno li chavalieri, io dirò ch'eranno parenti de lo Re Meliadus.)

Alora giurò la damaysella ch'ell'anderebe en tale parte que may non saperebeno novelle de ley nì del garçone. Alora cavalqua la damaysella col garçone en braçio e vàssene giù per lo desserto. Li chavalieri presseno la Redina e posseno la a cavallo e portonla ala ciptà e mostron la a tuto lo populo de la ciptà. E le donne de Leonis – vedendo la Redina qu'era morta e avea partorito – demandono li chavalieri, 'Onde è 'l filiolo qu'ella à facto, o masculo o femena ch'ella à facto? <che noy sapemo bi>[20] [fol. 93v] che noy sapemmo ben quando ela si partitte de la ciptà, ella era gravida. Imperò volemo vedere lo filliollo, o masquio o femena o morto o vivo ch'elli sia'.

Li chavalieri dissenno que non en ne sapon nulla, 'ché noy trovamo la Redina morta; e come noy la trovamo, choisì la racharmo qui'.

Ad aquelle parolle, fo venuto Merlino lo profetta e disse ali barone de Leonis, 'Si voy volete fare per mio segno, io v'ensegnarò retrovare lo Re Meliadus e lo filgliollo que la Redina à facto'. E li baroni repossono, 'Tuti noy faremo çò que voy comandarete'.

Alora disse Merlino lo profetta, 'Prendestde questi .ii. chavalieri e menate li en prissone, e fasere metere lo bando per tuto lo realme que tuti li chavalieri vengano <chi> armati'.[21] Encontenente fo facto çiò que disse Merlino.

Disse que li chavalieri foronno tuti veiniti alla piazza,[22] comandò Merlino per loro che tuti debanno andare el desserto ala torre de la Savia Donçella e prendere lo Re Meliadus e là dintro de la torre, ucidere la donçella: 'si non, per altra volta le ne tollerà'. E li chavalieri ferronno so comandamento.

---

[17]   This form is a linguistic trait of the Belluno area (Corti, 59).

[18]   Spellings with -au- can occur in the Pisa-Lucca area, in the Veneto and also in Franco-Italian texts (Corti, 56–7, 61–2).

[19]   MS è chavaliere, written in extenso. Emendation based on TR, p. 6: èe qui; TP, p. 130: è quie.

[20]   A scribal redundancy. These words were written at end of last line of fol. 93r, concluding with bi and a titulus (= 'bin'), but crossed out lightly by scribe. The scribe continued more correctly at the beginning of fol. 93v.

[21]   In MS, written clearly as two words: chi armati. Cf. TR, p. 8 and TP, p. 132: tutti armati.

[22]   MS alla prissione. Emendation based on TR, p. 8: i·ssu la piazza. Cf. TP, p. 132: alla corte.

to her and asked who was this lady who was dead. And the damsel said, 'This is Queen Eliabel, who died in childbirth'.

And the knights, upon seeing that this was the queen and seeing the little son that she had borne, one of the knights said to the other, 'Now we can be lords of the kingdom of Leonis because King Meliadus is lost and not to be found, and Queen Eliabel is dead, and the son that she bore is here. Therefore we can be lords of the kingdom of Leonis. Let's kill this boy that she bore and say no more about it'.

Then the damsel began to weep very hard and to beg the knights for God's sake not to kill the boy 'and I swear to you by the saints that I will go away somewhere, to such parts that you will not hear news of me nor of the boy'. (If anyone were to ask me who the knights were, I would say that they were relatives of King Meliadus.)

Then the damsel swore that she would go to such a place that they would never find out news of her nor of the boy. Then the damsel rode with the boy in her arms and went off into the wilderness. The knights took the queen and placed her on a horse and carried her to the city and showed her to all the people of the city. And the women of Leonis – seeing that the queen was dead and had given birth – asked the knights, 'Where is the child that she bore, whether male or female, that she had? [fol. 93v] – because we know very well that when she left the city, she was pregnant. Therefore we want to see the child, whether male or female, or dead or alive as it may be'.

The knights said that they knew nothing about it 'because we found the queen dead; and just as we found her, so we brought her back here'.

At these words, the prophet Merlin came and said to the barons of Leonis, 'If you want to follow my advice, I'll teach you how to find King Meliadus again, and the son that the queen had'. And the barons responded, 'We'll all do as you command'.

Then Merlin the prophet said, 'Take these two knights and lead them to prison, and proclaim throughout the realm that all the knights assemble, fully armed'. Immediately it was done as Merlin said.

Having said that the knights were all to come to the *piazza*, Merlin commanded them all to go to the wilderness, to the Tower of the Wise Damsel, and get King Meliadus; and there inside the tower, to kill the damsel: 'If not, she will seize him another time'; and the knights carried out his commandment.

Alora chiamò Merlino Governale e disse, 'Si tu vuolie esser choiçì bono homo come io credo, io ti darò lo segnore de Leonis a notricare lo[23] quale serà [lo] più valente chavaliere del mondo e lo più aventurosso. Emperò si tu vuolli emprometere de notricarlo bene e lealmente, io lo te darò en gardia'. Alora resposse Governalle e disse, 'Si voy lo me darete en gardia, io lo garderò [fol. 94r] lo più lealmente que io poterò'. (May si alchuno mi demanderà chi era Governale, io diria quel fo filliolo del Re de Gaules, partì si de lo so realme per unno chavaliere che avea morto.)

[3] May hora laysa lo conto de parlare da questa ventura, e torniamo a Merlino per devissare coma trovò Tristano ende la foresta. Partendo si Merlino e Guovernalle chon due notriçe, andoron de rietro al desserto e cavalcando pervieneno ala Fontana del Petrone, ende lo quale petrone avea litere entalliate. E Merlino[24] disse a Governale, 'Say tu quello que cheste litere dicanno?' Eli disse de no. E Merlino disse, 'Cheste litere dicanno choisì que asemblano loro parlamento li trey boni chavalieri del mondo de la bestia salvagia,[25] çoè l'uno Tristano e Lançeloto[26] e Galieaçat' (sic). (Queste parolle eranno scripte ende lo[27] petrone de la fontana.) 'E questo to segnore fi[e][28] Tristano, lo quale tu averay en gardia, si fie uno de questi chavalieri lo meliore del mondo e fie graçiosso qu'ogn'omo l'amerà. Queste parolle ti dicho perchè n'abi bona gardia, ché ancor farà bissongno a dame e damayselle, e a molti chavalieri canpare de morte per soa prodessa'.

E partendo si dala fontana |||[29] [fol. 94v] cavalcando, pervienegno a uno luogo onde era la damaysella con Tristano. Alora la damaysella vuolse fugire. E Merlino disse, 'Damaysella, non fugire!' Viene alora Merlino e presse Tristano e disse, 'Governale, prende Tristano'. E Governale lo presse en gardia e gardò lo poy tuto lo tempo de la soa vita. |||[30]

Apresso de queste parolle, si partireno de lo desserto e tornoronno ala ciptà de Leones. E quando foronno venuti ala ciptà, trovoronno [che] lo Re Meliadus era trovato.[31] E li baroni viderrono[32] Merlino; disseron alo Re, 'Echo choluy la (sic) profetta perqué t'aviemo trovato'. Alora lo Re Meliadus li fesse gra[n]de honore. E Merlino disse, 'Re Meliadus, abia bonna gardia de questo tuo filgliolo'. E lo Re demandò si·llo era sancto cristiano od à nome.[33] La damaysella disse que sì jero che la Redina quando viene a morte si li posse nome 'Tristano'. E alora disse lo

23   MS *le*. I have corrected it to *lo*. Lower case *o/e* is often hard to distinguish.
24   In MS, at far right edge of line: *merlni*. Scribe added a superscripted *o* over the *i*.
25   An apparent moralizing insertion not found in TR nor in TP.
26   In MS written with one *t*, but with a dot over the final -*o*.
27   MS *le*.
28   MS clearly *fio*; *fie* used twice later in the same sentence.
29   After the last line on the page are five blank lines; miniature never executed.
30   Scribe left four lines blank; miniature never executed. At center bottom of folio, there is a large, crudely drawn *I* trimmed in red.
31   Cf. TR, p. 10: *trovarono ke lo ree Meliadus si era tornato*.
32   Titulus written over the *r*.
33   Thus in the MS. Cf. TR, p. 10: *s'egli àe nome e·ss'egli èe fatto cristiano*.

Il Tristano Riccardiano *(Parodi's siglum 'F')*

Then Merlin called Governal and said, 'If you want to be such a good man as I believe you are, I will give you the lord of Leonis to raise, he who will be the most valiant knight in the world and the most fortunate. Therefore if you want to promise to raise him well and faithfully, I'll give him into your keeping'. Then Governal replied and said, 'If you'll give him into my keeping, I'll watch over him [fol. 94r] as faithfully as I can'. (But if anyone asks me who Governal was, I would say that he was the son of the King of Gaul; he left his realm because of a knight that he had killed.)

[3] But now the tale leaves off speaking of this adventure, and we return to Merlin to describe how he found Tristan in the forest. Leaving with two wet nurses, Merlin and Governal went back into the wilderness. And riding along they came upon the Fountain of the Stone, upon which stone there were letters engraved. And Merlin said to Governal, 'Do you know what these letters say?' And he said no. And Merlin said, 'These letters say thus: that the three best knights in the savage, evil world will assemble their parliament here: that is to say, the one is Tristan, and Lancelot and Galahad.' (These words were written upon the fountain's stone.) 'And this, your lord, will be Tristan, whom you'll have in your care, who will be one of these knights – the best in the world – and he will be so comely that everyone will love him. These words I say to you so that you take good care of him, because he will yet be of service to ladies and damsels and to many knights who will be spared from death by his prowess'.

And leaving the fountain, ||| [fol. 94v] riding along, they came upon a place where the damsel was with Tristan. Then the damsel wanted to flee, but Merlin said, 'Damsel, don't flee!' Then Merlin came and took Tristan and said, 'Governal, take Tristan!' And Governal took charge of him and guarded him then for the rest of his life. |||

After these words, they left the wilderness and returned to the city of Leonis. And when they had come to the city, they learned that King Meliadus had been found. And the barons saw Merlin; they said to the king, 'Behold the prophet because of whom we found you!' Then King Meliadus paid him great honor. And Merlin said, 'King Meliadus, take good care of this son of yours'. And the King asked if he had been baptized or named. The damsel said yes, 'I swear that the dying queen gave him the name "Tristan"'; and then the king said, 'But I'll

Re, 'E io li mutaray nome'. May encontanente disse Merlino alo Re, 'Abi bonna guardia de questo tuo figliolo ché per la soa prodessa camparanno molte dame da morte e molti chavalieri del mondo; per la soa prodessa fie no[m]i[n]ato[34] per tuto lo mondo'.

    Alora lo Re Meliadus chiamò Merlino ende ‖‖[35] [fol. 95r] la camera e dissi li, 'Chome ày tu nome?' Ed ello li disse, 'Alcuna gente mi chiammano Merlino profetta. Io venne en queste contrade più per amore de lo vostro filgliallo che per lo vostro, e per la bontà que serà en luy'. Alora disse lo Re, 'Credi tu che vallia nulla Tristano?' E li disse che fie uno de li meliore chavalieri del mondo. 'May laysa lo notrichare al Governale: colui èy lealle homo e gardarà lo benne en tenpo de sua vita'.

    Apresso disse Merlino alo Re Meliadus, 'Io t'acomando a Dio ché io non posso più estare qui, emperò che io viene con grande freta per amore del filialo vostro, e per deliberare te de la preysone onde tu eri encantato'.[36] E lo Re vuolle[37] dare a Merlino oro e argento[38] asay, ed elli non de ne volle[39] fare niente, ançi si partitte de lo Re encontenente e si se ne vày a soa via. E lo Re fesse trovare nottriçe[40] asay per allevare lo soe figliole e diede lo a Governale che lo fesesse bene notrichare molto lealmente. Lo Re [molto è alegro][41] di ciò que·lli avea decto Merlino – che lo so[42] filgliolo devea essere choçi gratiosso chavaliere – siqué non si recordava de la Redina Eliabella.[43]

[4] Demorando per uno tempo siché Tristano potea avere anni trey, alora lo Re presse un'altra molie la quale era molto gi[n]til donna. E poyqué fo venuta e[n]de la corte de lo Re e vide Tristano choisì bello garçone e bella creatura, encomençò ad avere grande ira de luy. E lo Re tienne tuto lo giorno Tristano en brachio. E la Redina n'era molto dolente e dissia enfra sí estesse, 'Quando [fol. 95v] n'averò uno sì bello?' E la nocte lo Re Meliadus giaque cola sua dama e 'ngravidela. E quando la Redina si sente gravida, molto fo alegra.

    E Tristano ch'è sì bello que neuno altro [fosse] più bello;[44] may lo Re Meliadus con li soy baroni ne fanno grande alegressa, vedendo chossì bello; e Tristano era magiore de quatro anni che li autry damayselli non eranno dama[?]i[45] de .vii. anni. E la Redina

---

34   MS *noiato*, with titulus over the *i*.
35   Four full lines blank at bottom of folio.
36   Here MS 1729 conserves a more complete reading than in MS 2543, edited by Parodi.
37   MS *vuolse*. Confusion of *s* / *l*.
38   MS *argerto*.
39   MS *volse*. Again, confusion of *s* / *l*.
40   Noun written at end of line as *not | triçe*, perhaps caused the doubling of the *t*.
41   Omission in MS. Insertion based on TR, p. 10: *molto èe allegro*; and TP, p. 134: *fue molto allegro di ciò*.
42   MS *fo*.
43   Scribe left two-thirds of the line blank to indicate end of the chapter.
44   Verb omitted in MS. Cf. TR, p. 10: *Ma Tristano è cosie bello e·nneuna altra criatura non può essere più di lui sì bello*.
45   Illegible word in MS. Clearly *dama*, then one unclear letter, followed by a 'dotted' *i*. Not found in TR nor TP.

Il Tristano Riccardiano (Parodi's siglum 'F')

change his name'. But at once Merlin said to the king, 'Take good care of this son of yours because his prowess will save many ladies from death – and many of the world's knights – because by his prowess, he will be renowned throughout all the world'.

Then King Meliadus called Merlin into ||| [fol. 95r] his chamber and said to him, 'What is your name?' And he said to him, 'Some people call me Merlin the prophet. I came into this country more for your son's sake than for your own, and for the goodness that will be in him'. Then the king said, 'Do you believe that Tristan will be worth anything?' And he [Merlin] told him that he would be one of the best knights in the world, 'but let him be raised by Governal: he is a loyal man and will watch over him well all his life'.

Then Merlin said to King Meliadus, 'I commend you to God's keeping because I can no longer stay here, given that I came in great haste for your son's sake and to deliver you from the prison in which you were enchanted'. And the king wanted to give him a lot of gold and silver, but he didn't want anything done about it; instead he left the king at once and went on his way. And the king sent for a lot of wet nurses in order to raise his son, and he gave him to Governal so that he would have him nourished well, very faithfully. The king was so happy about what Merlin had told him – that his little son would be such a fine knight – that he forgot all about Queen Eliabel.

[4] Some time later when Tristan must have been about three years old, the king took another wife who was a most noble woman. And after she had come into the king's court and saw Tristan, such a handsome boy and beautiful creature,* she began to take a great dislike to him, but the king held Tristan in his arms the whole day. The queen was very sorrowful about this and said to herself, 'When [fol. 95v] will I have one as beautiful as this?' and that night King Meliadus lay with his lady and impregnated her; and when the queen felt that she was pregnant, she was very happy.

And Tristan was so beautiful that no other could be more beautiful; and King Meliadus and his barons rejoiced greatly, seeing how beautiful he was; and Tristan was bigger at age four than other boys were at seven. And the queen

---

* Tristan's physical beauty was a well known trope in medieval literature and art. See Allaire, 'Arthurian Art in Italy', p. 215.

portò el filiolo el so[46] ventre ch'ella enchomençò a repausare e a gridare e chiamare Idio e la soa Matre che la debia aitare. E repausando, fesse uno filgliolo maschio: molto menoe granda alegressa la Redina, ||||[47] may lo Re non de mena coysì grande alegressa. Encontenente fesse trovare notriçe per notrichare lo garçone. E la Redina volendo coisì male a Tristano per le soe bellesse, disse enfra sé estessa, 'Bissonçia que io lo fassa ucidere'. May Guovernale che de queste cosse prende grande gardia, chonossia que la Redina hodia Tristano de tuto suo coro. E alora Governale chiamò Tristano: 'Hora ti comando ||||[48] [fol. 96r] che non debias bere nì ma[n]giar de neguna cossa che la Redina ti desse'. Tristano alora disse, 'Maystro, io farò chiò que voy me comandarete'. E alora torna Tristano [e] Guovernale ende la camera.

E tanto esteronno ende la chamera en tal maniera que Tristano potea avere anni .vii. E alora andò Tristano ende la sala del palaçio, tanto bello e avinente che l'uno al'autro homo prodo fosse.[49] E lo Re Meliadu<i>s presse Tristano en braçio e portò lo con luy ende la camera [e colcasse con lui e tenevasi][50] Tristano en braçio. E questo era d'estate ed era gr[an]do qualde siqué lo Re ||||[51] Meliadus gardando en una fenestra e vide una ampolla piena que parea bonno vino. E alora disse lo Re a Tristano, 'Prende aquella copa e dà mi da bere'. Tristano, que de queste non prende gardia, prende la copa e mete questo beveragio ende la copa credendo che fosse bonno vino, e porse lo alo re. E lo Re estesse la mano per prendere la copa.

E la Redina, vedendo prendere alo Re, enchominçò a cridare e a dire, 'Non bere, Re Meliadus!' E lo Re, dubitando di queste parolle, tessò la copa da sé [fol. 96v] [e disse], 'Perché non beverò?' E la Redina disse, 'Perché lo beverraçio non èi bonno per voy'. E lo Re disse, 'Perché estava [qui] quello beveragio?' E la Redina non sepe que dire, ançi encominçò tuta a tremare. E lo Re disse, 'Perqué er<r>a qui lo beveraçio?' e ancho[r] la Redina non responsse.

E alora chiamò lo Re tuti li soy baroni e disse quello, 'Era facto questo beveraçio o per me o per Tristano? E enperò vi comando que sia dato a bere ala Redina'. E la Redina disse que non lo beverà. E alora lo Re disse, 'Doncha, vuolli tu honcidere o mi o Tristano?' E alora disse que non volia honçidere luy. 'Donque, voley tu oncidere Tristano?' Ed ella disse que per luy era facto.

Alora comandò lo Re a tuti li suo baroni que debianno judicare chello que sia raysone da fare da ley, chome de femena que avea facto grando assesso. 'E si voy non judicarete la verità, io ve farò desstrugere'. Alora andoronno li baroni [perché][52] ebenno dubitança de lo Re. E videndo la Redina encolpata, diss<s>eron que avea servito d'essere destrutta. Encontenente comandò lo Re que fosse asscesso (sic) uno grande fuocho. E la Redina enchomençò fortemente a plangere, e le Dame e le damayselle.

---

[46] In MS clearly *fo*. Confusion of *s* / *f*.
[47] Scribe left seven blank lines at mid-page; miniature never executed.
[48] Scribe left three blank lines at bottom of folio.
[49] MS *fesse*. Probable corrupt reading. Cf. TR, p. 12: *bello e avenante ke neuno altro non si trova*.
[50] *Saut du même au même*. Cf. TR, p. 12.
[51] Beginning here, for twelve lines the text is copied on the left half of the column only, allowing an empty block of space on right; miniature never executed.
[52] Omission in MS. Insertion based on TR, p. 12.

carried her son in her belly until she began to give birth and to cry out and call upon God and his Mother to help her. And in giving birth, she bore a male child: it brought much great happiness to the queen, ||| but the king wasn't so very happy about it. Immediately he had wet nurses found to nourish the boy. And the queen, disliking Tristan so because of his comeliness, said to herself, 'It's needful that I have him killed'. But Governal, who watched these things very closely, knew that the queen hated Tristan with all her heart. And then Governal called Tristan: 'Now I order you ||| [fol. 96r] not to drink or eat anything that the queen gives you'. Tristan then said, 'Master, I will do what you command'. And then Tristan and Governal returned to his chamber.

And they stayed in their chamber in that fashion until Tristan must have been about seven years old, and then Tristan went into the great hall of the palace, as handsome and attractive as any nobleman could be. And King Meliadus took Tristan in his arms and carried him with him into his chamber. This was in summer, and it was very hot so that King ||| Meliadus, looking at a window, saw an ampule filled with what seemed to be good wine. And then the king said to Tristan, 'Get that cup and give me something to drink'. Tristan, who was not on his guard, took the cup and put that beverage into the cup – believing it to be good wine – and handed it to the king; and the king extended his hand to take the cup.

And the queen, seeing the king about to take it, began to scream and say, 'Don't drink, King Meliadus!' And the king, worried by these words, held the cup away from himself [fol. 96v] and said, 'Why shall I not drink?' And the queen said, 'Because the beverage isn't good for you!' And the king said, 'Why was that beverage there?' And the queen didn't know what to say; instead she began to tremble all over. And the king said, 'Why was the beverage here?' and again the queen did not answer.

Then the king called all his barons and said to her, 'Was this beverage made for me or for Tristan? Therefore I command you that it be given to the queen to drink', but the queen said that she wouldn't drink it. And then the king said, 'Well then, did you want to kill me or Tristan?' And then she said that she didn't want to kill him. 'Well then, did you want to kill Tristan?' And she said that it had been made for him.

Then the king commanded that all his barons must judge what was right to do with her, as a woman who had committed a great outrage. 'And if you do not judge rightly, I will destroy you'. Then the barons went aside to confer because they feared the king; but seeing the queen accused, they said that she deserved to be destroyed. At once the king commanded that a great fire be lit; and the queen began to weep loudly, as did the ladies and damsels.

E Tristano vedendo piangere le dame e le damayselle, demanda uno barone e disse li, |||⁵³ [fol. 97r] 'Honte èi venuto questo male que sì novellamente io <ve>vecho piangere tuti quanti?' E uno barone disse, 'Noy piangemo perché la Redina deve essere arsa, e perché ti volle⁵⁴ atoyssecare'. E alora si parte Tristano da lo barone e viene ende la sala dov'era lo Re con altri baroni asay. E Tristano s'inginòllo dinançi da lo Re patre so e disse, 'Messer, io ve demando uno dono'. E lo Re si meravillava de sò que Tristano li disse. E alora li disse lo Re, 'Dimanda so que tu vuolli, dolço mio filgliolo'. E alora disse Tristano, 'Enprometeti me voi sì choma Re e per la corona que 'n testa portae'. El patre disse que sì. Alora Tristano disse, 'Io ve demando que la Redina sia delliberata per mia amore'. Alora disse el Re, 'Qui tu [àe] ensegnato questo parollo, qué io so que per te non l'aveste sauputo dire'. E Tristano disse que si Dei li aùti, e li autri santi, che 'nulla persona non mey 'nsegnoe a dire queste parolle. Ma<i> io ve lo dicho, ché non èi neuna persona ende 'l vostro realme che tanto s'abia a dollere del male de la Redina quanto io; e s'ill'avesse [des]honore,⁵⁵ vo[y] l'averia. E s'illa avesse altro atessina,⁵⁶ io l'averia'.

E alora lo Re e tuti li soy baroni si meravillavanno del senno de Tristano, pensando com'elly rende cotale raysone de quello qu'ello avia decto, se dissendo non pote essere que si [fol. 97v] elumerà che non sia savio chavaliere. E alora disse lo Re, 'E io vuollio que la redina sia deliberata per tua amore. May tu non ày renduto a lei lo guissardone che si convenia del mal servichio'.

Molto se ne parla per lo realme de Leonis. E sì per la cortessia de Tristano dicendo tuti li baroni, 'S'illo viverà per longuo tenpo, non pote fallire qu'ello non sia prodo homo'. May la Redina, la quale èi deliberata per amore di Tristano, non pensa mai [se non]⁵⁷ come li possa dare morte a Tristano. |||⁵⁸

May Guovernalle, che chonossuto soa volontà de la Redina, si comandò a Tristano che non debia andare en la sala del palagio sensa luy e non debia mangiare nì bevere 'si non quello que io ti darò'. E Tristano responde e disse, 'Questo farò io volentier[i], maystro mio'. E alora si partite Tristano e Guovernale de la camera.

May la Redina, que de lo male pensa, reconçiò [fol. 98r] lo beveraçio per atoysegare Tristano. May uno giorno lo Re Meliadus era colchiato en lo lecto per dormire, e façia grando caldo. E la redina andava a·llecto per dormire con luy. E lo Re disse, 'Andate da me a dormire en vostra camera, ché en tut[o]⁵⁹ el tenpo de nostra vita, non dormirete comecho per quella che facto avete'. Alora si parte la Redina e tornia ala soa camera, e lo Re issite ende la sala ali soe chavalieri. |||⁶⁰

May la Redina non pensa se non ucidere Tristano: e avea reconçiato lo beveraço que non parea sì non bono vino e avea lo messo ende la chame[ra]. E

---

53 Three lines left blank at bottom of writing space.
54 MS *volse*. Confusion of *s / l*.
55 Emendation based on TR, p. 14: *disinore*; and TP, p. 136: *disnore*.
56 Unusual noun or corruption. MS has an additional phrase not in TR, p. 14 nor TP, p. 136.
57 Apparent scribal omission. Insertion based on TR, p. 14.
58 Scribe left nine and a half lines blank; miniature never executed.
59 MS *tute*.
60 Scribe left seven lines blank.

Il Tristano Riccardiano *(Parodi's siglum 'F')*

And Tristan, upon seeing the ladies and damsels weeping, asked a baron and said to him, ||| [fol. 97r] 'Whence has come this ill so suddenly? I see everyone crying'. And a baron said, 'We're weeping because the queen must be burned, because she wanted to poison you'. And then Tristan left the baron and came into the hall where the king was with very many other barons. And Tristan knelt before the king his father and said, 'Sire, grant me a boon'; and the king marvelled at what Tristan said to him. And then the king said to him, 'Ask what you wish, my sweet son'. And then Tristan said, 'Promise me as king and by the crown that you wear on your head', and the father agreed. Then Tristan said, 'I ask that the queen be delivered for my sake'. Then the king said, 'Who taught you these words? Because I know that you yourself would not have known how to speak them'. And Tristan said – may God help him, and the other saints – that 'no one taught me to say these words. But I say them to you because there is not a single person in your kingdom who should resent the queen's evildoing as much as I; and if she were dishonored, you would be as well; and if she suffered further outrage, I would bear it'.

And then the king and all his barons marvelled at Tristan's wisdom, thinking how he had pled his case by what he had said, seeing that it could not be otherwise than [fol. 97v] to reveal him to be a wise knight. And then the king said, 'I want the queen to be freed for your sake, even though you have not rendered unto her the just reward that her evil service merits'.

Everyone was talking about this throughout the kingdom of Leonis; and because of Tristan's courtesy, all the barons were saying, 'If he lives long enough, he cannot fail to become a valiant man'; but the queen who had been delivered for Tristan's sake never thought of anything except how she could bring about Tristan's death. |||

But Governal – who understood the queen's desire – commanded Tristan not to go into the great hall of the palace without him and not to eat or drink 'except what I give you'. And Tristan replied and said, 'I will do this willingly, my master'. And then Tristan and Governal left the chamber.

But the queen – who was only thinking of evil – prepared [fol. 98r] the beverage to poison Tristan. But one day King Meliadus had lain down in bed to sleep, and it was very hot; and the queen went to the bed to sleep with him; and the king said, 'Go from me and sleep in your own chamber because for the rest of our lives, you'll not sleep with me because of what you've done'. Then the queen left and returned to her room, and the king went into the hall to his knights. |||

But the queen thought of nothing except of killing Tristan: and she had prepared the beverage that seemed to be nothing but good wine and had it put

venendo uno gior<i>no una damaysella ende la camera de la Redina e avea lo filgliolo de la Redina en braçio – ed era gran chaldo – e lo fantino demandò bere. E la damaysella gardando[61] per la cassa over per la camera,[62] vide una anpolla que parea purro bonno vino. Presse l'anpolla e messe lo vino ende la copa. Credendo que fosse bonno vino, diede [fol. 98v] bere al fantino ch'[en]contenente[63] que ebe bevuto, lo fantino fo morto. E la damaysella enconten[en]te misse a metere grande grido e grande vo<i>sse siqué la Redina que v'era presso a queste camere <e> corse a queste rumore, e lo Re con altri chavalieri asay. E la Redina, quando vide que lo so figlliolo era mor[to], disse ala damaysella, 'Che t'òe io facto qué tu m'ày morto lo mio filgliolo?' Ed ella disse, 'Aì, donna, io non l'abo morto; ançi l'à morto quilli que fesse lo beveraçio'.

E alora disse lo Re, 'Chome, damaysella, ày tu morto lo mey filgliolo? Ell'è bissonçia che io ti fassa stringere'. Alora la damaysella encomençiò forte a plangere e avere grande paora. ||||[64]

Alora disse lo Re, 'Perqué l'ày morto?' E la damaysella disse que de quello beveragio non en sapia nulla, 'e però non son digna de morire. [fol. 99r] May quilli[65] en chonfeçioron a fare lo beveraçio è servita da morte'. E la Redina quando audite queste parolle, ebe granda paora perché la damaysella dicia lo vero. E lo Re [entendendo][66] quesste parolle, encontenente vide che la Redina era encolpata ad ha[67] queste cosse, e pare che Dio n'avesse fatto miracholo.

May lo Re si partite de la camera, e la Redina remasse con grande dolore e plange tutavia e dissendo enfra sé estessa, 'Ora èy morto lo mio filgliolo, volendo uccidere l'autro'. Molto si chiama lassa tapin<a>ella de queste ven[tu]re.[68] May quando vidi andare ||||[69] Tristano per la sala – tanto bello e tanto avine[n]te de tute bellesse ch'ogn'omo que lo vide s'inamorava[70] de luy tanto era graciossa e avinente – may la Redina quando lo vede, tutavia si contristava di luy.

May Tristano enchomençò a enperare de cavalchare e andare ala chaçia e a emperare de scrimire siché tuta gente si meravilliava de luy. E alora Tristano si veste [fol. 99v] di pagnni grossi per andare ala chaçia. May lo Re Meliadus fesse metere lo bando per tutto lo soe realme que tuti li soy baroni devessenno andar ala chaçia. E la matina fo a chavallo lo Re e li soe barone, e vanno alo desserto a chaçiare. Encontenente chomínçò la cassia: lo Re tiene dirietro a unno

---

[61] MS *gra(n)dando*. Odd scribal error, possibly influenced by the adjective *gran* in the line just above.
[62] Scribe self-corrects, here and elsewhere, by adding a gloss with *over* in the text.
[63] Several scribal errors in this section, notably the omission of letters.
[64] Eight lines left blank; a miniature never executed.
[65] Scribe wrote *quilli*, then struck out the first *l*.
[66] Apparent omission in MS. Emended with TR, p. 16 and TP, p. 138.
[67] Written with a space in MS. Ferrarese preposition *ha*; or perhaps a unique example of *adha* spelling (lenition), a Veneto trait. See TV, pp. 45, passim.
[68] Scribal error: first wrote *ven*, then scribbled out the next two letters, and ended word *-ire*. Cf. TR, p. 16: *disaventura*.
[69] Seven lines left blank; miniature never executed.
[70] An interesting variant reading. Cf. TR, p. 16: *sì si ne maravigliava*.

in her chamber. One day a damsel came into the queen's chamber and she had the queen's son in her arms – and it was very hot – and the little boy asked for a drink. And the damsel, looking through the chest, or rather, through the chamber,* saw an ampule that really seemed to be good wine. She took the ampule and put the wine into the cup. Believing that it was good wine, she gave [fol. 98v] a drink to the little boy so that immediately after he drank it, the little boy died. And the damsel at once set up a great cry at the top of her lungs so that the queen who was near these rooms ran to the noise, and the king with many other knights as well. And the queen, when she saw that her little son was dead, said to the damsel, 'What did I do to you that you've killed my son?' And she said, 'Ah, my lady, I didn't kill him; rather, whoever made the beverage killed him'.

And then the king said, 'What's this, damsel? Have you killed my son? Necessity demands that I have you tortured'. Then the damsel began to weep very hard and was very afraid. |||

Then the king said, 'Why did you kill him?' And the damsel said that she didn't know anything about that beverage 'and therefore I'm not worthy of death, [fol. 99r] but whoever prepared the beverage deserves to die'. And when the queen heard these words, she was very afraid because the damsel was telling the truth. And upon hearing these words, the king at once saw that the queen was guilty of these things, and it seemed that God had wrought a miracle about them.

But the king left the chamber, and the queen remained with great sorrow and weeping; yet she said to herself, 'Now my little son is dead because I wanted to kill the other'. She repeatedly called herself 'miserable' and 'wretched' because of this misfortune. But when she saw Tristan ||| going through the hall – so beautiful and so comely in every way so that everyone who saw him loved him (he was so very charming and comely) yet when the queen saw him, she always became sad about him.

But Tristan began to learn to ride and to go to the hunt and to learn to fence so that all the people marvelled at him. And then Tristan dressed himself [fol. 99v] in coarse garments to go to the hunt. King Meliadus had it proclaimed throughout his realm that all his barons must go on the hunt; and in the morning the king and his barons were on horseback, and they went to the wilderness to hunt. Immediately the chase began: the king kept after a stag, and Governal and

---

* Here and elsewhere, the scribe corrects an error by adding a gloss that contains the proper reading from his model.

servio,[71] e Guovernale e Tristano ennanti da lo Re. Cavalcando vieneno a uno prato e qui ne ussitte .viii. chavalieri armati. E quando trovoronno Guovernalle, dema[n]doronno, 'Ov'è Tristano?' e Guovernale disse que non si era. Alora dissenno li chavalieri, 'Dove èi Tristano?' e Governale non resposse a loro. E alora cavalchano li chavalieri e fierenno alo Re Meliadus e abateron lo a terra da cavallo morto. E Governale fugì enverso la ciptade – e Tristano – may neuno de li soe chavalieri non socchorenno lo Re Meliadus: chiascuno cominçò a fugire. |||[72]

[fol. 100r] Alora fo portato lo Re Meliadus ala ciptate. E alora enchominçiano a fare grando pianto per tuto lo soe realme, e benne lo devenno piangere tuti li soy baroni e li chavalieri per la prodessa qu'era en luy e per la soa cortessia. Asay ne piange la Redina e tute li autre dame e damayselle asay. E poy lo sepelinonno lo Re honorevollmente sichome si cho[n]venia.

[5] Or disse lo conto que poyqué Tristano fo facto chavaliere, ello fesse la vendeta del soe patre: ucise tuti li .viii. chavalieri li quale foronno ala morte de lo Re; e anchor non chiama si contento de questa vendìta de lo Re, ançi cavalchò in de la ciptate de honde eranno nati questi chavalieri, |||[73] la quale si chiama Presia,[74] e ançissi tuti li omini e le femene, e fessese la ciptà desfare infina alo fondamento. E tuto questo fesse Tristano per vendìta de lo soe patre lo Re Meliadus onqua non fo magiore vendìta per uno chavaliere chome Tristano fesse del soe patre.

[6] May tan[fol. 100v]to laysa lo conto de parlar da questa aventura que non apartienonno a nostra materia, e retorniamo a Tristano de choluy volemo devissare la storia veraçe. May la Redina, que non pensa si non chome possa fare morire Tristano, fesse fare uno grande ma[n]giare [e] convidò Guovernale[75] e Tristano. Disse Governale a Tristano, 'Dapoyqu'ella noy à convidato emperò qu'elli sonno assay de bonni baroni de suo realme a mangiare, vuollio que noy iandiamo perché parebe villania da la nostra parte sì noy [non] iandiamo; sì ti chomandò que tu non debia mangiare nì bevere si non so que io ti darò, nì de neuna vianda si[76] non quella que io ti farò dare'. Alora disse Tristano, 'Questo farò bene, maistro mio'.

Ala matina vienn\<n\>enno[77] alo mangiare; le viande foronno venute a çiaschuno. La Redina fesse presentare a Tristano starne e faysani e paoni \<e\> due arosti,[78] may Tristano de neuna non mangiava enfina a tanto che Governale non fesse venire la soa vianda. Alora enchomenchiò a mangiare; may de neuna vianda que la Redina mandoe, de neuna non mangioe. Vedendo, la Redina ne fo molto dolenta.

---

[71] TP, p. 138: *cervia*; *Tav. Rit.*, p. 40 n. 1: *cerbio, cervio* (modern Tuscan: *cervo*).
[72] Seven lines left blank at bottom of the page; miniature never executed.
[73] Seven lines left blank at mid-page; miniature never executed.
[74] TR, p. 18: *Bresia*; and TP, p. 138: *Brescia*. Not found in Carpentras, MS 404 (*Roman de Tristan*, ed. Curtis, vol. I, p. 136) nor in BnF, MS fr. 756, fol. 25v nor in TV.
[75] MS *guovernalo*.
[76] MS *fi*. Confusion of *s* / *f*.
[77] Useless titulus in first half of this verb. Scribe did write out -*nn*- twice.
[78] Cf. TR, p. 18: *istarne e ffagiani e due paoni arrostiti*.

Il Tristano Riccardiano *(Parodi's siglum 'F')*

Tristan were riding ahead of the king. Riding along, they came to a meadow from which seven armed knights came. And when they found Governal, they demanded, 'Where's Tristan?' and Governal said that he wasn't there. Then the knights said, 'Where is Tristan?' and Governal didn't answer them. And then the knights rode on and struck King Meliadus and knocked him to the ground from his horse, dead. And Governal fled toward the city with Tristan, but none of his knights aided King Meliadus: each one began to flee. |||

[fol. 100r] Then King Meliadus was carried to the city, and then they began to make a great lament all through his realm. And well should they weep – all his barons and knights – because of the prowess that was in him and because of his courtesy. The queen wept very much about it, and all the other ladies and damsels as well. And then they buried the king honorably, as was fitting.

[5] Now the tale says that after Tristan was knighted, he carried out the vendetta for his father: he killed all seven of the knights who were present at the king's death; and he still didn't consider himself happy about the king's avenging so he rode to the city where these knights were born ||| (which is called Brescia) and killed all the men and women, and had the city razed down to its foundations. And Tristan did all this to avenge his father King Meliadus, and there was no greater vendetta for a knight than the one Tristan undertook for his father.

[6] But [fol. 100v] at this the tale leaves off speaking of this adventure that does not pertain to our subject, and let us return to Tristan whose true story we want to narrate. But the queen, who thought of nothing except how she could put Tristan to death, had a great feast prepared and invited Governal and Tristan. Governal said to Tristan, 'Since she has invited us – because there are very many fine barons of her realm to dine as well – I want us to go, because it would be villainy on our part if we didn't go; so I command you not to eat or drink except what I give you, nor of any victual except what I've given you'. Then Tristan said, 'I will indeed do this, my master'.

The next day they came to the feast; the victuals were brought to everyone. The queen had Tristan served partridges and pheasants and two roast peacocks, but Tristan ate none of it except for what Governal had brought as his victuals. Then he began to eat; but of the victuals that the queen sent, he ate none of them. Upon seeing this, the queen was very aggrieved.

Dapoyqué foron partiti da le taule che·nno mangiate, e Governale chiamò Tristano ende la camera onde li disse molte parolle.[79] [fol. 101r] Governale disse a Tristano, 'A me pare que questa toa matrigna ti vuollia ançidere: emperçiò me pare que noy dobiamo partire de lo realme de Leones, dapoyqué lo Rey èi morto. Andemo alo Re Ferramonte de Guaules chi ne poteray enperare ciò que à bissonça a chavaliere. Queste parolle t'òe decte perché volria que tu deventasse bono chavaliere'.

Alora disse Tristano, 'Io sonno aparechate de fare tutto quello que voi[80] me comandarete'.

Alora Governale si perchaça e prende cavalli e horo e argento asay, e scudieri e·ffamilli; e fa lur iuirare de tener chredença de so que loro s'era comandato. Alo matina[81] si parte: Guovernale e Tristano montonno a cavallo sì privadamente que nullo de so realme non en sauperon nulla. Tanto cavalcharonno per loro çornate que pervenno ala corte de lo re Feramonto de Gaules. Venuti ala soa corte, Tristano [rimane][82] ende·lla corte; començo a servire dinanti alo Re. |||[83]

[7] A tanto avinente e tanto belle de tute cosse que tuti li chavalieri lo gardavano per maravilla. Disse uno enver l'autro que 'Dey non fe' unqua un più bello damaysello'; molto ne parla lo Re e tuta soa corte. May Tristano enchomençe a cavalchare e a rompere bigorti con chavalieri e damaçel[li] [fol. 101v] siché ende la corte non àe chavaliere nì damayselli que del chaçiare sapia tanto quanto luy, siqué Tristano poteva avere anni .xi.

May la filgliola de lo re Feramonte, videndo Tristano sì bello damaçello, ennamorò si da luy. E dissia enfra sé stesse, 'Però ch'io[84] avere potesse, non layserò que io non l'abia Tristano a mio volere uno giorno'. Estando la damaçella ende la dame, venne ende la sala del palaçio. Vide Governale e chiamò lo a sé. 'Governale, io ti vuolio manifestare lo mio coragio: vuolio que tu debias dire a Tristano que sia damaçello de mio amore per so non amo nì me nì altro tanto come faso lui'. E Guove[r]nalle disse que·llo farà ben quello messagio.

Siqué en queste parolle, viene L'Amorroldo de Landa,[85] chavaliere de lo realme de Longres[86] viene ala corte de lo re Ferramonte de[87] Gaules. Quando sepe que la venuta de L'Amorondo (sic), el Re Feramonte andò li encontra [con][88] grande conpania de chavalieri. Messe lo enne la ciptà com grande alegressa,

---

[79] At bottom of fol. 100v, four lines left blank; catchword, in a crudely drawn red ink cartouche: *Guouernale*.

[80] Scribe had written *quello vo que voi*, then struck out the first *vo*.

[81] Lack of article-noun agreement does occur in fourteenth-century Italian dialects.

[82] Omission in MS. Insertion based on TR, p. 20: *rimane*. Cf. TP, p. 140: *rimase*.

[83] Seven full lines left blank; miniature never executed.

[84] MS *chie*.

[85] On this name, see David J. Shirt, 'A Note on the Etymology of "Le Morholt"', *Tristania* I (1975), 14–18. For the toponym, I conserve all variant spellings as found in MS. Cf. TR, p. 20; TP, p. 140: *Irlanda* (Ireland).

[86] MS *Leones*, but below, *Longres*. Correction based on TR, p. 20: *Longres, Logres*. Cf. TP, p. 140: *l'Amoroldo d'Irlanda*.

[87] MS clearly written *che*. Emendation based on TR, p. 20.

[88] Cf. TR, p. 20: *andolli inkontro kon grande*.

Il Tristano Riccardiano *(Parodi's siglum 'F')*

After they had left the tables not having eaten [the queen's food], Governal called Tristan into his chamber where he told him many things. [fol. 101r] Governal told Tristan, 'It seems to me that this stepmother of yours wants to kill you: therefore, it seems to me that we ought to depart from the kingdom of Leonis, since the king is dead. Let's go to King Faramont of Gaul where you'll be able to learn what is needful for a knight. These words I have told you because I'd like you to become a good knight'.

Then Tristan said, 'I am ready to do all that you command'.

Then Governal set to work and got horses and much gold and silver, and squires and servants; and he made them swear to keep in confidence everything that he had commanded them to do. In the morning they left: Governal and Tristan mounted their horses so secretly that no one in the realm knew anything about it. They rode so much through the days that they came to the court of King Faramont of Gaul. Upon arriving at his court, Tristan remained in his court: he began to serve before the king. |||

[7] Tristan was so handsome and so pleasing in all things that all the knights looked at him in wonder. One said to the other that 'God never made a more handsome youth'; the king and his entire court talked about him a lot. But Tristan began to ride and to joust with knights and youths [fol. 101v] since in the court there was no knight nor youth who knew as much about hunting as he did, even though Tristan must have been about eleven years old.

But the daughter of King Faramont, seeing Tristan such a handsome lad, fell in love with him. And she said to herself, 'In order that I can have him, I won't leave off until I have Tristan to my will one day'. Being among her ladies, the damsel came into the palace hall. She saw Governal and called him to her. 'Governal, I want to reveal my heart to you: I want you to tell Tristan that he is the youth who has my love, because I don't love myself nor any other so much as I do him'. And Governal said that he would indeed deliver that message.

After these words, the Morholt of Ireland, knight of the kingdom of Logres, came to the court of King Faramont of Gaul. When he found out about the arrival of the Morholt, King Faramont went to meet him with a great company of knights. He led him into the city with great rejoicing and immediately had it

encontinente fesse meter lo bando per tuto lo realme que [tu]ti[89] li soy chavalieri vienessenno a corte de lo Re Feramonte. Comandò que fosse facto uno grande mançare. Facto fo quelo che comandò, la sera foron ale taule: lo Re venendo a mançare con tuti li soy chavalieri.

Tristano serve danançe alo re Feramonte. L'Amoroldo de Landa vedendo sì bello damaçello disse alo re, 'Qui è questo?' El Re resposse, 'Io non so qui sia, si non qu'el viene e[n] mia corte a servir'. Disse L'Amor[o]ldo, 'Dio lo fassa prodohomo, qué de le bellesse non à ello a·ffallire'.

Ende la corte de lo re Feramonte si avea uno follo, lo quale disse a L'Amoroldo, 'La soa bellessa ti costarà cara'. L'Amoroldo ne[90] [fol. 102r] comensò a ridere e farne befe.

Disse lo Re, 'Non dire, Amoroldo, qué l'autrier viene uno chavaliere que mançò con noy a ta<l>ula; diede al follo una cossa de cappone. Lo follo disse, 'Enpersò la prende perché tu non en daray may altrui'. La matina lavòsi lo chavaliere le mane, e·vvegne una damaysella; disse, 'Chavaliere, dona me un dono'. 'Demande que tu vuollie'. 'Dona me la toa espada'. Lo chavaliere li fesse dare. E la damayssella prende l'espada e dieli en su la tessta honde morì. Poché de molte aventure à decto lo follo veritade. Enperçò ti prreguo che tu ti gardi da luy'. L'Amoroldo ne començò a riderre e·ffar ne beffe.

La·ssera sennò con grande alegressa; lo Re Feramonte lo fa servir de so qu'à bessonça. La matina si partì L'Amoroldo con soa compania; lo Re l'acompagnò con soa gente. Alo partire li disse lo Re ch'elli si garde dalo domaysello sichome lo follo havia decto. Lo re Feramonte tornò al so palaçio.

[8] Ora laysa lo conto de L'Amorolldo di Landa e de soa compagnia perqué non apartiene a nostra materia, che benne lo saveremo trovare quando verrà lo tempo.

Governale chiamò Tristano [e disse],[91] 'Lieto ti poy tenere e aventurosso damaysello, qué tu sey amato de choysì bella damaysella sichome la filliola de lo Re Feramonte, la quale t'ama de tuto lo so amore'. Disse Tristano, 'Maisstro, conçellariaste me voi che io amasse la filliola de lo Re Feramonte di folle amore? Enpersò non l'amerò que torni en soa dassonore, qué a mio segnore ben serebe le folle[92] qu<u>ando proçaçesse de fare soa dessonore donde recievo grande ho[fol. 102v]nore'. Disse Guovernale, 'En tale manera refudi tu l'amor de la damaysella?' 'Sì, si non en tal manera che non l'amo de tale amore[93] chi como l'omo dive amare soa dama, may non qué io la vuolia amare de folle amore'.

---

[89] Apparent scribal omission of letters at end of line. Insertion based on TR, p. 20.

[90] MS *na*.

[91] Verb omitted in MS. Insertion based on TR, p. 22.

[92] Clear in MS, but see TR, p. 22: *bene sare'io folle*; TP, p. 142: *bene serei folle*.

[93] MS *non l'ame de tale amoro*. Scribe has confused the *o* / *e*, a common difficulty in reading such hands.

proclaimed throughout his kingdom that all his knights must come to the court of King Faramont. He commanded that a great feast be prepared. Having done as he commanded, that evening they were [seated] at the tables, the king coming to eat with all his knights.

Tristan served before King Faramont. Seeing such a handsome youth, the Morholt said to the king, 'Who is this?' And the king replied, 'I don't know who he is, only that he came to my court to do service'. The Morholt said, 'May God make him a valiant man, since he did not stint him in beauty'.

In King Faramont's court, there was a fool who said to the Morholt, 'His beauty will cost you dear'. The Morholt [fol. 102r] began to laugh and joke about this.

The king said, 'Don't say that, Morholt, because the day before yesterday a knight came who ate with us at table; he gave the fool a capon's thigh. The fool said, "I'll take it because you'll never give one of them to anyone else". The next morning the knight was washing his hands and a damsel came along. She said, "Knight, grant me a boon". "Ask what you will". "Give me your sword". The knight had it given to her. And the damsel took the sword and let him have it on his head whence he died. Since the fool has spoken the truth about many adventures, for this reason I beg you to guard yourself from him'. The Morholt began to laugh and make jokes about this.

That evening they made merry; King Faramont had him served with everything he needed. In the morning the Morholt left with his company; the king accompanied him with his people. At their leave-taking, the king told him to beware of the lad, just as the fool had said. King Faramont returned to his palace.

[8] Now the tale leaves off telling about the Morholt of Ireland and his company because it does not belong to our subject, yet we'll surely know where to find him when the time comes.

Governal called Tristan and said, 'You may consider yourself a happy and fortunate young man, since you are loved by such a beautiful damsel as the daughter of King Faramont who loves you with all her heart'. Tristan said, 'Master, would you advise me to love King Faramont's daughter with a mad love? Because I will not love her disrespectfully, because it would indeed be folly if I sought to bring dishonor to my lord from whom I receive great ho[fol. 102v]nor'. Governal said, 'In this way do you refuse the damsel's love?' 'Yes, if I don't love her in such a way that a man must love his lady, but not because I want to love her with a foolish love'.

[9] Ora disse el conto che queste parolle à decto Governale a Tristano per chognossere[94] so senno. Era ne molto alegro Governale de le parolle che Tristano ave decto, que hora cognosse quello s'è savio chavaliere. Alora si partino ambori de la camera e vienon ende la sala de lo palaçio. Tristano enchomençò a scrimire con li autri damayselli siché la filliola de lo re Feramonte, vedendo escrimere Tristano, tuta ardea de soa amore. Disse enfra sé estesse, 'Or l'avesse io e[n] mia camera!' ||[95] Dapoyqué si partite da l'escrimire, la damaiselle si perchosse anfre doe cammere. Tristano andoe de la sala de lo Re per passare al'autra parte de lo palaçio, passando tr'ambo[96] de queste camere. La damaysella, vedendo lo passare Tristano, corse e gittò li se enbraçio e a collo e començiò lo abaiçare siquome femina qu'èi passa de so amore. Tenendolo en tal maniera[97] Tristano, non pensando quelo qu'ella façia, [ella] gitò uno grande grido e dissia, 'Socor[fol. 103r]rete, chavalieri!' Questo dara[98] sichome <sicome> femina qu'era struta d'amore e [uscita] de materia[99] per hamore de Tristano. Mai li chavalieri audendo lo crido de la damaysella, corseno tuti a ley e trovoron la damaisella que avía abraçiato Tristano strittamente. Li chavalieri disseno, 'Que ày tu, damaysella, ché ài cridato?' Ella èi piena de paora e de verçongnia; disse, 'Questo damaisello me vuolle[100] far villania'. Alora disseno li chavalieri, 'Tristano, honde tu ày e recieve honore e cortessia E tu en so onta porchaçe de far li dessonore? Per mia fede, tu te ne pentiray!' |||[101] Lo Re comandò que fosse messo en presone.

May Guovernale non potea andare per lo palatia, sì era grande el romore. Uno de li chavalieri per uno dì disse<no>, 'Tòli <come ày amaistrato> lo to filliolo qué bene l'ày notrito!' Governale tornò ende la camera per verçonça non tornò per la sala. May pensando enfra sé metesmo, 'Melio que io lo fassa a·ssavere alo Re Feramonte de Tristano qu'ello sia destruto'. Allora si departe <dela salla> de la camera e vade en la sala de lo Re Feramonte. 'Io <vor> volria dire alquanto alchune parolle ende la chamera'. Alora si parte [fol. 103v] <Alora si partite> lo Re e Guovernale ende la camera. 'Io vuollio dire lo co[n]venente qu'è stato entre vostra filgliola e Tristano. Io ne jurarò sopra li Sancti Evvang[e]li de dire de la veritate'. (May si alcuno me demanderà come à nomme[102] la filgliola de lo Re Feramonte, io dirò que à nome Bellice.) 'Eli è vero que uno jorno andando per la salla, vostra figliola me chiamò e disse que io devesse dire a Tristano da soa parte sicome[103] l'amava de tuto so cuoro. Ditto queste parolle – disse – a Tristano, ello me disse que de queste cosse non farebe nulla. Enperçò ve preguo que voi debiate sapere la veritade de queste cosse'. Lo Re disse, 'Va' a toa vìa, ché io farò quello que rayson s'era'.

94   Written at end of line and difficult to read.
95   Five lines left blank; miniature never executed.
96   MS: *trabomo*. Emendation based on TR, p. 22: *e·ppassando intr'ambodue queste kamere*.
97   MS *maneia*, with the abbreviation for *r* written above the word.
98   Ink very light on this folio. Perhaps '*dava*'? Cf. TR, p. 22: *dicea*.
99   A somewhat corrupt phrase. Cf. TR, p. 22: *sì come femina la quale iera addivenuta pazza e uscita de la materia*.
100   MS *vuolse*. Confusion of *s* / *l* as elsewhere.
101   Five blank lines at mid-page; miniature never executed.
102   Useless titulus on this word.
103   MS *ci come*. Emendation based on TR, p. 24.

[9] Now the tell says that Governal said these words to Tristan in order to test his wisdom. Governal was very happy about the words that Tristan had said because now he knew that he was a wise knight. Then they both left the chamber and came into the palace hall. Tristan began to fence with other youths so that King Faramont's daughter, seeing Tristan fencing, burned all over with love for him. She said to herself, 'Now if only I had him in my chamber!' ||| As he was leaving after fencing, the damsel thrust herself in between two rooms. Tristan went through the king's hall in order to pass through to the other side of the palace, his route passing between these rooms. Seeing Tristan pass by, the damsel ran out and threw herself upon him – embracing his neck – and began to kiss him like a female who was mad with love for him. Holding Tristan in that fashion, not thinking of what she was doing, she let out a great cry and said, 'Help, [fol. 103r] knights!' This she did like a female who was destroyed by love and out of her mind for love of Tristan. But the knights, hearing the damsel's cry, all ran to her and found the damsel who had embraced Tristan tightly. The knights said, 'What's wrong with you, maiden? Why did you cry out?' She was full of fear and shame; she said, 'This young man tried to bring shame to me'. Then the knights said, 'Tristan, where you receive honor and courtesy, you – to your shame – try to bring dishonor upon her? By my faith, you'll repent this!' ||| The king commanded that he be put in prison.

But Governal couldn't go through the palace, so great was the uproar. One day one of the knights said, 'Take your youngster, you've raised him so well!' Governal returned to his room – out of shame – he didn't return to the great hall. But thinking to himself: 'It would be better for me to let King Faramont know about Tristan than to have him killed'. Then he left his room and went to King Faramont's hall. 'I would like to say a few words in your chamber'. Then [fol. 103v] the king and Governal went into his chamber. 'I want to tell you what went on between your daughter and Tristan. I swear upon the Holy Gospels to tell the truth about it'. (But if anyone asks me what was the name of King Faramont's daughter, I would say that she was called Belide.) 'It's true that one day while going through the great hall, your daughter called to me and said that I must tell Tristan on her behalf that she loved him with her whole heart. Having told these words' – he said – 'to Tristan, he told me that he would do nothing about these things. Therefore I pray you to know the truth of these things'. The king said, 'Go on your way, because I will do what reason demands'.

[10] Ora disse lo conto che [alo Re][104] Guovernale pare que abia dicta la veritate. Encontenente chiamò Belliçe ende la camera e disse, 'Bella figliola mia, che vendìta vuolie que fassa del damaisello lo quale ti vuolle[105] far villania?' Ela non resposse a queste cosse. E lo Re disse, 'Or ve pensi esta notte, e la matina me responderay'. Ala matina si leva lo Re, façi venire Tristano danançi, e uno nepote de lo Re lo quale avea morto uno chavaliere ende la corte de lo Re. Poy fe venire Belliçe danançe da sé. Lo Re disse, 'Prende una espada'.[106] Disse, 'Filiola, qui sono doe damayselli sicome tu vide. L'uno è toe parente, e amboro an serviti de morte. Per sò ti vuolio fare uno dono: che tu prende uno de[107] questi .ii. quale più ti plaçe [fol. 104r] en tu<t>a[108] parte. Quello que remarrà, farò li taliare la testa'. Bellice entendendo queste parolle, ci encomençò a pensare e a dire enfra sé estessa: 'S'io prendo Tristano, ora homo dirà que io sia falsa damaisella. S'io prendo mei chusino, lo Re taliarà la testa a Tristano. Si Tristano more, io non vuoli plus vivere'. Pensando en tale maniera, non sapia quale si devia prendere. Disse lo Re, 'Pre[n]de tosto, qué tu potray tanto estare che tu non aresti nì l'uno nì l'autro'. La damaysella pensando non sapia quale se devesse prendere.

Quale parte[109] disse que la damaysella arebe volentieri presso Tristano si non fosse per paora de lo Re. Alora disse lo Re, 'Prende tosto, filiola'. Alora Belliçe prende so coysino. Lo Re prende Tristano, messe mano al'espada, trayse la fuora de lo frodo, e disse, 'Tu ày presso to coysino em parte. Io tallaray la[110] testa a Tristano'. Alsò l'espada per ferrire a Tristano. Bellice disse, 'Re, non ferire ||||[111] qué io mi pento che io non pressi quello que volia'. Alora disse lo Re, 'Quello que prendeste, quello averay'. Alora disse la damaysella, 'Come non me volete dare?' Ela disse, 'Ora me date un dono lo quale io ve demandarò'. Lo Re disse, 'Demanda chiò que tu vuolli, a fora de Tristano'. 'Ora mi donate l'espada com voy volete onçidere Tristano'. Lo Re li diede [fol. 104v] l'espada. Ella posse lo pommo en terra e la ponta si posse drito al cuore. Alora disse alo Re Ferramonte, 'Or volete voy che io m'ançida o volete mi rendere Tristano? O ne emprima mi vuolio oncidere que vedere <la morte nì>[112] intalliare lì la testa a Tristano!' 'Come?' disse lo Re. 'Amate tu tanto Tristano quanto tu disse?' Ella disse, 'Io amo plus[113] lui che non fo nì me nì altrui'. Alora disse lo Re, 'Diede ala donçella Tristano' e comandò que fosse talaita (sic) la testa al chusino so de la damaysella. Facto fo soe que comandoe lo Re. Dapoyqué Tristano viene de la salla del palaçio dov'eran li chavalieri del mondo, si meravillavan de Tristano que s'era deliberato.

[104] Omission in MS. Insertion based on TR, p. 24: *Ora dice lo conto ke allo ree pare*.
[105] MS *vuolse*. Confusion of *s / l*.
[106] MS *espassa*.
[107] MS *da*.
[108] Cf. TR, p. 24: *in tua parte*.
[109] Apparently corrupt reading. Cf. TR, p. 26: *In questa parte dice lo konto*; TP, p. 144: *Ora dice lo conto*.
[110] MS *da*.
[111] Four lines left blank, just below mid-page; miniature never executed.
[112] Words not found in TR, p. 27 nor TP, p. 146.
[113] MS *ame pluy*, written with the abbreviation for -*us*.

Il Tristano Riccardiano *(Parodi's siglum 'F')*

[10] Now the tale says that it seemed to the king that Governal had told the truth. At once he called Belide to his chamber and said, 'My dear daughter, what vengeance do you want done to the young man who wanted to bring shame upon you?' She did not answer about these things. And the king said, 'Now think about it tonight, and in the morning answer me'. In the morning the king arose; he had Tristan brought before him and a nephew of the king who had killed a knight in the king's court. Then he had Belide come before him. The king said, 'Get a sword'. He said, 'Daughter, here are two young men, as you see: one is your relative, and both are deserving of death. For this reason I want to make you a gift: that you choose one of these two, which ever pleases you more, for yourself. [fol. 104r] The one that remains, I will have his head cut off'. Hearing these words, Belide began to think about it and to say to herself: 'If I choose Tristan, then people will say that I am a false maiden. If I choose my cousin, the king will cut off Tristan's head. If Tristan dies, I no longer want to live'. Thinking in this way, she didn't know which she ought to choose. The king said, 'Choose quickly, because if you wait too long, you'll have neither one nor the other'. The damsel – thinking – didn't know which she should choose.

In this part the tale says that the damsel would willingly have taken Tristan if it weren't for fear of the king. Then the king said, 'Choose quickly, daughter!' Then Belide chose her cousin. The king took Tristan, put his hand to his sword, drew it from its sheath, and said, 'You have chosen your cousin for yourself. I will cut off Tristan's head'. He raised the sword to strike Tristan. Belide said, 'King, don't strike! ||| – because I regret that I did not choose the one that I want'. Then the King said, 'The one you have chosen, you will have!' Then the damsel said, 'What, you won't give him to me?' She said, 'Now grant me a boon that I'll ask of you'. The king said, 'Ask what you will, except for Tristan'. 'Now give me the sword with which you want to kill Tristan'. The king gave her [fol. 104v] the sword. She placed the pommel on the ground, and the point she positioned straight at her heart. Then she said to King Faramont, 'Now do you want me to kill myself or do you want to give me Tristan? For I'd sooner kill myself than see Tristan's head cut off!' 'What?' said the king. 'Do you love Tristan as much as you say?' She said, 'I love him more than I ever did myself or anyone else'. Then the king said, 'Give Tristan to the maiden', and he commanded that the damsel's cousin be beheaded. It was done as the king commanded. After Tristan came into the palace hall where all the knights were, they marvelled that Tristan had been freed.

Guovernale chiamò Tristano ende la camera e disse lo convenente de la filliola del Re Ferramonte: 'sich'ella[114] t'ama de tuto so chuore. Si tu vuolie estare ende[115] la corte de lo Re Ferramonte, s'era mestieri que tu fasi la volontade de la filloila (sic); si non per altre fiate, n'averay dessonore. Enperò mi pare que noi si partissemo de questo realme dapoyqué Dio t'à campato de questo deissonore. Andiamo en Chornavala[116] alo Re Marcho que èi tuo çio, e non li dire to covenente de so que apertiene a nostra cavallaria. Non andar ti dissendo que tu sei so parente'. Tristano disse, 'Io songno apareçato de fare çio que voi volete'.[117] Alora si ne viene Tristano e Governale, e disse Tristano alo Re Ferramonte, 'Stato [fol. 105r] songno en vostra corte, chome voy sapete, ché mi [con]viene tornare en mio paisse. Enperçò ve preguo que voi me debiate dare chumiato'. Lo Re disse, 'Di sò sonno io molto dolente. Io volrey que tu non ti partisse en neuna manera. May dapoiqué io vego lo tuo vollere, io ti do cumiato, may tu me diray cui filholo foste'. ||||[118] Tristano disse, 'Non me dareste cumiato si io non ve dicho mio covenente?' Lo Re disse de non. Eli disse, 'Io abo nome Tristano. Lo Re Meliadus fo meo patre'. Dis[s]e lo Re, 'Tristano, bene dovey dire più tosto lo to covenente. Emperò non vuolia que tu ti parte de mia corte, ançe ti vuolio dare un dono: que tu sei segnore de tuto lo mei realme a toe segno e a tuta toa volontà'. (Lo Re Ferramonte àe gra[n]da ira perché non l'àe chonossut Tristano per lo tempo passato.) May Tristano disse que non remarrebe per neuna manera. Alora lo Re con grande dolore li diede cumiato.

[11] Ora disse lo conto que li barone e li chavalieri sonno molto dolente de la parte[n]ça de Tristano. La matina si leva [fol. 105v] Tristano, e fa compagnia lo Re e soi baroni, e aconpagnano Tristano. Alo partire lo Re professe[119] lo so realme a Tristano. Lo Re retornò a so palaçio; Tristano cavalçò ||||[120] lo giorno per so jornata tanto que pervegnon presso de Cornavallia.

[12] Dapoyqué Bellice sepe qu'era partito Tristano de lo realme de Gaules [e] andava per demorare en Cornavalia, enchomençò a fare lo magior plante che jamay fosse facto per una damaysella. Disse enfra sé metesmo, 'Ora sei partito quello que i[o] più amava più che me; nol vecho sicome io solia. Conosso que amore me costrenge en tal mannera que mia vita pocho po<r>te essere. Enperçò che io abo entesse que la morte èi la plus dolloysosa cossa que sia ne altrui possa sofrire, may a me tornarebe en dolçore dapoyqué 'l mio amore canpay de morte; però vuolio morire'.

114 Cf. TR, p. 26: *essai k'ella t'ama*; TP, p. 146: *e sai ch'ella t'ama*.
115 Scribe wrote *estare di ende*, then struck out *di*.
116 First time this toponym appears. Scribe wrote *-ll-*, then blacked out the first *l*.
117 MS *volote*. Confusion of *o / e*.
118 Beginning here, four blank, half-lines form a small square at right margin, then two full blank lines, then three half-lines blank forming a second small square at left margin (gutter); miniatures never executed.
119 MS: *porfesse*.
120 Here begins another small blank square, four half-lines high, at right margin (gutter).

Il Tristano Riccardiano *(Parodi's siglum 'F')*

Governal called Tristan into his chamber and told him how things stood with King Faramont's daughter, 'since you know that she loves you with her whole heart. If you want to stay in King Faramont's court, it behooves you to do his daughter's will; otherwise, you will be dishonored. Therefore it seems to me that we should leave this kingdom since God has saved you from this dishonor. Let's go to Cornwall to King Mark who is your uncle, but do not tell him your situation regarding our chivalry.* Don't go around saying that you are his relative'. Tristan said, 'I'm ready to do what you want'. Then Tristan and Governal went their way, and Tristan said to King Faramont, [fol. 105r] 'I have been in your court – as you know – so that it behooves me to return to my country. Therefore I pray you to grant me leave'. The king said, 'About this I am very sorrowful. I wouldn't like you to leave in any way; but since I see your desire, I grant you leave; but tell me whose son you are'. ||| Tristan said, 'You wouldn't grant me leave if I don't tell you my identity?' The king said no. He said, 'I am called Tristan. King Meliadus was my father'. The king said, 'Tristan, you really should have revealed your identity sooner. Therefore I don't want you to depart from my court, rather I want to grant you a boon: that you be the lord of my entire kingdom to do as you think best and according to your will'. (King Faramont was greatly angered because he didn't recognize Tristan after all this time.) But Tristan said that he would not remain in any way. Then the king – with great sadness – granted him leave.

[11] Now the tale says that the barons and knights were very sad about Tristan's departure. In the morning Tristan [fol. 105v] arose, and the king kept him company, and his barons accompanied Tristan. At their parting the king proffered his kingdom to Tristan. The king returned to his palace; Tristan rode ||| day after day until they [Tristan and Governal] came near Cornwall.

[12] After Belide found out that Tristan had left the kingdom of Gaul and was going to dwell in Cornwall, she began to make the greatest lament that had ever been made by a damsel. She said to herself, 'Now you have left! – he whom I loved more than myself; I won't see him as I used to. I know that love torments me in such a way that my life can't last long. Although I know that death is the most grievous thing that anyone can suffer, yet to me it will turn to sweetness since I have saved my love from death; for this reason, I want to die'.

---

* Here, scribe or his model has conflated two sentences, blurring their meaning. In such cases, I translate as accurately as possible. See footnotes to the Italian text for indications of problems in the MS.

Alora la damaysella chiamò uno escudieri lo quale era gintille homo. Fey lo jurar 'de tener credensa de so que i[o] ti darò'. Poi disse la damaysella que 'tu me façi uno messaçe a Tristano. Porteray li salute da mia parte. Daray li questo breve lo quale io ti daroe. Terray questa bracheta da mia parte la quale èi più bella e la melliore del mondo ní que avere potesse. Anchor li menaray lo mio destrier ch'è melior que avere potesse. May tuta fiata vuolio que tu li diche da mia parte ch'elli ti tengna con luy. Però [fol. 106r] enprima que tu ti parti, vuollio que vege la morte que io farò per la soa amore'.

Alora presse l'espada e posse lo pomo en terra ||||[121] e la ponta posse dritamente alo chuore, e disse, 'Dolço mio amore Tristano, io vuollio morire que io m'ançide per tua amore'. Encontenente si laysò cadere in sull'espada e fo morta encontenente la damaysella. Lo scudiery montò a cavallo e presse la bracçeta e lo breve, e partì si de la corte de lo Re Ferramonte.

Tanto cavalchoe per so jornata que çionçe Tristano a uno castello que si chiamava Titolin.[122] Guovernale, gardando si endaretro, vidi l'escudieri que cavallquava versso luy. Disse a Tristano, 'Echo uno chavaliere'. Tristano disse, 'Io l'aspettarò per[qué] uno homo non deve fogire'. A queste parolle l'esqudiere fo gunto. Saludò Tristano cortessamente, [e] elli li rende so salute. Apresso [disse], 'Ti saluto da parte de Bellace (sic), la figliola de lo Re Feramonte, lo quale ve manda per me questo destrieri e chesta bracheta, la quale èi la più bella e la melliore che si possa trovare, e sì me disse que me debiate venere con voy'. Tristano disse, 'Say tu mei nome o mio covenent<r>e?'[123] Eli disse que sì. 'Donqua ti comandi que tue non debi dire a nulla persona sença mia parollo'. Disse, 'Questo farò io volentiera'. Alora diede lo breve a Tristano. [fol. 106v] Tristano lo presse, e dissia choisì:

[13] 'Amis[124] mia, Tristano e bon chuore e de verayse amore, salut ti manda Bellices, la filiola de lo Re Ferramonte. Sapi, amicho, que dapoyqué sepi la toa partença lo quale tu eri facto lontagno contrate, io remassi con planto e con dolore dapoyqué tu da me eri partit<c>o.[125] Considerando tutavia de voy, non trovarmi chi a me potesse dare conforto de le mie pene. Sapi, amicho, considerando de la morte, sostenendo [do]lore,[126] recordando sì chome io potea morire con quella espada la quale lo Re ti vollia taliarre la testa, un[de][127] sapi que io ti mandi lo

[121] Beginning here, five half-lines left blank at the right; miniature never executed.
[122] MS consistently spells it this way. Cf. TR: *Tintoil*; TP: *Tintoille*.
[123] Perhaps on analogy with adverbs in *-mentre*.
[124] On this rhetorical opening, see Yseut's love letters to Tristan, in the Rossi *Canzoniere* of Biblioteca Apostolica Vaticana, Barb. Lat. MS 3953 (Lorenzo Renzi, 'Il francese come lingua letteraria e il franco-lombardo: L'epica carolingia nel Veneto', in *Storia della cultura veneta, I: Dalle origini al Trecento*, ed. Girolamo Arnaldi (Vicenza, 1976), pp. 563–90, on pp. 577–8); a false love letter from Gloriande to Amant in the *Roman de Tristan* (ed. Curtis, vol. I, p. 117) as well as BnF, MS 756, fol. 19vb. It is also found in medieval Veronese verse (Franco Riva, 'Lessico di antico veronese desunto da testi in versi (sec. XIII – sec. XVII)', *Accademia di Agricoltura, Scienze e Lettere di Verona. Atti e memorie* 5 (1953–54), 171–237, on 178); in TR, p. 30; and in two *Tavola Ritonda* manuscripts (*Tav. Rit.*, p. 62 n. 3).
[125] Perhaps a doubled *-tt-*; *c / t* often hard to distinguish in this hand.
[126] MS: *lo Re*. Cf. TR, p. 30: *non sostenni dolore*.
[127] In MS *Vn* with a superfluous titulus over the *n*. Cf. TR, p. 30: *Onde sappie*.

Il Tristano Riccardiano *(Parodi's siglum 'F')*

Then the damsel called a squire who was of noble blood. She made him swear to 'keep in confidence what I will tell you'. Then the damsel told him to 'carry a message from me to Tristan. Carry him greetings on my behalf. Give him this letter which I will give you. Take this hound on my behalf, which is the nicest and best in the world that anyone could have. In addition, lead to him my warhorse that is the best that one could have. But I also want you to tell him, for my sake, to keep you with him. Therefore [fol. 106r] before you leave, I want you to see the death that I will make for his love'.

Then she took the sword and placed the pommel on the ground ||| and positioned the point straight at her heart, and said, 'My sweet love Tristan, I want to die so I am killing myself for your sake'. Immediately she let herself fall upon the sword, and the damsel died at once. The squire mounted her horse and took the hound and the letter, and left King Faramont's court.

He rode so much through the days that he reached Tristan at a castle that was called Tintagel. Governal, looking behind him, saw the squire who was riding toward him. He said to Tristan, 'Look, a knight!' Tristan said, 'I'll await him because a man must not flee'. At these words the squire reached them. He greeted Tristan courteously, and he returned his greeting. Then he said, 'I greet you on behalf of Belide, the daughter of King Faramont, who sends me to you with this warhorse and this hound – which is the nicest and best that one can find – and she told me that I must come along with you'. Tristan said, 'Do you know my name or my identity?' And he said yes. 'Then I command you not to tell anyone without my permission'. He replied, 'This I will do willingly'. Then he gave the letter to Tristan. [fol. 106v] Tristan took it, and this is what it said:

[13] 'My *amis* Tristan, loved whole-heartedly and truly, Belide, the daughter of King Faramont, sends you greetings. Know, *ami*, that since I learned of your departure which you made for a distant country, I have remained in weeping and sorrow since you left me. Yet while thinking of you, I found no one who could give me comfort for my pains. Know, *ami*, thinking of death, suffering pain, remembering how I could have died with that sword with which the king wanted to cut off your head, therefore know that I am sending you my warhorse

mio destrieri e la mia bracheta la quale èi più bella e la miliore que si possa trovare perqué tu la debias denere[128] per mio amore. Enpersò sapi que io sonno morta con quella spada con la quale tu divie[129] essere morto'.
Tute queste parolle dissia lo breve.

[14] Quando Tristano ebe lecto lo breve chome era morta la filiola de lo Re Feramonte – e lo escudiere disse, 'Ella s'uccise per vostra amore' – molto n'è dolento Tristano.
Apresse cavalcando a Titolin, dapoyqué fonno alo palaso de lo Re Marcho, Tristano [e Governale][130] s'apressero danançi da lo Re e profersi li suo servicio. Lo Re gardando Tristano, vedendolo coissì bello, disse que son serviçi li plaçia asay. Alora remasse Tristano en so compagnia. Tuti li baroni di Cornavalia si meravillavanno de le bellesse de Tristano. Dissiano tuti comunamente que Dominiidio non fesse unqua uno più bello damaysello de luy. Molto si parla per [fol. 107r] tuta la terra siché lo Re Marcho non volea que neun lo serva, si non Tristano. Tuti li autre damayselli sonno a niente poyqué vene Tristano ende la corte. (Si alcuno mi demandarà si lo Re Marcho conossia Tristano, io diria de no. Quello non sapea so·nnome né so covenente.)

[15] Apreso di queste parolle, andoe a chaçiare con grandi compania. Tristano andoe con luy a chaçiare, may tuti li autri chavalieri e damaçelli non paren que sapianno de chaçia tanto come fae Tristano. Dapoy tornano ala terra, enchominçò a scrimire con cavalliery e damayselli siqué en pocho tenpo non trovava qui con luy volesse es[c]rimere. Apresso enchomençò a cavalchare e da menare arme con li autre chavalieri, siqué tuti li baroni de Cornavalia si meraviliavano dissian[131] que fa Tristano. (Potea avere anni .xv.)

[16] Alora viene L'Amoroldo de Landa con granda gente en Cornavalla per lo trabuto lo quale avea a recevere da lo Re Marcho per dieçe anni. Quelli de Cornavalla qui videronno la nave de L'Omoroldo de Landa enchomençeron a fare grando lamenta, dissendo, 'Mare, perqué non vieny una grande[132] tempesta ché tute queste nave andasseno a fondo, que tanto dolore arechano en Cornavalla'. Molte n'è dolento lo Re e tuti quilli de la soa[133] corte di questa aventura. L'Amoroldo presse porto a Titolin e si esmontò a terra de la nave. Mandoe .iii. chavalieri alo Re Marcho per demandare lo trabuto per dieçe anni. Quelli chavalieri [fol. 107v] forono giu[n]ti alo palayso de lo Re Marcho; disseno, 'A tu manda L'Amoroldo

---

128   Consonantal voicing used. Cf. TR, p. 30: *tenere*; *Tav. Rit.*, p. 63: *tenete*.
129   Cf. TR, p. 30: *dovei*. In MS confusion of high vowels *e* / *i*, here and elsewhere, e.g. *dive* (fol. 102v), *rie* (fol. 127v), *dibitti* (fol. 135v), *dibian* (fol. 155v).
130   The plural verbs indicate Governal's presence in the narrative.
131   Cf. TR, p. 32: *meravigliano di cioe ke facea*.
132   MS *quande*, written clearly.
133   MS *foa*. Confusion of *s* / *f*.

Il Tristano Riccardiano *(Parodi's siglum 'F')*

and my hound, which is the nicest and best that one can find so that you must keep it for my sake. For this reason, know that I died with that sword with which you were to have been killed'.

All these words spake the letter.

[14] When Tristan had read the letter – how the daughter of King Faramont had died – and the squire said, 'She killed herself for your love', Tristan was very sorrowful about it.

After riding to Tintagel, when they were at King Mark's palace, Tristan and Governal approached the king, and Tristan proffered him his service. The king – looking at Tristan, seeing him so handsome – said that his service would please him greatly. Then Tristan remained in his company. All the barons of Cornwall marvelled at Tristan's beauty. They all said among themselves that the Lord God had never made a more beautiful young man than he. They spoke of it so much [fol. 107r] throughout the land that King Mark didn't want anyone else to serve him, only Tristan. All the other youths were nothing since Tristan came to the court. (If anyone asks me if King Mark knew who Tristan was, I would say no: the fellow didn't know his name or his identity.)

[15] After these words, King Mark went hunting with a large company. Tristan went with him to hunt, but all the other knights and youths did not seem to know as much about hunting as Tristan did. After they returned to the land, Tristan began to fence with knights and young men so that in a brief time he found no one who wanted to fence with him. Afterward he began [to learn] to ride and to fight with weapons against the other knights so that all the barons of Cornwall marvelled at what Tristan was doing. (He must have been about fifteen.)

[16] Then the Morholt of Ireland came with many people to Cornwall for the tribute that he was supposed to receive from King Mark every ten years. Those of Cornwall who saw the Morholt of Ireland's ships began to make a great lament, saying, 'Sea, why doesn't a great storm come so that all these ships go to the bottom, since they are bringing such suffering to Cornwall?' The king was very sorrowful – and all those of his court – about this adventure. The Morholt put into port at Tintagel and descended to the ground from his ship. He sent three knights to King Mark to demand the ten-years' tribute. When those knights [fol. 107v] had reached King Mark's palace, they said, 'The Morholt of Ireland, the best

de Landa, lo melior chavaliere del mondo, qué ti apareche de paguar lo trebuto da ogi al terço giorno; si non, elo farà ardere la tua terra'. A queste parolle [...][134]

[E tutto] lo giorno armogionno chavalieri e damayselli per amor de Tristano. Magiore allegressa arebenno avuti que avesseno unqua se non fosse la tristicia l'avveran stati en tale maniera. Li 'nbaisatori retornoron a corte e disseno al Re Marcho que responde del trabuto, ||||[135] may lo Re Marcho non respose né neuno de li chavalieri.

Tristano, vedendo que lo Re Marcho non responde – né neuno de li chavalieri, Tristano si levò si ricto[136] e disse ali 'nbaysatori, 'Si li [n]ostri antichi che sonno estati ànno paguati lo trebuto a quilli de Landa, noy que siamo a valle nol volemo paguare. S'eli disse que noy lo debiam paguare, io ben apello ala batallia. Mostaròli per forçe d'arme come noy nol debiam pagare lo trebuto'. Quando li 'nbaysatori entesseno le parolle de Tristano, disseno, 'Re Marcho, disse per vostra parolla lo chavaliere so que disse?' Elli disse que sie.[137] Tristano s'inginòllo danachi da lo re e disse, 'Donate mi lo guante di la batallia con L'Amoroldo'. Lo Re li diede; Tristano lo rengr[fol. 108r]aciò. Li <n>enbaysatore disseno, 'Qui sette[138] voi que pre[n]dette la batallia con L'Amoroldo, perché L'Amoroldo non entrarebe a campo si voy non fossere de lingnaçio'. Tristano disse, 'Enperò non laysi illi la batallia conmecho, s'ill'è chavaliere e mi chavaliere, s'ill'è[139] filliolo de Re e io filgliolo di Re. Lo Re Meliadus de Leones fo mio parre, e lo Re Marcho aquie fie mio çio. Emperò la batalia non remarrà qué non fia tra·mme a luy'.

Allora si p[art]ino[140] li 'npbaysatori e tornono e disseno, 'Uno chavaliere ogi facto ende la corte de lo Re Marcho, lo quale volle entrar con voi a campo per questo trabuto, ché disse che non èi raysone que lo debianno pagare; ed èi lo più bello chavaliere que Dio fesseçe unqua'. Alora disse L'Amoroldo de Landa, 'Si è facto ogi chavaliere novello, deman serà morto. Have' voi pensato dove de' esser lo campo?' Li chavalieri respossero que non sapianno. L'Amoroldo disse, 'Tornate e stablite dove de' essere la batalia'. Alora tornoronno li chavalieri in de lo realme de Leonis a corte qu'eranno encompagnia de L'Amoroldo per vedere Tristano. Andoronno ala corte de lo Re Marcho. Dapoiché fonno ala corte, disseno li chavalieri a Tristano, 'Dove volete que sia la bataglia?' Tristano disse, 'Io vuollio que sia stablita en una issola, la quale si è presso da quie'. (Si alchuno me demanderà come à nome l'issola, io dirò ch'à nome L'Issola sença Av[e]ntura.)

---

[134] At this point, there is a lacuna that elides material found on TR, p. 32 and TP, p. 151. Here, Tristan learns about the required tribute, marvels at the cowardice of the Cornish knights, and asks to be dubbed to serve as their champion. In MS 1729 the narrative resumes as in TR, p. 36 and TP, p. 153.

[135] Five full lines left blank; miniature never executed.

[136] MS *levò suo ricto*. Correction based on TR, p. 36: *levossi ritto*.

[137] MS *fie*. Confusion of *s* / *f*.

[138] Not the number 'seven', this is the second person plural of the verb 'to be'. Form produced by hypercorrection. See also fol. 117v.

[139] MS *fille*. Confusion of *s* / *f*.

[140] MS *p(er)rino*. Scribe used the '*per*' abbreviation, but omitted the *t*.

knight in the world, is sending to you so that you prepare to pay the tribute on the third day from today; if not, he will have your land burned'. At these words [...]* And that whole day knights and youths fought with arms for love of Tristan. They would have had greater joy than they had if it weren't for the sadness they had in that fashion. The ambassadors returned to court and told King Mark to answer about the tribute, ||| but King Mark didn't answer nor did any of his knights.

Tristan, upon seeing that King Mark did not reply – nor any of his knights, Tristan rose up erect and said to the ambassadors, 'Even if our ancestors (who once lived) paid the tribute to those of Ireland, we who are here now do not want to pay it. If he said that we must pay it, I do indeed call for battle. I will show him by force of arms that we must not pay the tribute'. When the ambassadors heard Tristan's words, they said, 'King Mark, did this knight say what he said on your orders?' He said yes. Tristan knelt before the king and said, 'Give me the glove of combat with the Morholt'. The king gave it to him; Tristan thanked [fol. 108r] him. The ambassadors said, 'Who are you who undertakes the battle with the Morholt? – because the Morholt will not enter the field if you are not of noble lineage'. Tristan said, 'For this reason he will not put off fighting with me since if he is a knight, so am I; if he is the son of a king, I am the son of a king. King Meliadus of Leonis was my father, and King Mark here is my uncle. Therefore the battle will not be put off, because it will take place between me and him'.

Then the ambassadors left and returned to the ship and said, 'A knight made today in King Mark's court wants to enter the field against you about this tribute, since he says that it's not right for them to have to pay it; and he is the most beautiful knight that God ever made'. Then the Morholt of Ireland said, 'If he was only made a knight today, tomorrow he'll be dead. Have you thought of where the battle must be?' The knights replied that they didn't know. The Morholt said, 'Return and establish where the battle must be'. Then the knights who were in the Morholt's company returned to the kingdom of Leonis, to the court, in order to see Tristan. They went to King Mark's court. After they were at the court, the knights said to Tristan, 'Where do you want the battle to be held?' Tristan said, 'I want it to be held on an island that is near here'. (If anyone asks me what was the name of the island, I would say that it was called the Island without Adventure.)

---

* MS contains a lengthy ellipsis. For the missing contents, see TR, pp. 33–7.

[17] Dapoyqué li dui chavalieri videno Tristano, disseno l'uno de li chavalieri (lo quale à nome Cari[fol. 108v]es),[141] disse, 'Tristano non pò remanere [la batallia] que non fia pro chavaliere'. Tornonno li chavalieri a L'Amoroldo[142] e disseno che illi avean establta ende la Issola sensa Ventura 'de qui al terço jorno veramente qu'ende l'issola non passerà si non voi e luy'. Alora disse L'Amoroldo que questo li plaçia asay. Alora parle Galice a L'Amoroldo e disse, 'Io volrie ben per mia vuolla que la batalia non fosse tra voe e Tristano, ché io chonoscho bene ch'eli non potte remanere ch'eli non sia prodo chavaliere. Imperçò lauderia que fosse <c>[143] pasce tr'anbidoro[144] e lo trebuto fosse terminata di quie serto termine. Si voi vedeste Tristano, Dio non feçe unqua uno sì bello chavaliere'. Alora disse L'Amorolldo, 'E la battalia non potte remanere per neuna manera'.

Alquanto parla lo Re Marcho a Tristano: 'Io volrea que remasesse la batallia da te, e·lL'Amoroldo; si[145] lo trebuto demanda, io li doroe'. Tristano disse per tuto lo realme de Cornavalia non layserebe la batallia. Al terço giorno L'Amoroldo fo armato e montò a cav[a]llo, e tuti li soi chavalieri l'acompagnano fina ala riva del mare. Tristano presse soe arme e monta a cavallo (en su quello que Belliçe li donoe). Demandoe cumiato alo Re Marcho. Lo Re disse, 'Dapoyqué tu vuoli fare questa batalia, vuolio che tu me diche tuo covenente'. Tristano disse, 'Non me darete altramente cumiato?' Eli disse di no. Tristano disse, 'Mie nome fiè Tristano; lo Re Meliadus de Leones fo mio patre'. 'Come?' disse [lo Re]. 'Sei tu filgliolo di lo Re Meliadus de Leones, lo quale fo mio fratello? [fol. 109r] Certo, Tristano, bene dovei dire più tosto tuo covenente. Donqua questa batalia non faray enançi ben volgli pagare in tanti lo trebuto'. Tristano disse que la batalia non potte remanere in neuna manera. Alora [lo Re] lo comandoe a Dio. Quando li chavalieri entesseno que questo era Tristano, lo nepote de lo Re Marcho, c'andava ala batalia con lo meliore chavaliere del mondo, enchomençeron a fare lo maor pplanto – dame e damayselle – del mondo. Tuti plia[n]gevan per amore de Tristano. Lo Re Marcho l'acompagnia con tuti li soi chavalieri.

Quando foronno ala riva de lo mare, L'Amoroldo intrò ende la sua nave con lo so cavallo, e Tristano con la soa nave atressì<n>; e quando fo al'issola, el chaçiò la soa nave per lo mare. L'Amoroldo disse, 'Perqué ày tu chaçiata la toa nave per mare?' Tristano disse, 'Perché uno di noy deve remanere qui morto, ch'elli que remarrà potrà bene tornare en una nave'. Alora montonno a cavallo amburo li chavalieri. Disse L'Amoroldo a Tristano, 'Io ti vuolio perdonare questa batalia perqué io veguo que tu l'ày pressa per pocho senno'. Tristano disse, 'Si tu vuolli reffudare lo trebuto de lo Re, lo quale tu li dimandi, io layserò questa batalia. Si non li vuolli refudare, poy compliremo nostra batalia'. Alora disse L'Amoroldo, 'Quello que io ti dissia, si ti dissia perqué tue me pare tropo giovano chavaliere, non ché io vuollia refudare lo trebuto che io abo a recevere. Donqua non si

---

[141] MS *Caries, Galice*. Cf. TR, p. 38: *Gariette*.
[142] MS *ramolodo*.
[143] Scribe used a single *c* to fill out the line.
[144] MS *tranbi daro*. Emendation based on TR, p. 38: *intra voi due*.
[145] MS clearly *fi*.

[17] After the two knights saw Tristan, one of the knights (who was called Gareth) [fol. 108v] said, 'Tristan cannot fail to be anything but a valiant knight'. The knights returned to the Morholt and said that they had established that the battle be on the Island without Adventure, 'on the third day hence, of a certainty, so that no one will cross over to the Island except you and he'. Then the Morholt said that this pleased him greatly. Then Gareth spoke to the Morholt and said, 'By my faith, I do indeed wish that the battle was not between you and Tristan, because I know well that he cannot fail to be a valiant knight. For this reason it would be praiseworthy if there were peace between you both and if the tribute would be ended from here on at a certain date. If you saw Tristan – God never made such a beautiful knight'. Then the Morholt said, 'The battle cannot be put off in any way'.

King Mark spoke a bit to Tristan: 'I would like the battle between you and the Morholt to be put off; if he demands the tribute, I'll give it to him'. Tristan said that for the whole kingdom of Cornwall, he would not give up the battle. On the third day the Morholt was armed and mounted his horse, and all his knights accompanied him as far as the seashore. Tristan took his arms and mounted his horse (the one that Belide gave him). He asked leave of King Mark. The king said, 'Since you want to undertake this battle, I want you to tell me your identity'. Tristan said, 'Otherwise you won't give me leave?' He said no. Tristan said, 'My name is Tristan; King Meliadus of Leonis was my father'. 'What?' said King Mark. 'Are you the son of King Meliadus of Leonis who was my brother? [fol. 109r] In truth, Tristan, you really should have told your identity much sooner. Well then, you'll not go on with this battle inasmuch as I do indeed want to pay the tribute'. Tristan said that in no way the battle could be put off. Then the king commended him to God. When the knights heard that this was Tristan, King Mark's nephew, who was going into battle with the best knight in the world, they began to make the greatest lament – [with the] women and damsels – in the world. Everyone was weeping for love of Tristan. King Mark accompanied him with all his knights.

When they were at the seashore, the Morholt entered his boat with his horse, and Tristan with his ship similarly; and when they were at the island, he pushed his boat out to sea. The Morholt said, 'Why did you push your boat out to sea?' Tristan said, 'Because one of us must remain here dead; thus he who remains alive will easily be able to return in one boat'. Then both knights mounted their horses. The Morholt said to Tristan, 'I want to spare you this battle because I see that you have undertaken it unwisely'. Tristan said, 'If you want to refuse the king's tribute that you demand, I will give up this battle. If you do not want to refuse it, then we'll complete our battle'. Then the Morholt said, 'What I told you, I told you because you seem to me too young a knight, not because I want to refuse the tribute that I have to receive'. [And Tristan said,]* 'Well then, there

---

* Clarification based on TR, p. 40.

bissognia parlamento entre noy doe'. Alora disse Tristano, 'Chavaliere, [fol. 109v] guàrdate da me, qué io ti desfido!'

Alora s'alongano li chavalieri l'uno da l'autro, e viene l'uno enverso dal'autro. Amboro anderon a terra de cavallo; li cavvali (sic) andoron amboro de sopra ali chavalieri. Chiascuno molto si lamenta del colpo. Molto si meraviliav[a] L'Amoroldo de lo colpo de Tristano che li à dato. Tristano disse que unqua non recevete uno sì grande colpi per uno chavaliere. A tanto si alsano[146] anboro li chavalieri de terra; viene l'uno enverso l'autro e mettenno mane al'espade. |||[147] L'Amoroldo fiere a Tristano sopra al'escudo e diedi li sì gran colpo che ne portò uno grande pesço en terra. Tristano fiere a L'Amoroldo sobra al'elmo de tuta soa forssa. Passò l'ermo e la chufa de lo ferro. La ponta de l'espada si li missi el capo, siqué l'espata s'ingranò. Alo trayere, L'Amoroldo cade en terra e disse a Tristano, 'Non mi onchidere ché io mi chiamo vinto' – disse doe volte – 'may ti preguo che tue m'auti andare enfine ala nave'. Tristano disse que questo farae volontieri. Alora lo prende Tristano e menalo enfina ala nave. Dapoyqué fo ala nave, Tristano lo spengia en mare. L'Amoroldo [si ricordoe][148] d'una saeta atoysegata, quelli ferì Tristano ende [fol. 110r] la coysa. Tristano disse, 'Come, Amoroldo, ài me tu ferito?' Garda se ende la coissa: non pare che la ferita sia de niente.

Alora partì se L'Amoroldo de Connavalia (sic) e vae ala sua gente con tuti li chavalieri tornono en Landa molto doloyrossi. Quelli de Cornavalia disseno, 'Andate sensa may retornare'. May lo Re Marcho montò tosto a cavallo; emantenente mandoe per Tristano. Dapoyché lo Re fo venuto, lo Re e li soy chavalieri ne fan[n]o la magior festa e la m[a]giore alegressa che giamaye fosse facto per uno chavaliere.

[18] Ora disse lo conto [que] quando Tristano fo giunto a Titolin, molta gente li va encontro e fanno li gioa e festa. Durò questa festa de Tristano .viii. dì e .viii. nocte. Maie Tristano, lo quale èi ferito, enchomençò si a dolere[149] de la soa ferita sicome homo que non è sença grande enguoissa. Lo Re Marcho fe venire li mediçi per medicare Tristano. Gardano le ferite: non pare que abia niente, may disseno que lo guaranno molto tossto.

Tristano garite de tute li autre ferite salvo que de quella de la coissia que più medicava, e più pegiorava. Poy enchomençò a pegiurare e a pudire sì fortamente la ferita che nulla persona non potea estare ende la corte. Dapoyqué Tristano si sentitte quello pusse de la ferita, disse a Governalle, 'Maistro, dapoyché sono ferito en tal manera, que te pare?' (Governale vide que neuna persona non pote venire.) 'Io vuolio que tu vadi alo Re Marcho, e debias pregnare da mia parte che io me vuolio partire de la corte e andare estare ende 'l palaçio qu'èy ala riva [fol. 110v] de lo mare'. Poyqué Guovernale ebe decte queste parolle alo Re Marcho,

---

146 MS *sonano*. Reading differs from TR, p. 40.
147 Seven full lines left blank; miniature never executed.
148 MS omitted verb. Emendation based on TR, p. 40.
149 MS *dorere*. Rhoticism of the *l*.

Il Tristano Riccardiano *(Parodi's siglum 'F')*

is no need for further parlay between us'. Then Tristan said, 'Knight, [fol. 109v] guard yourself from me, because I challenge you!'

Then the knights moved away from one another and came charging at one another. Both went to the ground from their horses; both the horses fell on top of the knights; each one greatly lamented the blow. The Morholt marvelled greatly at the blow that Tristan had given him. Tristan said to himself that he had never received such a great blow from a knight. Then both knights rose up from the ground; then one came toward the other, and they put hands to swords. ||| The Morholt struck Tristan on his shield and gave him such a great blow that it carried a big piece of it to the ground. Tristan struck the Morholt on top of his helmet, with all his might. It passed through the helmet and the iron coif. The point of the sword struck into his head so that the sword splintered. On pulling it out, the Morholt fell to the ground; and he said to Tristan, 'Don't kill me because I consider myself defeated' – he said two times – 'but I beg you to help me go as far as the boat'. Tristan said that he would do this willingly. Then Tristan took him and led him as far as the boat. After he was in the boat, Tristan pushed it out to sea. The Morholt, remembering a poisoned arrow, wounded Tristan in [fol. 110r] his thigh. Tristan said, 'What, Morholt, have you wounded me?' He looked at his thigh: the wound didn't seem to be anything serious.

Then the Morholt left Cornwall and returned to his people with all the knights; they returned to Ireland, very sorrowful. The people of Cornwall said, 'Go – without ever coming back!' But King Mark quickly mounted his horse; he sent for Tristan immediately. After the king had come, the king and his knights celebrated greatly about him and had the most happiness ever because of a knight.

[**18**] Now the tale says that when Tristan arrived at Tintagel, many people went to meet him and rejoiced and celebrated greatly. This celebrating over Tristan lasted eight days and eight nights. But Tristan, who was wounded, began to suffer from his wound like a man who is not without great anguish. King Mark had physicians come to treat Tristan. They looked at his wounds: it didn't seem that he had anything serious, but they said that they would cure him very soon.

Tristan was healed of his other wounds, except for the one in his thigh that, the more they treated it, the worse it got. Then the wound began to worsen and to stink so strongly that no one could stay in the court. Since Tristan smelled that reeking from his wound, he said to Governal, 'Master, since I'm wounded in such a way, what do you think?' (Governal saw that no one could come near.) 'I want you to go to King Mark, and you must beg him for my sake to let me leave the court and go stay in the palace that is on the seashore'. [fol. 110v] After Governal told these words to King Mark, <and you must beg him for my sake>

<e debia lo pregnare da mia parte> ello feçe prendere una biria chavalchare[150] e fesse lo portare alo palagio che èi sopra dal mare. May Tristano non potte trovare consillio de suo male. Disse [a] Governale, 'Porta me ala fenestra qué io vuolio vedere lo mare'. Guovernale disse que non vuolia portare. (Si me demandasse alchuno perché Tristano volea andare ala fenestra, io dirò che si volea desperare.)

[19] Dapoyché vide [che non potea][151] andare, disse Tristano a Guovernale, 'Vàme alo Re Marcho e dìli che viengna a me'. Governale andò a lui e disse, 'Re Marcho, Tristano ve manda a dire que voy andete a luy a parlare'. Lo Re montò a cavallo e andò a luy. Tristano disse, 'Re Marcho, quando non posso trovare guarissone de questo mio malle, e m'è venuto vuolia de cerquare la ventura. Enperçò ve preguo que voy me faciate far una barqueta e metere i vianda per uno anno'. Alora disse lo Re che questo farà ello volentieri.[152]

Alora fesse fare la nave molto bella: fesse lì metere vianda per uno anno e fornimento si chome decto avea Tristano. Poy comandò che fia messo ende la nave una sua arpa e una sua violla. Poy vi fesse portare ala <la> nave luy. Lo Re Marcho e li soy barone l'acompagnerrono enfina ala riva de lo mare. Dapoy Tristano p[r]esse cumiato, lo Re e li soy barone e[n]come[n]çeronno forte a piangere de la partença de Tristano.

A tanto driçano le vele [fol. 111r] al vento. El tempo èy bonno e lo mare sensa tempesta. Lo Re Marcho e li suoy baroni esterano tanto ende su la riva de lo mare enfina que non poteno più vedere la nave de Tristano, e poy lo Re tornió a Titolin. (May si alcuno me demandarae perché Tristano entrò ende la nave, io dirò ch'ello l'intrò più per hendendemento de morire che de guarire.)

[20] Molto èy dolento lo Re Marcho e tuti li soe barone de la partença de Tristano. Dicano comunamente: 'Si Tristano more, Cornavalia èi destruta'. May Tristano lo quale è [con] Governale, andoronno tuto lo giorno qu'è[153] molto bello tempo. May la nocte metesma è començoe una grande tempesta. May Tristano si laysi portare al tempo, may grande paora ànno de morire. Estetenno en mare, sostenendo gran pena e dolore asay, tanto que una nocte ariveronno a terra. Quando Governale vide terra, disse a Tristano, 'Noy siemo presso a uno castello'. Tristano enchomінçò a regraciare Idio que l'avea messo a terra. Alora comandò a Guovernale che debia legnare la nave ali autri ligny que sonno ende·llo porto.

[21] Ora disse lo conto que Tristano e Governale steti en mare .viii. messe. (Si alcuno me demandarà onde Tristano arivoe, io dirò che arivoe en Milanda ala corte de lo Re Languis, chuygnato de L'Amoroldo, lo quale morìo de la ferita la quale Tristano li diede.) Dapoyché la nave di Tristano fo ançiata, prende l'arpa e cominçò a sonare; ed era presso alo giorno. Fesse sono[154] [fol. 111v] tanto

---

[150] MS [Se?]orria. First two letters unclear, the first is capitalized. Cf. TR, p. 42: *bara kavalkarese*.
[151] Omission in MS. Emendation based on TR, p. 42.
[152] Scribe wrote seven red *c*s to fill out the line.
[153] Scribe wrote *quei*, then lightly struck out the incorrect final *-i*.
[154] Scribe wrote five letters, then cancelled out the third, leaving *fono*. Confusion of *s* / *f*.

Il Tristano Riccardiano *(Parodi's siglum 'F')*

he had a horse litter brought and had Tristan carried to the palace that overlooked the sea. But Tristan could find no relief for his suffering. He said to Governal, 'Carry me to the window because I want to see the sea'. Governal said that he didn't want to carry him. (If anyone asks me why Tristan wanted to go to the window, I would say that he wanted to kill himself from despair.)

[19] When he saw that he could not go, Tristan said to Governal, 'Go to King Mark on my behalf and tell him to come to me'. Governal went to him and said, 'King Mark, Tristan is sending to ask you to go and speak to him'. The king mounted his horse and went to him. Tristan said, 'King Mark, since I can't find a cure for this pain of mine, I wish to seek my fortune. Therefore I pray you to have a little boat made for me and to put in it enough victuals for a year'. Then the king said that he would do this willingly.

Then he had a very nice ship built; he had food for a year and supplies put in it as Tristan had said. Then he commanded that his harp and his viol be put in the ship. Then he had [Tristan] carried to the ship. King Mark and his barons accompanied him as far as the seashore. After Tristan took his leave, the king and his barons began to weep hard about Tristan's departure.

In that moment they raised the sails [fol. 111r] to the wind; and the weather was fine and the sea without storms. King Mark and his barons stayed on the seashore until they could no longer see Tristan's ship, and then the king returned to Tintagel. (But if anyone were to ask me why Tristan entered the ship, I would say that he entered it more with the intention of dying than of being cured.)

[20] King Mark was very sad about Tristan's departure as were all his barons. They were all saying: 'If Tristan dies, Cornwall is destroyed'. But Tristan, who was with Governal, went along all day because it was very fine weather, but the very same night a great storm began. But Tristan let himself be carried along by the weather, and they were greatly afraid of dying. They stayed at sea, enduring great hardship and much suffering, until finally one night they reached land. When Governal saw land, he said to Tristan, 'We're near a castle'. Tristan began to thank God who had brought him to land. Then he commanded Governal to tie up the ship to the other boats that were in the port.

[21] Now the tale says that Tristan and Governal were at sea for eight months. (If anyone asks me where Tristan arrived, I would say that he arrived in Ireland at the court of King Anguin, the brother-in-law of the Morholt who had died of the wound that Tristan gave him.) After Tristan's ship was seen to, he took his harp and began to play; and it was nearly dawn. He played [fol. 111v] so sweetly that

dolçame[n]tre que lo Re Languis lo udia de la camera. Entendendo lo sono de l'arpa, parveli tanto dolçe a udire qu'illo si levò del letto e vestì<r>si e andoe ala finest[r]a, la quale era sopra allo porto del mare. Qui ve·sstete tanto infine que Tristano sonoe. Possa layse lo sonare. Tristano messe uno grande grido e disse, 'Lasso, [sono] morto!' En tal manera queste parolle entende ben lo Re Languis. Encontenente chiamò .iiii. bayleri e disse lo Re, 'Andiate a quello porto e demandiate qui è quilli que à sonate'. Li damayselli vanno e fanno chello que lo Re comandoe a loro. Non si potte tenere: lo re andò loro dirietro con altra gente. Si vienono a Tristano, salutì lo cortessamente, ed eli rende so salut. Lo Re disse, 'Qui sete voi?' Tristano disse, 'Chavaliere aventurosso'. Disse lo Re, 'Io vuolio che tu viegne a stare ende 'l mio palagio'. Tristano disse que non potea andare. Alora comandoe lo Re que fosse portato a braçio. Facto foe sò que lo re commandò e fo vi posto giù[155] Tristano. (May si alcuno mi demanderà si illi lo chonosianno, io dirò de no, o saupesse soa condiçione.)

[22] Ad queste parolle lo Re fesse venire Ysota la bronda, la quale era soa fillola, ed era tanto bella ed avinente de tute cosse. Lo Re disse, 'Figliola, chi [fol. 112r] àe uno chavaliere aventurosso, enperçò vuolio que tue ti porchaçi de soe gurissone'. Yssota la bronda medicava la ferita de Tristano. Yssota vedendo que Tristano pur pegiorava, encomenço forte a dolere. Yssota comandoe que Tristano fosse portato fuora[156] al sole. Facto foe chiò qu'ella comandoe. Yssota disse, 'Si la tua ferita fie atoisseguata, seguro si è de garire; si non èi atoysegata, non ti poterò garire'.
Tanto la sgardò la ferita en giù e 'n su che truova que la ferita èi atoysequata. Alora prochaçò Yssota de trovare de quelle cosse que·ffanno mestieri a quella ferita. Fa venire erbe per fare enpiastre de farina e ponere ala ferita siché sentir en pocho dì[157] melliorare la dolore. Disse [Tristano], 'Damaysella, pare questa mediçina m'abia giurate'. May tanto si proçaçia Yssota che Tristano fo garito. E si li disse, 'Chavaliere, sàltassi tue ancora'. Tristano disse di no. Yssota disse, 'Salta, chavaliere, più que tu poe, qué io ti vuollio vedere'. Alora saltò Tristano .xxii. piè; la ferita aperçe. La damaysella enchomençò a medicare Tristano.

[23] Ora disse lo conto che Yssota fesse saltare Tristano perqué non li parea ben garito. Yssota disse, 'Salta, chavaliere, un'altra vuolta: le più que tue pòeti'. Tristano saltò .xxxii. piede. Yssota disse, 'Tu sey bene garito. May io non vidi ancor chavaliere que saltasse tanto come fa<r>te voy!' E molta era alegra de Tristano[158] da[fol. 112v]poyché sentito qu'ello èi garito de la soa ferita, may non quel sia tornato en soa bellessa nì en soa colore nì en soa fortessa, sich'ello potesse sofrire arme. Dapoyché Tristano venne fora ende la sala del palaçio là dov'eranno asay

---

[155]   MS *su*.
[156]   MS *fuara*. The scribe more often writes *fora*, but also *fuora*.
[157]   MS *do*.
[158]   Clear in MS, but see TR, p. 46: *Tristano èe molto allegro*.

Il Tristano Riccardiano *(Parodi's siglum 'F')* 43

King Anguin heard it from his chamber. Hearing the sound of the harp, it seemed to him so very sweet to hear that he arose from his bed and dressed and went to the window that was above the seaport. Here he remained as long as Tristan was playing. Then he left off playing. Tristan let out a great cry and said, 'Alas, I am dead!' In this way King Anguin clearly understood these words. Immediately he called four bailiffs, and the king said, 'Go to that port and ask who is that man who's playing'. The young men went and did as the king commanded them. He could not restrain himself: the king went along behind them, with other people. They went to Tristan, greeted him courteously, and he returned their greeting. The king said, 'Who are you?' Tristan said, 'A knight of fortune'. The king said, 'I want you to come and stay in my palace'. Tristan said that he wasn't able to go. Then the king commanded that he be carried in their arms. It was done as the king commanded, and Tristan was set down there. (But if anyone asks me if they knew him, I would say no, nor did they know his condition.)

[22] At these words, the king summoned Yseut the Blonde, who was his daughter, and she was so very beautiful and comely in all things. The king said, 'Daughter, here [fol. 112r] is a knight of fortune, and for this reason I want you to set about healing him'. Yseut the Blonde treated Tristan's wound. Yseut, upon seeing that Tristan still kept getting worse, began to grieve greatly. Yseut commanded that Tristan was carried outside into the sun; it was done as she commanded. Yseut said, 'If your wound is poisoned, your recovery is assured; if it isn't poisoned, I will not be able to heal you'.

Then she looked at the wound so hard, up and down, that she discovered that the wound was poisoned. Then Yseut set about finding some of those things that were useful for that wound. She had herbs brought in order to make flour plaster and placed it on the wound so that in a few days, he felt the pain getting better. Tristan said, 'Damsel, it seems that this medicine has cured me', but Yseut was still trying very hard so that Tristan would be cured. And she asked him, 'Knight, would you be able to jump yet?' Tristan said no. Yseut said, 'Jump, knight, as far as you can because I want to see you'. Then Tristan jumped twenty-two feet; the wound opened. The damsel began to treat Tristan.

[23] Now the tale says that Yseut made Tristan jump because he did not seem completely healed. Yseut said, 'Jump, knight, another time, as much as you are able'. Tristan jumped thirty-two feet. Yseut said, 'You are indeed cured, but I never saw a knight who could jump as far as you!' And she was very happy about Tristan since [fol. 112v] he felt recovered from his wound, but not so much that he had regained his beauty nor his color nor his strength so that he would be able to bear arms. After Tristan came out into the palace hall where there were very

chavalieri, ciascheduno si meravillavano de le soe bellesse. Disse l'uno al'autro que s'illo avesse chollore, el tanto più bello chavaliere de luy non si trovarebe.

[24] Molto parlano li chavalieri di fare torniamento. Lo Re di Scorçia fesse metere lo bando che volia fare torniamento. Da inde ala potesta[159] chalunque chavaliere volesse conbatere d'arme fosse e-Milanda[160] al tempo que decto era. Dapoyché lo torniamento aproximò, li chavalieri vanno alo torniamento. Lo Re Languis disse a Tristano, 'Volie tu ve[n]ire alo torniamento de lo Re de Scorçia?' Tristano disse, 'Io non potrey portare arme; may si voy volete que io vengna con voy, io venirò volentieri'. Lo Re disse, 'Io non vo ad aquesto torniamento per combatere, inperçò vuolio tua compagnia'. Alla matina si partite lo Re e Tristano e li autri chavalieri asay: chavalcano alo torniamento. Cavalcando presso a uno castello, trovonno uno chavaliere e uno escudieri en so compagnia. Lo escudieri que vidi Tristano enmantenente esmontò a terra da chavallo e 'nginolieli si ali piede[161] [fol. 113r] e baysòli li piedi. Tristano chando[162] vidi disse, 'Gàrdati non lo dire a persona mio covenente ní 'l mio nome'. Elli disse que bene lo farà.

[25] Ora disse lo conto que lo chavaliere quilli à trovati avea nome meser Gualvagno, nepote de lo Re Artus. Lo escudieri disse, 'Ello èi bene vero che alo matino meser Galvagno me volle[163] fare chavaliere, may dapoyqué io vos ài trovato, vuollio que voy me debiate fare chavaliere'. Tristano disse che alo matino ello lo farà chavaliere.

Alora chiamò lo senesqualcho e comandò que alo matino abia aparechiato sò que fae mestieri a fare chavaliere. La sera viennengno alo alberguo alo castelo. Lo Re lo fesse servire de sò que fae mestieri. Dapoyché ebenno cenato, lo Re chiamò Tristano e disse, 'Chonosse tu quello chavaliere?' E lo disse de sì, 'e à nome Meser Galvagno, nepote de lo Re Artusso, ed è prode chavaliere e cortesse'.

Alora andoe lo Re Languis a luy e demandoe de lo Re Arturo e de la Redina Genevra chome laysanno[164] li boni chavalieri. Asay parlavano la sera de lo realme de Longoes.

Ala matina si leva Tristano e fa chavaliere lo soe escudiery e dònali arme e cavali; e poy fo prode e francho chavaliere ||||[165] [fol. 113v] (May Tristano l'ançisse ende l'esquiere de lo Sacradalle <per> dessaventurossamente.) Apresso cheste parolle si parte Tristano – e lo Re Languis e meser Galvagno – e pervenneno alo torni[a]mento de lo Re de Scorcia lo quale era a campo con lo Re de Cento

---

159   Corrupt reading in MS. Cf. TR, p. 46: *da indi a la Pentacosta*.
160   Scribe most often writes *Landa*. Cf. TR, p. 46: *Inn-irlanda*.
161   Catchword at center bottom in a crudely drawn red cartouche: *ebayselo li piedi*.
162   Thus in the MS. Cf. TR, p. 46: *quando*.
163   MS *vosse*. Confusion of *s* / *l*.
164   Probable scribal misreading of the verb. See TR, p. 48: *la fanno*.
165   Six full lines left blank at bottom of writing space. Child's drawing of a person's head and shoulders in darker brown, non-text ink. Beneath the head, more of the body, apparently on a charging horse, was added in dry point.

Il Tristano Riccardiano *(Parodi's siglum 'F')*

many knights, everyone marvelled at his beauty. One said to the other that if he had better color, a more handsome knight than he would not be found.

[24] The knights were speaking a great deal about having a tournament. The King of Scotland had it proclaimed that he wanted to hold a tournament. From then to Pentecost, whatever knight wanted to fight with arms must be in Ireland at the time that was stated. Since the tournament day was approaching, the knights were going to the tournament. King Anguin said to Tristan, 'Do you want to come to the King of Scotland's tournament?' Tristan said, 'I wouldn't be able to bear arms; but if you want me to come with you, I'll gladly come'. The king said, 'I'm not going to this tournament in order to participate; for this reason I want your company'. In the morning the king and Tristan and very many other knights departed; they rode to the tournament. While riding near a castle, they found a knight, and a squire in his company. The squire – who saw Tristan – immediately dismounted from his horse and knelt at his feet [fol. 113r] and kissed his feet. Tristan, when he saw him, said, 'Be careful that you don't tell anyone my identity nor my name'. He said that he would indeed obey this.

[25] Now the tale says that the knight whom they found was called Sir Gawain, King Arthur's nephew. The squire said, 'It is indeed true that Sir Gawain wanted to make me a knight in the morning; but since I have found you, it's you who must make me a knight'. Tristan said that in the morning he would make him a knight.

Then King Anguin called the seneschal and ordered him to prepare all that was needful to create a knight in the morning. In the evening they came to the lodging at the castle. The king had himself served with what was needful. After they had dined, the king called Tristan and said, 'Do you know this knight?' And he said, 'Yes, he is called Sir Gawain, King Arthur's nephew, and he is a valiant and courteous knight'.

Then King Anguin went to him and asked about King Arthur and about Queen Guenevere, and how their good knights were faring. That evening they spoke much about the kingdom of Logres.

In the morning Tristan rose and knighted his squire and gave him arms and horses; and afterward he was a valiant and brave knight. ||| [fol. 113v] (But during the Quest for the Holy Grail, Tristan killed the squire, accidentally.) After these words, Tristan left – and King Anguin and Sir Gawain – and they came to the tournament of the King of Scotland who was on the field – with the King of the Hundred Knights on the other side – with his company. This knight is Sir

Chavalieri da l'autra parte en soa compagnia. Questa chavaliere è messer Galvagno, e li fratelli de Lançeloto[166] Astor de Mare [e] Meser Brando (sic);[167] Gariet e Danello Salvaçio, Saromus,[168] e altri bongni chavalieri asay. Dapoyqué lo torniamento fo enchomenchiato, lo Re de Cento Chavalieri ferite alo Re de Scorçia. Encominçono a me[te]re per terra li chavalieri; metenno mane ale spade e comi[n]çiano a dare grandi colpi. May lo Re de Scorçia ferite alo Re de Cento Chavalieri. Uno chavaliere ròmpelli la lançia adosso; altro male noli fesse nì movere de la sella. La batallia enchomençò aspera e dura enfra l'una parte e l'autra. Durò la batallia per grando tempo e ora de lo giorno. ||||[169] Lo Re de Cento Chavalieri combatea con soa compagnia e chaçiò fora del campo lo Re de Scorçia con sua compaçgna[170] per forsa d'arme. Dapoyqué lo Re de Scorçia [fol. 114r] foe torniato ende schonfita con tuta la soa gente, uno chavaliere viene da la sua parte lo quale p[orta]va[171] tute le 'nçie nere[172] de lo Re e portava due spade. (May si alchuno me demamdare (sic) chome avea nome aquello chavaliere con le 'nsi[e] nere[173] que portava le doe spade, io diroe que à nome Palamides lo Pagano; però portava le .ii. espade <e> perché illo non era ancor abatuto da nullo chavaliere.)

[26] Dapoyqué Palamides fo al torniamente, enchominçiò abatere chavalieri e cavalli per terra. Dapoyché ebe rota la lançia, e' mete manno al'espada e cominçiò a dare grandi colpi siché neuno chavaliere potea andare enançi da luy. En pocha d'ora messe endesconfita lo Re de Cento Chavalieri con tuta sua cognpagnia per forçe d'arme: chaçiò fuore de tuto lo torniamente, siché tuta la gente enchomençiò a gridare, 'Tuto lo torniamento àe vinto lo chavaliere de le doe espade!' (May lo Re de Cento Chavalieri – dapoyqué fo esconfito – fesse gridare uno altro torniamento da inde a .xxx. die.)

[27] Alora si partenno tuti li chavalieri, e honni homo si prende cumiato. May lo Re Languis chavalcando dirietro a Palamides – tanto cavalchò que l'ebe junto – disse, 'Chavaliere, io ti demando uno dono'. Lo chavaliere disse, 'Demanda sò che ve plaçe'. Lo Re disse che [fol. 114v] tu v[ie]gne albergar mecho'. Lo chavaliere disse, 'Io farò la vost[r]a vo[lun]tade'.

Alora cavalchò lo Re – e Tristano e Palamides e tuti [li][174] soy chavalieri. Si ne parla per tuto lo realme de meser Palamides. Dapoyqué fonno presso da lo castello de lo Re Languis, tuti li soi chavalieri li venianno encontra a fare grande festa. Dapoyqué fonne alo palaçio, lo Re comandoe que fossenno poste le taule a

---

[166] Simplification in the MS. Cf. TR, p. 48: *meser Galvano e Leonello, fratello di Lancialotto, e Istor da Mare.*

[167] Properly, *Bordo* (from the French tradition, *Bors*). TR, p. 48: *Boordo.*

[168] Clear in the MS, but see TR, p. 48: *Oddinel lo Selvaggio e Esagris.*

[169] Seven full lines left blank; miniature never executed.

[170] Spelling error, likely caused by line break: *co(m)paç | gna.*

[171] Damage to MS renders three internal letters difficult to read.

[172] Cf. TR, p. 48: *segne nere.*

[173] MS *lenSiere* with one titulus.

[174] Letters damaged, ink lost at top corner of *verso*. Corresponds to the damaged area on the *recto*.

Il Tristano Riccardiano *(Parodi's siglum 'F')*

Gawain, and Lancelot's brothers* Hector of the Fens [and] Sir Bors; Gareth and Dodinel the Savage, Segris, and very many other good knights. After the tournament had begun, the King of the Hundred Knights struck at the King of Scotland. They began to hurl knights to the ground, they grabbed their swords and began to give great blows. But the King of Scotland struck at the King of the Hundred Knights. One knight broke his lance against him; no other harm did he cause him nor did he move from the saddle. The battle began, cruel and harsh, between one side and the other. The battle lasted a long time and throughout the day. ||| The King of the Hundred Knights was fighting with his company and chased the King of Scotland and his company from the field by force of arms. After the King of Scotland [fol. 114r] had returned in defeat with all his people, a knight came from his side who was wearing the king's all-black insignia and who was carrying two swords. (But if anyone asks me what was the name of that knight with the black insignia who was carrying the two swords, I would say that he was called Palamides the Pagan, and he was carrying two swords because he had not yet been unhorsed by any knight.)

[26] After Palamides was at the tournament, he began to knock knights and horses to the ground. After he had broken his lance and put his hand to his sword, he began to give great blows so that no knight was able to go against him. In a short time he put the King of the Hundred Knights and his whole company into defeat; by force of arms, he chased them entirely away from the tournament, so that all the people began to shout, 'The Knight of the Two Swords has won the whole tournament!' (But the King of the Hundred Knights – since he was defeated – had another tournament proclaimed for thirty days hence.)

[27] Then all the knights departed, and each one took his leave. But King Anguin riding behind Palamides – he rode hard to catch up with him – said, 'Knight, grant me a boon'. The knight said, 'Ask what you please'. The king said, [fol. 114v] 'Come to lodge with me'. The knight said, 'I will do as you wish'.

Then the king rode on, with Tristan and Palamides; and all his knights throughout the whole kingdom were talking about Sir Palamides. When they were near the castle of King Anguin, all his knights came to meet him to celebrate greatly. After they were at the palace, the king commanded that tables be set up

---

* 'Brothers' could indicate 'cousins'. 'Old French "cousin" and "neveu" [...] were sometimes used with wider meanings than they have today' (West, pp. xiii, 187).

Palamides, may Palamides si dessarmoe en una camera. Li baroni de Landa que sepenno que questo era lo chavaliere che à vinto lo torniamento, enchomençoron a servirlo e farli grande festa e grande honore.

Dapoyqué foronno poste le taule, lo Re fesse venire Ysota davançi da luy. Quando Yssota fo venuta davançi da luy, tanto bella ||||[175] e tanto avinente de tute cosse, lo Re li comandoe che debia servire ala sua taula. Palamides s'inamoroe de ley perché era sì bella ed avinente de tute cosse che fa uno mestieri. Dapoyché si levanno da taula, Palamides [fol. 115r] garda pur la damisella siché Tristano si ne fo aveduto. EnchomInçò anche ad resguardare la damissella siché Palamides chonossia bene che Tristano l'ama de tuto so core. (May Tristano odia Palamides, e Palamides odia luy.) [M]ay[176] Branguina disse a Yssota, 'May si tu fosse messe a partito de questi .ii. chavalieri, quale prenderesti en prima tra lo nostro chavaliere o l'autro chavaliere che dichonno ch'è sì prodo chavaliere?' Yssota disse que 'si lo nostro chavaliere fosse prode chavaliere d'arme chome io credo, volrei en prima luy; si non fosse sì prode, volrey en prima l'autro'. E·stando en queste parolle, Palamides dema[n]doe cumiato alo Re perché lo termine aproximava d'andare alo torniamento. Lo Re li diede chu[m]iato.

[28] [B][177] Alo matina si partitte Palamides e vàssene alo torniamento. Lo Re fesse metere bando per tuto lo realme che tuti li soe chavalieri s'apareçano[178] de fare batallia con luy. May Palamides, lo qualle per la soa prodessa fa tanto d'arme que non trova nullo chavaliere che ali soy colpi possa sufrire, e' chomença a chaciare li chavalieri de la Taula Retonta, e Re Languis. [fol. 115v] A pocha d'otta li missi tuti ende sconfita. Alora lo populo enchomençiò a gridare e a dire: 'Tuto à vinto lo torniamento lo chavaliere con le 'nsiegne niere[179] che porta [le][180] due espade!'

[C] May Tristano dapoyché ebe auditto d[ire][181] che Palamides avea vinto lo torniamento, fo da la parte de lo Re Langu[i]s e de la parte de li chavalieri de la Taula Retonta. Enchomençiò a ferire ende le squere de li chavalieri honde era Palamides. Tristano abatette .iii. chavalieri sensa rompere lançia. Al quarto colpo fiere a Palamides, e abattello luy e lo cavallo, e poy messe manno al'espada e [chomençiò] a dare grandi colpi entre li chavalieri. Fesse tanto per soa prodessa che messe en eschonfitta lo Re de Schorçia con tuti li soy chavalieri, siché tuto lo povolo gr<a>ida, 'E tuto à vinto lo chavaliere de l'arme bianche!' Palamides, che [à] grande verguonça, e' si si parte da lo torniamento.

---

[175] Seven full lines left blank, mid-sentence; miniature never executed.

[176] Upper corner of this folio is damaged as are adjacent folios. Damaged area extends from fols 114 to 117 *recto* and *verso*. Ink and some letters were lost as a result. Fol. 114r was carefully patched during modern restoration.

[177] Between paragraphs 28 and 32 inclusive, the plot segments are out of order. The same misordering had occurred in TR, §§28–33. My capital letters in square brackets indicate the more logical order according to TP, §§104–106; and TV, §§97–102.

[178] Apparently superfluous titulus over the *-eç-* middle of word.

[179] MS *piere*. Corrected with TR, p. 52: *niere*.

[180] Loss of two letters due to damage.

[181] More letters illegible due to damage.

for Palamides, and Palamides disarmed himself in a chamber. The barons of Ireland, who knew that this was the knight who had won the tournament, began to serve him and celebrate greatly and pay him great honor.

After the tables were set up, the king had Yseut come before him. When Yseut had come before him, so very beautiful ||| and so very comely in all things, the king commanded her to serve at his table. Palamides fell in love with her because she was so beautiful and comely in all things that were needful. After they arose from the table, Palamides [fol. 115r] looked so intently at the damsel that Tristan noticed it. He, too, began to stare at the damsel so that Palamides knew very well that Tristan loved her with all his heart. (But Tristan hated Palamides, and Palamides hated him.) Brangain said to Yseut, 'If you were to choose between these two knights, which would you take first: our knight or the other knight that they say is such a valiant knight?' Yseut said that 'if our knight were as valiant a knight-at-arms as I believe, I would want him first; if he were not so valiant, I'd want the other one first'. And while they were talking, Palamides asked leave from the king because the time to go to the tournament was approaching. The king gave him leave.

[28] [B]* In the morning Palamides left and went on his way to the tournament. The king proclaimed through the whole kingdom that all his knights prepare themselves to do battle with him. But Palamides, who by his prowess did so many feats of arms that he found no knight who could withstand his blows, began to chase the knights of the Round Table and King Anguin. [fol. 115v] In a short time he defeated all of them. Then the people began to shout and say: 'The knight with the black insignia who carries two swords has won the whole tournament!'

[C] But Tristan, when he had heard it said that Palamides had won the tournament, was on the side of King Anguin and on the side of the Round Table. He began to strike into the ranks of knights where Palamides was. Tristan unhorsed three knights without breaking his lance. On the fourth blow, he struck Palamides and knocked down him – and his horse – and then grabbed his sword and began to give out great blows among the knights. He did so much by his prowess that he defeated the King of Scotland with all his knights, so that all the people shouted, 'The knight with the white arms has won everything!' Palamides left the tournament, greatly ashamed.

---

*   From §§28 to 32 inclusive, the plot segments are out of order, a misordering that also occurs in TR. Capital letters in square brackets indicate the correct narrative order according to TP, §§104–106. See also TV, §§97–102.

[29] Ora[182] disse lo conto que quando Tristano ebe messe ende sconfita lo Re de Schorçia e abatette Palamides, gli guarda per lo torniamente: vide que Palamides s'era partito e andato via. Tristano brocha de speroni alo destrieri e viene derietro a Palamides; elo lo giunto en uno bello prato. Disse a Palamides, 'Gàrdate da me, ché io ti offendo! – que io sonno [fol. 116r] lo chavaliere che tu trovasti ende la corte del Re Languis. May ogi [s]i para chi serà buonno chavaliere e qui serà digno d'avere l'amore de la bella Yssota'.

Dapoyché Palamides entesse le parolle che Tristano [avea][183] decto, volse la tessta del cavallo enver luy e messe mano al'espada. Tristano, lo quale viene enversso de lui con la spada en mano, e' fierì a Palamides e diedi li sì grande colpi su ende l'e[r]mo che lo fe andare en terra da cavallo. Eli estette en terra per grande hora che non si potea levare. ‖‖[184] (May si alchuno me demanderà come Tristano viene alo torniamento, perché non viene con lo Re Languis, perché ello volea fare la soa chavallaria sì privatamente que nulla persona lo saupesse.)

[30] [A] May Tristano, lo quale remasse ende la corte que lo Re Languis, andoe alo torniamento. Eli [fol. 116v] era tanto pensoso che non sapia que si fare ed era remasso solo ende la corte. Estando choissì pensoso, disse Bra[n]guina (lo quale era chameriara <di> de M[adonna][185] Yssota), 'Chavaliere, perché estate coysì pensosso?' Tristano disse, 'Io songno deloyrosso e pensoso de cossa che io non mi·ppote ajudare'. E Branghina disse, 'Ditte me quello che voy avete, che io ve·nne aitaroe al mio poterre'. E alora disse Tristano, 'Si tu me vuolie iurare de tenerre me chredença, io ti diroe tuto lo mio choraçio'. Branguina li juroe de tener li credensa. Tristano disse, 'Io andarea volentieri ad aquesto torniamento s'io[186] avesse arme e chavalli e doe eschudieri che mi fessenno compangn[i]a'. Branguina disse, 'Per questo non laysarete voy, che voy non audiare'. Allora l'apresso[187] Branguina e mènelo ende una camera; aperse due caisse lo quale eranno [piene][188] <di> de l'Amoroldo le 'nsegne tute bianche. Queste arme avea facto l'Amoroldo e non l'avea anche portate. Tristano si s'armoe de queste arme. Dapoyché fo armato, si prende .ii. destrieri lo quale eranno estati di l'Amoroldo. E Branguina disse, 'Pilliate .ii. mie fratelli che ve achompagnano'. En tal maniera andoe Tristano encontra Palamides alo torniamento: de loro facti [fol. 117r] bene l'audirete apresso. Neuncha per nessuno t[en]po[189] non foe facto tanto d'arme e·Milanda. Bene ne parla de luy oni bonno chavaliere.

---

[182] Large red initial on *Ora* indicates a new narrative section.
[183] Loss of word due to paper damage. Cf. TR, p. 52: *avea dette*.
[184] Scribe left eight and a half lines blank; miniature never executed.
[185] Letters lost due to damage.
[186] MS *fio*. Confusion of *s* / *f*.
[187] Thus in MS. Cf. TR, p. 54: *lo prese*.
[188] Insertion based on TR, p. 54.
[189] Two letters illegible due to a stain.

Il Tristano Riccardiano *(Parodi's siglum 'F')*

[29] Now the tale says that when Tristan had defeated the King of Scotland and unhorsed Palamides, he looked for him throughout the tournament: he saw that Palamides had left and gone away. Tristan spurred his horse and went after Palamides and reached him in a lovely meadow. He said to Palamides, 'Be on guard against me, because I challenge you! – because I am [fol. 116r] the knight whom you found in King Anguin's court, but today it will be apparent who is a good knight and who will be worthy of having the love of the beautiful Yseut'.

When Palamides heard the words that Tristan had said, he turned his horse's head toward him and put his hand on his sword. Tristan came toward him with sword in hand and struck Palamides and gave him such great blows on his helmet that he knocked him to the ground from his horse. Palamides remained on the ground for a long time because he was unable to get up. ||| (But if anyone asks me why Tristan came to the tournament – why he didn't come with King Anguin – it was because he wanted to display his chivalry so secretly that no one would know it.)

[30] [A] But Tristan, who remained in King Anguin's court, went to the tournament. He [fol. 116v] was so very pensive that he didn't know what to do, and he remained alone in the court. Seeing him so pensive, Brangain (who was Lady Yseut's chambermaid) said, 'Knight, why are you so pensive?' Tristan said, 'I am sorrowful and pensive about something that I can't help'. And Brangain said, 'Tell me what's wrong with you so that I can help you to the best of my ability'. And then Tristan said, 'If you want to swear to keep my confidence, I will reveal my whole heart to you'. Brangain swore to him to keep faith. Tristan said, 'I would willingly go to this tournament if I had arms and horses and two squires who would keep me company'. Brangain said, 'This will not prevent you from going'. Then Brangain took him and led him to a chamber: she opened two chests that were full of the Morholt's solid white arms. (The Morholt had had these arms made and hadn't even worn them.) Tristan armed himself with these arms. After he was armed, he took two warhorses that had belonged to the Morholt. And Brangain said, 'Take two of my brothers, for they will accompany you'. In this fashion Tristan went to encounter Palamides at the tournament: of their feats [fol. 117r] you will assuredly hear next. Such feats of arms had never been done in Ireland: well might every good knight speak of him!

[31] [D] En questa parta disse lo conto dapoyqué Tristano ebe aquistato lo torniamento – sichome èi decto de sopra[190] – partì si illo encontenente con li soy escudieri e vàssenne alo castello de lo Re Languis. Cavalcando en tale manera, trovoe una damaysella. Ele venia de lo realme de Longres: vidi Tristano, si lo pressò a salutare. Eli rende soe saluti cortesamente. La damaysella disse, 'Io ve preguo per cortessia de voy, che voy me dicate chi conquestò la Dolorossa Gardia'. Disse Tristano que non sapia niente. ||[191] La damaysella enchominçò a squardare le arme de Tristano: vide qu'eranno tute rotte e trevalliate per lo compbatere. Disse la damaysella, 'Voy seyte lo chavaliere que conquistoe la Dolorossa Guardia'. Tristano disse, 'Io non sonno disso'. 'Donque, ve preguo que voy me debiate dire vostro covenente'. Tristano disse que non lo dirae en neuna manera. 'Io ve preguo che voy ve debiate levare l'ermo [fol. 117v] de capo siché io ve possa vedere lo visso'. Tristano si levò l'ermo e mostrò li lo visso. La damaysella disse, 'Bene vego io que voy non sette desso chello que io vado sercando, may voy me parete d'uno tempo e d'una bellessa cho[me luy]'.[192]

A tanto si parte la damaysella, e Tristano cavalcha en[verso] lo castello. Cavalcando perviene a una fontana; chi si dessarmoe e repausoe li arme e choma[n]doe ali eschudieri che de queste cosse non de nesseuno dire nulla. Elli dissenno que bene lo faranno volentiery. Tristano si parte e vàssene alo palagio e trove Branguina; ella fesse gra[n] fessta a Tristano. Branguina disse, 'Chi à vinto lo torniamento?' Tristano disse, 'Io non so'. Bra[n]guina disse, 'Lo chavaliere de le .ii. espade à vinto lo torniamento?' Tristano disse, 'Non credo che l'abia vinto a questa fiata'.

[F] A tanto laysa lo conto[193] de Branguina que non pote sapere de Tristano quello qu'ella volia. Possa demandoe li fratelli chi à vinto lo torniamento. 'Lo chavaliere de l'arme bianche, ed e' à tanto facto d'arme unqua non fesse chavaliere e[n] Milanda que tanto fessesse d'arme. Dapoyqué lo Re Languis ebe perduto lo torniamento, ello per sua prodessa esconfite lo Re de Scorçia e tuti li soy chavalieri, e abate Palamides trey volte'. Branguina, quando entende le parolle, fo molta alegra; encomençò a servire Tristano de sò ch'e[fol. 118r]lla potea.

[32] [E] Ora disse lo conto che quando Palamides foe abattuto da Tristano [per][194] lo colpo de l'espada, enchominçò a fare lo magior pianto che çamay fosse fatto per uno chavaliere. Enchominçò sé a chiamare, 'Lasso, tapino! Ora non potree portare arme de quie a uno anno e uno die. Si potesse portare arme, per aventura, combatrey con luy'. Poy gittò l'esbergo, lo scudo e tute le arme. Disse que giamay quelle arme non portarae dapoyqué sì malamente si è desavenuto. Apresso queste parolle, si parte Palamides e va a sua via, facendo grande rumori.

---

190   An earlier scribe noticed the narrative sequencing problem and added this gloss, also found in TR, p. 54: *sì come detto èe di sopra*.

191   Seven half-lines blank, flush right, for a drawing never executed. The text is on the left half of each line.

192   Damage in MS results in complete loss of some letters, here and next sentence.

193   Cf. TR, p. 56: *lascia lo parlamento Braghina*.

194   Omitted word in MS. Insertion based on TR, p. 56.

[31] [D] In this part the tale says that when Tristan had won the tournament – as was told above* – he left immediately with his squires and went on his way to the castle of King Anguin. Riding along in this fashion, he found a damsel. She was coming from the kingdom of Logres: she saw Tristan; she approached to greet him. He returned her greeting courteously. The damsel said, 'I pray you, by your courtesy, to tell me who conquered Dolorous Guard'. Tristan said that he knew nothing about it. ||| The damsel began to examine Tristan's arms: she saw that they were all broken and damaged by combat. The damsel said, 'You are the knight who conquered Dolorous Guard'. Tristan said, 'I'm not the one'. 'Well then, I pray you to tell me your identity'. Tristan said that he wouldn't tell it in any way. 'I pray you to remove the helmet [fol. 117v] from your head so that I can see your face'. Tristan lifted off his helmet and showed her his face. The damsel said, 'I clearly see that you aren't the one whom I am seeking, but you seem to me of the same age and appearance as he is'.

In that moment the damsel departed, and Tristan rode toward the castle. As he was riding along, he came upon a fountain; here he disarmed and set down his arms. And he commanded his squires to not say anything about these things to anyone, and they said that they would indeed do this willingly. Tristan left and went on his way to the palace and found Brangain; she greeted Tristan joyously. Brangain said, 'Who won the tournament?' Tristan said, 'I don't know'. Brangain said, 'Did the Knight of the Two Swords win the tournament?' Tristan said, 'I don't believe that he won it this time'.

[F] In that moment the tale leaves off telling about Brangain who couldn't find out from Tristan what she wanted. Then she asked her brothers who won the tournament. 'The White Knight – and he did such feats of arms as no knight in Ireland ever did, such were his feats of arms! After King Anguin had lost the tournament, he by his prowess defeated the King of Scotland and all his knights, and he unhorsed Palamides three times'. Brangain, when she heard their words, was very happy; she began to serve Tristan with anything that [fol. 118r] she could.

[32] [E] Now the tale says that when Palamides was unhorsed by Tristan's sword blow, he began to make the greatest lament that had ever been made by a knight. He began to call himself a miserable wretch. 'Now you won't be able to bear arms henceforth for a year and a day. If I could bear arms, by some chance, I would fight with him'. Then he threw down his hauberk, his shield and all his arms. He said that he would never again carry those arms since it had gone so badly for him. After these words, Palamides left and went on his way, making great sobs.

---

* An apparent gloss added by an earlier scribe to address the misordered segments. These words also appear in TR, pp. 54.

Estando uno pocho, la damaysella – la quale avea parlato a Tristano – trovoe Messer Calvagno. Quando si trovono ensieme, la damaysella disse a me[se]re[195] Galvagno, 'Sapereste me dire novelle de lo chavaliere que ossise la Dolorossa Gardia?' Elo disse de no.

Ora laysemo queste parlare e torniamo al facto de Tristano, chome li s[i] diviene.

[33] Disse lo conte que quando Yssota sepe que Tristano ebe vinto lo torniamento, foe molta alegra. Emantenente perchaçoe de li fare uno bagno per tale quello si repossesse perché non li parea que fosse benne garito. E fo facto soe comandamento encontenente e fo fatto lo bagno e Tristano fo posto dintro. E estando en grande gioya e 'n alegressa que avea Yssota de Tristano, [fol. 118v] e però menava li gran festa.

Estando en queste parolle, vi è a mano l'espada de Tristano a Yssota; e·lla [Redina] si l'aves[s]e vedere, e vide que ela avia rota la ponta, onde ella si pensoe en sé, dissendo, 'Serea questo choluy[196] che onçisse l'Amoroldo mio fratello?'[197] Ela vae onde ella avea reposto la ponta qu'ella trovoe ende la testa de L'Amoroldo que si diede Tristano [ala][198] batalia. E posse la ponta su en l'espada e conosse quella era dessa. E contenente corse adosso a Tristano con l'espada en mano, dissendo, 'Tristano, nepote de lo Re March[o] de Cornavalia, ora non ti vale più to nome celare, ché tropo ti sei cellato, daché ucideste l'Amoroldo [de] Landa a tradimento! May ell'è bissonça que tu mori de mia mane!' Alora li vae adosso la Redina: con l'espada en mano, vae per ferire Tristano, <mc>[199] |||

[34] May Tristano – lo quale era en lo bagno – de queste cosse non cura niente. Tuto li dame e damisselli que facianno trastulio a Tristano enchomençono a cridare, 'Mora lo chavaliere!' La Redina andava a ferire Tristano, may l'escudieri – lo quale trovò l'espada – lo scudieri la tenea ad aquesta Raina.[200] [fol. 119r] Ve viene lo Re, e li soy baronni trovonno la Redina con l'espada en mano. Ela, quando vide lo Re, ela disse, 'Vendica me, Re Languis, de Tristano, nepote de lo Re Marcho de Cornavallia, lo quale uccisse l'Amoroldo mio fratello a tradimento'. Alora disse lo Re, 'Dama, laysate questa vendìta a me, perché non si cho[n]viene a voy'.

[Alora disse lo Re: Chome è, chavaliere? Sei tu Tristano?][201]

Tristano disse, 'Alchuna gente mi chiama coysì'. Alora disse lo Re, 'Ucidisti tu l'Amoroldo a tradimento?' E Tristano disse, 'Io lo ferive[202] ala batalia sichome

---

[195] MS *mere*. Scribe omitted the *ser* abbreviation.
[196] MS *choloy*.
[197] MS *fratella*.
[198] Letters partially lost due to small hole on the page.
[199] Scribe started to form the next two letters (*ma*), then stopped to leave spaces for miniature and continued below the space. Eight full lines left blank; miniature never executed.
[200] MS *Raino*.
[201] Ellipsis in MS. Emendation based on TR, p. 64.
[202] Thus in MS. Cf. TR, p. 64: *lo feretti*; TP, p. 166: *l'uccisi*.

Il Tristano Riccardiano *(Parodi's siglum 'F')*

A while later, the damsel who had spoken with Tristan found Sir Gawain. When they met up, the damsel said to Sir Gawain, 'Would you be able to tell me news of the knight who seized Dolorous Guard?' He said no.

Now let's leave off speaking of this and return to the deeds of Tristan as is fitting.

[33] The tale says that when Yseut found out that Tristan had won the tournament, she was very happy. She at once set about preparing him a bath so that he could recover because it didn't seem to her that he was entirely healed; and her command was followed at once and the bath was prepared and Tristan was placed in it. Given the great joy and happiness that Yseut had because of Tristan, [fol. 118v] for this reason she celebrated greatly with him.

While they were conversing, Tristan's sword was there at hand before Yseut. She* had seen it and saw that it had its tip broken whereupon she thought to herself, saying, 'Could this be he who killed the Morholt, my brother?' She went to where she had stored the tip that she had found in the Morholt's head, with which Tristan had wounded him in battle; and she placed the tip on the sword and knew that it was the same sword. And immediately she ran up to Tristan with the sword in her hand, saying, 'Tristan, nephew of King Mark of Cornwall, now it no longer does you any good to conceal your name because you have concealed yourself for too long, given that you killed the Morholt of Ireland treacherously, but it behooves you to die by my hand'. Then the queen rushed at him: with the sword in her hand, she went to strike Tristan. |||

[34] But Tristan – who was in the bath – was not at all worried about these things. All the ladies and damsels who were entertaining Tristan began to cry out, 'Death to the knight!' The queen was going to strike Tristan, but the squire – the one who had found the sword – held onto this queen. [fol. 119r]. The king and his barons came there, and they found the queen with the sword in her hand. When she saw the king, she said, 'Avenge me, King Anguin, on Tristan, nephew of King Mark of Cornwall, who killed the Morholt my brother treacherously!' Then the king said, 'Lady, leave this revenge to me because it is not suited to you'.

[Then the king said, 'What's this, knight? Are you Tristan?']

Tristan said, 'People call me so'. Then the king said, 'Did you kill the Morholt treacherously?' And Tristan said, 'I wounded him in combat chivalrously; but if

---

* This portion of the narrative is greatly abbreviated to the extent that it is not immediately clear that it is the queen, not Yseut, who notices the broken sword.

chavaliere. May si alcuno chavaliere àe en vostra corte che vuollia dire che io l'auçisse a tradimento, io ben apello ala batallia ala corte del Re Arturo'. E lo Re a queste parolle non resposse niente. May lo Re, gardando a Tristano, disse, 'Chavaliere, per trey cosse io ti perdono: la prima perché io ti trovay ende la navissella quasi come morto a mia corte. Recoveraste e aveste garissone, siché io non vuollio destrugere l'onore de li autri chavalieri del mondo.[203] La terça perch'io ti campay da morte. E si io t'ançidesse, bonno homo diria che io fosse traditore; e per queste trey cosse, poy partire de mia corte salvo e securo quando a voy piacherà'.

Alora Tristano engraçiò lo Re de questo donno asay. Enchontenente comandò a Guovernalle que trovosse una nave 'perché io vuolio tornar en Cornavalia'. E Guovernale trovoe una nave e apareçe tute cosse che fanno mestieri. E Tristano demandoe chumiate alo Re Languis e partiti si de la corte, e mènnene secho amboro li fratelli di Branguina. [fol. 119v] E dapoyqué Tristano foe ende la nave, si riçoe le velle al vento e prende la via d'andar en Cornavalia. Lo tenpo èi bello, lo mare sensa tempesta siché en nove giorno (sic), fo giunto en Cornavalia. E quando foe al porto, fesse a sapere alo Re Marcho sichome ello era tornato sano e garito. E lo Re de queste cosse fo molto alegro e encontenente montò a chavallo, luy e li sue bar[oni],[204] e andanno encontro a Tristano. E lo Re quando vide Tristano ende la via, si l'abraçie e·ffese li granda çioa; e cavalcanno, vienenno alo palagio de Titolin. E qui esmo[n]torono e trovoron dame e damayselli che fanno grande alegressa a Tristano; e tuti li chavalieri e baroni de Cornavalia ne fanno grande fessta de la tornata de Tristano perché s'era partito de Cornavalia ferito quasi com morto. ‖‖[205]

[35] Ora laysa de parlare de Tristano e torniamo a uno nano che viene ala corte de lo Re Marcho, lo [fol. 120r] quale era filgliolo de Re. El patre l'avea chaçiato via perché li parea guobo[206] denançi e dirietro, siché li parea che fosse uno fantasma. E lo Re Marcho li fesse grande honore perqué era filgliolo de Re e sapea endevinare. E disse <a>lo Re al nano, 'Che ti pare che debia essere da me?' E lo nano disse, 'Re Marcho, voi avete en vostra corte uno chavaliere, lo quale è 'l vostro nepote, che ne farae granda dessonore'. E lo Re disse, 'Di' me lo nome che io lo faroe estrugere'. E lo nano disse, 'Voy non uccidereste pur luy, may oncidereste molti chavalieri e dame le quale ancho per soa prodessa camparanno da morte'. E lo Re disse, 'Da questa dissognore poterremenne aitare?' E lo nano disse, 'Per nullo modo non ve ne potette aitare, may voy non dovete curare de queste parolle perché fie sì graçiosso chavaliere a tuta gente che de sua prodessa che tutto lo mondo ne parlarae'. E lo Re disse, 'Dapoyqu'ello fie sì graciosso chavaliere, non potrebe avere tanto dessognore nì tanto dapnagio che io non lo suffrà per amore de la sua chavallaria'.

---

[203] MS omits words that introduce the second reason. Cf. TR, p. 64: *guarigione, e l'altra si è k'io non vorrei distruggere lo fiore di tutti i cavalieri del mondo.*
[204] Final letters illegible due to damage.
[205] Seven full lines left blank; miniature never executed.
[206] Apparently superfluous titulus over the *u* on this word.

Il Tristano Riccardiano *(Parodi's siglum 'F')*

there is any knight in your court who wants to say that I killed him treacherously, I call him to combat at King Arthur's court'. And the king, at these words, didn't answer at all. But the king, looking at Tristan, said, 'Knight, I pardon you for three things: the first because I found you in the little boat, almost dead, at my court. [The second is because] you recovered and were cured, therefore I do not want to destroy the honor of the other knights in the world. The third is because I saved you from death. And if I killed you, good people would say that I am a traitor; and because of these three things, you may leave my court, safe and sound, when it may please you'.

Then Tristan thanked the king very much for this gift. Immediately he ordered Governal to find a ship 'because I want to return to Cornwall'; and Governal found a ship and prepared all the things that were needful. And Tristan asked leave of King Anguin and left the court, and they took with them both of Brangain's brothers. [fol. 119v] And after Tristan was in the ship, he raised the sails to the wind and set off on the route to go to Cornwall. The weather was fine, the sea calm so that in nine days he arrived in Cornwall. And when he was in port, he had King Mark informed that he had returned, safe and healed. And the king was very happy about these things and mounted his horse, he and his barons, and they went to meet Tristan. And when the king saw Tristan along the road, he embraced him and rejoiced greatly. Riding along, they came to the palace of Tintagel; and here they dismounted and found ladies and damsels who made merry because of Tristan; and all the knights and barons of Cornwall rejoiced greatly about Tristan's return because he had left Cornwall wounded and almost dead. |||

[35] Now it leaves off speaking of Tristan, and let us return to a dwarf who came to King Mark's court, who [fol. 120r] was a king's son. His father had chased him away because he had a hump before and behind, so that it seemed that he was a gnome, but King Mark paid him great honor because he was a king's son and he knew how to prophesy. And the king said to the dwarf, 'What do you think will befall me?' And the dwarf said, 'King Mark, you have in your court a knight who is your nephew, who will bring about great dishonor'. And the king said, 'Tell me his name so that I will have him destroyed'. And the dwarf said, 'You will not kill him at all, but you will kill many knights and ladies who, due to his prowess, will be spared death'. And the king said, 'Will we be able to help save ourselves from this dishonor?' And the dwarf said, 'In no way can you help yourselves about it, but you mustn't concern yourself about these words because he'll be such a fine knight to all the people that the whole world will speak about his prowess'. And the king said, 'Since he'll be such a fine knight, he could not have so much dishonor nor so much harm that I wouldn't bear it for the sake of his chivalry'.

E poy disse alo nano, 'Io volio que tue estias en mia corte e prende ciò que ti fae mestieri'. E lo nano si partitte dalo Re e andoe ende la sa[fol. 120v]la del palaçio. E quando li donne lo videnno, enchomençono a fare beffe de luy, e dichanno, 'Un[de][207] èi strita questa fantasma ch'èi venuta a corte?' E lo nano a queste parole non resposse neuna cosse. E gardando enfra li autri chavalieri, vide Tristano que non v'era ussato de vedere. E demandoe qui era chello chavaliere choissì bello. E uno escudieri disse ch'à nome Tristano, nepotte de lo Re Marcho. E lo nano encontenente si partìo da lo escudieri e andoe alo Re e presse cumiato da luy. E lo [Re] disse, 'Nano, perché ti parti?' El nano disse, 'Perché a me èi venuto uno messagio que debo io fare'. E lo Re li diede chumiato, e lo nano vae ala soa via e alo soe chamino.

[36] Ora disse lo conto che dapoyqué Tristano foe tornato a corte, lo Re fesse mete[r] uno bando per tutto lo realme che tuti li chavalieri que ànno damisselle vienanno ala corte a pena d'essere destruti. E questo fesse per una damissella che li amava – la quale avea nome la Damissella de l'Auqua de l'Espina – perch'ella venisse a corte, ché la volea requedere d'amore. Dapoyqué foronno venuti li baroni e chavalieri, dame e da[ma]yselle a corte, e lo Re qua[n]do vidi la Damaysella de l'Auqua de l'Espina, fesse li grande honore. E encontenente choma[n]doe que fosseno messe le taule. E dapoyché foronno messe le taule, lo Re fo molto dolente per[fol. 121r]qué non si potea parlare ala damaysella.

[37] Ora disse lo conto que dapoyché la damaysella vide Tristano, pare[208] li molto bello e de messura sì chello e[n]començoron fortamente a esguardare. E Tristano gardando ala damissella, e la damissella pensava enfra sé, e dissia que da Yssota en fora, non era più bella damissella de ley. May tanto esguarda la damissella a Tristano, e Tristano ala damissella, qué per lur esgardare chognoçe l'uno la volontà de l'autro. E gardando en tal manera, disse la damaysella enfra sé estesse, 'Ora sogno ben aventurossa damissella, dapoyqué sonno amata de choissì alto e bello chavaliere'. E coysì chiascuno de loro chiamò si paguato[209] l'uno de l'autro. E dapoyché ebenno mangiato, la damissella venne a Tristano e disse, 'Chavaliere, eccho la damissella che v'ama de tutto soe chore'. E Tristano disse, 'Damissella, gran merçede quando voy l'endignaste a dire. E però sapiate che io sonno chavaliere de vostra amore'. A tanto [finirono][210] lo loro parlam[e]nte sensa più dire, |||[211] [fol. 121v] e a questa fiata l'uno se departe dal'autro. E la damaysella tornoe a soe albergo con suo chavaliere, e tuti li autri chavalieri tornano a lur alberguo. E la damissella chiamoe uno soe eschiavo, 'Domane[212] mi farae uno mesagio a Tristano, nepote de lo Re Marcho, e diray da mia parte que demano vegne a me de sera ala fontana de l'Auqua de

---

207   MS *vn* with a titulus over *n*. Cf. TR, p. 66: *onde*.
208   MS: *bare*.
209   Cf. TR, p. 68: *pacato*.
210   Verb omitted in MS. Emendation based on TR, p. 68.
211   Five full lines blank at bottom of writing space; miniature never executed.
212   Four minims clear in MS: *Dennane*. Cf. TR, p. 68: *Domane*.

Il Tristano Riccardiano *(Parodi's siglum 'F')*

And then the king said to the dwarf, 'I want you to stay in my court and have whatever is needful to you'. And the dwarf left the king and went into the palace hall. [fol. 120v] And when the ladies saw him, they began to make fun of him, and said, 'Where did this gnome come from who has come to court?' And at these words, the dwarf didn't say a thing. And looking among the other knights, he saw Tristan whom he was not accustomed to seeing; and he asked who was that knight who was so handsome; and a squire said that 'he's called Tristan, nephew of King Mark'. And at once the dwarf left the squire and went to the king and asked to take leave from him. And the king said, 'Dwarf, why are you leaving?' And the dwarf said, 'Because I just remembered a message that I must deliver'. And the king granted him leave, and the dwarf went on his way and on his mission.

[36] Now the tale says that after Tristan had returned to court, the king had proclaimed throughout his kingdom that all the knights who had sweethearts must come to court, on pain of death. And he did this because of a damsel whom he loved – who was called the Damsel of Thornwater – so that she would come to court, because he wanted to request her love. After the barons and knights had come to court, with their ladies and damsels, the king – when he saw the Damsel of Thornwater – paid her great honor. And immediately he commanded that the tables be set up. And after the tables had been set up, the king was very sorrowful [fol. 121r] because he was unable to speak to the damsel.

[37] Now the tale says that after the damsel saw Tristan, he seemed to her very beautiful and well-formed, so that they began to look at each other intently. And while Tristan was looking at the damsel, the damsel was thinking to herself and saying that, except for Yseut, there was no more beautiful damsel than she was. But the damsel looked at Tristan so much – and Tristan at the damsel – that from their stares each one understood the will of the other. And while looking in this manner, the damsel said to herself, 'Now I am truly a fortunate damsel, since I am loved by such a high-born and handsome knight'. And thus each of them considered himself satisfied by the other. After they had eaten, the damsel came to Tristan and said, 'Knight, behold the damsel who loves you with her whole heart'. And Tristan said, 'Damsel, many thanks for deigning to say so; and by the same token, know that I am the knight of your love'. At that point they spoke no more ||| [fol. 121v] and in the same moment they parted from one another. The damsel returned to her lodging with her knight, and all the other knights returned to their lodgings. And the damsel called one of her slaves: 'Tomorrow you will take a message from me to Tristan, King Mark's nephew: tell him for me that I ask him to come to me in the evening to the fountain of Thornwater, and tell him

l'Espina, e tuta fiata vengna bene armato de tute arme perché homo non sae le venture que possenno venire'. E lo nano montoe a cavallo e viene ala corte del Re Marcho. E quando vidi Tristano, si lo chiamò a sé e disse, 'La Damaysella de l'Auqua de l'Espina ve manda mille salute. E manda ve a dire questa sera vegnate a ley alo giardino de la fontana, e vegnate bene armato de tute arme per molte aventure che vegnano[213] ali chavalieri'. E Tristano, quando endesse cheste parolle, fo molto alegro e disse alo nano, 'Io songno aparechiato de fare lo comandamento de la damissella e de venire a quella hora che li plaçerae'. E a tanto foron le parolle que Tristano si [è] partito da lo nano e andoe al suo palagio. E chomandoe ali soy escudieri che apareçhessanno le soy arme e conçhessanno li destrieri, si[ché] quando volroe cavalcare, li trovi prestamente.

[38] [fol. 122r] Ora disse lo conto que lo Re Marcho vidi bene quando lo nano parloe a Tristano. Encontenente chiamò lo nano ende la camera e disse, 'Nano, io vuolio que tu me digue che enbaysata ày facto a Tristano, mei nepote – qué tanto ày consellato con luy – e chi ti mandoe'. E lo nano disse, 'Meser, chesto non diroe io perché non serea cortessia dire altrui le private parolle che mi·ssonno date, e comandate che io non lo debia dire'. Alora disse lo Re, 'Come, nano, non me diray tu quello che ti demandaroe?' E lo nano disse, 'Io non ve diroe le prevate parolle que io debo tenere che altri lo sapi'. E lo Re disse, 'Si tu non le me dirae, io ti tallerò la testa'; e alsò le mane con l'espada per ferire lo nano molto iratamente. E lo nano ebe grande paora e disse, 'Meser, non me uciditte, ché io ve diroe lo messagio che io fesse a Trisstano'. Enchontenente li disse tuta l'enbaysata che avea facto a Tristano. E lo Re disse, 'Nano, io requesta tua dama d'amore molte fulte, neanque non potey avere da ley una bona parolla! Ben pare che sia femine[214] da pocho valere perché tutto giorno prende el peçhio, e choisì à ella facto. Ella àe ora laysatto me – que sonno alto e possente Re – e àe presso Tristano ch'è uno fanchollo che non [fol. 122v] sae nì valle[215] nulla cossa. May bissogno èi che io lo (sic) fasse estrugere'. E lo nano disse, 'Meser, si voy façere destrugere una dama perché ama Tristano, voy non farete raigione que voy vedete tuto giorno che uno grande Re ama una povera damaysella, e per amore una Redina ama uno povero damaysello. E però l'amore non guarda paragio, may vae secondo aventure le porta; siqué donqua la mia dama non deve per questa chaysone essere destruta'.

[39] E[n] questa parte disse lo conto che lo Re vedia bene che lo nano dissia veritade, may sì grande l'envidia àne de Tristano soe nepote che disse, 'Bissogno che io combata con luy'. E alora disse lo Re alo nano, 'Tu poy ben fare siché io averoe tua dama, ed ella non serae destruta'. E lo nano disse, 'Questo faroe io volentieri si è en tal modo che io non sia chiamato traditore'. E lo Re disse, 'En che manera tu lo poe fare siché non de seray represso? Tu anderay con Tristano

---

213 Long, extraneous titulus over middle of this word.
214 Scribe used idiosyncratic abbreviation: *feie* with ~ above the last two letters. Cf. TR, p.70: *femina*.
215 Rice paper patch over upper right corner covers several words in first five lines.

as well to come well-armed with all his weapons because one doesn't know what misfortunes may arise'. The dwarf mounted a horse and came to King Mark's court. And when he saw Tristan, he called him over and said, 'The Damsel of Thornwater sends you a thousand greetings, and she is sending to ask you to come to her at the garden of the fountain this evening, and come well-armed with all your weapons because many adventures happen to knights'. And Tristan, when he heard these words, was very happy and said to the dwarf, 'I am ready to do as the damsel commands and to come at whatever time may please her'. And then with these words Tristan parted from the dwarf and went to his palace; and he ordered his squires to prepare his arms and ready the horses so that when he would want to ride, he would quickly find them.

[38] [fol. 122r] Now the tale says that King Mark saw clearly that the dwarf had spoken to Tristan. At once he called the dwarf to his chamber and said, 'Dwarf, I want you to tell me what message you carried to Tristan, my nephew – because you consulted with him such a long time – and who sent you'. And the dwarf said, 'Sire, I'll not tell this because it wouldn't be courteous to tell others the private words that were given to me, and I was commanded not to reveal them'. Then the king said, 'What, dwarf, you won't tell me what I asked you?' And the dwarf said, 'I will not tell you the private words that I must keep others from knowing'. And the king said, 'If you won't tell me, I'll cut off your head'; and he raised his sword with both hands in order to strike the dwarf, most angrily. And the dwarf was very afraid and said, 'Sire, don't kill me, because I'll tell you the message that I took to Tristan'. Immediately he told the whole message that he had carried to Tristan. And the king said, 'Dwarf, I have requested your lady's love many times; I couldn't even have one kind word from her! It certainly seems that she is a worthless female because she always chooses the worst, and so she has done. She has now left me aside – I, who am a noble and powerful king – and has chosen Tristan who is a boy who doesn't [fol. 122v] know anything nor is he worth anything: it behooves me to destroy her'. And the dwarf said, 'Sire, if you have a lady destroyed because she loves Tristan, you will not being doing right: for you always see that a great king loves a poor damsel; and because of love, a queen loves a poor lad. And thus love has no regard for rank, but goes according to how Fortune carries it; so for this reason my lady must not be killed'.

[39] In this part the tale says that the king clearly saw that the dwarf was speaking the truth, but he had such great jealousy of Tristan his nephew that he said, 'It behooves me to fight with him'. And then the king said to the dwarf, 'You can surely manage it so that I will have your lady, and she will not be destroyed'. And the dwarf said, 'This I will gladly do, yes, in such a way that I'm not called a traitor'. And the king said, 'In this way you can manage it so that

chome tu ày promesso; e io montaroe a cavallo de tute arme. E andoròmmene[216] al passo de l'Aqua de l'Espina ch'io[217] ne espeytaroe tanto que venrae Tristano; e quie conbateroe con luy e meterò lo a terra del cavallo per forse di arme; e poyché io l'averò abatutto, vuolli [fol. 123r] che me menne[218] ala damaysella e meteray me con ley en luoguo de Tristano'. E lo nano disse, 'Come <non> sapete[219] voy que choisì legieramente e possente abaterete voy Tristano? Jà disse l'omo che èi gintille e prodo chavaliere, e de sua prodessa molto si parlla. E però io ve consillio che voy non mettiate vostra persona en aventura de morte e per chotalle caysone'. E lo Re disse, 'Nano, per mia fede, tu me vedray sì prodo chavaliere che te ne meravillarae de mia prodessa' – e a tanto finiame lo loro parlamento. E lo Re remasse ende la camera, e lo nano issite de fuora ende la sala del palagio. ‖‖[220]

E Tristano, quando lo vidi, disse, 'Io sonno apareçiato de venire tute le fiate che ti piaçerà'. E lo nano disse que l'ora non era anchora venutta, 'may espett<t>ate tanto que sia notte, e poy andaremo a nostra via'.

E lo Re Marcho qu'èy remasso [fol. 123v] ende la chamera, chiamoe uno eschudieli e disse li, 'Vae e aparechia mi le mie arme, e fae conçiare lo mey destrieri, qué io vollio que tu me sfasse (sic) compangnia; may ben ti guarda que queste parolle non debie manifestar a neuna persona del mondo! – e io farò dire ali chavalieri chome sonno amalato novellamentre d'una grieve malantie e farò achumiatare tuti li buoni <e> chavalieri chome sonno amalato'. E lo scudieri disse que questo faroe ille volentieri. E alora si parte l'eschudieri e comença di pensare ende le parolle che lo re li avea decte (may bene chonossia que so segnore era fello.) Apresso queste parolle la notte foe fatta, e lo Re fa dare chumiato a tuti li soy baroni e fae dire a loro qu'ello èi feramente malato.

Alora tuti li soy baroni retornoron a lur[221] alberguo; e lo Re s'aparechiò e presse soe arme e dapoyqu'ello foe armato, ello si partìo de la corte e andoe al soe giardino e qui n'espeçtoe lo soe eschudieri. E estando per uno pocho, l'eschudieri vengne al giardino con li chavalli. E lo Re montoe a chavallo, e lo schudieri li portava la lançia e l'eschudo. E partendo da lo giardino, cavalchoe verso lo giardino de l'Auqua de l'Espina. E quando foron giunti, [fol. 124r] e lo Re disse al'eschudieri, 'Aspecta mi quie afina che chavaliere erante viegna <Alora>[222] li quali vegnano en nostra terra'. 'May dapoyché voy volete combatere con loro, aspettate li fora del nostro realme, siché voy no[n] siate chiamato traditore'. E lo Re disse, 'Io non especto altro que questo passo'. E alora esmontoe lo Re da chavallo.

E esstando per pocha d'ura, e Tristano viegne con lo nano. E lo Re, encontene[n]te che lo vide, presse l'eschudo e la lanchia e montoe a chav[a]llo e disse, 'Chavaliere,

---

[216]   MS has titulus over the first *m*.
[217]   MS *chie ne*.
[218]   MS *mene* with titulus over the first *e*.
[219]   Extraneous *non*. See TR, p. 72: *Kome sapete*.
[220]   Seven full lines left blank at mid-page; miniature never executed.
[221]   MS *luy*.
[222]   Apparently superfluous word. Not found in TR, p. 72 nor in TP, p. 168.

Il Tristano Riccardiano *(Parodi's siglum 'F')*

you aren't taken to task: you go with Tristan as you promised and I'll mount my horse, fully armed. And we'll go to the ford at Thornwater where I'll wait until Tristan comes along; and here I'll fight with him and knock him to the ground from his horse by force of arms. And after I have unhorsed him, I want [fol. 123r] you to lead me to the damsel, and you'll put me with her instead of Tristan'. And the dwarf said, 'How do you know that you will so easily and powerfully strike down Tristan? People are already saying that he is a noble and valiant knight, and much is said of his prowess. Therefore I advise you to not put your person in danger of death nor for such a reason'. And the king said, 'Dwarf, by my faith, you will see in me such a valiant knight that you'll marvel at my prowess'. And in that moment they finished speaking, and the king remained in his chamber, and the dwarf went outside of it into the hall of the palace. |||

And Tristan, when he saw him, said, 'I'm ready to come any time that you wish', but the dwarf said that the hour was not yet come, 'but wait until it's night, and then we'll go on our way'.

King Mark, who had remained [fol. 123v] in his chamber, called a squire and told him, 'Go and prepare my arms and have my warhorse readied, because I want you to keep me company; but guard yourself well because you must not reveal these words to anyone in the world! And I'll tell the knights that I have newly become ill from a grave malady, and I'll take leave of all the good knights, as I am ill'; and the squire said that he would do this willingly. And then the squire left and began to think over the words that the king had told him (and he truly knew that his lord was wicked). After these words, it became night; and the king gave leave to all his barons and had them told that, of a certainty, he was ill.

Then all his barons returned to their lodgings, and the king readied himself and took up his arms. And after he was armed, he left the court and went to his garden and here he awaited his squire. After he had been there a short while, the squire came to the garden with the horses; and the king mounted his horse, and the squire carried his lance and his shield for him. And upon leaving the garden, they rode toward the garden of Thornwater. When they arrived, [fol. 124r] the king said to the squire, 'Wait for me here until an errant knight comes, those fellows who come into our territory'. [The squire said,] 'Since you want to do battle with them, await them outside of our kingdom so that you are not called a traitor'. But the king said, 'I will wait nowhere but at this ford'; and then the king dismounted from his horse.

And after the king had stayed there a short time, Tristan came along with the dwarf. And the king – as soon as he saw him – took up his shield and lance and

gàrdate da me, ché io ti desfido!' E Tristano, quando entesse ch'era apellato ala batallia e non chonossende chi fosse lo chavaliere, disse enfra sé metesmo que non èi altro che de ferrire e non fare altro. E alora brochanno li desstrieri l'uno enverso de l'aut[r]o, |||[223] e lo Re Marcho fierì a Tristano sobra al'esqudo e passò li l'esqudo e l'asberguo, e fesse li piacha ende lo (sic) carne, e la lançia si[224] rompò en pessi. E Tristano [fol. 124v] ferite alo Re sopra[225] l'eschuto e passòli l'esberguo e messe li lo ferro de la lancia ende le spalle derietro e messe lo a terra de lo cavallo. La lançia si rompò en pessi, e lo Re achadere tramortito.

Adesso <e> Tristano disse al nano, 'Ora andiamo a nostra via, qué de quostuy siemo noy deliberati'; e partitti si en tale manera che giugnono alo giardino de la fontana de l'Auqua de l'Espina. Eli esmontanno da chavallo, e [Tristano] dessarmò (si e non si faiça la ferita; soe fo perché non ende <c>churava[226] may dessarme si per vedere si era pericholossa). E poy se risse e disse al nano, 'Vae a tua dama e disse li che io sonno chi[227] e espetto so comandamento'.[228] Alora si parte lo nano e vae ala sua dama e trovòla qu'era en letto però ch'era grande hora de la notte passata. E la damissella, quando vidi lo nano, disse, 'Ov'è Tristano?' E lo nano disse, 'Dama, elle è al giardino: espetta to comandamento'.[229] E la damissella disse, 'Vae tosto e di' che vengna'. E alora tornò lo nano a Tristano e disse li soe que·lla damaysella avea decto e comandato.

A tanto montoe Tristano a chavallo e venne al palaçio de la dam[a]yssella, e quie ne smontoe; e andoe ala chamera de la damissella e trovoe la colchiato ende lo letto. E Tristano si dissarmoe e poy li si colchò con ley en letto. (E la ferita l'in-[230] [fol. 125r] sanguenoe tutto lo letto implire de sangue de la ferrita que·llo avea data lo Re Marcho.) E quando fo el letto, chomi[n]çhono a fare granda alegressa l'uno con l'autro. E la damissella chome[n]chiò abaysare Tristano, e steteron amboro e·ffessenno luro chomandamento pian<t>imento d'amore. E poy enchomi[n]çiono a parlare de molte aventure. E quando eranno en chotale solaçio (e non sapendo la damissella <del sangue> niente del sangue ch'era uscito a Tristano), echo venne lo nano e disse, 'Levate suso, Tristano, ché meser segnore lo Re viene <e> nella chamera!' E Tristano, quando entesse quelle parolle, presse l'arme e demanda chumiato ala damissella, e poy montò a cavallo e partiti si da lo palaçio.

E lo marito de la damissella montoe susso alo palaçio dov'era la chamera de lo palayso de la damissella e fesse rachare candelle per vedere lume. E lo chavaliere, gardando alo lecto, vide qu'era pieno de sangue. Ed ello disse ala damissella, 'Honde ven[n]e questo sangue ch'èi coissì frescho?' E la damissella – piena de paora – disse, 'Questo sangue [è] usito del mio nasso che tuta nocte non àe [fol. 125v] fatto altro'. E lo chavaliere disse, 'Dame (sic), queste parolle non ànno più mestieri perché d'altra parte èi venuto chesto sangue che de vostro nasse: già non è ditte mi

---

223   Six full lines left blank; miniature never executed.
224   MS *fi*. Confusion of *s* / *f*.
225   MS *sapra*.
226   Scribe wrote *c* at end of line, then repeated it on the entire word on the next line.
227   Sense: *qui*.
228   MS *comandanento*.
229   Cf. TR, p. 74: *aspetta tutto vostro komandamento*.
230   Catchword at center bottom, in a crudely drawn red cartouche: *sanguenoe*.

mounted his horse and said, 'Knight, be on your guard, because I challenge you!' And Tristan, when he heard that he was called to battle and not knowing who the knight was, said to himself that there was nothing else to do but to fight. And then they spurred their warhorses, one toward the other, ||| and King Mark struck Tristan on his shield and it passed through his shield and his hauberk and made him a wound in his flesh; and the lance broke into pieces. And Tristan [fol. 124v] struck the king on his shield and it passed through his hauberk and he put the lance's iron tip through to the back of his shoulders and knocked him to the ground from his horse. The lance broke to pieces and the king fell, senseless.

Now Tristan said to the dwarf, 'Now let's go on our way, because we're delivered from this fellow'; and they left in such fashion that they arrived at the garden of the fountain of Thornwater. They dismounted from their horses, and Tristan disarmed himself (and he didn't bind his wound because he wasn't worried about it, but he did disarm himself to see if it was dangerous). And then he laughed and said to the dwarf, 'Go to your lady and tell her that I am here and await her command'. Then the dwarf left and went to his lady. And he found that she was in bed, because a great portion of the night had passed. And the damsel, when she saw the dwarf, said, 'Where is Tristan?' And the dwarf replied, 'Lady, he's in the garden: he awaits your command'. And the damsel said, 'Go at once and tell him to come'. Then the dwarf returned to Tristan and told him what the damsel had said and commanded.

In that moment Tristan mounted his horse and came to the damsel's palace, and here he dismounted; and he went to the chamber of the damsel and found her lying in bed. And Tristan disarmed himself and then climbed into bed with her (and his wound [fol. 125r] bled: the whole bed filled with blood from the wound that King Mark had given him). And when he was in bed, they began to make merry with each other. The damsel began to kiss Tristan, and they stayed together and fully obeyed love's commandment; and then they began to talk about many adventures. While they were enjoying such solace (and the damsel not knowing anything about the blood that had flowed from Tristan), lo and behold! – the dwarf came and said, 'Get up, Tristan, because my lord the king is coming to the chamber!' And Tristan, when he heard those words, took up his arms and asked leave of the damsel, and then mounted his horse and left the palace.

The damsel's husband went up to the palace where the damsel's chamber in the palace was and had candles brought in order to have light; and the knight, looking at the bed, saw that it was full of blood. And he said to the damsel, 'Whence came this blood that is so fresh?' And the damsel – full of fear – said, 'This blood came out of my nose, for all night it didn't [fol. 125v] do anything else'. And the knight said, 'Lady, these words are of no use because this blood came from somewhere other than your nose: you haven't yet told me the truth!'

encontenente la veritade!' E la damissella e[n]chomençiò a jurare, e dissia che coysì era la veritade chome decto avea. E alora lo chavaliere messe mano al'espada per metere si paora ala damissella. 'O tu me dirae la veritate – chi foe lo chavaliere que giache techo – o io to uccidere encontenente!' Alora la damissella ebe grande paora. 'En prima que voy m'ançidate, io ve dirò lo nome del chavaliere'. Alora disse, 'Ello fo Tristano, nepote de lo Re Marcho, lo quale si partìo ora da quie'. Alora disse lo chavaliere, 'Dama, per mia fede, malo ày pensato quando en mia vita prochassiste dessognore; may per mia fede, voy cara la compprareste!' Alora disse, 'Ditte mi per quale via vae lo chavaliere'; e la damissella disse, 'Ello vae dirietro a Titolin'. Alora Lanbique[231] presse l'escudo e la lançia, e montò a cavallo e vae dir[i]etro a Tristano.

E cavalcando en tal manera, e Tristano enchomençò a dire enfra sé metessmo, 'Ora sonno io bene dessaventurosso chavaliere, quando coissì tosto me ne co[n]viene partire dal mio [fol. 126r] amore'; molto si conplange Tristano enfra sé metesmo de questa dessaventura. May Lanbis che cavalqua verso a Tristano molto astivamente,[232] elo [à] veduto Tristano alo resplandore de la luna. Ed ello li disse, 'Tristano, gàrdate da me, ché i[o] te desfido!'; e Tristano, qua[n]do à udito lo chavaliere que l'apellava ala batallia, encontenente diriçoe la testa[233] de lo cavallo verso de luy e messe mano al'espada. E Lanbuigues ferìo <e> Tristano sobbra de l'eschudo e diedi li sì grande colpo qu'ello li passò l'eschudo e l'essbergo, e ferì lo siché [la] lançia si rompoe en pieçi. May quando Tristano si sentite ferito, ferite a Lanbigues sopra l'ermo con l'espada e diedi li sì grande colpo che li passoe l'elmo e la cuffia[234] del ferro, e fesse li granda piagua el capo. E a traere que fesse de l'espada a sé, Lanbigues cade a terra da cavallo siché ala chadere tramortivo. E Tristano disse, 'Chavaliere, non combateremo noy più?'; e Lanbigues non resposse. Ed alora – credendo Tristano che fosse morto – e alora disse, 'Chavaliere, per mia fede, si tu m'ài [fol. 126v] ferito, io non credo que gare te ne posse vantare'. E alora se ne torna Tristano e vae al soe palaçio.

E quando Guovernale vidi Tristano qu'era ferito, enchomi[n]chiò a fare grando pianto, dissendo, 'Ai, lasso! que mala gardia abo presso de voy qué siete in tal manera ferito! May si io avesse sauputo la vostra andata, voy non sereste ito sensa me'. E Tristano disse, 'Dolço maistro mio, non temette che io non abo ferita che io non garisscha legiaramente'. May encontenente vienenno li medici e chominçano a gardare le ferite de Tristano e d'ogni parte e trovagno que la ferita che recevete dirietro era più pericholossa que non era quella che li diede lo Re Marcho, e trovanne la ferita de lo Re Marcho più pericholossa que quella de Tristano.

Dapoyqué lo Re sepe que Tristano g[i]acea (credente qu'elle giachesse per la ferita[235] quello li diede), ello disse al'eschudieri che l'avea acompagnato al'Auqua de l'Espina, disse lo Re al'eschudieri, 'Tu credevi que io avesse lo pegiore de lo chavaliere erante de la batallia, may tu poy bene [fol. 127r] vedere

---

[231] MS contains many variants on this character's name, all of which I show without further comment. For the original French spellings, see West, p. 185.

[232] Scribe wrote *asq(ua)uamente*, incorporating the *q(ue)* abbreviation, but also wrote out *-ua-*. On fols 131r and 132v, scribe wrote more correctly, although again with an extra syllable, *astivatamente*. Emendation based on TR, p. 76: *astivamente*.

[233] MS *lançia*.

[234] MS clear: *leschufa*. Apparent misreading or conflation of *eschudo* and *cuffia*.

[235] MS *ferira*.

And the damsel began to swear and say that such was the truth as she had said. And then the knight put his hand to his sword in order to frighten the damsel. 'Either you tell me the truth – who was the knight who lay with you – or I'll kill you at once!' Then the damsel was greatly afraid. 'Before you kill me, I'll tell you the knight's name'. Then she said, 'He is Tristan, King Mark's nephew, who left here just now'. Then the knight said, 'Lady, by my faith, you thought ill when you sought to bring dishonor to my life; but by my faith, you'll pay for it dearly!' Then he said, 'Tell me by which road the knight went'; and the damsel said, 'He went straight toward Tintagel'. Then Lambegues got his shield and his lance, and mounted his horse and went after Tristan.

While riding along in that fashion, Tristan began to say to himself, 'Now I am truly an unfortunate knight, when it behooved me to leave my love so soon'; [fol. 126r] Tristan lamented a lot to himself about this misfortune. But Lambegues was riding toward Tristan very fast, and Tristan saw him in the moonlight. And he said to him, 'Tristan, guard yourself from me because I challenge you!' And Tristan, when he heard the knight who was calling him to battle, immediately directed his horse's head toward him and grabbed his sword. And Lambegues struck Tristan on his shield and gave him such a great blow that it passed through his shield and his hauberk, and he wounded him so that his lance broke to pieces. But when Tristan felt himself wounded, he struck Lambegues on the helmet with his sword and gave him such a great blow that it passed through the helmet and the iron coif and made a great wound in his head. And when Tristan pulled his sword back to himself, Lambegues fell to the ground from his horse so that he fell, senseless. And Tristan said, 'Knight, aren't we fighting any longer?'; but Lambegues did not answer. And then Tristan – believing that he was dead – said, 'Knight, by my faith, even though you have [fol. 126v] wounded me, I don't believe that you can hardly boast about it'. And then Tristan returned on his way and went to his palace.

And when Governal saw Tristan, who was wounded, he began to lament greatly, saying, 'Ah, alas! What poor care you have taken of yourself since you are wounded in this fashion! But if I had known about your leaving, you would not have gone without me'. And Tristan said, 'My sweet master, don't worry because I have no wound that will not heal quickly'. But at once physicians came and began to look over Tristan's wounds and all over his body, and they found that the second wound that he received was more dangerous than the first which King Mark had given him; and they found that King Mark's wound was more dangerous than Tristan's.

After the king found out that Tristan was lying in bed, wounded (believing that he was lying there because of the wound that he had given him), he said to the squire who had accompanied him to Thornwater – the king said to the squire, 'You believed that I had the worst of the battle from the errant knight, but you can clearly [fol. 127r] see that I have the ability to do combat with an

che io abo podere de combatere con uno chavaliere erante e per amore de donna, qué ve<v>de que Tristano non potre levare per la ferita che io li abo facto'. E lo eschudieri, quando entesse queste parolle, parve a luy che dissesse la verità. E lo eschudieri disse, 'Vero que voy esstate mellio che Tristano, may voy foste abattutto da cavallo, e Tristano non è'. E lo Re disse, 'Io vuolio andare a vedere choma illo estae. |||[236]

E quando foe giu[n]to al'albergo[237] de Tristano, disse, 'Dolchio mio nepote, chome estae?' Ello disse, 'Io estoe mellio que altra gente non si credanno'. E lo Re disse, 'May poy tu vedere qu'en questo realme abi chavaliere que t'abia facto questo. May tuta fiata vuollio que tu mi digue qui fo [fol. 127v] lo chavaliere che ti ferìo'; e Tristano [disse], 'Io non so, may io lo saperò tosto'. E alora credendo lo Re que lo dissise per luy, ebe gran paora. Alora si partì lo Re da Tristano e andoe al soe palaçio molto pensosso, e Tristano guaritte en .xx. dì de quelle ferite que non potte portare arme. (E sapiate che Tristano non chonobe lo Re quando combatite con luy, may lo Re chonobe tropo bene Tristano e diedi li due rie colpi. May Tristano fo quello che n'ebe mellio che lo Re Lanbugues, lo quale ne giaque .vii. messe fortamente agravato de la ferita lo quale ebe da Tristano quando l'abatette da cavallo.)

[40] In questa parte disse lo conto que dapoiqué Tristano fo garrito che potea portare l'arme, enchominçoe andar a corte alo Re Marcho. Lo Re Marcho mandoe per tuti li soi baroni e chavalieri que fossenno a corte con le lur dame e damisselle en pena d'essere destruti; e questo fa da lo Re Marcho per amore de la Damissella de l'Auqua de l'Espina. May quando lo comandamento vengne a Lanbigue, si ebe granda paora d'andare a corte per temença de Tristano, [fol. 128r] e disse ala damissella en che manera venroe a corte. Ed ella disse, 'Non sapete voi la veritade qu'è stato entre mi e Tristano? Enperò non vuolio io venire a corte'.

Alora disse Lanbigues [...][238] E la damissella a Lanbigues, 'Non temere che io ti rende[r]oe ben sechuro de Tristano'. Alora si parte Lanbigues con la damissella, e viegnneno a corte del Re Marcho; e lo Re fesse loro grande honore per amore de la damissella. E lo Re comandò che fossenno messe le taule. En pocha d'ora comandò que fossen messo due pavallione ala marina. Fatto fo so comandamento e pressenno li pavalloni, andoe lo Re con li baroni – e con le dame e damissele – ala marina [a] mangiare.

E dapoyché tuti sonno a taula e mangiando con grande alegressa, viene uno chavaliere errante armati de tuti arme. E cavalcando enverso li pavalloni e gardando enfra li chavalieri, vide lo Re Marcho e disse, 'Chavaliere errante sonn' io. Vado cercando lontane aventure per lontani paesi, e sono gi[fol. 128v]ovano chavaliere; neancho non demanday neuno dono a neuno Re; e però ve demando uno dono achoisì veramente que quello che io demanderoe, io la possa menare là unque a me piacherà'. E lo Re disse, 'Chavaliere, adimanda chiò que

---

[236] Six full lines left blank; miniature never executed.
[237] MS *alesbergo*.
[238] *Alora* has a red capital *A* and a guide letter *a* in margin indicate a new paragraph. The beginning of this incomplete utterance suggests additional dialogue not preserved in TR nor TP.

Il Tristano Riccardiano *(Parodi's siglum 'F')* 69

errant knight – and for the love of a lady – because you see that Tristan can't get up due to the wound that I gave him'. And when the squire heard these words, it seemed to him that he was telling the truth. And the squire said, 'It's true that you're better than Tristan, but you were unhorsed and Tristan wasn't'. And the king said, 'I want to go see how he is'. |||

When he had reached Tristan's lodging, he said, 'My sweet nephew, how are you?' He said, 'I'm better than some people would think'. And the king said, 'So you can see that in this kingdom we have a knight who did this to you, but still I want you to tell me who was [fol. 127v] the knight who wounded you'. And Tristan said, 'I don't know, but I'll find out soon'. And then, believing that he said it on his account, the king was greatly afraid. Then the king left Tristan and went to his palace, very pensive; and Tristan was healed of those wounds in twenty days during which he could not bear arms. (And know that Tristan didn't recognize the king when he fought with him, but the king knew only too well who Tristan was and gave him the two cruel blows; but Tristan was the one who had the best of King Lambegues, who lay abed seven months gravely ill from the wound that he had from Tristan when he unhorsed him.)

[40] In this part the tale said that after Tristan was healed so that he could bear arms, he began to go to King Mark's court. King Mark commanded that all his barons and knights assemble at court with their ladies and damsels on pain of being destroyed; and King Mark did this for love of the Damsel of Thornwater. But when the commandment reached Lambegues, he was greatly afraid of going to court for fear of Tristan, [fol. 128r] and he asked the damsel in what manner they could go to court. And she said, 'Don't you understand the truth about what was between Tristan and me? For this reason I don't want to go to court'.

Then Lambegues said [...]. And the damsel replied to Lambegues, 'Have no fear because I'll protect you most securely from Tristan'. Then Lambegues departed with the damsel, and they came to King Mark's court; and the king paid them great honor for the damsel's sake. And the king commanded that tables be set up. A short while later he commanded that two pavilions be set up on the seashore. His command having been carried out and the pavilions taken, the king went with his barons – and with their ladies and damsels – to the seashore to eat.

And after they were all at table and eating with great cheer, a fully-armed errant knight came along. And riding toward the pavilions and looking among the knights, he saw King Mark; and he said, 'I am an errant knight. I go seeking far-off adventures in distant lands, and I'm a [fol. 128v] young knight; nor have I ever asked a single boon to any king; and yet I am asking you for a boon in such a way that what I ask, I can take her wherever I please'. And

a te piaçerà niche[239] tu vuolli'. Elli disse, 'Vuollio questa damissella'; e posse la a cavallo suso en uno bello palafreno e prende soe camino. |||[240]

[41] Ora disse lo conto que quando Lanbigues vidi que lo chavaliere andoe via – e con la damissella – prende le arme e montoe a chavallo[241] e andoe dirietro alo chavaliere e gio[n]sso lo en uno bello prato. E quando lo vide, si l'esscridoe e dissi li chavaliere, 'Gàrdati da me, ché io te sfido!' Alora lo chavaliere driçoe la testa del chavallo enverso Lanbigues, e abaysanno amboro le lançe e vienon si a ferire. Lo chavaliere [fol. 129r] ronpe la lança a Lanbigues e cade a terra e fortamente chello èy enaverato; e lo chavaliere, lo quale à nome Bordo,[242] si·nn'andò con la damissella. |||[243] (May Tristano sarebe[244] volentieri a co[m]batere con lo Bordo,[245] ma laysava per temensa del Re Marcho, qu'ello sapea bene che lo Re l'amava de tuto soe chore; e però non andoe a combatere con luy.)
Estando en tal manera, passando li due chavalieri eranti apresso li pavallogni armati de tuti arme e andananguo (sic) per la via dritta alo desserto d'Irlanda e non salutoron lo Re Marcho nì neunno de la soa corte. |||[246] [fol. 129v] Alora disse lo Re March[o] a Bendin,[247] 'Va' dirietro a quelli chavalieri e di' lur da mia parte come estae lo Re Arturo[248] e di' che vegnano a me'. Alora Bendin (sic) montoe a cavallo e entende dirietro ali chavalieri. E tanto cavalchoe en tal manera quelli giu[n]sse en una grande valle, e disse loro, 'Chavalieri, lo Re Marcho ve manda a dire que vegnate a luy, ch'ello ve vuolle a dimandar de novelle'. E li chavalieri disseno que lor debia aperdonare 'e schussasseci alo Re Marcho per sò que noy non possamo ora venire a luy perqué andiamo a una ventura. May [a] la nostra tornata, torneremo a luy volentieri'. Alora disse Bendin, 'Questo èi villania de non tornare dirietro al Re!' E li chavalieri disseno que non tornalrebeno en nessuna manera. [E Bendin disse,][249] 'Sì, farete, ché io ve menaroe per forsa vuallate voy o non'. Alora Bendin presse le renne (sic) del chavallo d'uno de li chavalieri. E lo chavaliere disse, 'Bendin, per mia fede, tu

---

239   MS clearly reads *niche*. The passage differs from TR, p. 78 and TP, p. 172.
240   Six full lines blank; miniature never executed.
241   Scribe incorrectly wrote the abbreviation for *chavaliere*. Correction is mine.
242   MS *Bordo*, throughout the episode §§41–4. At some point in the transmission process, a copyist likely used only the initial *B.*, which was expanded incorrectly by a later copyist. I show as in the MS without further comment. For the larger textual tradition, see TR, p. 80: *Blanore*; TP, p. 172: *Branoro di Gaules*, Lancelot's nephew. Of the two variants, *Blanor* is more accurate (West, p. 41).
243   Seven full lines left blank; miniature never executed.
244   MS *si rebe*. Emendation based on TR, p. 80: *sarebe*.
245   The redactor has added a definite article to this name, here and below, almost like an epithet; perhaps on analogy with *l'Amoroldo*. Also, var. *el Bordo* (fols 132v, 133r).
246   At bottom of ruled writing space, seven more full lines left blank on the same folio. In this MS, it is rare to have two illustrations on a single page.
247   In this episode, scribe wrote *Bendin*, var. *Beldin*, perhaps due to misreading a Gothic upper case *G* in his model. Cf. TR, p. 80 ff.: *Ghed(d)in*; TP, p. 172: *Gedis*.
248   MS *artulo*. Cf. TR, p. 80: *lo ree Arturi*.
249   MS missing words. Insertion based on TR, p. 80.

Il Tristano Riccardiano *(Parodi's siglum 'F')*

the king said, 'Knight, ask what will please you, as you wish'. And he said, 'I want this damsel'; and he placed her upon a fine palfrey and set off on his way. |||

[41] Now the tale says that when Lambegues saw that the knight was going away – and with his lady! – he took up his arms and mounted his horse and went after the knight, and he reached him in a lovely meadow. When he saw him, he shouted at him and said to the knight, 'Guard yourself from me, because I challenge you!' Then the knight directed his horse's head toward Lambegues, and both of them lowered their lances and came to strike at one another. The knight [fol. 129r] broke his lance against Lambegues, and he fell to the ground very hard so that he was injured. And the knight, who was called Blanor, went off with the damsel. ||| (But Tristan would have gladly fought with Blanor, but did not permit himself for fear of King Mark, because well he knew that the king loved her with his whole heart; and for this reason he did not go to fight with him.)

As things stood like this, two fully-armed errant knights were passing near the pavilions, going along the direct route to the wilderness of Ireland, but they didn't greet King Mark nor anyone in his court. ||| [fol. 129v] Then King Mark said to Ghedin,* 'Go after those knights and ask them for my sake how King Arthur is and tell them to come to me'. Then Ghedin mounted his horse and went after the knights. And he rode so hard in that fashion that he caught up with them in a big valley, and he said to them, 'Knights, King Mark is sending to bid you to come to him because he wants to ask you for news'. And the knights said that he must forgive them, 'and make our excuses to King Mark insofar as we cannot come to him now because we're going on an adventure; but on our return, we'll gladly return to him'. Then Ghedin said, 'This is villainy not to go back to the king!' But the knights said that they would not return in any way. And Ghedin said, 'Yes, you will do it, because I will bring you by force, whether you want to or not'. Then Ghedin grabbed the reins of one knight's horse, and the knight said, 'Ghedin, by my faith, you're not very courteous nor wise since you think

---

* MS *Bendin*, var. *Beldin*. My translation as *Ghedin* respects the broader textual tradition.

non sey bene cortesse nì savio quando per forsa [?]ende[250] crede menare: non crede que da te io mi possa aitate quando io volroe?' E[n]contenente messe mano al'espada [e disse,] 'Laysa me, chavaliere!' E Bendin non resposse nie[n]te, may ancho tutavia lo menava. E lo chavaliere alsoe l'espada e ferite Beldin (sic) e diede li sì grande colpo que lo messe a te[rra][251] del cavallo. [fol. 130r] Alora si partinne li chavalieri e vanno ala lur via. May Beldino si relevò al piutosto qu'ello poe e tornoe verso ali pavalione.

[42] E en questa parte disse lo conto che dapoyché la damissella andava con lo Bordo, vide che Tristano non lo sochorea, mandò li una damissella per dire li vilania. E dapoyqu'ella fo gionta ali pavaliogni, chomençò a esgardare lo Re e tuti li soy chavalieri sensa neysuno salutare. E regardando en tal manera, disse lo Re, 'Damissella, molto si avete regardato e sensa dire nulla cossa'. E la damisella disse, 'Io non si veguo quello chavaliere che io volia'. E lo Re disse, 'Decto me quello che voy volete, e io lo ne faroe venire, s'illo è en mia corte'. E la damissella disse que '[vuolio][252] Tristano, vosstro nepotte'. E dapoyché foe venut[o],[253] ella li disse, 'Tristano, tu sey lo male venuto |||[254] sichome lo più falso chavaliere e non lealle che sia al mondo. May si lo Re Marcho chonossesse le toe [ma]leçensa,[255] come io façio, ello non ve voldria vedere'. E poy disse, 'Io t'ò decto queste parolle perché mi fo [fol. 130v] chomandato <E si me tornaroe endirietro chel mi foe chomandato> e si me tornarò endirietro[256] a mia dama ch'ella lo mi chomandoe'. E lo Re disse, 'Damissella, dìme che t'à desservito Tristano, mio nepote, ché l'ày decte tanta villania'. E la damissella non resposse, may encontene[n]te si partite dali pavaliogni e andoe a sua via. E tanto chavvalcha[257] que gio[n]sse la Damissella de l'Auqua di l'Espina.

May Tristano, lo quale remasse al pavalione, fo molto dolente de la villania che avea uditta; e enconte[nente] montoe a cavallo e presse arme, e Governale li fae compagnia. E partì si dali pavaligni e calvalchoe en tal manera. E Governale disse, 'Chome, Tristano, se' messo en questa ventura?' E Tristano disse, 'Per trovare la Damissella de l'Auqua de l'Espina'. E cavalcan<qua>do trovonno Bel<u>din tuto pieno de sangue. E Tristano disse, 'Beldin, qui t'àe ferito?' e Beldin disse, 'Àme ferito due chavalieri eranti'. |||[258] [fol. 131r] Alora disse Governale, 'Per mia fé, Beldin, io so che neuno chavaliere erante non t'arebe

---

[250] First letter may be *q*. This folio contains many probable errors. Reading unlike TR, TP.
[251] Hard to read. Ink running dry and third letter overwritten.
[252] MS missing verb. Cf. TR, p. 82: *Io voglio Tristano, vostro nepote*.
[253] Final vowel is overwritten. Resembles *æ*.
[254] Six full lines left blank; miniature never executed.
[255] MS *ojileçensa*, first letters hard to read. Perhaps *oji* should be *mi* (*ma*) due to misreading the hand of the model. Cf. *Geste Francor*, ed. Zarker Morgan, vol. 2, p. 1295 from Old French *leçerie* (trickery, treason). This would correspond to TR, p. 82: *mislealtade*.
[256] Redundancy is in MS. At top of new page, ink was running dry and pen needed sharpening. Scribe rewrote words with slight variants at top of *verso*. A type of self-correction.
[257] As elsewhere, scribe wrote a letter at end of line and then repeated it at the beginning of the next, resulting in -*vv*- spelling.
[258] Five lines left blank at bottom of writing space for miniature, never executed.

Il Tristano Riccardiano *(Parodi's siglum 'F')*

you can lead us by force. Don't you think that I can free myself from you when I want?' Immediately he drew his sword and said, 'Let me go, knight!' And Ghedin didn't answer at all, but was still leading him along. And the knight raised his sword and struck [Ghedin] and gave him such a great blow that he knocked him to the ground from his horse. [fol. 130r] Then the knights left and went on their way, and Ghedin got up as soon as he could and returned toward the pavilions.

[42] And in this part the tale says that after the damsel went off with Blanor and saw that Tristan was not coming to her aid, she sent a damsel to him to berate him. And after she had reached the pavilions, she began to look for the king and all his knights without greeting anyone. While she was looking around in that fashion, the king said, 'Damsel, you've been looking around and without saying a thing'. And the damsel said, 'I don't see that knight whom I want'. And the king said, 'Tell me whom you want, and I'll have him come here, if he is in my court'. And the damsel said, 'I want Tristan, your nephew'. After he had come, she said to him, 'Tristan, you are ill-met ||| as the most false and disloyal knight that there is in the world! But if King Mark knew of your treachery as I do, he wouldn't want to see you'. And then she said, 'I have said these words to you because I was [fol. 130v] commanded to, and so I will turn back to my lady who commanded me to do it'. And the king said, 'Damsel, tell me how Tristan, my nephew, has done you a disservice for which you have spoken so villainously to him'. And the damsel didn't reply, but immediately left the pavilions and went on her way. And she rode so much that she reached the Damsel of Thornwater.

But Tristan, who had remained at his pavilion, was very sorrowful about the villainy that he had heard; and immediately he mounted his horse and took his arms, and Governal kept him company. And he left the pavilions and rode in this fashion. And Governal said, 'Why, Tristan, have you set out on this adventure?' And Tristan replied, 'In order to find the Damsel of Thornwater'. And as they were riding along, they found Ghedin, all full of blood. And Tristan said, 'Ghedin, who wounded you?' And Ghedin replied, 'Two errant knights wounded me'. ||| [fol. 131r] Then Governal said, 'By my faith, Ghedin, I know that no errant knight would have wounded you if he had not had reason to do so'. Then Ghedin said,

ferito si tu non avesse lura lo perché'.[259] Alora disse Beldin, 'Ello èi ben vero che lo Re Marcho mi mandoe indirietro perché li volia demandare novelle del realme de Longres, e io dicendo loro queste novelle, non vollono[260] tornare. E io presse lo freno del cavallo de uno de li chavalieri, e io – che lo chavaliere volia menare – certo cont[r]a soe volere; per questa chaysone me ferinon'.[261] Alora disse Guovernalle, 'Per mia fede, Beldin, tu non ere savio quando per forse voley menare li chavaliere eranti; enperò, Tristano, io non vuollio que tu prende la batallia nì non chonsillio que tu combate con luy. Garo che non conbatereste con raisone'. E Tristano disse, 'Io non conbaterò contra raysone dapoyché Bendin fo ferito, essendo dessarmato'.

Apresso queste parolle, si partì Tristano e cavalchoe verso li chavalieri aranti (sic) molto ast<r>ivatamente. E cavalcando en tale manera si vidi li chavalieri erranti a uno prato presso a una foressta. Tristano disse, 'Gardate voy da me, ché io ve sfido!' Li chavalieri, quando entessi ch'erano apellati ala batalia, volseno[262] le teste de li cavalli verso a Tristano. E Tristano abaysò [fol. 131v] la lancia e viene a ferrire uno de li chavalieri. E lo chavaliere fere a Tristano sobra l'eschudo de tuta soa forsa siché la lancia si ronpe en pesse, may non l'esmontoe da cavallo. May Tristano ferì a lui l'eschudo e l'esbercho, e mese li la lançia – cioè lo ferro – ende le coste senestre e gitò lo a terra da cavallo e retrayse se la lancia sensa rompere; e lo chavaliere cade tramortito. E l'autro chavaliere, quando vide lo conpagno a terra da cavallo, driçoe la testa del cavallo verso Tristano; e Tristano verso de luy. E lo chavaliere ferì a Tristano e rompe li la lancia adosso: altro male non li fesse. May Tristano ferì a luy e messe lo a terra del cavallo. |||[263]

Alora disse a Bendin Tristano, 'Ora torna a corte quando ti piaçhe, e diray al Re che li chavalieri non vollon[264] tornare per te; may ben ti garda che tu non dire nulla de queste cosse'.

Alora tornò Beldin a corte, e Beldin si [fol. 132r] meravillava de Tristano molto, che coissì e delliberati de due chavalieri eranti, perché non credea que Tristano fosse de sì gran forssa. E dapoyqué fo giunto alo Re Marcho, disse, 'Meser, li chavalieri non vuolleno[265] tornare per me, ançi me feriron vilanamente; e io trovoe Tristano tornando. Si mi chiamay ello; si me deliberoe da queli chavalieri'. Molto si meravillava lo Re Marcho di Tristano che coissì tosto si deliberò de .ii. chavalieri eranti e chominçò avere grande paora de luy.

[43] May hora laysa lo conto de parlare di Re Marcho, e torniamo per devissare de Tristano: chome si deliberò del chavaliere que menava la Damissella de l'Auqua de l'Espina. May li chavalieri que foron abatuti de Tristano disse,

---

259   Ink running out, but *lura* is clear. Cf. TR, p. 82: *non avessi fatto lo 'mperchee*.
260   MS *volsono*. Confusion of *s / l*.
261   Clear in MS. Cf. TR, p. 82: *fedirono*.
262   MS *vosseno*. Confusion of *s / l*.
263   Five and a half lines blank, over halfway down on the page; miniature never executed.
264   MS *volson*. Confusion of *s / l*.
265   MS *vuolseno*. Confusion of *s / l*.

'It's very true that King Mark sent me after them because he wanted to ask them news about the kingdom of Logres, but when I told them this, they didn't want to return. And I took hold of the rein of one of the knight's horses, and I did this because I wanted to bring the knight along, certainly against his will. For this reason they wounded me'. Then Governal said, 'By my faith, Ghedin, you weren't wise since you wanted to conduct errant knights by force; therefore, Tristan, I don't want you to undertake the battle nor do I advise you to fight with him. You would hardly be fighting justly'. And Tristan said, 'I won't be fighting unjustly given that Ghedin was wounded while unarmed'.

After these words, Tristan left and rode toward the errant knights, very hastily. And riding along in that manner, he saw the errant knights in a meadow near a forest. Tristan said, 'Guard yourselves from me, because I challenge you!' The knights, when they heard that they were called to battle, turned their horses heads toward Tristan. And Tristan lowered [fol. 131v] his lance and came to strike one of the knights; and the knight struck Tristan on his shield with all his might so that the lance broke to pieces, but he did not unhorse him. But Tristan struck him on his shield and hauberk, and he put his lance – that is, the iron tip – into his left ribs and hurled him to the ground from his horse, and withdrew his lance without breaking it; and the knight fell, senseless. And the other knight, when he saw his companion unhorsed, directed his horse's head toward Tristan; and Tristan toward him. And the knight struck Tristan and broke his lance against him: he did him no other harm; but Tristan struck him and knocked him to the ground from his horse. |||

Then Tristan said to Ghedin, 'Now return to court when it pleases you and tell the king that the knights didn't want to come back with you; but take good care not to say anything about these things'.

Then Ghedin returned to court, and Ghedin [fol. 132r] marvelled greatly about Tristan who had thus delivered himself from two errant knights because he didn't believe that Tristan had such great strength. And after he had rejoined King Mark, he said, 'Sire, the knights did not want to return with me; instead they wounded me villainously; and I found Tristan while I was returning. I called him to me, and he delivered me from those knights'. King Mark marvelled greatly about Tristan, who had so quickly delivered himself from two errant knights, and began to fear him greatly.

[43] But now the tale leaves off speaking of King Mark, and we return to tell about Tristan: how he delivered himself from the knight who was leading away the Damsel of Thornwater. The knights who were struck down by Tristan said,

'Chavaliere, de que paesse sette?' E Tristano disse, 'Io sonno de Cornavallia'. E li chavalieri disseno, 'Ora siemo noy più que vituperati parqué noy siamo abatuti de coissì vil gente chome quilli di Cornavallia; e enperò non porteremo più arme enfine que li nostri conpagni de la Taula Retonda noy non sapiamo chelli non siano abatuti da coisì vil gente chome quilli de Cornavallia'. E a[fol. 132v]lora enchomi[n]çono a gitare tute le lur arme. E Tristano de queste cosse si facia meravillia e dissi a loro, 'Chavalieri, dapoyché voy non volete le vostre arme, prendete le mie e portate le con voy'. Alora disseno li chavalieri, 'Noy siemo asay vituperati e non vuoliamo portare le vostre arme per avere più dessognore'.

E a tanto si parte Tristano de li chavalieri e cavalcha molto astivatamente. Cavalcando en tale manera, si vide el Bordo alo entrar del castello, e avea en soa co[n]gpagn[i]a la Damissella de l'Auqua de l'Espina. E quando la vidi, disse Governale a Tristano, 'Cavalchiamo tosto, qué io vedo la Damissella que ve disse villania e 'l chavaliere que la menava'. [Tristano disse,] 'Enperò molto mi tarda che io sia ala batallia con luy'.²⁶⁶ Disse Governale a Tristano, 'Chome? Combaterete voy con luy? E[n] lo castello [è]²⁶⁷ già la damissella: non è vosstra dama'.

[44] Ora disse lo conto que Tristano rende cotal raisone a Governale e disse, 'Maistro mio, io bene entesse qu'è ussansa de li chavalieri eranti en chotal che chascaduno chavaliere lo potte apellare de batalia. E dapoyché noy seremo fuora del castello, io apellarò lo chavaliere de batalia'. E Governale disse, 'De queste cosse mi chiamo asay contento'.

Alora cavalcha Tristano [fol. 132 *bis, recto*]²⁶⁸ enverso lo castello ed albergò²⁶⁹ en qua d'una donna que non avea marito, may avea uno so filliolo qu'era prode damissello. E Tristano, quando fo dessarmeato, lo damissello lo volle²⁷⁰ chonossere, e disse li, 'Chavaliere, foste voy ancho en Landa?' E Tristano disse de no. E lo damissello disse, 'Per mia fede, voy me semelliate pur a uno chavaliere que vince lo torniamento en Landa e sco[n]fite lo Re de Schorçia con tuta la soa gente, ed abbate Palamides lo bono chavaliere de le .ii. espade; e fesse en quello dì tanto d'arme che bene se ne contarae da homni chavaliere; e tornava ende la corte del Re Languis'. E Tristano disse, 'Io non sono quello chavaliere que tu disse, may bene vuolria essere nomato de tanta prodessa quant'illi'. E lo damissello disse, 'Voi li semilliare melio d'essere quello che io àe decto que nullo que may si vedesse'. A tanto feniamo²⁷¹ lur parlamento, e chello damissello fa servire Tristano de sò ch'eli à bessog[n]a.

Ala matina si leva Tristano – e Governale – e pre[n]de soe arme e vae a una capella per udire la messa. E poyqu'ebe udita la messa, mo[n]tò a cavallo e partì si de lo damissello e chomi[n]çò a chavalchare. E [fol. 132 *bis, verso*] cavalcando en tal manera, giu[n]çe lo chavaliere en uno bello prato, e la nocte era nevigato.

---

²⁶⁶   Narrative simplification. Cf. TR, p. 84.
²⁶⁷   Insertion based on TR, p. 86: *Nel kastello èe giae la damigella*.
²⁶⁸   The later medieval owner missed numbering this folio. A modern librarian added '*bis*'.
²⁶⁹   MS *e dalmergoe*. Emendation follows TR, p. 86: *e venne ad albergare*.
²⁷⁰   MS *volse*. Confusion of *s* / *l*.
²⁷¹   Clear in MS. Cf. TR, p. 86: *si finano loro parlamento*.

Il Tristano Riccardiano *(Parodi's siglum 'F')*

'Knight, from what country are you?' And Tristan said, 'I'm from Cornwall'. And the knights said, 'Now we are more than dishonored because we were beaten by such vile people as those of Cornwall; and therefore we will no longer bear arms until we find out that our companions of the Round Table were also beaten by such vile people as those of Cornwall'; and [fol. 132v] then they began to throw away all their arms. Tristan marvelled at these things, and he said to them, 'Knights, since you don't want your arms, take mine and carry them with you'. Then the knights said, 'We are so very dishonored, and we don't want to carry your arms in order to have more dishonor'.

At that Tristan left the knights and rode off very quickly. Riding along in that manner, he saw Blanor at the entrance of the castle, and he had in his company the Damsel of Thornwater. And when he saw her, Governal said to Tristan, 'Let's ride quickly, for I see the damsel who spoke villainously to you and the knight who is leading her along'. Tristan said, 'And for this reason I can't wait until I'm engaged in battle with him'. Governal said to Tristan, 'What? Are you going to fight with him? The damsel is already in the castle: she is not your lady'.

[44] Now the tale says that Tristan granted that Governal was right and said, 'My master, I well understand that it is the custom of errant knights insofar as that each knight can summon him to battle; and after we are outside the castle, I will summon the knight to battle'. And Governal said, 'About these things, I consider myself most content'.

Then Tristan rode [fol. 132 *bis, recto*] toward the castle, and he took lodgings there with a woman who had no husband, but one of her sons was a valiant young man. And when Tristan was disarmed, the young man wanted to learn his identity and said to him, 'Knight, were you ever in Ireland?' And Tristan said no. And the young man said, 'By my faith, yet you seem to me a knight who won the tournament in Ireland and defeated the King of Scotland with all his people and struck down Palamides the Good, Knight of the Two Swords; and that day he did such feats of arms that every knight will quite rightly recount them; and he returned to King Anguin's court'. And Tristan said, 'I am not that knight of whom you speak, but I would certainly like to be known for such prowess as he'. And the young man said, 'You resemble that fellow of whom I told you better than anyone I ever saw'. Just then they finished their conversation, and that young man had Tristan served with what he needed.

In the morning Tristan arose – and Governal – and he took up his arms and went to a chapel to hear mass. And after he had heard the mass, he mounted his horse and left the young man and began to ride. And [fol. 132 *bis, verso*] riding along in this manner, he caught up with the knight in a lovely meadow, and in the night it

E Tristano gridoe alo chavaliere e disse, 'Chavaliere, gar[da] te da me, qué io ti sfido!' E lo chavaliere, quando entesse qu'era apellato ala batallia, volsie[272] si enverso Tristano; e chiaschaduno enchominça a dare del campo l'uno al'autro, e abaysano le lançe e vienon se a ferire. E chiaschaduno ronpoe la soa lança, cioè perqué li colpi foron grandi, siché amboro li cavalli cadeno en terra, e li chavalieri cadono riti. E encontenenti anboro messenno mane al'espada e chominçonno a ferire e a dare grandi colpi sobra l'escudo, siché chia[s]caduno si meravilava de la forsa l'uno da l'autro. E tanto conbateronno fine que si repossenno uno pocho e de lur vuolia. E dapoyqué foron repausati, cominçano l'autro asalto e, sichome a più volte adiviene che lo più possente vince e quelo qu'èi <più> meno perde,[273] e cossì addiviene al Bordo, lo quale non è de la forsa nì de la vista de Tristano. E disse enf[r]a sé estesso, 'I'òe conbatuto con Meser Lanceloto del Lac, mio fratello, e con [fol. 133r] altri chavalieri, may uncha sì grandi colpi non sufersi chome sostiegni da questo chavaliere; e vegio bene qu'al dirietro de la batalia, non poterò sufrire con luy'.

Alora si trayse endirietro Bordo e disse a Tristano, 'Chavaliere, tanto mi·ssono conbatuto con voy che io vegio bene que voy siete lo meliore chavaliere del mondo; e però volrey sapere vostro nome, e io en primamente ve diroe lo mio nome siché [si] io vincho la batalia, saperò qui ò vinto. E si voy vincerete me, saperete chi averete vinto'. E Tristano disse, 'Ditte me lo vostro nome'. Ello disse, 'Io abi nome Bordo'. Ed elli disse, 'I'ò nome Tristano, per la chuy mano tu dey morir'. El Bordo disse, 'Que[s]ta batalia èi remasse entre[274] noy, perché io non conbaterò più con voy perqué io voy ay tanto uditto noiare[275] e prodessa e de cortessia que io ve layserò questa batalia'. Adonque disse Tristano, 'Adonche mi renderete la damissella. E si voy non la mi volete rendere, io voy apello ala batallia'. E Bordo dissi, 'Io ve farò tanto per honore de chavallaria: che·lla damissella viegna entre [fol. 133v] noi doy, e quello è quello ch'a ley più piaçierà si possa prendere'. Alora disse Tristano, 'Questo asay mi piaçe'.

A tanto viene la damissella in meçio de li chavalieri; disse la damissella, '[Tristano],[276] asay t'oe amato più che nullo chavaliere, ma co[n]siderendo que mi ni layssasti menare e non me socoresti, vo me ne andare con questo chavaliere, ché con voy non venroe io may!' Quando Tristano entesse le parolle, fo molto dolente, e partì si da lo chavaliere. |||[277]

[45] (Ora disse lo conto che si Tristano avesse sauputo o creduto che la damissella l'aveste abandonato en tal manera, ello arebe conpiuto sua batalia.) Apreso queste parolle, Tristano e Governale tornoron a Titolin. Quando lo Re sepe que Tristano venia, fo molto alegro. Encontenente li andoe encontra con li soe baroni poyché vide Tristano, may lo chore suo non li vuolia bene e gran paora

---

[272] MS scribe wrote *vorsie*, then overwrote the *r* with an *l*.
[273] Simplification of a more complex passage, with some loss of meaning.
[274] MS *antre*.
[275] Thus in the MS. Cf. TR, p. 88: *nominare*.
[276] MS omits name as found in TR, p. 88.
[277] Four full lines left blank, mid-page; miniature never executed.

Il Tristano Riccardiano *(Parodi's siglum 'F')*

had snowed. And Tristan shouted at the knight and said, 'Knight, guard yourself from me, because I challenge you!' And the knight, when he heard that he was called to battle, turned toward Tristan; and each one began to take his position on the field, one against the other, and they lowered their lances and came to strike. And each one broke his lance, that is to say because their blows were great, so that both the horses fell to the ground, but the knights landed on their feet. And immediately both of them put their hands to their swords and began to strike and to give great blows on their shields, so that each of them marvelled at the other's strength. And they fought so much until they rested a while, as they desired. And after they had rested, they began another assault and, since at times it happens that the most powerful wins and he who is less powerful loses, so it happened to Blanor who didn't have Tristan's strength or quickness. And he said to himself, 'I've fought with Sir Lancelot of the Lake, my brother, and with [fol. 133r] other knights, but never have I suffered such great blows as I am sustaining from this knight; and I clearly see that at the end of the battle, I won't be able to withstand him'.

Then Blanor withdrew and said to Tristan, 'Knight, I have fought so much with you that I clearly see that you are the best knight in the world; and for this reason I would like to know your name; and I'll tell you my name first so that if I win the battle, I'll know whom I have defeated; and if you defeat me, you'll know whom you have defeated'. And Tristan said, 'Tell me your name'. And he said, 'My name is Blanor'. And he said, 'My name is Tristan, by whose hand you must die', but Blanor said, 'This battle between us is ended because I will no longer fight with you, since I have heard so much praise for your prowess and courtesy that I leave the battle to you'. Then Tristan said, 'Well then, give me back the damsel; and if you do not give her back to me, I'll call you to battle'. And Blanor said, 'I'll do this much for you, for the honor of chivalry: the damsel will come between [fol. 133v] us two, and he who is the one that pleases her more may take her'. Then Tristan said, 'This pleases me greatly'.

In that moment the damsel came into the midst of the knights; the damsel said, 'Tristan, I loved you more than any other knight, but considering that you let me be led away and did not aid me, I'll go on my way with this knight, because I'll never come along with you!' When Tristan heard her words, he was very sorrowful and departed from the knight. |||

[45] (Now the tale says that if Tristan had known or believed that the damsel would have abandoned him in such fashion, he would have finished his battle.) After these words, Tristan and Governal returned to Tintagel. When the king found out that Tristan was coming, he was very happy. Immediately he went to meet him with his barons since he saw Tristan, but his heart did not wish him

avea de ley (sic). E dissia enfra sì estesse que si Tristano demora en Cornavalia 'seguro posso essere de perdere la[278] vi[fol. 134r]ta dapoich'ello èi choysì francho chavaliere d'arme'. Apresso queste parolle, lo Re Marcho introe ende la sala e chiamò Tristano a sé, e disse, 'Nepote, io vuolio que ti sia en piacere de dire me e a questi chavalieri le chavallaria che tu ày facto dapoyché chavaliere ti fesse'. E questo disse, 'Re Marcho, questo non seria cortessia per voy nì per me de recordare queste cosse'. E lo Re disse, 'Io ti comando [per lo saramento] che tu me [se]y tenuto[279] che tu lo me debie dire'.

E Tristano con grande dolore chominçioe a recordare. E dapoych'el ebe recordato, disse, 'Re Marcho, ora m'avete fato dire un pogcho desognore quando m'avete facto dire quelle cosse che i'ò facto'.

Alora lo Re dubitò più de Tristano ||||[280] dapoych'ebe entesse le soe prodesse. Apresso cheste parolle, lo Re sen'andoe ende la chamera e chominçoe a pensare en che modo potesse delongnare Tristano da sé e mandarlo en tal parte che non tornasse giamay en Cornavalia. E pensando, non trova via per la quale cioe e' potesse fare. Alora [fol. 134v] chiamò due baroni lo (sic) quale molto si fidava; disse a loro tutto soe entendemento. E li baroni quando ebenno entesso lo Re, dissengnò al Re tuto lo modo per lo quale devesse essere destruto Tristano. Dapoyché[281] [lo] Re ebe entesso lo consillio de li baroni, si mandoe per tuti li soy baroni e chavalieri; e fesse coma[n]dare a Tristano che vengnesse[282] dinançi da luy. Dapoyqué Tristano fo venuto, disse lo Re, 'Dolçio mio nepote, molte fiate m'ày re[pr]esso[283] però che io non abo presse molie. Ora per tua gracia me io entendimento di prenderla, quando a ti piaçe'. E Tristano disse al Re, 'Se per me potesse avere cossa che vi piaçia, io ve farò lo mio podere'. E lo Re disse a Tristano, 'Prometellomi tu chome chavaliere'. E Tristano disse, 'Certa, sie'. E lo Re l'ingracio asay de questo dono. E disse Tristano, 'Adonqua, dimandaroe a voy quello que bissogno me fae'. E lo Re disse, 'Ello èi ben vero che voy e tuti li mey baroni m'avesso [demandato] perché io non abo pillato mollie; però lo vuolio prendere. E vuolio una damissella la qualo (sic) m'avete laudato più volte de bellessa, ciò è Ysota la Bronda, filliola del Re Languis de Landa'. E Tristano disse, 'Io ne farò mio podere'.

E alora [fol. 135r] disse lo Re a Tristano, 'Hora t'aparechia e prende oro e argento quanto a ti piaçe, e prende conpagny de chavalieri <d> e de damayselli chome voy volete, e façete che io abia la damisselle'.

Dapoyqué Tristano ebe entesse le parolle che lo Re li avia decte, fo molto dolorosso e dissia enfra sé esstessi, 'Ora ben veguo che lo Re Marcho mi manda enver Landa più per la mia morte que per la mia vita' – enperò sie dissese de no[n] vuole vi andare en questa aventura – 'dapoyché lo enpromesso. Honi

---

278   Catchword at center bottom of fol. 133v, in a crudely drawn red cartouche: *ta dapoi*.
279   MS *comando che tu mey tenuto*. Emendation based on TR, p. 88.
280   Five full lines left blank; miniature never executed.
281   MS *cho*.
282   MS clear: *venqnesse*.
283   Letters hard to read. Possibly superscripted *a* or an abbreviation including an *r*. Does not correspond to TR, p. 90 nor to TP, p. 176.

well and he was very afraid of him. And he said to himself that if Tristan dwelt in Cornwall, 'I can be sure of losing my life [fol. 134r] since he is such a brave knight at arms'. After these words, King Mark entered the hall and called Tristan to himself and said, 'Nephew, I want you – if it may please you – to tell me and these knights the chivalrous deeds that you have done since I knighted you'. And this fellow said, 'King Mark, this would not be courteous for you nor for me to recall these things'. But the king said, 'I command you by the oath that binds you to me to tell me'.

Tristan with great sorrow began to recount his deeds; and after he had recounted them, he said, 'King Mark, now you've made me speak rather dishonorably since you've made me tell those things that I have done'.

Then the king worried more about Tristan ||| since he heard of his prowess. After these words, the king went away into his chamber and began to think of some way in which he would be able to remove Tristan far from himself and to send him into such a place that he would never return to Cornwall; but by thinking, he found no way by which he could do it. Then [fol. 134v] he called two barons whom he trusted greatly; he told them all his thoughts. The barons, when they had heard the king, laid out for the king an entire plan by which Tristan should be destroyed. After the king had heard his barons' advice, he sent for all his barons and knights; and he had Tristan commanded to come before him. After Tristan had come, the king said, 'My sweet nephew, many times you have taken me to task because I have not taken a wife. Now, thanks to you, I intend to take her, when it may please you'. And Tristan said to the king, 'If, thanks to me, you could have something that pleases you, I will do my best for you'. And the king said to Tristan, 'Do you promise me as a knight?' And Tristan said, 'Certainly, yes'. And the king thanked him greatly for this boon. And Tristan said, 'Well then, I'll ask you what it is that you need me to do'. And the king said, 'It's very true that you and all my barons have asked me why I have not taken a wife; for this reason I want to do it. And I want a damsel whose beauty you have praised to me many times, that is Yseut the Blonde, daughter of King Anguin of Ireland'. And Tristan said, 'I'll do my best about it'.

And then [fol. 135r] the king said to Tristan, 'Now prepare yourself, and take as much gold and silver as you please, and take a company of knights and young men as you wish, and make it so that I have the damsel'.

After Tristan had heard the words that the king had said to him, he was very sorrowful and said to himself, 'Now I clearly see that King Mark is sending me toward Ireland more for my death than for my life' – and for this reason he told himself that he didn't want to go on this adventure – 'yet I promised him.

homo dirie que fosso desliali chavaliere, e enperò en prima mi vuolio metere en aventura de morte che essere tenuto chavaliere messliallo, cioè per rimare d'esse[r] chiamato deslealle'. E a questo s'acorda Tristano, e disse a Re Marcho, 'Dapoyqué èi vostro piaçera que io mi meter |||[284] en aventura per avere Yssota, metarò mi e faroe mio podere perché abiate la damissella'.

[fol. 135v] E lo Re disse a Tristano, 'Io ti chomando per quello che mi sey tenuto que prende ciò que ti fa bissog[n]ia, e aparechia toa nave e dibitti recolare[285] con quella conpagna que a ti piaçe de menare. E debiti partire de Cornavalia e non tornare afina tanto che non mi vienge la damissella, cioè Yssota'. E Tristano disse, 'Re Marcho, io farò vostro comandamento'; e mandò per chavaliere e per damisselli de Cornavalia (e debe ne fare venire en nomero de cinquanta). E dapoyqué foron venuti ende la sala del palaçio, disse <lo Re> loro, 'Ello èi ben vero' – disse Tristano – 'che lo Re Marcho m'acomanda da sua parte que io ve comandi che voy me debiate far conpagnia a una ventura la quale fae mestieri de conquistare e per forse d'arme, e questa ventura siè el realme de Landa'.

E li chavalieri chomínçano a fare gran lamento entendendo queste parolle, e diçiano, 'Ora videamo noy apertamento che lo Re Marcho manda noy en Landa con Tristano perché noy siamo morti, ché noy potemo ben sapere que Tristano uccisse l'Amoroldo de Landa; e si noy andiamo en questo realmo, tuti vecirimo (sic) morti. May Tristano potrà canpare per soe prodesse, luy e noy. Però, segnori, inançi si laysiamo estrugere que noy andiamo enver Landa'.

E quando Tristano entesse queste parolle, si disse, 'Segnori [fol. 136r] chavalieri, non ve sgumentate, qué per aventura averemo melio che voy non credete. E io ve prometo come[286] chavaliere que tuti li chavalieri que voy trovarete, vuollio que voy n'abiate honore; e tute gioe e altre aventure que avenire possagno, vuollio que sianno al vostro comandamento. Cierto de queste cosse devereste essere alegro, quando siete mandato a choysì alta ventura sichome prendere filliola de Re – e per forse d'arme; e si non per forse d'arme, potemo menare afine questa ventura. Noy seremo nomiati sobra tuti altri chavalieri del mondo'.

E li chavalieri resposeno e disseno, 'Tristano, voy si avete promesso grande dono de vostre chavallarie; may tuta fiata sapete bene che en tuti parte di mondo, noy non siemo odiati quanto en lo realme de Landa; e però noy <non> volemo venire en questa parte là on[de] noy saperemo bene de recevere morte enanti si volemo laysare estrugere'. May Tristano tanto prometi ali chavalieri que ala fine disseno, 'Tristano, noy faremo vostro comandamento'.

[46] Ora disse lo conto che li chavalieri non s'arendiano andare con Tristano si non perqué si confidavanno ende le prodesse de Tristano. E Tristano encontenente presse una nave e·ffesse la conçiare choma si cho[n]ve[fol. 136v]ne: fesse i metere pavalione e arme e altri arnessi asay. E comandoe ali <d>chavalieri e ali damisselli que debiano essere en soa conpagnia que da inde al terço dì si ànno recolti ala lor nave con lo lor arnessi, 'sapiendo qual decto termino io vuolio

---

[284]   Four full lines blank; miniature never executed.
[285]   MS *Recoare* with an *l* inserted later. See below (fol. 136v): *recollar*.
[286]   MS *coma*.

Everyone will say that I am a disloyal knight. And for this reason I would first put myself into a fatal adventure than to be held a disloyal knight, that is to forestall being called disloyal'. Tristan realized this, and he said to King Mark, 'Since it is your will that I put myself ||| at risk in order to have Yseut, I will risk myself and I'll do everything in my power so that you have the damsel'.

[fol. 135v] And the king said to Tristan, 'I command you by the fealty due me that you take whatever you need and prepare your ship, and gather whatever company it pleases you to take along. And you must leave Cornwall and not return until such time as you may come with the damsel, that is Yseut'. And Tristan said, 'King Mark, I will do as you command'; and he sent for knights and young men of Cornwall (and he must have had about fifty of them come). And after they had come into the hall of the palace, he told them, 'It is very true' – said Tristan – 'that King Mark commanded me for his sake to order you to keep me company on an adventure which requires conquest and force of arms, and this adventure is in the kingdom of Ireland'.

The knights began to make a great lament upon hearing these words, saying, 'Now we clearly see that King Mark is sending us to Ireland with Tristan so that we die, because we can surely know that Tristan killed the Morholt of Ireland; and if we go to this kingdom, we'll all be dead; yet Tristan will be able to save himself and us by his prowess. For this reason, lords, before letting ourselves be destroyed, let's go on toward Ireland'.

And when Tristan heard these words, he said, 'Sir [fol. 136r] knights, don't be frightened, because with luck we'll come out better than you believe. And I promise you – as a knight – that from all the knights you find, I want you to have honor from them; and of all the joys and other adventures that come to pass, I want them to be at your command. Certainly, you must be happy about these things since you are being sent on such a noble adventure as to obtain the daughter of a king, and by force of arms; and if not by force of arms, we can bring this adventure to a close. We will be renowned above all the other knights in the world'.

And the knights replied and said, 'Tristan, you have promised a great boon by your chivalric deeds; but nonetheless you know well that, in all the parts of the world, we are not hated as much as in the kingdom of Ireland; and yet we want to go to this place where we surely know that we'll receive death rather than wanting to remain and be destroyed'. But Tristan promised so much to the knights that, in the end, they said, 'Tristan, we will do as you command'.

[46] Now the tale says that the knights would not have submitted to going with Tristan if not for the fact that they entrusted themselves to Tristan's prowess. At once Tristan got a ship and had prepared what was needful: [fol. 136v] he had pavilions and arms and a lot of other equipment put on board. And he commanded his knights and young men to rejoin his company, that the third day hence they must be gathered at their ship with their equipment, 'knowing that on

partire'. May tute le dame e damisselle de Cornavalia, entendendo come Tristano e li .l. chavalieri si partivanno qué devon andare ende le parte de Landa, là on[de] quelli de Cornavalia sono più odiati che en tuto li autre parte del mondo, e' chomençono a fare gran lamento e dissendo tuti comunamente che lo Re per ucidere Tristano e tuti li soy compagni manda per Yssota en Landa perché sono enemissi.

May Tristano s'aparecha per recollar si ala nave con li soy baroni e damisselli, e cominçono a menare grande alegresse de questa aventura, e disse enfra sé estesse, 'Ben chonosscho che lo Re Marcho non mi manda en questa aventura per mio bene, qué si de queste cosse mi potesse remanere con mio honore, volentieri lo farey. May po[y]qué io l'ò promesso, debo me ne alegrare dapoyqué sonno messo en l'aventura d'avere filiola de Re e per forsse d'arme. Ora potrò sapere si io potrò neuna coss[fol. 137r]<ss>e d'arme. E si io non debo volere darme mollie che io moia quando ò li boni chavalieri che con li rey viva con li malvasi de Cornavallia'.[287] E[n] cotal manera si conforta Tristano.

May enpresse de questo parolle lo termene s'apressa, e Tristano si recolie verso la nave con tuti li soy chavalieri e damisselli que <non> andar con luy. E lo Re Marcho l'acompagna fina ala nave[288] del mare con tuti li soy baroni. Alo partire que'l Re fesse, si disse a Tristano, 'Fa' tanto che io abia la damissella che io t'abo decto'. E Tristano disse, 'Meser, io ne farò lo mio podere'. E a tanto si partitte lo Re e andoe a soe palaçio. E Tristano comandò al may[s]tro marinaio que fassa la più dritta via que poe per andare ver Landa. El marinaio encontenente driçoe la vela. El tenpo èy bono, e 'l mare sensa tenpesta sì con ligno vae per mare con gioa. |||[289]

May la note enchomençoe lo mare una grande tenpesta siché ebeno granda paora de morire, tanto que lo vento portò loro en lo realme di [fol. 137v] Longres, tanto quelli foron al por[to] de Longres. E Tristano dimanda li marinari, 'Onde siamo noy?' E li disseron, 'Noy siamo el realme de Longues'. E Tristano fa metere fori li pavalione come chavalieri erranti si volesseno conbatere con noy.[290] Alora disse Tristano, 'Io coisì vuolio'. Alora li conpagni avean gran paora che chavalieri non passaseno.

[47] A tanto vegneno due chavalieri ensieme qu'erano missi de Gamelloti sensa chonossere l'uno l'autro. Elino era[n] facto chavalieri novello, e videno questi pavaliogni estessi ala marina, cavalchone en quelle parte; e quando foron presso ali pavalione, demandoron g[i]ustra ali chavalieri a guissa de chavalieri eranti. E tanto disseno li chavalieri ch'eranno enviati el realme de Longres. Disseno [a Tristano][291] che 'li chavalieri que sono làye dimandano giustra ali

---

[287] MS *Connavallia*.
[288] Thus in the MS. This passage is longer and does not correspond to either TR, p. 90 or TP, p. 177.
[289] Five full lines left blank; miniature never executed.
[290] *Saut du même au même* in MS. The narrative is more complete in TR, p. 90: '*sse passaserono cavalieri erranti, sì vorreberono kombattere, e noi non vorremo kombattere, noi*'.
[291] Emendation based on content of TR, p. 92.

Il Tristano Riccardiano *(Parodi's siglum 'F')*

the aforesaid day I want to depart'. But all the ladies and damsels of Cornwall, upon hearing how Tristan and the fifty knights were leaving because they had to go to the region of Ireland where those of Cornwall were more hated than in all the other parts of the world, began to make a great lamentation, all of them agreeing that 'in order to kill Tristan and all his companions, the king is sending for Yseut in Ireland, because they are enemies'.

But Tristan readied himself to assemble at the ship with his barons and young men, and they began to display great happiness about this adventure. And Tristan said to himself, 'I know very well that King Mark is not sending me on this adventure for my health, so that if I could put off these things with my honor, I would gladly do it. But since I promised him, I must take cheer about them, given that I am setting off on an adventure to get the daughter of a king, and by force of arms. Now I'll be able to find out if I'm worth anything [fol. 137r] at fighting; and if I must not want to get myself a wife, then may I die since I have good knights who with the wicked are living with evildoers of Cornwall'.

But after these words, the established date was approaching, and Tristan went on his way toward the ship to meet with all his knights and young men who were going with him; and King Mark accompanied him as far as the seaworthy ship with all his barons. On the leave-taking that the king took, he said to Tristan, 'Do all in your power so that I have the damsel that I told you about'; and Tristan said, 'Sire, I will do my best'. And at that the king left and went to his palace. And Tristan commanded the ship's master to take the most direct route that he could to go to Ireland; and the seaman immediately set sail, and the weather was fine, and the sea without storms so that he sailed on the ship with joy. |||

But at night a great tempest began so that they were greatly afraid of dying. So strong was the wind that it carried them to the kingdom of [fol. 137v] Logres, so far that they were at the port of Logres. And Tristan asked the seamen, 'Where are we?' And they told him, 'We're in the kingdom of Logres'. And Tristan had the pavilions set up outside, 'as errant knights do if they would like to fight with us'. Then Tristan said, 'Such do I want'. Then his companions were greatly afraid that knights might indeed pass by.

[47] Meanwhile, two knights from Camelot had met up without recognizing each other. They were newly-made knights and, upon seeing these pavilions stretched along the seashore, they rode over to that place; and when they were near the pavilions, they demanded to joust with the knights in the fashion of errant knights. And then the knights said that they had been sent to the kingdom of Logres. They told Tristan that 'the knights who are over there are demanding to joust with knights,

chavalieri, e dichano qui sono quilli chavalieri'. E alora [Tristano] si fae portar le arme e vàssene ali chavalieri. E quello che prima fo facto chavaliere laysay venire enversso Tristano e percossìli siqué li ronpoe la lançia en su la targia. E Tristano percossì a luy seché (sic) lo porta a terra da cavallo. A tanto si laysa avenire lo novello chavaliere e fierì a Tristano e ronpe li la la[n]çia adosso. E Tristano fierì a luy e passòli la targia e l'e[fol. 138r]sberguo e messe li la lançia per le carne e messelo a terra da cavallo.

Alora dissenno li chavalieri a Tristano, 'Chavaliere, chi sete voy che si avete abatuti?' E Tristano disse, 'Voi non potete sapere mio nome'. E li chavalieri disseno, 'De que paesse sette voy?' E Tristano disse, 'Io sonno de Cornavalia'. 'Oì, Dey', disseronno quilli, 'Chi vi t'à menati li chavalieri de Cornavalle a g[i]ostrare ende 'l realme de Longres?' 'Cierto', disse l'uno, 'dapoyqué fo facto chavaliere, queste èi la prima ventura che chavaliere m'avegne. Donqua non voy[292] g[i]amay portare arme quando li chavalieri de Cornavalia m'anno vinto! Doncha non porterò giamay arme enfina que io non sonno con li conpagni de la Taula Retonta, e siemo abatuti per mano de li chavalieri de Cornavalia sichome sono io'. E alora gitoe lo chavaliere novello tute l'arme e andòsene fassendo lo magiore [pianto] <delo> del mondo.[293] E l'autro conpagnone non gitoe soe arme, may partì si. Alora si ànno veduto li chavalieri de Cornavalia sichome Messer Tristano que s'ey deliberati de due chavalieri que coissì bono d'arme ebe de Longrues, e si tienono asay più sechuri[294] per la bontà de Tristano.

[48] Alora giu[n]çe[295] en quello metessmo porto una nave que venia suso lo Re Languis de Landa – con .xl. chavalieri en soa compania – el quale era apellato de tradimento da Bramor,[296] choissino de Lanceloto, ch'e' Re avea morto [fol. 138v] o facto morire en soa corte en Landa a uno chavaliere, lo quale chavaliere era de Re Bando de Banucho<a>.[297] E quando lo Re Languis vidi al porto li pavalioni en terra, disse enfra suo chuore, 'Or fosse questo Tristano de Cornavalia! – ché si luy trovasse, io camperia de morte de Bramor che si è bono chavaliere, ché contra luy non poterò re[s]istire'. Alora fo decto alo Re, 'Ell'è Tristano de Cornavalia'. A tanto demandoe lo Re, 'Ovv'è Tristano?' Fone li ensegnato, e viene lo Re enversso de Tristano molto alegramente e [Tristano] verso luy; e fo l'uno e l'autro grande festa. E chominçò a dire que novelle ello avea. ||| [298] E lo Re disse, 'Io l'òe rie, may ogimay[299] l'averò bone da qu'io t'ò trovato, qué al tempo que voy e noy faciamo lo torniamento ende lo realme de Landa – sichome tu say – si viene uno chavaliere en mia corte

---

[292] Cf. TR, p. 92 and TP, p. 178: *voglio*.
[293] Omission in MS emended with TR, p. 92: *facendo la magiore pianto del mondo*.
[294] MS *segnore*. Emendation based on TR, p. 92: *sicuri*.
[295] MS *giuçe* or *ginçe*. See TR, p. 92: *giugne*.
[296] Lancelot's cousin who accused King Anguin is properly *Blanor* (West, p. 41).
[297] Scribe wrote a superscript *a* at the end of this name.
[298] Five full blank lines; miniature never executed.
[299] MS *omni may*. TR, p. 92: *oggimai*.

and they say that they are knights'. And then Tristan had his arms brought and went out to the knights. And the one who had been knighted first let himself come toward Tristan and struck him so that he broke his lance on his targe; and Tristan struck him so that he carried him to the ground from his horse. In that moment the second new knight let himself come and struck Tristan and broke his lance against him; and Tristan struck him and ran him through the targe and the [fol. 138r] hauberk and put his lance into his flesh and knocked him to the ground from his horse.

Then the knights said to Tristan, 'Knight, who are you who have beaten us?' And Tristan said, 'You may not know my name'. And the knights said, 'What country are you from?' And Tristan said, 'I am from Cornwall'. 'Oh, God', those fellows said, 'who has brought knights from Cornwall here to joust in the kingdom of Logres?' 'In truth', said one, 'since I was knighted, this is the first chivalric adventure that I have met with. Therefore I don't ever again want to bear arms since the knights of Cornwall have defeated me! Therefore I will never bear arms until I'm with the companions of the Round Table and they are struck down by the hand of Cornish knights as I am'; and then the new knight threw down all his arms and went off making the greatest lament in the world. And the other companion did not throw down his arms, but he surely did leave. Then the knights of Cornwall saw how Sir Tristan was delivered from two knights who were as good at arms as any that Logres had, and they felt much safer because of Tristan's ability.

[48] Then in that same port a ship arrived that had aboard King Anguin of Ireland – with forty knights in his company – who had been accused of treachery by Blanor,* Lancelot's cousin, for having murdered [fol. 138v] – or having had put to death in his court in Ireland by a knight – one of King Ban of Benwick's knights. And when King Anguin at the port saw the pavilions on the ground, he said in his heart, 'If only this were Tristan of Cornwall! Because if he could be found, I would be spared from Blanor who is a good knight, because I won't be able to withstand him'. Then the king was told, 'He is Tristan of Cornwall'. At that the king asked, 'Where is Tristan?' He was pointed out to him. And the king came toward Tristan very happily, and Tristan toward him, and they rejoiced greatly together. And Tristan began to ask what news he had. ||| The king said, 'I have bad news, but this very day I will have good news, given that I found you: because at the time that you and we had the tournament in the kingdom of Ireland – as you know – a knight came to my court, of King Ban of Benwick's lineage,

---

* MS consistently misuses *Bramor* for Lancelot's cousin and Anguin's accuser. My emendation follows the French prose *Tristan*. See West, p. 41.

del parentato de Re Bando de Benichio, ed ey li fisse honore de quello che io podey. Lo chavaliere fo morto en mia corte, e non so en che manera. Or m'à apellato Bramor a corte del Re Arturo de batallia, e io so[300] bene che con Bramor defender [fol. 139r] mi non posso, chè tropo èi bono chavaliere. May ti prego per l'amor che io ti porto e per alchuno servicio que io t'ò facto e que io fare ti potesse, che tu mi debie fare esta batalia per me. E io ti prometerò come chavaliere che io en le morte del chavaliere non ebe colpa'.

[49] E Tristano disse, 'Alora io lo faroe volontieri questa batallia. E jurarete mi su le Sancti Evvangeli que voy de la morte del chavaliere non aveste colpa, e darete me uno dono lo quale io ve demandaroe'. E lo Re disse, 'Qualunque ti poterò fare'. E Tristano disse, 'Si voy non lo mi potete fare, non lo mi farete'. A tanto foron acordati. E fanno gran fessta li chavalieri di Cornavalia e e' tessino ogimay[301] per campati le loro perssone che si tenian en prima tuti morti.

[50] A tanto andava Tristano solaciando con li chavalieri de li pavalioni. Tanto susso e tanto andoe che viene una damissella que portava uno eschudo al collo. Eran dipinto dintro unno Re e una Redina |||[302] [fol. 139v] a oro<ro> e 'l campo arsuro, e era operto l'eschudo per meçio fino ala bocha del chavaliere e de la donna. E alora Tristano saludò la damissella, e la damissella Tristano; e alora disse Tristano ala damissella, 'Di' me, per amore de te, que quosse sonno queste de chesto chavaliere e de questa Redina?' Disse la damissella a Tristano, 'Cierto, voy me parete chavaliere de grando affare: io ve ne dirò parte. Questo eschudo si era mandato, e non lo trovo a Gamelloto la persona a chuy era mandato. Vado chi ond'ello è.[303] E quilli è uno chavaliere e una dama che s'amavanno de granda amore e non ebenno a fare ongna l'uno con l'autro, e sonno chome voy videte quie – e non credeno que neuno sapia lo lor facto. E quando elli non[304] averan conpiuto il loro amore, si se chuderà l'escudo e serà coysì forte ende 'l megio sichome en altra parte'.

A tanto si parte la damissella sensa più dire e cavalca fine al'intrada d'uno boscho; ed ebe trovato uno chavaliere, ed illo li disse, 'Damissella, da' me l'eschudo che ày'. Ella disse que non farae. Alora li tolse lo chavaliere l'escudo qu'ella avea e diedi li de molte bossie, over colpi,[305] ala damissella. E la damissella torna |||[306] [fol. 140r] endirietro a Tristano. E Tristano, quando lo vide, disse, 'Damissella, que ày tue?' Ella li disse tuto lo facto, e Tristano chiamò Guovernalle e fasse venire l'arme; encontenente li foe araghata. E disse Tristano alo chavaliere, 'Si tue vuolio conbatere, ora te n'apello'. Alora lo chavaliere disse che sie.

Alora<ri> lo chavaliere ferite Tristano e rompite li la lanc[i]a adosso, e Tristano ferite lo chavaliere e chaçiete lo a terra da cavallo. E Tristano disse, 'Damissella,

---

300 MS *fo*. Confusion of *s* / *f*.
301 MS *gionny*. Cf. TR, p. 94: *si tengono ogimai*.
302 Six full lines left blank at bottom of writing space; miniature never executed.
303 Cf. TR, p. 94: *andai cercando quivi ov'egli èe*.
304 Pleonastic use of *non*, not a negation.
305 Here as elsewhere, the scribe uses *over* to self-correct a word he had previously written.
306 Two lines left blank at base of writing space, but not enough space for a miniature.

and for that I paid him such honor as best I could. The knight was killed in my court, but I don't know in what manner. Now Blanor has summoned me to King Arthur's court to do battle, and I know well that [fol. 139r] I can't defend myself with Blanor who is such a good knight. But I pray you, for the love that I bear you and for any service that I have done you and that I could still do for you, to undertake this battle for me. And I will promise you, as a knight, that I had no fault in the knight's death'.

[49] And Tristan said, 'Well then, I'll undertake this battle for you, if you will swear to me on the Holy Gospels that you weren't guilty of the knight's death and will grant me a boon that I will ask of you'. And the king said, 'Whatever I may be able to do for you'. And Tristan said, 'If you can't do it for me, don't do it for me'. To this they agreed. And the knights of Cornwall rejoiced greatly, and this very day they considered their persons saved because earlier they held themselves all dead men.

[50] After that Tristan was going along, enjoying himself with the knights from the pavilions; and he went so far along that a damsel came who was carrying a shield at her neck. On it was painted a king and a queen ||| [fol. 139v] in gold on an azure field, and the shield was split open down the middle as far as the mouths of the knight and the lady. And then Tristan greeted the damsel, and the damsel Tristan; and then Tristan said to the damsel, 'Tell me, for your sake, what things are these, about this knight and about this queen?' The damsel said to Tristan, 'In truth, you seem to me a knight of great deeds: I will tell you, in part. This shield was sent, and I did not find in Camelot the person to whom it was sent so I'm seeking him here. And these are a knight and a lady who love each other greatly and have had no more contact one with the other than you see here, and they don't believe that anyone knows about their doings; but when they will have consummated their love, the shield will close itself and be as sturdy in the middle as elsewhere'.

At that the damsel left without saying any more and rode as far as the entrance to a wood; and she found a knight, and he said to her, 'Damsel, give me the shield that you have', but she said she would not. Then the knight seized the shield that she had from her and gave the damsel many slaps, or rather, blows; and the damsel returned ||| [fol. 140r] back to Tristan. And Tristan, when he saw her, said, 'Damsel, what's wrong with you?' and she told him the whole story. Tristan called Governal and had his arms brought; they were brought to him at once. And Tristan said to the knight, 'If you want to fight, I am challenging you now'. Then the knight said he did.

Then the knight struck Tristan and broke his lance against him, and Tristan struck the knight and knocked him to the ground from his horse. And Tristan said, 'Damsel,

prende l'eschudo'. E Tristano disse, 'Chavaliere, lo ti viene a dire tue no<no>me'. |||[307] Eli disse, 'Fiderae mi tu la persona ed io vel diroe'. E Tristano disse, 'Io de ne fido'. Ed ello li disse, 'Io sono Breus'. (E quando Tristano lo sepe, non lo volerà aver fidato per una ciptate!) E alora li comanda Tristano que vada a Meser Galvagno 'per mio preysono, da mia parte'. Alora disse Breus que non lo ne mandasse[308] per Dio, ançi l'ançidesse – disse elli a Tristano. E Tristano disse, 'Io ti ne manti perquè ello t'oiçida quando io t'abo fi[fol. 140v]dato'.

Alora li viene Breus fina ali pavalione, preguando lo que non lo li mandasse; a tanto pur fo mestieri quello vi andasse. E la damissella si contoe novelle a Tristano sichome lo Re Arturo e la Redina non eran a Gamelloto, may eravi de quelli del Re Bando de Benuçi tuti – salvo Lançeloto – e che espetavano de far batallia con lo Re Languis de Landa; ed era vi remasso lo Re Achano, e lo Re de Cento Chavalieri. Recordoe <a>[309] Tristano tuta l'aventura de l'eschudo e de la damissella e de Breus, e·ffesse ne grando solacio. E contanno alora sichome lo Re Achano debia judicare la batalia da luy a Bramor: 'però andiamo, que melio èi aspaçiare sene[310] per tenpo che tardi'. Asò s'acordano de fare. Alora montoe a chavallo lo Re Languis con .xl. chavalieri – tuti vestiti a seta: eli s'adornano che pare ben Re. E Tristano avea drapi asay e non vuolle[311] andare, si non armato; e uno chavaliere li porta l'eschudo e uno altro la lançia. Alora disse che neuno non diga soe nome.

[51] Ora gio[n]sse lo Re Languis a Gamelletto, e giunçeron quilli que di' judicare la batalia. E lo Re Languis disse, 'Io sonno venuto a defender mi del tradimento che io sonno apellato sichomo leale chavaliere e qu'io non ebe colpa [fol. 141r] de la morte del chavaliere que io sonno encolpato'. E Tristano disse, 'Io per lo Re Languis dicho que de la morte de lo chavaliere non ebe colpa. Enperò io sonno aparech[i]ato di conbater con lo chavaliere que li a pone queste cosse'. Alora Tristano v'à dato lo g[u]anto a Bramor, e Bramor lo recevete.

A tanto issite fora tuta la gente de Gamelloto ala batalia, e Tristano contra e intra al travalio, e Meser Bordo, e con ello Astor da Mare [e] Meser Broberis de Gaules. E chiamano Bramor en una camera e disson li, 'Or ti cho[n]viene essere bono chavaliere siché non requi onta a cassa che noy non ensemo ussati'. Disse, 'Que chavaliere èi Meser Lanceloto?' Elli disse, 'Voy mi vederete'.[312] Ed illi dissenno, 'Tu ày a fare con uno gioiosso chavaliere al nostro parere'.

[307] Six full lines blank; miniature never executed.
[308] MS *mandasso*.
[309] In the MS, it seems that the damsel is recounting this, which is illogical. Cf. TR, p. 96: *igli ricontoe Tristan*. Also in TP, p. 182: *contò Tristano tutta la ventura*.
[310] The spelling *spaçiarsi* is also found in comense dialect (see *La Spagna in rima del manoscritto comense*, ed. Giovanna Barbara Rosiello, *Il cavaliere del leone* 3 (Turin, 2001), p. 553). The Tuscan form is *spacciare* (see *I cantari di Fiorabraccia e Ulivieri: testo mediano inedito*, ed. Elio Melli, Biblioteca di Filologia Romanza della Facoltà di Lettere e Filosofia dell'Università di Bologna 3 [Bologna, 1984], p. 257).
[311] MS *vuolse*. Confusion of *s* / *l*, as elsewhere.
[312] MS is abbreviated here. Cf. TR, p. 98 for the fuller narrative.

take your shield'. And Tristan said, 'Knight, it behooves you to tell your name'. |||
And he said, 'If you guarantee my safety, I'll tell you'. And Tristan said, 'I guarantee it'. And he told him, 'I am Breus'. (And when Tristan found out, he would not have spared him for a whole city!) And then Tristan commanded him to go to Sir Gawain 'as my prisoner, for my sake'. Then Breus said that he shouldn't send him there 'for God's sake'; instead that Tristan should kill him, so he said to Tristan. But Tristan said, 'I'm sending you there so that he will kill you, since I have spared you'.

[fol. 140v] Then Breus came with [Tristan] as far as the pavilions, begging him not to send him to [Gawain]; and yet it really was needful for him to go there. And the damsel recounted news to Tristan, how King Arthur and the queen were not at Camelot, but there were all those of King Ban of Benwick – except for Lancelot – and that they were waiting to do battle with King Anguin of Ireland, and King Acanor had remained there, and the King of the Hundred Knights. Tristan recounted the whole adventure of the shield and about the damsel and about Breus, and he was greatly amused by it. And then they recounted how King Acanor had to adjudicate the battle between him and Blanor: 'for this reason let us go, for it's better to get ourselves going sooner than later'. This they agreed to do. Then King Anguin mounted his horse, with forty knights all dressed in silk so ornately that they did indeed seem kings; and Tristan wore much finery (but he only wanted to go armed), and one knight carried his shield for him and another his lance. Then he said that no one should tell his name.

[51] Now King Anguin arrived at Camelot, and all those who must judge the battle. And King Anguin said, 'I have come to defend myself from the treachery for which I have been accused, as a faithful knight, and that I was not guilty [fol. 141r] of the knight's death for which I am accused'. And Tristan said, 'I speak for King Anguin when I say that he had no fault in the knight's death. For this reason I am ready to fight with the knight who has accused him of these things'. Then Tristan gave the glove of combat to Blanor, and Blanor received it.

Then all the people went out of Camelot to the battle, and Tristan with them – and he entered the trial – and Sir Bors, and with him Hector of the Fens and Sir Blioberis of Gaul. And they called Blanor into a chamber and told him, 'Now it behooves you to be a good knight so that you don't bring unaccustomed shame to our house'. They said, 'Do you know what a knight Sir Lancelot is?' He said, 'You will see me'. And they said, 'You'll have your hands full with an accomplished knight, in our opinion'.

A tanto si viegnono a campo e viegnonno ensieme ala batalia e danno si del campo tan[to] con fa mestieri. E fieron si de le lançe, pecto per pecto e de li cavalli l'uno con l'aut[r]o, e li chavalieri vissagio per vissagio ||||[313] [fol. 141v] siché chiascaduno cadeno, e li cavalli. Alora si leva chiascadumo chavaliere sichome prodi e arditi, e 'nchominçano lo primo asalto[314] siché nessuna persona non li potte biasmare. E chiaschaduno si pilla volont[i]er[i] a lena e forssa.

Or si levan Tristano el secondo asalto e disse, 'Chavaliere, tropo siemo repausati'; e chominçano alo secondo asalto sì bene e sì forte che molte mallia vanno per terra, e li schudi ve sonno molti trevalliati, e chiaschaduno si possa volontieri <E> de lo secondo asalto. Alora Leonello e Bordo e Meser Astore e li autre fratelli de Bramor vedeno palessamente que Bramor n'àe lo pegiore de la batalia. Allora disse Bramor a Tristano, 'Io volio que ti plaçia de dire me tuo nome, e io ti dirò prima lo mio: perché si tu m'ançide, saperay qui tue averay morto; e si onçiderò te, saperò qu'io averò morto'. A tanto disse Tristano, 'Or di' lo toe nome'. E lo chavaliere disse, 'I'ò nome Bramor, chussino de Lanceloto'. E Tristano disse, 'E io sono Tristano de Cornavalia'. Alora fo molto alegro Bramor quando sepe que conbatea con chotale chavaliere. E disse Bramor, 'Perché io remagna perdente, no[n] me èi dessognore'.

[52] Alora si leva Tristano e cominça la batalia forte e dura; e del[fol. 142r] lo terço asalto, si viegneno descop[r]endo le carne. Alora Bramor recevete uno grande collpi da Tristano chome chavaliere de grande vertue, sich'ello cade a terra enginollie li si ali piede e possa reverto en terra. E Tristano li disse, 'Chome, conpagnone, non conbateremo noy più?' E lo chavaliere disse, 'Per mia fé, *non*,[315] que io non posso più re[s]istire'. A tanto si ne vae Tristano davançia alo Re Achano e alo Re di Cento Chavalieri e disse, 'Segnori, lo chavaliere àe tanto bene facto que non si poe biasmare. Prego ve che metette passe da me e di lo chavaliere', e deliberate lo Re Languis da quello che aposto li foe. Alora si trayseron a consil[lio] li due Re; e disseno, 'Chavaliere, tu sey segnore d'andare o d'estare al tuo piaçere'. Disseno, 'Echo lo più cortese chavaliere del mondo que vuolle passe chon l'omo vinto' – e soe dichanno li due Re – 'el Re Languis è bene deliberato [de] sua enquesta'.

Alora si viene Tristano al soe destrieri e gieta si ve susso sensa metere pè en estaffa e con l'espada nuda en mano, e recha en mano lo freno e vàssene con gran salti del destrieri. Alora disse tuta la gente, 'Noy credevamo quel chavaliere [fol. 142v] fosse molto ferito, ed ello èy montato en tal manera a chavallo sensa metere piè ende l'estaffa!' Alora chiaschuno disse, 'Questo èy lo più valente chavaliere del mondo: non ase[m]bra que abia conbattuto'.

A tanto viene lo Re Languis de Landa e disse, 'Segnori, date mi parolla che io mi parta, qué si lo mio chavaliere v'andasse sensa me, io non lo p<r>oteria[316] poy trovare'. Alora disse lo Re Achanno, 'Ditte mi lo nome de lo chavaliere; poy

---

313 Five full lines left blank at bottom of writing space.
314 MS *alsaltio*.
315 In MS written with a titulus. Gallicism.
316 MS *proreria* or *proteria*, fourth letter hard to read (faded ink and ink blot on this word).

Il Tristano Riccardiano *(Parodi's siglum 'F')* 93

At that point they came to the field, and they came together to the battle and took their positions on the field as was needed. And they struck each other with their lances, and the horses one against the other chest to chest, and the knights face to face ||| [fol. 141v] so that each one fell down, with the horses. Then each knight got up as valiant and bold men do and began their first assault so that no one could criticize them. And then, by resting, each one willingly regained energy and strength.

Now Tristan began the second assault and said, 'Knight, we have paused too long'; and they began the second assault so well and so strongly that many pieces of chain mail flew to the earth, and their shields took a lot of punishment from it, and each of them paused willingly from the second assault. Then Lionel and Bors and Sir Hector and the other brothers of Blanor clearly saw that Blanor was having the worst of the battle. Then Blanor said to Tristan, 'I want you to tell me your name, if you please, and I'll tell you mine first so that if you kill me, you'll know whom you have killed; and if I kill you, I'll know whom I have killed'. At that Tristan said, 'Now tell your name'. And the knight said, 'I am called Blanor, cousin of Lancelot'. And Tristan said, 'And I am Tristan of Cornwall'. Then Blanor was very happy when he found out that he was fighting with such a knight; and Blanor said, 'Although I may end up losing, it does not dishonor me'.

[52] Then Tristan arose and began the battle, hard and fierce; and in [fol. 142r] the third assault, [their torn mail] was revealing their flesh. Then Blanor received a great blow from Tristan, like a knight of great worth, so that he fell to his knees on the ground at Tristan's feet and then fell backwards onto the ground. And Tristan said to him, 'What, comrade, aren't we fighting any longer?' but the knight said, 'By my faith, *non*, because I cannot stand any more'. At that Tristan went before King Acanor and the King of the Hundred Knights and said, 'Lords, the knight has done so well that one cannot fault him. I pray you to make peace between me and the knight, and to deliver King Anguin from what was placed upon him'. Then the two kings withdrew to take counsel, and they said, 'Knight, you may go or stay at your pleasure'. They said, 'Here is the most courteous knight in the world, who wants to make peace with the defeated man' – this the two kings said – 'and King Anguin is completely delivered from his accusation'.

Then Tristan came to his horse and threw himself into the saddle – without putting his foot in the stirrup – and with his naked sword in hand. And he gathered up the reins and went along with his warhorse making great bounds. Then all the people said, 'We believed that knight [fol. 142v] was badly injured, but he mounted his horse in such fashion, without putting his foot in the stirrup!' Then everyone said, 'This is the most valiant knight in the world: it doesn't even seem that he has fought'.

In that moment King Anguin of Ireland came and said, 'Lords, grant me leave to depart, because if my knight were to go away without me, then I wouldn't be able to find him'. Then King Acanor said, 'Tell me the knight's name; then go

andate con Dio'. E lo Re Languis disse, 'Io non l'audo[317] dire'. 'Per mia fé', disse lo Re Achano, 'en tal manera non ve partirete'. Alora disse lo Re Languis, 'Lo chavaliere si è Tristano de Cornavalia, filliolo del Re Meliadus'.

A tanto si parte lo Re Languis e quanto ne potre andare apresso a Tristano con tuta soa gente. Ed <avide>[318] a poci giorni lo gio[n]ssi e sonno si retrovati ala marina ali pavaliogni. E trovano li chavalieri de Cornavalia, e fanno grande feste, e fanno chome alo Re encontrato. Alora disse lo Re Languis a Tristano, 'Che faray, Tristano, o de lo andare u dello estare?' E Tristano pensa enfra sé metessmo que pare a luy lo melliore andare enver Landa con luy que sensa luy. Alora disse Tristano alo Re Languis [fol. 143r] ch'ello volea andar con luy en Verlanda. Molto ne foe lieto e gio[io]sso lo Re.

Encontenente montono a [la nave][319] e viegneno tanto per lur giorn<i>ate[320] che sonno gionti en Landa. E quando gi[un]sse la nave al porto e videno l'ensegne del Re Languis, tuta la gente trahea al porto e videno che lo Re tornava con sua gente (credendo tuta gente que lo Re Languis non tornasse may, però qu'ello conbateia con uno bono chavaliere). Lo Re Languis dessende a terra con la soa gente ||||[321] e con Tristano; li chavalieri e li baronie e la Redina [e] Yssota la Bronda, e dichono tuti, 'Meser lo Re, voi siate ben tornate, lo Dio merçe'. Alora disse lo Re, 'S'io son tornato, laudor e la gracia e la mercede ne rendete a questo chavaliere, ché io si torna[fol. 143v]to[322] per soa bontà e per mia no, e aquestuy ne sapiate grado, ché per la soa bontà e per la sua prodessa, sì, sonno tornato'.

Alora viene la Redina e Yssota la Bronda a Tristano – e le dame e damisselle, chavalieri e baroni – e·ffacian tuti gran festa a Tristano; e vasto è la festa e l'alegresse .viii. giorni. A tanto lo Re fa rassonare[323] – per comandamento de Tristano – tuti li baroni de Landa e le dame e le damiselle debianno venire a corte. A tanto feronno asenbrati en uno palasio. Alora disse Tristano al Re, 'Io vuolio demandare lo dono lo quale io ve quissi'. Alora disse lo Re, 'Demanda que tu plaçe'. E disse Tristano, 'Io vuolio Madona Yssota la Bionda per molie del Re Marcho de Cornavalia'. E lo Re disse, 'Demande la tu per te o per lo Re Marcho?' E Tristano disse, 'Io la vuolio pur per lo Re Marcho'. E lo Re disse, 'Io la vuolio pur dar a te e altruy noe'. E Tristano disse, 'Io la vuolio pur ales tuto[324] per lo Re Marcho, ché io lo ho promesso'. E lo Re Languis disse, 'Promette me tue queste cosse sichome chavaliere?' E Tristano disse de sie. Alora prende lo Re Madonna Yssota la Bionda per la mano, e Tristano la sposò per lo Re Marcho. E t[r]aysse si Tristano verso de la donna sichome era lur ussata en quella parte. E

317   Cf. TR, p. 100: *Io non lo soe dire*. TP, p. 186: *Io no·llo so*.
318   Thus in MS. Word not found in corresponding passage in TR nor in TP.
319   MS *chavallo*. Cf. TR, p. 100: *vaselli*; TP, p. 186: *navi*.
320   Fifth letter written with three minims.
321   Seven full lines left blank; miniature never executed.
322   At end of recto, MS: *torno*. Correction mine.
323   Cf. TR, p. 102: *radunare*; TP, p. 186: *fa chiamare*.
324   Cf. TR, p. 102: *Io la voglio <u>pur</u> per lo ree*; TP, p. 186: *Io la voglio <u>al postutto</u> per lo re*. Emphasis added.

with God'. And King Anguin said, 'I don't dare say'. 'By my faith', said King Acanor, 'if such is the case, you'll not leave'. Then King Anguin said, 'The knight is Tristan of Cornwall, son of King Meliadus'.

In that moment King Anguin left and went as fast as he could go after Tristan, with all his people. And in a few days he caught up with him; and they found each other again at the seashore, at their pavilions. And they found the knights of Cornwall and celebrated greatly, and they did this as they met the king. Then King Anguin said to Tristan, 'What will you do, Tristan, either go or stay?' Tristan thought to himself that it seemed to him better to go on toward Ireland with him than without him. Then Tristan said to King Anguin [fol. 143r] that he wanted to go with him to Ireland. The king was very happy and joyful about it.

Immediately they got on board the ship and they went so far through their journeyings that they arrived in Ireland. And when the ship arrived at the port and they saw the insignia of King Anguin, all the people approached the port and saw that the king had returned with his people (all the people having believed that King Anguin would never return, given that he was fighting with a good knight). King Anguin went down to the ground with all his people ||| and with Tristan; the knights and the barons and the queen and Yseut the Blonde and everyone said, 'My Lord the King, welcome back, thanks to God'. Then the king said, 'If I have returned, render praise and give thanks for it to this knight; because I have returned [fol. 143v] due to his ability and not my own, and to this fellow you must be grateful since by his ability and his prowess I have indeed returned'.

Then the queen came over to Tristan, with Yseut, and the ladies and damsels, knights and barons; and they all celebrated greatly over Tristan; and the celebration and joy lasted eight days. At that time the king had it proclaimed – by order of Tristan – that all the barons of Ireland and their ladies and damsels must come to court. Then they assembled in a palace. Then Tristan said to the king, 'I want to ask the boon which I required of you'. Then the king said, 'Ask what you please'. And Tristan said, 'I want My Lady Yseut the Blonde as wife of King Mark of Cornwall'. And the king said, 'Are you asking for her for yourself or for King Mark?' And Tristan said, 'I do indeed want her for King Mark'. But the king said, 'Yet I want to give her to you and to no one else'. And Tristan said, 'In the end, I truly want her for King Mark because I promised him'. And King Anguin said, 'Do you promise me these things as a knight?' And Tristan said yes. Then the king took My Lady Yseut the Blonde by the hand, and Tristan wed her in King Mark's stead, and Tristan withdrew from the lady as was their custom in

[fol. 144r] enchominçano l'armeçare grande sichome may si vidésse. E fanno li chavalieri de Cornavalia grande festa perché èi facta de la guera gran pasce que molto ne sonno alegre li chavalieri. |||[325]

[53] Or[326] si viene aconsando e aparecchiando Tristano de tornare en Cornavalia con la damissella e con la sua gente; aparechiansi d'ire per mare. Alora donò la Redina a Madonna Yssota la Bionda molte giose e molte pietre preciosse sichome a tal donna sì cho[n]venia, e mena ne Yssota Brachina per sua[327] privata camerera over damissella. E quando montano su en la nave Tristano e Madonna Yssota, e tuti li chavalieri e li schudieri vanno armeçando ala marina e facendo gran gioia,[328] e le dame e damisselle facendo lur gran festa e solaçio.

A tanto si chiamò la Redina Governale e Branchina perché vede che colloro sonno reponitore [fol. 144v] <sonno reponitore> de l'oro e de l'argento e de le lur giosse tute. E disse lur, 'Tenete questi due flanqui[329] d'argento che èi pienno de beveragio d'amore, e gardate lo bene. E qu[a]ndo lo Re Marcho irà con Yssota la Bionda e[n] la prima <che> sera, date ne lur a bere; e quello che remane, gitate lo via'. Elli dichano che ben lo faranno. A tanto si parte Tristano e Yssota, e tuti si danno bon tempo.

Estando uno giorno, Tristano e Yssota e' guçavanno a schachi e non pensavano altro che bene l'uno con l'autro. (Già lur chuore non pensava follia d'amore.) Honde avendo gioçati ensieme giochi due ed eranno sobra al terço gioguo, et era grando caldo. E Tristano disse a Governale e a Branqu[i]na che lur desse a bere. Presse li fia[s]chi del beveragio e diede lur a bere non chonossendo che fosse isse. Governale presse una copa, e Branguina messe lo en la copa. E Governale diede lur a bere, prima a Meser Tristano. Ello la beve piena ché li façia gran sete. E l'autra copa diede a Yssota, e [fol. 145r] bevela e scoloe la copa en terra. E cade ne una choçia, e [el cane][330] lichoe la copa per grande sete che li facia. Adesso canbiò Tristano lo suo coragio, e non fo più en quello segno ch'era de prima – e Yssota lo semillante – e chomínçano a gardare l'uno l'autro. Enançi que conplissano quello gioghi, si si levaronno e andoron sene anboro en una camera e comínçano quello giogo que tuto lo tenpo de la lur vita gioçano volontieri. |||[331]

Or sen'andoe[332] Governale e Branguina che avean dato lo beveraçio amorosso a Tristano e a Yssota, e tenon si encolpati.

---

[325] Six full lines left blank just above mid-page; miniature never executed.
[326] Large red initial *O* signals the love potion episode.
[327] MS *fua*. Confusion of *s* / *f*.
[328] MS *giaa*.
[329] MS *fla* with titulus and *q(u)* abbreviation. Cf. TR, p. 102: *fiaschi*.
[330] MS omits the noun. Cf. TR, p. 104.
[331] Five and a half lines left blank; miniature never executed.
[332] Cf. TR, p. 104: *si n'adiede*; TP, p. 188: *s'avede*.

those parts. And [fol. 144r] they began a joust, as great as one ever saw, and the knights of Cornwall celebrated greatly because a lasting peace was made from the war, so that the knights were very happy about it. |||

[53] Now Tristan began readying himself and preparing to return to Cornwall with the damsel and with her people: they were preparing to go by sea. Then the queen gave My Lady Yseut the Blonde many jewels and many precious stones as was suitable for a lady of such rank, and she brought Brangain to Yseut to have as her trusted chambermaid, or rather damsel. And when Tristan and My Lady Yseut went aboard the ship, all the knights and squires went to the seashore, displaying feats of arms and cheering wildly; and the ladies and damsels were rejoicing and making merry for them as well.

In that moment the queen called Governal and Brangain aside because she saw that those two were custodians [fol. 144v] of the gold and silver and of all their jewels. And she told them, 'Keep these two silver flasks which are full of a love potion and guard them well; and when King Mark is about to go with Yseut the Blonde the first evening, give them to drink of it; and what remains, throw it away'. And they said that they would do so. Just then Tristan and Yseut departed, and everyone wished them good weather.

Sailing along like that one day, Tristan and Yseut were playing chess, and they weren't thinking of anything but good, one toward the other. (Their hearts had not yet thought of mad, foolish love.) Whence having played two games together, they were into the third game, and it was very hot. And Tristan bade Governal and Brangain to give him something to drink. Governal took the beverage flasks and gave them to drink, not realizing what they were. Governal got a drinking cup, and Brangain put it in the cup. And Governal gave them a drink, first to Sir Tristan. He drank deeply because he was very thirsty. And he gave the other cup to Yseut, and [fol. 145r] she drank it and poured out the cup onto the ground; and a drop of it fell, and the dog licked the cup because of the great thirst that he had. Now Tristan's heart changed, and he was no longer in the same mind as he was before – and Yseut similarly – and one began to look the other. Before they had completed that game, they rose and went off together into a chamber and began that game that for the rest of their lives they willingly played. |||

Now Governal and Brangain realized that they had given the love potion to Tristan and Yseut, and they held themselves at fault.

[54] A tanto andoron ala nave valicanto el tenpo de gran fortuna. [Ed allora sì s'acomandano a][333] Dio e li soy sancti que l'aytanno, e piançeano li marinari tuti. Al quarto giorno andonno chome porta la fortuna. Si si foron arivati al'Issola de Giganti, che qualunche chavaliere estranio v'ariva, si cho[n]viene che senpre may [fol. 145v] stia en preysone.

A tanto viegneno .xii. chavalieri al porto e disseno, 'Venite a terra ché voy siete tuti pressonieri'. Alora cominçano[334] tuti a piangere. E Yssota pia[n]çe e disse a Tristano, 'Ày mi menato de mia terra chie per essere preysonna quie?' Alora disse Tristano, 'Io meterò manno a conbatere fine a tanto che io averò de la vita en su questa nave; e dapoyché io non poterò più, Dio ve consillio'. Ancho Yssota disse, 'Moremo en tal modo?' Tristano [disse], 'Madonna, io non so que altro ve possa fare. Vi di[rò][335] se non afina que io poterò tenire l'espada en pogno, non vennero a mene'.[336] A tanto prendonno consillio que 'en preysone averemo alchuno remedio mellio che laysar si tuti ucidere in tal modo'.

A tanto sonno pressi tuti preysoni, e sonno messi ala porta[337] end'el Castello de Plio.[338] (E Yssota si apiatò l'espada de Tristano; tanto le altre cosse foron tute tolte.) E sonno intrate dintro ale altre porte e foronno messi dintro da lo castello e poneno mente per la[339] [fol. 146r] preysone qu'era en meço del casstello; e veramente parea lur pessima e vera sichome preyssone chu v'era messo, non en uissia mae,[340] nì vivo nì morto. La nocte, estano dintro, lo dì aproximò; e [passano][341] quella note con gran dollia.

Al matino si vienegno .ii. chavalieri a sapere come estanno li preysoni. A tanto si mette ennaçi Tristano e disse ali chavalieri, 'Devemo noy estare qua intro sempre may, o potemo noy essere a termine[342] neuno o per alchuna ventura?' E li chavalieri disseno, 'Sie, en tal manera si chie entre voy avesse uno tale chavaliere – lo quale non si par vedere – ch'elli fosse sì forte che per sua forsa e prodesse vinçesse el nostro signore; e la sua dama fosse sì bella – o più – che la sua'. Alora Tristano disse, 'Chi è uno che s'aracharae[343] bene la sua persona con quella di vostro segnore e àçi donna que èi più bella che la vostra'. Li chavalieri disseno, 'Chome, chavaliere? Non è homo el mondo que con lo nostro segnore potesse con luy conbatere per defender si, altro que Lançeloto'.

[55] A tanto laysa ch<i>e lo conto dicono (sic) chome è chella ventura, e 'n qual modo, e perché quello castello era apellato 'Lo Castello de Plio'. Alora

---

333   Omission in MS. Insertion based on TR, p. 104.
334   MS *cominçana*.
335   Two letters covered by ink blot.
336   Clear in MS, but see TR, p. 104: *non vi verroe meno*.
337   MS *al porto*.
338   MS, here and below, *plio*. Cf. TR, p. 107: *Proro*.
339   Catchword in brown text ink, at center bottom (no red cartouche): *preysone*.
340   Cf. TR, p. 104: *non n'uscirae mai*.
341   Verb omitted in MS. Cf. TR, p. 104: *passano quella notte*.
342   Word is split over end of line with superscripted *r* and abbreviated: *at^r|mo*. Cf. TR, p. 104: *a·ttermine*.
343   Cf. TR, p. 106: *arrischierebe*.

Il Tristano Riccardiano *(Parodi's siglum 'F')*

[54] At that point they were making their passage by ship, the weather changed and became very stormy. And then they commended themselves to God and the saints to help them, and all the sailors were weeping. By the fourth day they were going wherever the storm carried them. Thus they arrived at the Island of Giants (and know that whatever foreign knight arrived there, it behooved him – forever after – [fol. 145v] to remain in prison).

In that moment twelve knights came to the port and said, 'Come down to the ground because you are all prisoners'. Then they all began to weep. And Yseut was weeping and said to Tristan, 'Have you brought me from my land so that I be a prisoner here?' Then Tristan said, 'I will remain on this ship to fight as long as I have life; and when I am no longer able, God protect you'. Again Yseut said, 'Will we die in this fashion?' Tristan said, 'My lady, I don't know what else I can do about it. I can only tell you that as long as I'm able to hold my sword in my fist, I will not fail you'. In that moment they decided that 'in prison we will have some chance of remedy; it's better than letting ourselves all be killed in such fashion'.

Just then they were all taken prisoner and were led to the gate of the Castle of Weeping.* (And Yseut concealed Tristan's sword in her clothing; yet all the other things were taken from them.) And they entered inside by other doors and were put inside the castle. And they examined the [fol. 146r] prison (which was in the middle of the castle), and it really seemed to them – sad, but true – how any prisoner who was placed there never got out, not dead or alive. While being inside, night seemed day; and they passed that night with great sorrow.

In the morning two knights came to find out how the prisoners were. In that moment Tristan went forward and said to the knights, 'Must we stay in here forever or will we be able to leave at some determined date or by some happenstance?' And the knights said, 'Yes, in this way: if here among you there is such a knight – which we don't seem to see – who was so strong that by his strength and prowess he could defeat our lord; and if his lady were as lovely – or more so – than our lord's'. Then Tristan said, 'Here is one who will indeed risk his person with that of your lord, and he has a lady who is more lovely than yours'. The knights said, 'What, knight? There is no man in the world who could fight with our lord to save himself, other than Lancelot'.

[55] At this point the tale leaves off to tell how that adventure came to be, and in what way, and why that castle was called 'The Castle of Weeping'. Then

---

* In MS rhoticization of the *l: Proro*. Cf. *Roman de Tristan*, ed. Curtis, vol. II, p. 70: *Plor* (of weeping).

chomínçanno a dire li chavalieri lo facto a Tristano, e dichonno sichome [fol. 146v] chello segnore li messe questo ussato:

'En questa isola si fo giganti ed ebe nome Dialices, e messe chesto ussato perché al tempo de Josep Abaçimaçia, andava predicando la fé de Cristo. E viene en questa issola e avea çià la magior parte rachata ala soa fede. E ancho credendo che Jossepo andando li gran gente dirietro del povolo, si trovate en uno desserto una crosse sopra che dissia sichome Giossepe en quella issola devia predicare, overo en chello luogo, de la fede de Cristo. Alora vide Dialices che tuta soa gente avea perduto en tal modo. Si pensò en che modo lo potesse reçov[er]are a so diedi lay pensoso. Dialices avea .xii. fillioli gioveni, molti belli de lur persona. Estando una nocte tuti li fillioli [de] Dialices – e eranno en lecto – tuti li pressi e a tuti tallió loro la testa e gittonoli en la piaça per aysenplo, ché oni homo n'avesse paora de luy e perch'ello potesse rechoverare soa terra e soa gente.

Alor ebe la gente grandissima paora, vedendo la forsa de Dialiçes e l'enequità sua. Alor fesse gran parlamento, e disse calunqua persona credesse [fol. 147r] a Josseppe, si farebe de luy chome à facto de li fillioli. Alora fesse una grande hoste e presse Giossepe e tuta sua gente e fesseli tuti degollare. E possa chominçò a fare questo castello, e fesse lo fondare su en l'ossa e su le corpora de questoro e de li fillioli atressie; e coysì rechoverò sua terra e soa gente en tal modo qué li strangieri <en tal modo che li strangieri> li avean facto questo dapno. E però comandò che tuti <E> li strangieri che arivassero en quello porto fossero messi en preysone en chel castello e nonne devesseno may issire, saulvo que si enfra loro avesse uno chavaliere che vinçesse lo segnore di l'issola. E qualunque èi vinçitore, si remangna segnore de l'issola e debia talliare la testa a una de le dame, cioè a chalunqua èy più layda. E en tale manera lo vinçidor<or>e remane segnore de l'issola e de campare; e la simelle costumansa siè che giamay non se ne partere (sic) deve. E en tal manera potereysste campare, e si si avesse chavaliere che con lo nostro Re volesse conbatere e avesse la sua donna più bella que la nossa'.

[56] Alora disse Tristano venire avanti [fol. 147v] a Yssota, e mostra la ali chavalieri. Disse lur, 'Que ve pare de la dama?' Ed elli disseno, 'Bene si pote passare'. 'E io conbatrò col vostro segnore e per lo mio desliberamento e de mia conpagnia'. E li chavalieri disseno come ch' 'al mondo non è neysuno che conbatesse col nostro segnore soferissa en batallia, salvo que Lançeloto'. Ora disseno li chavalieri a Tristano [. . .]³⁴⁴ 'Ora m'avete facto dire un pocho de villania'. Ora fo messe Tristano e Yssota en uno bello palagio e facto lor asçio.

Alor sen'andonno li chavalieri al segnore de l'issola, e disseno li, 'Branor, a voy co[n]viene mantener nostra ussansa, qué tra li preysoni que pilliamo eri

---

344   Apparent *saut du même au même* or corruption in the MS. Cf. TR. p. 108: *E Tristano disse: 'Io per mee non vieterei bataglia a Lanciolotto. E ora sì m'avete fatto dire una grande villania'*.

Il Tristano Riccardiano *(Parodi's siglum 'F')*

the knights began to tell the whole story to Tristan, and they told how [fol. 146v] that lord set up this custom:

'On this island there was a giant, and he was called Dialices, and he set up this custom because at the time of Joseph of Arimathaea, he was going around preaching the faith of Christ, and he came to this island and had already brought the major part of the people to his faith. And still believing that Joseph was going along with a great horde of people behind, they found in a wild place a cross upon which it said how Joseph was supposed to preach on that island – that is to say, in that place – the faith of Christ. Then Dialices saw that he had lost all his people in that way. He thought of what way he would be able to get them back: he gave himself over to thinking about this. Dialices had twelve young sons, very handsome in their persons. And one night all the sons of Dialices – they were in bed – all of them were taken, and he cut off each one's head and threw them into the *piazza* as an example so that everyone would be afraid of him and so that he would be able to recover his land and his people.

Then the people were very greatly afraid, seeing the power of Dialices and his iniquity. Then he had a great parliament, and he said that to each person who believed [fol. 147r] in Joseph, he would do to him as he had done to his sons. Then he assembled a great army and captured Joseph and all his people and had them decapitated. And then he began to build this castle, and he set its foundation on top of the bones and bodies of these and of his sons as well; and thus he recovered his land and his people in such a way, because foreigners had brought this harm upon him. And for this reason he commanded that all the foreigners who arrived in that port were put in prison in that castle and must never get out, except if there were among them a knight who could defeat the lord of the island; and whoever was victor, he would remain lord of the island and he would have to cut off the head of one of the ladies, that is whoever was the uglier. And in this way the victor would remain lord of the island and be saved; but according to the custom, he must never leave there. And in this way you may be able to save your life, if there were a knight who would want to do combat with our king, and if he had a lady more beautiful than ours'.

[56] Then Tristan told Yseut to come forward [fol. 147v] and showed her to the knights. He said to them, 'What do you think of the lady?' And they said, 'She may well pass'. Tristan said, 'And I will fight with your lord, both for my freedom and that of my company'. And the knights said that 'in the world there is no one who, if he fought with our lord, would withstand him in battle, except for Lancelot'. Now the knights said to Tristan, [...]* [And Tristan said,] 'Now you have made me speak a bit villainously'. Now Tristan was put – with Yseut – in a lovely palace and made comfortable.

Then the knights went off to the lord of the island and told him, 'Brunor,** it behooves you to uphold our custom because among the prisoners that we captured

---

*   Omission in the MS. See TR, pp. 107–9 for a more complete reading.
**   The redaction consistently calls the giant *Branor*. I have emended this to *Brunor*, according to the French prose *Tristan* tradition (West, pp. 54, 126).

si àe uno chavaliere que vuolle co[n]batere al'ussato de l'issola'. ||| ³⁴⁵ E Branor disse, 'Ancho per me la vostra ussansa non fosse, io vuollio la mantenere'. E li chavalieri disseno, 'Or da par Dio, ala matina al son del corno, [fol. 148r] serete fora del castello con vostra dama'. A tanto si partittono li chavalieri e vanno a Tristano e danno li tutto soe arme, salvo l'espada (ché la espada apietò Yssota); e foronno al campo. El corno sona, ed esse fora Branor e la soa dama. Lo conto disse que la donna de Branor era grande e bella sichome donna ch'era trata de giganti, may non si pote apellare di bellessa co[m] Yssota. E la dama de Branor è devento tuta pallida de paora sichè decto fo que Yssota era più bella.

A tanto estando anboro le dame allato, la batalia si chominçono anboro li chavalieri e danno si del campo. (E Branor, sire d[e L]ontane Payse, è patre de Galioto lo Bruno.) E vienon si dare ende le targe de le lançe e de li petti de li cavalli. E començano la batallia sì forte e dura sichè li cavalli e li chavalieri vanno reverti per terra de li chavalli. E poy si levano li chavalieri con lur targe en braço e con l'espada en mano. ||| ³⁴⁶ [fol. 148v] Cominçano lo primo asalto sì duramente que çiaschaduno si meravillava de Tristano, sì bene lo fae, ché B[r]anor èi bene magior de luy uno chobito e segnoreçava Tristano molto. May Tristano èi bene savio conbatetore che la fa sì bene que chiachaduno si possa volontieri del primo asalto per piliare forsa e alena. Ciaschaduno si fa meravillia de Tristano quando si porre racare con Branor.

Or si levano li chavalieri, cominçano l'autro asalto e conbateno tropo forte e duro che molti malglie e arbergui vano per terra. E Yssota cambia so visso, çioè [s'inpalidò],³⁴⁷ perché si vide canbiare la batallia. May che disse lo conto de Tristano que èi savio conbatetore e de gran<di> durata, e viene menando Branor a destra e a sinistra; e Tristano chonosse bene che àe lo melio di la batalia. E' fiere uno colpo a Branor sopra l'ermo; e Branor non pote regire lo colpo: laysò si andare reverto en terra sìchome homo che molto sangue àve perduto. E Tristano disse, 'Conpagno<no>, non conbateremo noy più?' E Branor disse, 'Io sonno presso ala morte'. A tanto non parlò più Branor, ed elli è isito lo fiato.

[57] Alor disse Tristano, 'Segnori, io sonno deliberati per questa batalia'. [fol. 149r] Elli disseno che non era fina 'a tanto che voi talliate la testa ala donna de Branor'. E Tristano disse, 'Come? Talleroe io la testa ale donne?' Elino disseno che sie, 'Coysì ve cho[n]viene a fare si volete essere deliberato'. A tanto viene Tristano verso la donna e talloe li la testa con l'espada ||| ³⁴⁸ e mandòla molto de longo. En tal manera fo deliberato Tristano.

E presso è menato ende 'l castello onde estava Branor. Ed elli è facto gran honor e grande festa sichome dengno fare al so segnore. Alor disse Tristano,

---

³⁴⁵ Eight full lines left blank; miniature never executed.
³⁴⁶ Eight blank lines at bottom of writing space; miniature never executed.
³⁴⁷ Verb omitted in MS. Resolution based on TR, p. 108.
³⁴⁸ Six full lines left blank at mid-page; miniature never executed.

yesterday, there is a knight who wants to fight according to the custom of the island'. ||| And Brunor said, 'Even though your custom was not established by me, I want to uphold it'. And the knights said, 'Now, by God, in the morning at the sound of the horn, [fol. 148r] you will be outside the castle with your lady'. In that moment the knights left and went to Tristan and gave him all his arms, except for the sword (because Yseut had concealed the sword); and they were at the field of battle. The horn sounded, and Brunor and his lady* came out. The tale says that Brunor's lady was large and handsome (being a woman descended from giants), but she had no claims to beauty as did Yseut; and Brunor's lady became quite pale with fear since she had been told that Yseut was more beautiful.

Then, with both the ladies standing to one side, both the knights began the battle and took their positions on the field. (And Brunor, lord of the Faraway Lands, was the father of Galehot the Dark.) And they came on, letting themselves have it on their targes with their lances and with their horses' chests. And they began the battle so harsh and cruel that the horses and the unhorsed knights fell over backwards onto the ground. And then the knights got up with their targes on their arms and with their swords in their hands. ||| [fol. 148v] They began the first assault so harshly that everyone marvelled at Tristan who was doing so well, because Brunor was a good cubit taller than he and towered over Tristan by a lot. But Tristan was truly a shrewd fighter who did so well that each of them gladly rested from the first assault to regain strength and energy. Everyone marvelled at Tristan since he was able to withstand Brunor.

Now the knights got up, began another assault and fought so hard and cruelly that many pieces of their chainmail and hauberks flew to the ground. And Yseut's face changed – that is to say, she became pale – because she saw the battle shifting. But the tale says of Tristan that he was a shrewd fighter and of great endurance, and he went driving Brunor to the right and to the left; and Tristan knew well that he was having the better of the battle. And he struck a blow upon Brunor's helmet; and Brunor could not withstand the blow: he let himself fall backward onto the ground, like a man who had lost a great deal of blood. And Tristan said, 'Comrade, will we fight no more?' and Brunor replied, 'I am near death'. At that point Brunor spoke no more, and his breath left him.

[57] Then Tristan said, 'Lords, I am liberated by this battle', [fol. 149r] but they said that it was not ended 'until you cut the head off Brunor's lady'. And Tristan said, 'What? Must I behead ladies?' They said yes, 'Thus it behooves you to do if you want to be liberated'. In that moment Tristan went toward the lady and cut off her head with his sword ||| and sent it very far away. In this manner Tristan was liberated.

And then he was led into the castle where Brunor had stayed, and he was met with great honor and great rejoicing as is worthy to do for one's lord. Then

---

*   Brunor's wife, unnamed in the MS, was *la Bel(l)e Jaiande* (var. *Joiande*) in the French prose *Tristan* (West, p. 34).

'La mia gente deve estare en preyson<on>e ende lo Castello de Prodo?' E li chavalieri disseno che sie, 'salvo che voy sete segnore<Re> e potete fare a vostro senno, salvo que non s'andavo partire illi nì voy'. E Tristano disse, 'Chome? Debo<i> io gardare la vostra terra tuto lo tenpo de mia vita?' E li chavalieri disseno que sie. A tanto fesse traere li chavalieri fora de preisogne del [fol. 149v] Castello de Prodo, e sonno segnore d'andare e di onçillare e de cassiare per l'issola a lor senno.

Or si sta Tristano en su el castello reale de su l'issola e segnoreça la terra e tiene en sua familia Governale e Branguina; e altri non ussavano d'apressare alo palaçio. E apagavonno sì bene Tristano e Yssota de quella vita que facianno che may altro non demandavano a Dey. E non si recordano de lur parenti nì de lur gente, e non èi lur avisso che altro mondo sia che quello.

[58] Or laysa lo conto di Tristano e di Yssota, e torniamo a una filliola che avea Branor. E prende lo corpo del suo patre e la testa de la sua matre e mete li en su la nave. E parte si con essa de Lontana Yssola, e passa ala *terra ferma* el reallme de Naugales ch'era de Galeoto lo Bruno, el filliolo de Branor, sire d[e L']ontana Yssola. E fa fare una biera <e fa la portar a una biera> e fa la portare a gente da piedi e fa i metere lo corpo del patre <d>e de la matre. E viene [a] Galioto lo Bruno, so fratello, per mostrar li lo dapnaçio e çiorchò lo gran tenpo e non lo potte trovare; e demandòne tuti li chavalieri eranti de luy. E quando viene uno tenpo passando per la ter[r]a del Re de Cento Chavalieri sotto uno [fol. 150r] castello que si chiama lo Castello de l'Encantatrisse, e qui n'abitava lo Re de Cento Chavalieri. E la damissella avea con sí quatro damisselli e due damayselle; e gardan si davanti vi[de]ron[349] venire uno chavaliere ad arme roçinosse. E la damissella demanda, 'Chi è lo chavaliere?' E lo chavaliere li rissposse qu'era d'estrangno paesse. E la damissella disse, 'Saperiate [dire] mi novelle de Galioto lo Bruno, lo prinçe d[e L]ontana Issola?' E lo chavaliere disse, 'Perché ne demandate?' E la damissella disse, 'Perché io li vuolria dire uno so gran dapnage que li è devenuto questi giorni: che Tristano de Cornavalia èi venuto al'Issola de li Giganti e à morto soe padre Branor. Echo lo corpo so en questa bara, ed èvi la testa de la sua matre'. ||| [350] Alor disse lo chavaliere, 'Io sono desso', E la damissella lo garda. (Non lo conossia perché grando tempo era estato che non lo avea veduto.) Or si leva Galioto lo Bruno l'ermo, e la damissella lo conosse e chominça [fol. 150v] a fare gran dolia chome damissella may fessesse. Alor disse Galeoto, 'Lo piangere non vale nulla'. Mandoe adesso per lo Re de Cento Chavalieri al Castello di l'Encantatrisse, qu'elo era soe fidele. E quando lo Re vide lo messagio, si si mostrò molto dolente de quella ventura. E presseno Branor e sotereron lo a una badia e fessen li gran honore.

---

[349] Cf. TR, p. 112: *vide venire*.
[350] Six full lines left blank; miniature never executed.

Tristan said, 'Must my people remain in prison inside the Castle of Weeping?' And the knights said yes, 'except for you who are lord and can do as you wish, except that neither they nor you will leave'. And Tristan said, 'What? Must I watch over your land for the rest of my life?' And the knights said yes. In that moment he had the knights brought out of the prison of the [fol. 149v] Castle of Weeping, and they were free to move about and to go hawking and to hunt throughout the island as they wished.

Now Tristan remained up in the royal castle of the island and ruled the land, and he kept as his familiars Governal and Brangain, but no others were accustomed to going near the palace. And Tristan and Yseut were so well satisfied with that life which they were leading that they never asked God for another thing, and they remembered nothing about their relatives nor about their people; and in their view, there was no other world but that one.

[58] Now the tale leaves off telling of Tristan and Yseut, and let's return to a daughter* that Brunor had. She took her father's body and her mother's head and put them aboard a ship, and she left the Faraway Islands by ship and crossed to the *terra ferma* of the kingdom of North Wales that belonged to Galehot the Dark, the son of Brunor, lord of the Faraway Island. And she had a bier built and had it carried by people on foot and had her father's body and mother's head placed in it. And she was going to Galehot the Dark, her brother, to show him the harm, but she searched a long time and could not find him; and she asked all the errant knights about him. And after a while, she came to be passing through the land of the King of the Hundred Knights, below a [fol. 150r] castle that was called the Castle of the Enchantress; and here the King of the Hundred Knights was living. And the damsel had with her four young men and two damsels, and they looked ahead and saw a knight with rusty arms coming. And the damsel asked, 'Who is the knight?' And the knight answered her that he was from a foreign land. The damsel said, 'Would you be able to tell me any news of Galehot the Dark, the prince of the Faraway Island?' And the knight said, 'Why do you ask about him?' And the damsel said, 'Because I would like to tell him of a great harm that has come to him these days: that Tristan of Cornwall came to the Island of Giants and killed his father Brunor. Behold his body on this bier, and here is his mother's head'. ||| Then the knight said, 'I am he'; and the damsel looked at him. (She didn't recognize him because it had been a long time since she had seen him.) Now Galehot the Dark removed his helmet, and the damsel recognized him and began [fol. 150v] to make the greatest lament that a damsel ever did. Then Galehot said, 'Weeping is of no use'. He sent for the King of the Hundred Knights at the Castle of the Enchantress, because the king was his loyal vassal; and when the king saw his message, he showed himself to be very sorrowful about that adventure. And they took Brunor and buried him in an abbey and paid him great honor.

---

*   Brunor's daughter, unnamed in the MS, was *Delice*, in the French prose *Tristan* (West, p. 54).

[59] Alor disse Galioto que vuolle andare al'Issola de Giganti[351] a vendichare la morte del soe patre e de la matre. Alora comandoe allo Re de Cento Chavalieri que s'aconpangne con cento chavalieri de li meliore che pote avere e che debian ire al'Issola de li Giganti. Alor disse el Re a Galioto que debia ire per Lançeloto ché facia questa batalia per luy, 'ché [de] Tristano abo udito contare de tropo prodesse siché ad aqueste aventure non ve ne potrey aitare altro chavaliere ch'eli'. E Galioto disse, 'Io mi pensava qu'altro non mi potea contrare de la mia usança de l'Issola'. Ora disse lo conto que Galioto disse, 'Io vuolio andar puro io'. E commandò al Re de Cento Chavalieri che debia fare so comandamento. E lo Re disse que lo farae.

A tanto si parte Galioto con conpagna de <de> due eschudieri solamente e viene sene verso lo porto[352] el più tosto que poe. E qua[n]do giu[n]se al porto, si chiamoe una nave [fol. 151r] la quale andava en Landa; e Galioto susso vi montoe, e li marinari andavanno e[n]ver lur <c>chamino.[353] Dapoyqué foron en mare e avianno lo tenpo bono alo lur chamino, e Galioto si parla al patrone de la nave e disse que lo porti al'Issolla de Giganti. Disse lo patrone, ||| [354] 'Non sapete voi la mala usança | de l'Issola: que nullo estranio | che vi chapita que non sia pr|esso? Però non vi volria portare | en neuna manera de mo[n]do!' Alor disse Galioto que sì farae, 'e si tu non mi portarae per amore, tu me portarae a forsa'. Ed ello disse que non farae per so chomandamento. Alor messe Galioto mano[355] al'espada e viene contra al patrone de la nave e fierì lo de gran forsa que li levoe la testa de l'espalle, e a parechi de li autri marinari si fae lo semillio. Alor comanda ali autri marinari che encontenente debian andare al'Issola de Giganti.

Alor li marinari per paora si presseno lo camino verso l'Issola de Giganti. E tanto andaronno per lur giornate que pervegneno al Castello de Prodo; |||[356] e poyché foron | gionti al porto, [fol. 151v] echo venire .xii. chavalieri armati; e vignono contra lur al porto e demandono quilli de la nave per chuy parolla eranno venuti al porto.[357] E' [dissero,] 'Desmontate di su la nave e venete su al castello e fare[t]e vosse ussansa'. E Galioto esmontò a terra de la nave. Encontenente fo ali chavalieri, e li chavalieri presseno Galioto e menanlo al castello. E dapoyqué fo al castello, li chavalieri lo voleanno metere en preysone. A tanto parlò Galioto e disse, 'Segnore, io sono venuto per far l'ussansa de vostra terra e nostra, e per altro non vienne quae si non per conbatere con lo vostro chavaliere'. A tanto respondeno li chavalieri a Galioto, 'Adunque conbaterete voy con Tristano de Cornavalia, nepote de lo Re Marcho'. Ello disse, 'Per altro non si sonno venuto quae, si non per conbatere con luy'.

---

[351]   MS *gigaiti*.

[352]   MS *porte*.

[353]   As elsewhere, scribe wrote first letter of word at end of line and then wrote it again at beginning the next.

[354]   A rare case of two small miniatures, never executed, on a single page. Five half-lines blank, flush right; miniature never executed. From this point on, the scribe sometimes has short lines of text, broken to frame the blank space. I indicate such line breaks with a single vertical line (|).

[355]   MS *mane*.

[356]   Three lines two-thirds blank, flush right, at bottom of writing space.

[357]   MS *porte*.

[59] Then Galehot said that he wanted to go to the Island of Giants to avenge the deaths of his father and mother. Then he ordered the King of the Hundred Knights to accompany him with one hundred knights of the best he could have and said that they must go to the Island of Giants. Then the king told Galehot to send for Lancelot so that he would undertake this battle for him, 'because I have heard such great prowess recounted about Tristan that no other knight than he could help you in this'. And Galehot said, 'I was thinking to myself that no other evil could befall me from my custom of the Island'. Now the tale says that Galehot said, 'Yet I myself want to go'. And he commanded the King of the Hundred Knights to carry out his command, and the king said that he would do it.

In that moment Galehot left, with only two squires in his company, and came toward the port as quickly as he could. And when he reached the port, he summoned a ship [fol. 151r] that was going to Ireland; and Galehot climbed aboard; and the sailors went on their way. After they were at sea and were having good weather for their trip, Galehot spoke to the ship's master and told him to take him to the Island of Giants. The master said, ||| 'Don't you know the evil custom of the Island: that any foreigner who happens along is captured? Therefore I wouldn't want to take you there for anything in the world!' Then Galehot said yes, he would do it, 'and if you won't take me out of love, you'll take me due to force'; but he said that he would not follow his command. Then Galehot took his sword and went up to the ship's master and struck him with such great force that he took his head off from his shoulders, and he did the same to several of the other sailors. Then he commanded the other sailors to go at once to the Island of Giants.

Then the sailors – out of fear – set their course toward the Island of Giants, and they went so far through their days that they came upon the Castle of Weeping. ||| And after they had reached the port, [fol. 151v] behold! – twelve armed knights were coming; and they came up to meet them at the port and asked those on the ship by whose word they had come to the port. And they said, 'You will come down from the ship and come up to the castle and follow our custom'; and Galehot came down to land from the ship. As soon as he was before the knights, the knights took Galehot and led him to the castle. And once he was at the castle, the knights wanted to put him in prison. In that moment Galehot spoke and said, 'Lords, I have come to follow the custom of your – and our – land; and for no other reason did I come here, except to fight with your knight'. To that the knights answered Galehot, 'Well then, you'll fight with Tristan of Cornwall, King Mark's nephew'. And he said, 'For no other reason have I come here: only to fight with him'.

[60] Alora si partono li chavalieri, e vanno a Tristano e salutan lo, e dichono lo, 'Si è venuto uno chavaliere que vuolle conbatere con voy sichome èi nostra ussansa'. E Tristano disse, 'Qui è lo chavaliere?' Eli dichonno que non sanno qui sia. May [uno] disse, 'Quillo èi venuto per conbatere con voy'. A tanto resposse Tristano, 'Aparechiato sono de fare vostra ussança. Dapoyché batalia vuole, de batallia non li faliroe io çiaemay;[358] tutavia ve preguo que lo saludete da mia parte, ché io credo que sia lo più valente chavaliere del mondo, [fol. 152r] over[359] del realme de Longues'. A tanto respondono li chavalieri, 'Questo messagio faremo noy volontier[i]'. Or si partono li chavalieri e viegnon encontra ala nave ov'era Galioto, lo sire d[e L]ontana Isola. E quando sonno venuti danançi a luy, si lo salutano da parte de Tristano e dichono, 'Dapoyqué batalia volete, de batalia non voy venrà meno'. Giae alor disse Galioto que Tristano lo mandava salutare per dispeto[360] de luy.

[61] A tanto disse lo conto que poyqué Tristano remasse co[n] Yssota e con Guovernalle, molto si esconforta Yssota de quela ventura <di> conpagnando si de tanto solaçio qua[n]to avianno ensieme,[361] èi lur venuta questa dessaventura. 'May chalunque chavaliere fosse estato del realme de Longres fosse estato di questa ventura, non me serey partita da Tristano. May ora per d'essa ventura, si è venuto lo melior chavaliere del mondo en quessto luogo'. Credendo Yssota che fosse Lançeloto, molto si conpiange Yssota e Governale, e 'n quella notte non presso possa; may Tristano tutavia si conforta non ne chura çia perso fosse Lançeloto, ch'eli àe grandi volontae de conbatere con luy, magior que de nessuno del realme de Longres. 'E sì li pase el volia, pace averà; e si batalia volrrà, de batalia non li faliroe io giae a mio podere'.

Al'arba si vieste Tristano e armò sie, e monta [fol. 152v] a chavallo e viene encontra alo castello; e Guovernale li porta l'esqudo e la lancia, e Yssota remane. E quando Tristano fo giunto al porto onde era lo chavaliere e vidi que già era montato a cavallo, non li falla si non la giustra. E Tristano si parla a Governale, 'Vae e demanda chome à nome lo chavaliere: s'illo èi Lanceloto come io credo, io non volria conbatere con luy potendo aver paçe'.

A tanto si parte Governale e viene alo chavaliere e saluta lo cortessamente; e lo chavaliere li rende soe salut. E Governale disse, 'Tristano de Cornavalia, nepote del Re Marco, si ve manda a dire que voy li dichate vostro nome.' Alor resposse lo chavaliere, 'I'ò nome Galioto, sire d[e L]ontana Yssola. Quello m'àe morto mio patre e mia matre. E però sonno venuto chie per conbatere con luy'. A tanto torna Governale a Tristano: 'Elli si à[362] nome Galioto, sire d[e L]ontana Issola, e èi venuto chie per prendere vendìta de voe'. E quando Tristano entesse qu'era Galioto, el più alto p[ren]ce del mondo e 'l più valente, disse enfra sé metesmo, 'Or sonno[363] io lo più aventurosso chavaliere del mondo, dapoyché io sonno a campo con choisì alto prençe'. E molto si conforta Tristano da questa ventura.

358 Cf. TR, p. 114: *giamay*.
359 Here and elsewhere, scribe uses *over* ('or') to add a self-correcting gloss.
360 MS clearly *per disporo*. Cf. TR, p. 114: *dispetto*.
361 MS *enfieme*. Confusion of *s* / *f*.
362 MS *fia*. Confusion of *s* / *f*.
363 MS *fonno*. Confusion of *s* / *f*.

Il Tristano Riccardiano *(Parodi's siglum 'F')*

[60] Then the knights left and went to Tristan and greeted him and told him, 'A knight has come who wants to fight with you as is our custom'. And Tristan said, 'Who is the knight?' They said that they didn't know who he was, but one said, 'That fellow has come to fight with you'. At that Tristan answered, 'I am prepared to follow your custom. Since he wants battle, I will never fail to give him battle; yet I pray you to greet him on my behalf because I believe that he is the most valiant knight in the world, [fol. 152r] or rather, in the kingdom of Logres'. To that the knights replied, 'We will gladly take this message'. Now the knights left and went up to the ship where Galehot, the Lord of the Faraway Island, was. And when they had come before him, they greeted him on Tristan's behalf and said, 'Since you want battle, he will not fail to give you battle', but then Galehot said that Tristan was sending him greetings to insult him.

[61] At this point the tale says that since Tristan remained with Yseut and with Governal, Yseut was greatly discomfited about that adventure, having shared so much solace as they had together, and now this misfortune came to them. 'But whatever knight he may have been – had he been of the kingdom of Logres, through this adventure I would not have been parted from Tristan. But now, due to this adventure, the best knight in the world has come to this place'. Believing that it was Lancelot, Yseut lamented greatly with Governal and that night she could not rest; but nonetheless Tristan was comforted: he cared not at all if this were Lancelot because he had a great desire to fight with him, greater than with anyone in the kingdom of Logres. 'And if he wants peace, peace he will have; and if he wants a battle, I'll not at all fail him in battle, to the best of my ability'.

At dawn Tristan dressed and armed himself and mounted [fol. 152v] his horse and came to meet him at the castle; and Governal carried his shield and lance for him; and Yseut remained. And when Tristan had reached the port where the knight was and saw that he was already mounted on his horse, there was nothing left for him to do but to joust. And Tristan spoke to Governal, 'Go and ask the knight's name: if he is Lancelot, as I believe, I wouldn't want to fight with him, being able to have peace'.

At that Governal left and went to the knight and greeted him courteously; and the knight returned his greeting. And Governal said, 'Tristan of Cornwall, nephew of King Mark, is sending to you to ask you to tell him your name'. Then the knight replied, 'I am Galehot, lord of the Faraway Island. That fellow killed my father and my mother, and for this reason I have come here to fight with him'. At that Governal returned to Tristan: 'His name is Galehot, lord of the Faraway Island, and he has come here to avenge himself on you'. And when Tristan heard that it was Galehot, the noblest prince in the world and the most valiant, he said to himself, 'Now I am the most fortunate knight in the world since I'm taking the field with such a noble prince'. And Tristan comforted himself greatly about this adventure.

A tanto cavalcha Galioto enverso Tristano e disse, 'Sire chavaliere, gàrdate da me, ché io te desfido!' Alor pre[n]de Tristano [fol. 153r] la lançia e l'eschudo; e prendeno del canpo quello ch'è bissogna e abaysano le lançe e vienon si a ferire, e fieron si de tuta la lor forsa siché li lançe volonno en pessi. E poy si trayseno li chavalieri vissagio per vissagio, l'uno con l'autro, siché chiadescuno vae a terra da cavallo, e li chavalieri vanno sotto da li chavalli, e sono lor de sobra siché chiascaduno si dolosse e si dole de questa caduta. |||[364] Apresso si levano li chavalieri lo più tosto que posseno – sichoma homini de gran possa e de gran legeressa[365] – e metono mano[366] al'espada e fanno grande asalto l'uno con l'autro, e danno sì grande colpi l'uno al'autro siché en pocho d'ura no ne ià neuno che non abi ferite asay, siché chiadascuno si fae meravilia l'uno de l'autro.

E tanto durò lo primo asalto que Yssota – stava <ala> per mura[367] del castello, e stava a vedere la batalia de due chavalieri sì for[fol. 153v]te – e garda e vide lo soe amicho en chotal batalia, e vide li grandi colpi menare a Tristano siché Tristano enchina alcuna volta. E quando Yssota vide que Tristano n'àe lo peço, alor si pote vedere lo soe visso facto choma erba. E quando vidi que Tristano n'àe lo meliore, alor si pò vedere lo soe visso più bello que rossa de magio. E tuta si canbia Madona Yssota chome la batalia e chonosse bene de l'aventura de lo venire qual derietro de la batalia. (Galeoto non potrà sufrire con Tristano.)

May que ve diroe de li due chavalieri que non pensano ad acheste cosse? May chiascaduno pensa al soe conpagnone, a dar sì grandi colpi d'una mano e de l'autra; e<i> durarae la batalia en tal manera que Galioto si meravillava de la forsa de Tristano. E Tristano disse enfra sé metesmo qu'al derietro de la batalia non poterà sofrire con luy. Molto si meravilia de questa batalia Galioto e que perdia molto sangue de le ferite que avea siché pareçi chavalieri<e> ne serian già morti. May tuta gente que gardava la batalia si meravillavano chome potreno tanto sofrire d'arme que non sono già morti li due chavalieri che conbateno.

Echo ti venire due chavalieri armati a chavallo! Disseno ali chavalieri de l'Issola que stavan a judicare la batalia, disseno, 'Or siamo estruti e vituperati de la nostra [fol. 154r] usansa del Castello de Prodo; ed èy destruto lo nostro castello e desfato quando la nossa gente èi morta, salvo li preysoni d'estragno paese que sonno laysati; e tuto questo dapnagio à facto lo Re de Cento Chavalieri, lo quale si viene con cento chavalieri; ed àe facto lo dapnagio que decto v'è'. E quando li chavalieri que devian judicare la batalia entesseno queste cosse, chiascuno chominçoe a fugire e tieneno lor chamino; e anbeduro li chavalieri remasseno soli ala batalia.

---

[364] Eight full lines left blank; miniature never executed.
[365] Clear in MS: *legesere(ser)* with *ser* abbreviation at end. Cf. TR, p. 118: *leggerezza*.
[366] MS *mane*, as above.
[367] Cf. TR, p. 118: *i·ssu le mura*.

Il Tristano Riccardiano *(Parodi's siglum 'F')*

At that moment Galehot rode up to Tristan and said, 'Sir Knight, guard yourself from me because I challenge you!' Then Tristan took up [fol. 153r] his lance and shield, and they took their positions on the field as was needed, and they lowered their lances and came at each other to strike, and they struck each other with all their might so that the lances flew to pieces. And then the knights charged each other, face to face, one against the other, so that each one went to the ground from his horse, and the knights fell under their horses – and the horses were on top of them – so that each of them lamented and ached from this fall. ||| Afterward the knights arose, as soon as they could – like men of great strength and of great agility – and put hands to swords and made a great assault one with the other; and they gave such great blows one to the other so that in a short time there was neither one of them who didn't have many wounds, so that each one marvelled at the other.

And the first assault lasted so very long that Yseut – she was on the wall of the castle and she was there to see the fierce battle between the two knights [fol. 153v] – and she watched and saw her *ami* in such a battle, and saw the great blows aimed at Tristan so that at times Tristan bent over. And when Yseut saw that Tristan was having the worse of it, then one could see her face become as green as grass. And when she saw that Tristan was having the better of it, then one could see her face more beautiful than a rose in May. And the whole while My Lady Yseut changed as the battle did, and she was well aware of the outcome that awaited after the battle. (Galehot could not withstand Tristan.)

But what shall I tell you about the two knights who were not thinking of these things? Each one was thinking of his companion, to give such great blows on one side and the other. The battle was going on so long in that way that Galehot marvelled at Tristan's strength; and Tristan said to himself that at the end of the battle, he would not be able to withstand him. Galehot marvelled greatly about this battle and that he was losing a lot of blood from the wounds that he had, such that quite a few knights would have already been dead from them. But all the people who were watching the battle marvelled at how they could withstand so much armed combat that the two knights who were fighting were not already dead.

Behold, two armed knights coming on horseback! They said to the knights of the Island [of Giants] who were about to judge the battle, they said, 'Now we are destroyed and vituperated because of our [fol. 154r] custom of the Castle of Weeping; and our castle will be destroyed and unmade when our people are dead, except for the prisoners of foreign lands who will be freed; and all this harm was done by the King of the Hundred Knights, who is coming with one hundred knights, and he has done the aforesaid damage'. And when the knights who were supposed to judge the battle heard these things, each one began to flee and go his way; and both knights [Galehot and Tristan] remained alone in battle.

[62] Or si conforta Yssota que vede que Tristano n'àe lo melio de la batalia. E chome estano en tal manera, echo venire lo Re de Cento Chavalieri, armato a cavallo, con una bandiera en mano de le arme de Galioto; e apresso di luy vienenno .x. chavalieri armati a cavallo. E quando Yssota vide questi, dubitò molto de Tristano; may tutavia si conforta de la prodesse sua. E quando Galioto vidi venire la sua ensegniere e li soi chavalieri, disse a Tristano, 'Or ti cho[n]viene a morire en le mie mane, qué non poy canpare! Echo li mey chavalieri lo quale vegnanno per oucidere te'. Alor respose[368] Tristano e disse, |||[369] [fol. 154v] 'Io so que voy non dite queste parolle si non per metere mi paora, ché voy siete sì alto chavaliere e sì prode, e que non sufrereste en neguna manera di monndo que nostra batalia si desfinissa per altri chavalieri que de due noy. *Entre noy .ii. fo cominçata e·ssere finita debie essere, né già d'altro chavaliere non prenderò gardia si non de voy.*[370] May sì tanto posse que io vencha la batalia, e li vostri chavalieri volianno conbatere mecho ad uno a uno, già de batalia non lur faliroe io'.

A tanto viene lo Re de Cento Chavalieri con la lançia en mano per ferire Tristano e colie[371] una lanç[i]a de la parte de Galioto, e lo Re trapassa oltra. |||[372] Alor comanda Galioto al Re de Cento [Chavalieri] que en queste cosse non si debia entremetere, 'e laysa fenire la batalia entre noy due'. A tanto vedendo Tristano la cortessia de Galioto e pensando l'ofens<i>a[373] que li avea facto (sichome illo avea morto el patre e la matre), si si fesse enançi e prese l'espada e diede la a Galiotto. [fol. 155r] E pensando le grande hofensa qu'ello avea facto, soè d'ançidere soe patre e sua matre, si disse a Galiato (sic), 'Io ve prego sichome a chavaliere e lo più alta prinçe del mondo che soè que io fessi, si fisse per deliberar me e mia conpagnia, e·ffessi l'ussansa de l'Issola de Giganti'.

E Galioto entende[n]do queste parolle e la cortessia de Tristano, e considerando que avea lo pegior de la batalia, [disse,] 'Per tanto ti perdono tua vita, perché io vegio que tu sey de li melior chavaliere del mondo. E considerando la prodessa tua, si[374] ti perdono mio mal talento, sichome tu ày morto mio patre e mia matre'.

Alor gitono li chavalieri li schudi e levonno si l'ermo e abraçion si ensieme con granda honore anbeduro li chavalieri. E dapoyqué Yssota vide la |||[375] pasce entre li chavalieri, | si n'àe alegressa, ne|uno non demande! | E vienon se ne con conpagn[i]a de due eschudieri, e li due damisselli menava Galioto e Tristano e tuta sua conpagnia, e fa lor granda alegressa. Encontenente fesse cercare tuta l'issola per medici per far curare le piague de Galioto e quelle de Tristano.

---

[368] MS *reposse*.
[369] Four full lines blank at bottom of writing space; miniature never executed.
[370] At the top of fol. 154v, scribe has written additional words in the margin using a light brown ink, different than the rest of the page, and has shown the insertion point with a # symbol. This type of self-correction is not found elsewhere. The inserted text corresponds to TR, p. 120; and TP, p. 202.
[371] Cf. TR, p. 120: *si colse*.
[372] Seven full lines left blank at mid-page; miniature never executed.
[373] In the next sentence, MS reads *hofensa*. Cf. TR, p. 120: *affensione*.
[374] MS *fi*. Confusion of *s* / *f*.
[375] Scribe left four half lines blank, flush right; miniature never executed.

Il Tristano Riccardiano *(Parodi's siglum 'F')*

[62] Now Yseut took comfort because she saw that Tristan was having the better of the battle. And as things stood in that manner, look who's coming: the King of the Hundred Knights, armed on horseback, with a flag in his hand that bore Galehot's device; and behind him were coming ten armed knights on horseback. And when Yseut saw these fellows, she was very worried about Tristan; but still she took comfort in his prowess. When Galehot saw his insignia coming – and his knights – he said to Tristan, 'Now it behooves you to die at my hands because you cannot be spared! Behold my knights who are coming to kill you!' Then Tristan answered and said, ||| [fol. 154v] 'I know that you're only saying these words to frighten me because you are such a noble knight, and so valiant, and because you wouldn't allow for anything in the world that our battle would be finished by other knights than we two. Between us two it was begun and it must be finished, nor will I be on guard of any other knight if not of you. But as soon as I win the battle, and your knights want to fight with me one by one, I will certainly not fail to give them battle'.

In that moment the King of the Hundred Knights was coming – with lance in hand – to strike Tristan, and Tristan made a leap toward where Galehot was, and the King passed beyond. ||| Then Galehot commanded the King of the Hundred Knights not to meddle in these things, 'and let the battle be finished between us two'. Whereupon Tristan, seeing Galehot's courtesy and thinking of the offense that he had done him (since he had killed his father and mother), went forward and took his sword and gave it to Galehot. [fol. 155r] And thinking of the great offense that he had done, that is of killing his father and his mother, he said to Galehot, 'I pray you as a knight and the noblest prince in the world, that what I did was done in order to liberate myself and my company, and I did it according to the custom of the Island of Giants'.

And Galehot, upon hearing these words and Tristan's courtesy, and considering that he was having the worse of the battle, said, 'For such I pardon you your life, because I see that you are among the best knights in the world; and considering your prowess, I forgive you my ill will, since you killed my father and my mother'.

Then the knights threw down their shields and removed their helmets, and both the knights embraced each other with great honor. And since Yseut saw the ||| peace made between the knights, if she was happy about it, let no one ask! And [she] came there in the company of two squires – and the two youths led Galehot and Tristan away, and all his company – and she rejoiced greatly for them. Immediately she had the whole island searched for physicians to cure the wounds of Galehot and those of Tristan; those of

Eronno asay più pericolosse quelli de Galioto que chelli di [fol. 155v] Tristano; e Tristano garite en dì .xv., e Galioto pognoe a garire più d'uno messe.

Alor Galioto parlò a Tristano e disse, 'Io ve pregu per honor de voy e de cavallaria e per le cosse que voy più amate nel mondo, e da questo ve pregu que voi m'enprometate que[376] al più tosto que voy ve poreste partire dal Re Marcho, vegnate a me en Gaules, qué lo magior dessiderio òe, soè de vedere[377] voy e Meser Lançelotto del Lac; e s'io anbedoro ve posso metere ensieme,[378] alor serò io lo più alto segnore del mondo'. Alor respose Tristano a Galioto; eli li promesse como chavaliere.

A tanto si parte Tristano, e Yssota e Governale e Branguina e tuti li autre chavalieri de Cornavalia. E Galioto li fae conpagnia fina alo porto del Castello de Prodo. Alor disse Tristano a tuti li baroni e chavalieri que tuti dibian tornare en una nave, e çiascaduno hobeditto lo so comandamento. Alor disse Galioto a Tristano que non debia laysar per nulla che non vada a luy en Gaules sicome promesso li avia; e Tristano disse ch'ello farae volontieri. [fol. 156r] A tanto si parte Galioto da Tristano, e si la comanda Tristano a Dey. E Tristano monta en su la nave, e li maistre marinar[i] driçano le vele al vento e fanno la più dritta via que possono verso Cornavalia.

[63] Or laysa quie lo conto de Tristano, e torniamo a Galioto al'Issola de Giganti. E scrisse una litera al Re Arturo e a Madona la Redina Genevra e a tuti li chavalieri eranti de Longres,[379] e d'altro paesse, e disse la letera en questo modo:

'Io, Galioto, segnore d[e L]ontane Issole, a voy [Re Arturo e a][380] Madonna la Redina Genev<b>re, salut. Per mei litere ve manifesto que io con mey chavalieri passay al'Issola de Giganti per tollere la mala ussansa, la quale era en quello luoguo, e avea la tolta e desfata lo Castello de Prodo, e quampati (sic) li preissonieri lo quale erano en quello castello. E io per vendicarmi de sò che mi fesse Tristano de Cornavalia <e li autri chavalieri>, e chuori encontra cuore.[381] E sapiate, Re Artus e Madona Redina Genevra e tuti li autri chavalieri del vostro realme ch'el mondo non soe tanta prodessa nì tanta cortessia nì tanta bellessa. E tuta la gentilessa que dire si potte fie en chostoro, soè en Lançeloto e en Tristano e 'n Madona la Redina Genevra e 'n Mado[fol. 156v]na Yssota la Bionda'.

E questa foe la leterra que Galioto mandoe al Re Arturo.

E quando la letera fo gionta ala corte del Re Arturo, alor viene davanti ali chavalieri. Molto se n'alegra lo Re e la Redina e tuta la corte [entendendo]: 'li quali chavalieri sono quisti: Tristano e Lancelloto, e le donne la Redina Genevra

---

[376] MS clear: *One*.
[377] MS *verere*.
[378] MS *enfieme*. Confusion of *s / f*.
[379] Scribe first wrote *de gaules*, expunctuated it and continued correctly.
[380] Correction based on TR, p. 122.
[381] MS: *couroe*. Apparently corrupt reading in MS. TR, p. 122 reads more logically: *E io per vendicarmi di cioe ke Tristano m'avea fatto, sì combattei co·llui cuore per cuore*. See also TP, p. 204: *Et per vendicarmi di ciò che Tristano di Cornovaglia m'avea fatto, combattetti co·llui cuore a cuore*.

Il Tristano Riccardiano *(Parodi's siglum 'F')*

Galehot were much more dangerous than those of [fol. 155v] Tristan; and Tristan healed in twenty-five days, but Galehot took more than a month to heal.

Then Galehot spoke to Tristan and said, 'I pray you for the sake of your honor and of chivalry and for the things that you love most in the world and by this, I pray you to promise me that as soon as ever you are able to leave King Mark that you come to me in Gaul, because the greatest desire that I have is to see you and Sir Lancelot of the Lake; and if I can have both of you together, then I would be the noblest lord in the world'. Then Tristan replied to Galehot: he promised him as a knight.

At that time Tristan departed, and Yseut and Governal and Brangain and all the other knights of Cornwall; and Galehot kept them company as far as the port of the Castle of Weeping. Then Tristan told all the barons and knights that they all must return to the ship, and each one obeyed his command. Then Galehot told Tristan that he must not for any reason fail to come to him in Gaul as he had promised, and Tristan said that he would gladly do it. [fol. 156r] In that moment Galehot left Tristan, and he commended Tristan to God. And Tristan climbed aboard the ship, and the master sailors directed the sails into the wind and set the most direct course that they could toward Cornwall.

[63] Now the tale leaves off about Tristan, and we return to Galehot on the Island of Giants. And he wrote a letter to King Arthur and to My Lady the Queen Guenevere and to all the errant knights of Logres and of other lands; and the letter said in this fashion:

'I, Galehot, lord of the Faraway Islands, to you King Arthur and to My Lady the Queen Guenevere, [send] greetings. By my writing, I inform you that I with my knights crossed to the Island of Giants in order to remove the evil custom, the which was in that place; and I have removed it and destroyed the Castle of Weeping and spared the prisoners who were in that castle. And in order to avenge myself for what Tristan of Cornwall and the other knights did to me, I fought, matching my courage to his. And know, King Arthur and My Lady Queen Guenevere and all the other knights of your kingdom, that in the world there is not so much prowess nor so much courtesy nor so much beauty.* And all the gentility of which one could speak is in those, that is to say, in Lancelot and in Tristan and in My Lady the Queen Guenevere and in My Lady [fol. 156v] Yseut the Blonde'.

And this was the letter that Galehot sent to King Arthur.

And when the letter had reached King Arthur's court, then it came to be read before the knights. The king and queen and the whole court rejoiced about 'which knights are these: Tristan and Lancelot, and the ladies Queen Guenevere

---

* This trope praising the two best knights and the two most beautiful women in the world is somewhat unclear due to abbreviations or *sauts*. Translation is verbatim.

e Yssota la Bionda'. Questo dicia la letera e contava, grande alegressa en corte del Re Artù (e magior ne seria estata si ve fosse estato Lançeloto a corte del Re Arturo en Longres).

[64] Ora laysa lo conto de parlare del Re Artus, e torniamo al facto que non apertiene ora a dire en questo libro. Alor Galioto ebe estruta la mala ussansa de l'Issola di Giganti; tanto <tanto> tenpo demoroe ende l'issola quanto pognoe a garire de le soe piague. E poy si partitte de l'issola e tornoe en soe realme con sua gente. E pocho tenpo demora en sua terra ch'ello morìo, honde ne foe gran danpno de luy e sì alto prinçe morìo en tal manera. E gran dolore ne [menano][382] a corte del Re Arturo e si è en tuta parte<te>. [fol. 157r] E quando Tristano ouditte che Galioto era morto, fo ne molto dolente de questa ventura 'perché andato serei a luy en Gaules sichome promesso li avia'.

[65] A tanto torna lo conto a Tristano per devissare chomo tornoe o arrivoe en Cornavalia con Yssota. E tanto vae Tristano con soa conpagn[i]a que giunsseroно al porto de Titolin en Cornavalia. E poyché ebenno presso porto, escende Tristano en terra e mandoe uno eschudieri al Re Marcho. E disse alo schudieri, 'Saluta mi lo Re Marcho e tutti li baroni, e di' li chome i'ò menata Yssota la Bionda, filliola del Re Languis de Landa; ed èi, con tuta soa conpagnia, sano ed e alegro'.

E qua[n]do lo Re Marcho entesse queste novelle, fo tropo dolente, soè perché Tristano era tornato en Cornavalia. E disse ali soy chavalieri (perché non paresse ch'è dolente ne fosse de sua tornata), 'Montate a chavallo e andate ala marina a conpagnare Tristano e Yssota la Bionda!' Alor monta lo Re a cavallo con li soy baroni e chavalieri, e vànsene ala marina al porto. E poyché fonno çiu[n]ti in quella parte, e lo Re vidi Yssota – qu'era coysì bella – e tutta soa conpagnia, Marcho – reponendo Yssota a niente qu'era coysì bella[383] – disse enfra suo chuore, [fol. 157v] 'Ora[384] èi Tristano lo più leale chavaliere del mondo <E> que essere potesse en nessuno modo e tenpo dapoyché [la] à menata choisì com'io li disse'. E però li fae grande honore e disse, 'Dolçe mio nepote, voy m'avete sì ben facto qué avete demostrato que sey lo più leale chavaliere del mondo'.

Alor andoe lo Re con tuta sua cognpagnia enverso Titolin, <verso> Yssota la Bionda e <per> Tristano,[385] e vie[ni]sse lì e nela terra con tuta la sua conpagnia con grande alegressa; e poy foron venuti a palagio; e lo Re Marcho vidi Yssota cotanto bella e tanto avinente. Encontenente fesse fare litere e mandoe messagio per tuta Cornavalia a tuti chavalieri e baroni, a povere e a richi, e da homni[386]

---

[382] Verb omitted in MS. Insertion based on TR, p. 124.
[383] MS has additional words not found in TR.
[384] MS *Ore*.
[385] Probable corrupt reading or omitted words here.
[386] MS *honi* with long titulus over the word. Cf. *om(n)i* on fol. 159r.

and Yseut the Blonde'. This the letter said and recounted; and there was great rejoicing in King Arthur's court (but it would have been greater if Lancelot had been at King Arthur's court in Logres).

[64] Now the tale leaves off speaking of King Arthur, and let's return to a matter that does not belong to what this book is telling now. When Galehot had destroyed the evil custom of the Island of Giants, he dwelt as long on the island as it took to be healed of his wounds; and then he departed from the island and returned to his kingdom with his people. And he had only dwelt in his land a short while when he died, whence there was great harm to his kingdom because such a noble prince died in such a way; and there was great mourning about it at King Arthur's court as well as everywhere else. [fol. 157r] And when Tristan heard that Galehot was dead, he was very sorrowful about this adventure 'because I would have gone to him in Gaul as I had promised him'.

[65] At this point the tale returns to Tristan to describe how he returned and arrived in Cornwall with Yseut. Tristan went so far with his company that they reached the port of Tintagel in Cornwall. And after they had entered port, Tristan descended to the ground and sent a squire to King Mark. And he told the squire, 'Greet King Mark and all the barons on my behalf, and tell them that I am bringing Yseut the Blonde, daughter of King Anguin of Ireland; and he, with his whole company, is healthy and happy'.

When King Mark heard this news, he was too sorrowful, that is, because Tristan had returned to Cornwall. And he said to his knights (so that it didn't appear that he was suffering about his return), 'Mount your horses and go to the seashore to accompany Tristan and Yseut the Blonde!' Then the king with his barons and knights mounted their horses and went along the shore to the port. And after they had reached that area, and the king saw Yseut – who was so beautiful – and her whole company, Mark – comparing Yseut to nothing, because she was so beautiful – said in his heart, [fol. 157v] 'Now is Tristan the most loyal knight in the world that could ever be in any way or time since he has brought her, just as I told him'. And for this reason he paid him great honor and said, 'My sweet nephew, you've done so very well for me because you've shown that you are the most loyal knight in the world'.

Then the king went with his whole company toward Tintagel, with Yseut the Blonde and Tristan, and came there and entered the land with his whole company, with great happiness; and then they came to the palace, and King Mark saw Yseut so very beautiful and so lovely. At once he had letters written and sent messages throughout Cornwall to all knights and barons, to poor and rich, and

altra persona da quello realme, que da inde a otto[387] giorni chascuno fosse a Titolin perché volia prendi Madonna Yssota la Bio[n]da, filliola del Re Languis de Landa, per sua molie e enchoronala del realme de Cornavalia. E dapoeché (sic) lo chomandamento fo andato per tute le parte, chiascaduno s'apareça e viene a Titolin. E dapoyqué foron asenbrati, si chominçano a fare gran festa e la magior alegressa que dapoyqué Dey foe issesse entra<entre> loro. Ora non tema neuno de Cornavalia enfine que Tristano èi vivo e àe facta la passe quelli de Cornavalia con quelli de Landa, che çamae non li dev'essere guera.[388] [fol. 158r] Grande gioa ne menano li chavalieri e le dame e le damisselle de Cornavalia.

Lo giorno de le nosse èy passato.[389] Apresso l'autra dì si cominçano le nosze grandi solaçio e grandi [...][390] per tuti le parte del soe realme. E lo Re enchoronò Yssota de tuto lo realme de Cornavalia con grando solacio. Ora passa lo giorno de la nosse, e la nocte apressa que lo Re si corcha con Yssota, ensieme en la camera. |||[391]

Alor Tristano e Governale e Branguina foron ensieme en la camera a consilio, dicendo Tristano, 'En che manera potremo fare que lo Re non sapia nostre chovenente? – que voy sapete bene com lo vae lo facto nostro entre noy due'. Alor respose Governale e disse, 'Or laysate queste cosse a Branguina <A branguina> e a me'. Disse, 'Noy vi metremo tal consillio que queste cosse non si sapranno niente'. Alor parla Governale a Brançuina. Quello volia que Branguina si colcasse con lo Re; enpromesse li gran gioa. [fol. 158v] Alor respose Branguina e disse, 'Io sonno apareçata de fare tutto quello que mi chomandarete'.

E la nocte apresxima, e lo re si vuolle[392] colchiare con Yssota. Alora viene Yssota ende la camera, e le donne e le donçelle l'aconpagnò per meterla a lecto. E dapoyché Yssota fo corçata, e non remase en la camera si non Governale e Branguina. E non tarda garie che lo Re viene ende la camera, e Tristano li fae conpagnia. E dapoyché lo Re fo entro la camera, si s'aparegia per ire a lecto. E dapoyché fo a letto, Tristano este[n]guoe li lumi. |||[393] El Re Marcho disse a Tristano, 'Per que chaysone àe e[s]tinguate lo lume?' E Tristano respose e disse, 'Questo è l'ussato de Landa, que quando nessuna pouçella si corcha con suo segnore la prima nocte, fanno esti[n]guati tuti li lumy perché le puçele [fol. 159r] sonno vergnonosse la prima nocte de lor segnore; e questo è una matessa[394] che si fae en Landa. E la matre de Madona Yssota sel me disse e preguòmene asay que io lo fessese'. Alor respose lo Re Marcho e disse, 'Bene agia cotal ussança'.

---

[387] MS *onto*. TR, p. 124: *ad otto dì*; TP, p. 206: *ad .x. dì*.
[388] MS *grera*. Catchword at center bottom in a crudely drawn red cartouche: *G(r)uande gioa*.
[389] This is somewhat illogical. Cf. TR, p. 126: *si s'apressa*.
[390] Omission of a noun. Reading is unlike TR, p. 126 or TP, p. 208 or TV, pp. 210–11.
[391] Five full lines left blank, mid-page; miniature never executed.
[392] MS *vuolse*. Confusion of *s* / *l*.
[393] Seven full lines left blank; miniature never executed.
[394] This unusual noun is also found in *comense* dialect. See *Spagna in rima*, ed. Rosiello, p. 545: *mateza* ('madness' or 'stupidity').

to every other person of that kingdom, that eight days from now everyone should be at Tintagel because he wanted to take My Lady Yseut the Blonde, daughter of King Anguin of Ireland, as his wife and crown her queen of the kingdom of Cornwall. And after the command had gone everywhere, everyone prepared to come to Tintagel. And after they had assembled, they began to rejoice greatly and to be still happier than if God had descended among them. Now no one in Cornwall was afraid as long as Tristan was alive and had made peace between those of Cornwall and those of Ireland, so that there must never be war between them. [fol. 158r] The knights and ladies and damsels of Cornwall had great joy because of this.

The day of the wedding passed. After the next day, they began the wedding festivities and great [...] through all the parts of his kingdom. And the king crowned Yseut queen of the whole kingdom of Cornwall, with great merriment. Now the wedding day passed, and the night was approaching when the king would lie with Yseut, together in the chamber. |||

Then Tristan and Governal and Brangain were together in the chamber taking counsel, Tristan saying, 'In what way will we be able to manage it so that the king doesn't find out our situation? – because well you know how the affair between the two of us is going'. Then Governal replied and said, 'Now leave these things to Brangain and to me'. He said, 'We'll offer you such counsel about these things that no one will find out anything'. Then Governal spoke to Brangain: that fellow wanted Brangain to lie with the king; he promised her great joy.* [fol. 158v] Then Brangain replied and said, 'I'm ready to do all that you command me'.

Night was approaching, and the king wanted to lie with Yseut. Then Yseut came into the chamber, and ladies and damsels accompanied her to put her to bed. And after Yseut was in bed, no one remained in the chamber except for Governal and Brangain. And it wasn't much later that the king came into the chamber, and Tristan kept him company. And after the king was inside the chamber, he prepared himself to go to bed. After he was in bed, Tristan extinguished the lights. ||| And King Mark said to Tristan, 'For what reason have you extinguished the light?' Tristan replied and said, 'This is the custom of Ireland, that whenever any maiden lies with her lord the first night, they have all the lights extinguished because maidens [fol. 159r] are bashful the first night with their lord; and this is a mad thing** that they do in Ireland; and Lady Yseut's mother told it to me and begged me very much that I would do it'. Then King Mark replied and said, 'Blessed be such a custom'.

---

*   In the MS the singular noun means 'joy'. Cf. TR, p. 126: *gioie* (plural: 'jewels').
** Translation follows the MS *matessa*, a wording radically different from that of TR, p. 126: *kortesia* (courtesy, kindness).

E quando Tristano dissia queste parolle, a·ttanto Governale messe a lecto Branguina a lato da Re Marcho; e Madona Yssota si partì, e omni[395] persona de la camera. E lo Re giache con Branguina, credendo si atrouare la Redina. E dapoyché fo solaçato tanto qua[n]to a luy parve, e lo Re comanda que li lumi sonno[396] assesi. E Tristano, lo quale èi apresso de la camera, encontenente intrò dintro; e Governale encontenente presse la Redina e messela entro el lecto; e Branguina si partite e viene ala sua camera (e lo Re de queste cosse non sepe niente). Molto era lo Re lieto enfra soe core, credendo aver giachuto con la Redina e trovala pussella. Encontenente foron li lumi assesi, e lo Re fa alumir lo lecto sichome l'usança de Cornavalia. E dapoyché lo Re vide la certança de la Redina, fo molto alegro en soe chuore. E comandoe che omni[397] homo si partisse de la camera. La note si trapassa lo Re con grande alegresse.

Ala matina si leva [fol. 159v] lo Re Marcho, vestì si e asetta si e viene endi (sic) la sala del palagio. E qui ne trovoe chavalieri e barony asay de Cornavalia. E vedendo lo Re Marcho Tristano, si lo chiamò a sé e disse, 'Bello nepote Tristano, io chonosso la tua leança e la fratellança e la tua franquessa de la toa chavallaria. E però si ti daroe uno dono: che io vuolio que tu sey segnore de tuto lo realme de Cornavalia di fare a tuo senno, salvo de la corona en fuora; e questo ti prometo, vegendo questoro'. E Tristano si l'insiginolia ali piedi e 'ngraçiellò asay de questo dono qu'ello li avia fatto. May ne sonno alegri li ||||[398] chavalieri de Cornavalia | que dato àe lo Re | Marcho a Tristano, e | chiascuno disse, 'Re | Marcho, benedito | siate voy da Dio | da questo donno que avete fato! E fine que Tristano fie en Cornavalia, estaremo bene con voy'. Alor resposse lo Re Marcho, 'Seguro potemo estare ed essere da omni[399] bono chavaliere'. E grande èi la gioa que menanno li chavalieri de Cornavalia per amore [fol. 160r] de loro segnore lo Re.

[66] E lo Re Marcho per grande amore tuto lo giorno si consillioe con Branguina Si<j>ché la Redina Yssota, vedendo lo consilio que Branguina facia con lo Re, ebe grande paura che non dissesse al Re sò qu'era estato da ley a Tristano. ||||[400] E disse enfra sé estesso que | bissongno era que la fessesse | morire. Alor la Redina fe | chiamare due soy servi que | avea menato de Landa con ley. Eranno venuti, e fesse lor giurare li soi comandamenti de sò que li comandaroe a loro, elli enteneranno credença. Elli disseno que lo faranno volontieri a lor podere. Alor disse <meeser> Madona Yssota[401] che s'aparechessano, siqué ala matina andassenno al boscho con Branguina. E dapoyqué l'avesseno el profondo del bossquo che la devesseno ucidere, 'E non laysate per neuna pietate nì merchede

---

[395] MS *omi*, also with titulus.
[396] MS *sena*, written with a titulus to indicate: *sen(n)a*.
[397] MS *oi* with titulus over *i*.
[398] Six half lines left blank toward gutter (to the right side of *verso*); miniature never executed.
[399] Again, MS has *oi* with titulus.
[400] Five half lines left blank, right flush; miniature never executed.
[401] Scribe first wrote *Madona bra*, then struck out *bra*.

Il Tristano Riccardiano *(Parodi's siglum 'F')*

While Tristan was saying these words, in that moment Governal put Brangain to bed alongside King Mark; and Lady Yseut left, as did every person in the chamber; and the king lay with Brangain, believing that he had found the queen. And after he had taken as much pleasure as he desired, the king commanded that the lights were lit. And Tristan, who was near the chamber, immediately entered inside; and Governal immediately took the queen and put her into the bed; and Brangain left and went to her chamber (and the king knew nothing of these things). The king was very happy in his heart, believing that he had lain with the queen and found her to be a maiden. At once the lights were lit, and the king had the bed illumined as was the custom of Cornwall. And once the king saw the certainty about the queen, he was very happy in his heart; and he commanded that everyone should leave the chamber. The king passed the night with great happiness.

In the morning [fol. 159v] King Mark arose, dressed and prepared himself, and went into the hall of the palace; and here he found a great many knights and barons of Cornwall. And upon seeing Tristan, King Mark called him to himself and said, 'My fine nephew Tristan, I recognize your loyalty and brotherhood and the valor of your chivalry. And for this reason I will give you a gift: I want you to be lord of the whole realm of Cornwall, to do with as you think best – except only for the crown; and this I promise you, before these as witnesses'. And Tristan knelt at his feet and thanked him so much for this gift that he had made him. The knights of Cornwall were happy about ||| what King Mark gave to Tristan, and each one said, 'King Mark, may you be blessed by God for this gift that you have made! And as long as Tristan is in Cornwall, we will be fine with you'. Then King Mark replied, 'We can all be safe and secure from every good knight'; and great was the joy that the knights of Cornwall showed for the sake [fol. 160r] of their lord the king.

[66] King Mark – out of great love – was always consulting with Brangain so that Queen Yseut, seeing the counsel that Brangain was taking with the king, was greatly afraid that she would tell the king what had been between her and Tristan; ||| and she said to herself that it was needful that she have her killed. Then the queen had summoned two of her servants whom she had brought from Ireland with her. They came, and she made them swear that about what she would order them to do, they would maintain in confidence. They said that they would gladly do it, to the best of their ability. Then Lady Yseut said that they should prepare themselves so that in the morning they would go to the wood with Brangain and after they had her in the depths of the wood that they must kill her 'and do not

ch'ella voy cheresse'. Elli disseno que lo faranno quando li è en piachere <che lo farenno>. (May molto si meravilliano de queste cosse que Madona Yssota à lor comandato.) A tanto la Redina fae apellare Branguina e si li comanda que la matina monte (sic) a chavallo en su lo soe palafreno. 'E mena en tua conpagnia questi [fol. 160v] due servi que vegnono con noy de Landa, e vàne el bossquo. Cerchami de le erbe que tu say, qué io vuollio far bangno'. E Branguina de queste cosse non prende garda. Disse, 'Madona, io lo farò volontieri'.

Ala matina si leva Branguina e visti si e aparechia sé, e cavallcha su en uno bello palafreno, e mena en soa conpagnia li due servi. E chavalchano en quelle parte onde melio credea de trovare l'erbe che Madonna Yssota li avia comandato. E chavalcando en tal manera, disseno li servi a Branguina, 'Noy non andiamo bene'. Alor prendono la via d'andar al desserto. E Branguina disse, 'Noy non and[i]amo ||||[402] per bona via da trovar | herbe'. E li servi disseno, | 'Noy andiamo bene'. E | tanto andorono en tal | manera que foron giu|nti en una gra[n]de valle e profonda ende lo deserto, là onde eranno serpente e leoni e autre rie bestie.

Alora li servi l'ap[r]esseno e gi<a>tanla da cavallo. Alor disse Branguina, 'Per che manera voy me desmontate da cavallo?' E l'uno de li servi disse, 'Ello éy bissono que tu moire (sic) en questo desserto; e [fol. 161r] però t'avemo menata quie per unçiderti'. Alor disse Branguina, 'Façete voy achesta cossa per voluntà di la Redina?' Elli respossemo che sie. Alor chomimça fortamente a piangere. E l'uno de li servi disse <l'uno> al'autro, 'Ucidela!'; e l'autro disse, 'Ucidela tue!' Alor disseno li servi che ne paria a lor gran peccato. Disse ora, 'Ài tu facto nulla a Madonna Yssota?' E Branguina disse noe, 'salvo che due damisselle si partiron de lor terra e venianno en estragno paese, e chiascaduna avea uno fiore de fiordelisso a gardare; e l'una perdete la soa fioredelisso per soa mala gardia. E quella que lo gardoe bene lo soe fiordelisso, si prestoe lo soe fiordeliso ad aquella che lo perdere per soe mala gardia, onde quella que lo prestoe ne deve morire. En tal manera, moroe io questa volta. Cheste parolle voy abo decto perché voy li dicate ala Redina. Or fate de me sò che voy piaçe. Poyché Madona vuolle que io moia, io vuolio morire'.

E li servi si consillano anbedoro. Disse l'uno al'autro, 'Ligamla[403] ad aquesto desserto, e venranno le bestie salvaçe che la manceranno en questo desserto, qué a me pare grando pecchato ucider la'. Alor sonno acordati [fol. 161v] a[n]bedoro li servi, e presseno Branguina e liaganla a piede d'uno arbore, e lo soe palafreno a piede de ley. E presseron una soa gonella e vegneno a uno luoguo onde avea bestie salvaçe e onçisseno una; e de quello sangue, ensanguinoe le lur espade per uno; e de quello sangue paresse que fosse de quello de Branguina perché paresse che l'avesse morta. E tallieron la gonella per tal que paresse que l'avesseno morta. E laysarono la en <m>[404] el deserto. ||||[405] E dapoy s'en tornano, e retrovanno la Redina Yssota.

---

[402]   Five half lines blank at gutter; miniature never executed.
[403]   MS: *ligala* with titulus. Cf. TR, p. 130: *Leghialla*.
[404]   MS has clear *m*, with spaces before and after. TP, p. 212: *nel deserto*. Not in TR.
[405]   Six full lines left blank; miniature never executed.

Il Tristano Riccardiano *(Parodi's siglum 'F')*

fail out of any pity or mercy that she would ask you'. They said that they would do it since it was her pleasure <that they would do it>. (But they marvelled greatly about these things that Lady Yseut had commanded them.) In that moment the queen had Brangain summoned, and she commanded her that in the morning she mount her palfrey, 'and take in your company these [fol. 160v] two servants who came with us from Ireland, and go into the wood. Look for the herbs that you know about, because I want to prepare a bath'. And Brangain took no heed of these things. She said, 'My lady, I will do it willingly'.

In the morning Brangain arose and dressed and prepared herself, and she rode on a lovely palfrey, and she took in her company the two servants. And they rode into those parts where she best believed she would find the herbs that Lady Yseut had commanded her. And riding along in that manner, the servants said to Brangain, 'We're not going the right way'. Then they took the route to go to the wilderness. And Brangain said, 'We're not going ||| on a good route to find herbs'. And the servants said, 'We're going fine'. And they went so far in that way that they reached a large and deep valley in the wilderness, where there were serpents and lions and other wicked beasts.

Then the servants took her and threw her from her horse. Then Brangain said, 'For what purpose have you pulled me from my horse?' And one of the servants said, 'It's necessary that you die in this wilderness, and [fol. 161r] for this reason we have brought you here: to kill you'. Then Brangain said, 'Are you doing this thing at the will of the queen?' They replied yes. Then she began to weep very hard. And one of the servants said to the other, 'Kill her!' and the other said, 'You kill her!' Then the servants said that it seemed to them a great sin. Now he said, 'Have you done anything to Lady Yseut?' And Brangain said no, 'except that two damsels left their land and came to a foreign country; and each one had a lily flower to guard, and one lost her lily due to her carelessness. And that one who guarded her lily well loaned her lily to the one who lost it due to her carelessness, whence that one who loaned it must die because of it. In this way, I will die this time. These words I have told you so that you tell them to the queen. Now do with me as you please: since my lady wants me to die, I want to die'.

The servants took counsel together. The one said to the other, 'Let's tie her up in this wilderness, and wild beasts will come and eat her in this wilderness, because it seems to me a great sin to kill her'. Then they were in agreement, [fol. 161v] both the servants; and they took Brangain and tied her to the foot of a tree, and her palfrey at her feet. And they took one of her skirts and came to a place where there were wild beasts and killed one; and with that blood one of them bloodied their swords – and that blood seemed to be Brangain's – so that it would seem that [they] had killed her. And they cut the skirt in such a way so it seemed that they had killed her; and they left her in the wilderness; ||| and after they returned, they found Queen Yseut.

Ella disse, 'Si dice niente quando viene a mor<t>ire?' E li servi disseron que sie, ch'ella comandoe sua anima a Dio e a Sancta Maria e ali sancti che li devesseno aytare. E contoe com due damisselle si partiron de lor realme e anderon en estragne paesse. E chiascaduna avea una fiore[de]lisso, e l'una lo [fol. 162r] perdete per soa mala gardia. E quella [que] lo gardoe bene, prestoe la a quella que lo gardoe malle. 'E en tal manera, moroe io'. Alor Madona Yssota disse ali servi, 'Diss'ella altro?' E li servi disseno de no. Alor si meravillia Madona Yssota de la soa cortessia, e disse ali servi, 'Andiate e menate me lo soe corpo, ché io li vuolio fare honore ala morte quando non li abo facto en la vita'. Or montano a chavallo li servi e chavalchano en quella parte onde abianno laysata Branguina. E comensçano a cerguare de qua e de lae per Branguina. Non lo potetono retrovare. E chominçano a cerquare en omni[406] lato. Non li possano trovare en neuno lato siché·lla nocte lur sopraviene e remasseron en lo deserto.

[67] Or laysa lo parlar de' due servi, e volio devissare lo condo de Branguina en que modo foe diliberata del deserto. E quando Branguina piançea fortamente e metea gran gridi, e chiama Idio e la soa Matre que la devesse aytare. En tal manera andava uno chavaliere armato a lege de chavaliere erante. Lo chavaliere, odendo la rumore de la damissella, chavalca [fol. 162v] en quelle parte per sapere chi fosse. E tanto chavalcha que perviene chi ov'era Branguina. E venendo presso a Branguina onde era piue spunosso en quella parte, ed era Branguina ligata a uno arbore. E quando Branguina vide lo chavaliere, enchominçoe a pregare per amore de chavallaria, e pregòli que la devesse deliberare.

A tanto lo chavaliere la selçe, e poy li demanda s'illa àe neuno cavallo. Alora Branguina si li mostroe lo cavallo. Lo chavaliere menoe lo cavallo a Branguina e messe la a cavallo; e torna lo chavaliere per lo so cavallo e cavalcha co[n] Branguina, e demanda que parte vuole andare. Alora Branguina disse che la menasse a uno monesterio ch'ella vuolle servire Idio e la soa Matre. 'Dapoyqué io non posso essere con quella donna que io amo più sopra tute li autre cosse del mondo, io non vuolio servire altro que Dio'. Alor disse lo chavaliere que la menarebe a uno monestero. ‖‖[407] [fol. 163r] (May si alchuno mi demanderà chi era lo chavaliere, io dirò qu'era Palamides lo bruno[408] chavaliere.)

A tanto cavalchano en tal manera che giu[n]sseronno a uno monestero al'ora de prima. Alora disse Branguina, 'Chome s'apella lo monestiero?' E Palamides disse que s'apella lo monestieri reale 'perché tieny le dame que v'intrano si sonno filioli de richi e de grandi baroni'. Alor Palamides chominça a gardare Branguina e chonoveba qu'era Branguina la damissella qu'era de Mona Yssota. Fòne molto alegro. (May si quello giorno non si fae a chonossere.) ‖‖[409] May le donne de lo monestero si fanno tuto el giorno gran festa a Branguina, e Palamides li fae granda honore.

---

406   MS again, *oi* with titulus.
407   Five full lines and most of a sixth left blank at bottom of writing space.
408   Cf. TR, p. 132 and TP, p. 214: *lo buono*.
409   Six full lines left blank.

Il Tristano Riccardiano *(Parodi's siglum 'F')*

She said, 'Did she say anything when she was about to die?' And the servants said yes, that she commended her soul to God and to Saint Mary and to the saints to help her. And she recounted how two damsels left their kingdom and went into a foreign country; and each one had a lily, and the one [fol. 162r] lost it due to her carelessness; and she who guarded it well, loaned it to she who guarded it badly 'and in this way, I will die'. Then Lady Yseut said to the servants, 'Did she say anything else?' And the servants said no. Then Lady Yseut marvelled at her courtesy, and she told the servants, 'Go and bring me her body, because I want to pay honor to her in death when I have not done it in life'. Now the servants mounted their horses and rode into that place where they had left Brangain, and they began to search here and there for Brangain; they couldn't find her again. And they began to search everywhere. They couldn't find her anywhere so that night was overtaking them, but they remained in the wilderness.

[67] Now the tale leaves off speaking of the two servants, and I want to describe the tale of Brangain, in what way she was delivered from the wilderness. When Brangain was weeping very hard and emitting great cries, she called upon God and his Mother to help her. Meanwhile, a knight, armed in the fashion of an errant knight, was going along. The knight, upon hearing the damsel's noise, rode [fol. 162v] into those parts to find out who it was. And he rode so much that he came there where Brangain was; and coming near to Brangain – where it was the most thorny in that part of the wood, there was Brangain tied to a tree. And when Brangain saw the knight, she began to beg him for chivalry's sake, and she begged him to liberate her.

In that moment the knight dismounted, and then he asked her if she had a horse at all. Then Brangain showed him the horse. The knight led the horse to Brangain and put her on the horse; and the knight returned to his horse and rode off with Brangain; and he asked her to what place she wanted to go. Then Brangain said that he should take her to a monastery,* because she wanted to serve God and his Mother. 'Since I cannot be with that lady whom I love more than all the other things in the world, I want to serve no one but God'. Then the knight said that he would take her to a monastery. ||| [fol. 163r] (But if anyone asks me who the knight was, I would say that he was Palamides, the good** knight.)

They rode along in that manner so far that they reached a monastery at the hour of prime. Then Brangain asked, 'What is the monastery called?' And Palamides said that it was called the Royal Monastery 'because the ladies who entered there are daughters of the rich and of great barons'. Then Palamides began to look at Brangain, and he recognized that she was Brangain, the damsel who was with Lady Yseut. He was very happy about it. (But that day he did not yet identify himself). ||| The ladies of the monastery made a festive welcome the whole day to Brangain, and Palamides paid her great honor.

---

* In Italian, *monastero* (var. *monistero*) indicated an institution for nuns or monks. See *Il Novellino* 62, p. 70; Boccaccio, *Decameron*, ed. Quaglio, vol. 2, p. 780: Day 9, Story 2.
** MS reads 'the brown (or dark) knight' which, although Palamides was of 'Saracen' descent, is not his normal epithet. Translation adopts the readings of TR, p. 132; and TP, p. 214.

Ala matina si leva Palamides e monta a chavallo e vae en Cornavalia enverso Titolin. E viene el desserto ad una font[an]a [fol. 163v] el quale è al passo del deserto de Titolin. Al'aqua [de la][410] fontana Madonna Yssota molto sovenno venire a solasarçi con lo Re e con le donne perché la fontana era molto bella e dilectovole.

[68] Or laysa lo conto de parlare de Palamides e torna al Re Marcho.

[69] Alora chomanda lo Re Marcho que sianno messi .v. pavaliogne ala marina; fo facto soe[411] comandamento. E poy montoe a chavallo el<le> Re – e la Redina e altri chavalieri e donne – e chavalchano ala marina. E lo Re si parte con sua congpagnia; e la Redina si parte con altre donne, e vanno ala fontana que tanto era dilectivole. E poyqué foron ala fontana, posseno si a sedere; e chomençone a fare grande piante per amore de Branguina. Enfra quisti pianti, tornoron li servi ala<la> Redina; e disse loro, 'Si trovaronno Branguina, o morta o viva?' E li servi disseron che noe, che non la trovareno en neuno modo del mondo.

[70] Alor la Redina e[n]chominça a fare magior pianto que danançi, over da prima. E disse ali servi, 'Doncha, non l'avete trovata nì morta nì viva? Disse me encontenente' – disse la Redina – 'si voy l'ançideste'. E li servi, [fol. 164r] avendo gran paora, disseno, 'Noy non la uçidemo, ançi la laysamo viva el desserto a piede d'uno arbore'. E poyché la Redina ebe entesso qu'ella era viva, diede chumiato ali servi. E poy gittò unno gran sospiro e disse, 'Or lassa, Branguina, quanto sonno dolorossa!'

En tanto viene Palamides, lo quale era al passo de la fontana del bosquo. Vedendo que la Redina si lamentava de Branguina en tal manera, ||||[412] <[c]he dono>[413] trayse si ennançi e disse, 'Madona la Redina, chi ve re[n]desse Branguina, que dono li dareste voy?' E la Redina disse, 'Si tu Branguina me mene, jà tale dono no[n] me demanderay che tu non li abe'. Alor respose lo chavaliere, 'Prometete me voy chome Redina?' Ed ella respose e disse que sie. E Palamides [fol. 164v] disse, 'Enançi que sia trey giorni si ve la menaroe sanna e salva'.

[71] A tanto Palamides monta a chavallo e partì si de la Redina e chavalcha verso lo monestiero reale per la più rieta via che poe. E tanto chavalchoe che perviene alo monestiero ov'era Branguina. E le donne de lo monestere, quando videno Palamides, fesseli grande honore – e Branguina especialmente, conossendo qu'era lo chavaliere che l'avia deliberata de la morte; e Palamides disse che non era esso.[414]

410   MS *le*.
411   MS *foe*. Confusion of *s* / *f*.
412   Eight full lines blank; miniature never executed.
413   Guide letter *c*, but no *c* was written in the normal text. After the blank space, the text begins *he dono*. These words correctly belong to Palamides' utterance in the next line.
414   Palamides' reply, an apparent humility topos, is not found in TR, p. 134.

Il Tristano Riccardiano *(Parodi's siglum 'F')*

In the morning Palamides arose and mounted his horse and went into Cornwall, toward Tintagel. And in the wilderness he came to a fountain [fol. 163v] that was at the ford of the wilderness of Tintagel. Lady Yseut very often came to the fountain's water to enjoy herself with the king and with her ladies because the fountain was very beautiful and delightful.

[68] Now the tale leaves off speaking of Palamides and returns to King Mark.

[69] Then King Mark commanded that five pavilions be set up on the shore; his command was carried out. And then the king mounted his horse – and the queen and other knights and ladies – and they rode to the shore. And the king went off with his company; and the queen went off with other ladies and came to the fountain that was so delightful. And after they were at the fountain, they sat down; and the queen began to weep greatly for love of Brangain. In the midst of this weeping, the servants returned to the queen; and she said to them, 'Is Brangain found, dead or alive?' And the servants said no, that they did not find her in any way in the world.

[70] Then the queen began to make a greater lament than before, or rather, than at first. And she said to the servants, 'So then, you haven't found her, neither dead nor alive? Tell me at once' – said the queen – 'if you killed her'. And the servants, [fol. 164r] greatly afraid, said, 'We didn't kill her; instead we left her alive in the wilderness, at the foot of a tree'. And when the queen had heard that she was alive, she granted leave to the servants. Then she let out a big sigh and said, 'Now alas, Brangain, how very sorrowful I am!'

In that moment, Palamides (who was at the ford of the fountain in the wood) came over, seeing that the queen was lamenting about Brangain in that fashion. ||| He drew forward and said, 'My Lady the Queen, what gift would you give to whomever restored Brangain to you?' And the queen said, 'If you bring Brangain to me, there is truly no gift that you could ask of me that you would not have'. Then the knight replied, 'Do you promise me as queen?' And she replied and said yes. And Palamides [fol. 164v] said, 'Before three days have passed, I will bring her to you, safe and sound'.

[71] In that moment Palamides mounted his horse and left the queen and rode toward the royal monastery by the most direct route that he could. And he rode so much that he came to the monastery where Brangain was. And the ladies of the monastery, upon seeing Palamides, paid him great honor; and Brangain did so especially, knowing that he was the knight who had delivered her from death, but Palamides said that it wasn't him.

[72] Alor Palamides si trayse l'ermo fore del capo.
[. . .]⁴¹⁵
espectanto en pocho l'ora que Palamides andava enverso la tore, si s'adormentò per la gran fatigua que avea auto la nocte cavalcando. E estando en questo modo eli<n> dormendo, echo venire Tristano – e Governale – verso le torre. Si trovoron Palamides dormendo. E quando Tristano vide que Palamides dormia, disse a Governale, 'Va' e chiamalo che viena ala ||||⁴¹⁶ [fol. 165r] batalia che io l'aspecto'. Governale andoe a Palamides, e Palamides non odia de queste cosse nulla. Alor [Governale] se volta a terra e presse lo per l'ermo e chome[n]çia lo a tirare. E tanto lo tiroe que lo esvellioe. E poyché foe esvelliato, disse, 'Dolço pençieri aveste ora estato ché li parea essere chon la sua dama a tanto conpimento d'amore'. Ello disse, 'Eschudieri, si tu fosse chavaliere, tu l'achatareste caro chiò que facto mi ày!' E Governale re[s]posse e disse, 'Ora estate su ji<u>amay e prendete le arme – qué 'l tuo pensieri ti è venuto fallaçe – qué Tristano t'apella ala batalia'. ||||⁴¹⁷ E Palamides si⁴¹⁸ leva encontenente su e presse suo eschudo e soa lançia, e monta a chavallo e viene ala giusta con Tristano.

[73] Alor desfidò l'uno l'autro, e viegnon si a ferire l'uno l'autro [fol. 165v] E p[r]essono le lançe e fieron se sì forte che chiascadono andoe a terra da cavallo, siché a chiaschaduno à bissoncha de cadere a terra de cavallo. Encontenente si levan su e meteno [s]y mane al'espade e fieron sy siché en pocho d'ora nonn·è mae neuno que non abi asay ferite; e grande mestieri fae alor pausare più che de conbatere.

E Madona Yssota, la quale è ala fenestra e vede che Tristano chonbate, molto n'è alegra perché li conbate per amor soa e per so deliberamento; may molto èy dolenta quando vidi <vidi> li gran colpi che Palamides dae a Tristano; e molto si desconforta Madona Yssota del primo asalto.

Dapoyqué foron repousati, li chavalieri achominçano lo seconde asalto. E Tristano chominça a ferire Palamides di sì gran força e dàli sì gran colpi che en poucho d'ora, chominça a menare Palamides a soa volontà. E Madona Yssota, vedendo la batalia e chonoysendo l'aventura la quale avegnano (sichome dama que n'era usata), vidi e chonosse bene che Palamides n'àe lo peçiore de la batalia, che ala fine non potrà durare con Tristano. May li chavalieri si laguano⁴¹⁹ altro che de parolle lo quale si danno grandi colpi [fol. 166r] e d'una mano oe de l'autra. E si chonosse bene Palamides qu'alo ferire Tristano non è soe amicho; e chonosse Palamides ch'alo derietro, non potrà durare a Tristano e non credea que en Tristano fosse tanta forsa.

---

415   Lengthy narrative ellipsis. See TR, pp. 134–46 and TP, pp. 216–26 for missing content.
416   Four full lines left blank at bottom of writing space.
417   Seven full lines left blank.
418   MS *fi*. Confusion of *s* / *f*.
419   Cf. TR: *si servono*.

[72] Then Palamides pulled his helmet from his head.
[...]*
awaiting for a short while after Palamides had gone toward the tower, he fell asleep from the great exhaustion that he had from riding that night. And while he was sleeping in this way, behold Tristan coming – and Governal – toward the tower! They found Palamides sleeping. And when Tristan saw that Palamides was sleeping, he said to Governal, 'Go and call him so that he comes to ||| [fol. 165r] battle, because I await him'. Governal went to Palamides, but Palamides didn't hear anything of these goings-on. Then Governal jumped to the ground and took him by the helmet and began to pull it, and he pulled it so hard that he woke him. And after he was awakened, Governal said, 'You were having sweet thoughts <now get up> because you seemed to be with your lady at the moment of fulfilling your love'. Palamides said, 'Squire, if you were a knight, you would pay dearly for what you've done to me!' Governal replied and said, 'Now get up, if ever you will, and take up your arms! – since your thoughts are fallacious – because Tristan is calling you to battle'. ||| And Palamides arose at once and took his shield and his lance, and he mounted his horse and came to joust with Tristan.

[73] Then the one challenged the other, and they came to strike one another. [fol. 165v] And they took their lances and struck each other so hard that each one went to the ground, unhorsed, so that it behooved each one to fall to the ground from his horse. Immediately they got up and put hands to swords and struck each other so that in a short time there was no one who did not have a lot of wounds; and then they really needed to rest more than to fight.

Lady Yseut, who was at the window and saw that Tristan was fighting, was very happy about it because he was fighting for her love and for her deliverance; but she was very sorrowful when she saw the great blows that Palamides was giving to Tristan; and Lady Yseut was very discomfited by the first assault.

After they had rested, the knights began the second assault. And Tristan began to strike Palamides with such great force and gave him such great blows that, in a short time, he began to move Palamides around at will. Lady Yseut, seeing the battle and realizing what Fortune might bring (like a lady who was quite accustomed to it) saw and clearly knew that Palamides was having the worse of the battle, that in the end he would not be able to endure against Tristan. But the knights concerned themselves with other than words, for which they gave each other great blows, [fol. 166r] with one hand or the other. And Palamides clearly knew from Tristan's blows that he was not his friend; and Palamides knew that, in the end, he would not be able to endure against Tristan; and he didn't believe that there was such power in Tristan.

---

* Lengthy narrative ellipsis in the MS. Cf. TR, pp. 135–47; and TP, pp. 217–27.

[74] Quando Madona Yssota vidi conbatere li chavalieri e vedea lor prodessa, disse enfra sé estessa, 'Qualuncha de questi chavalieri morisse, ne seria gran danno'. Alor si parte Madona Yssota da la fenestra e viene ala porta e·ffese baysare lo ponte e andoe entre li chavalieri. Governale disse, 'Madonna, metete passe entre li chavalieri, ché non mo[i]a uno en tal manera'. E Yssota disse, 'Questo farò volontir[i] io, s'io poterò'. ||||[420] Alor chomanda la Redina ali chavalieri e disse loro, 'Laysate quest<e>a batalia'; e li chavalieri feronno so chomandamento. Encontenente disse la Redina a Palamides, 'Laysa questa batalia, ché io volio que tu me fasse uno messagio, lo quale ti diroe'. E Palamides resposse e disse, 'Jo farò [fol. 166v] çò che mi comandarete'. Alor disse la Redina,[421] 'Io ti chomandi che tu vadi ala corte del Re Artù e salutalo mi luy, e la Redina Genevra e tuti quelli de soa corte. E direte loro qu'en tuto lo mondo non sono si non due chavalieri e due dame'. Alor disse Palamides, 'Questo faroe io volontieri'. (May ben chonossia que la Redina lo mandava più per alongar lo da sé que per altro.) Alor si parte Palamides de la Redina per fare lo messagio que comandato li era.

E Madona Yssota prende Tristano e Governale, e mèneli entre la torre; e regarda li le piague de Tristano e trovò che non avea danno neuno. Alor disse Tristano a Madona Yssota che parea lor, que en questo ponto, si potian partire con meno de dissonore, 'ché voy sapete lo covenente che èi enfra voy e me: che voy non ve potette tener da me nì io da voi'. Alor disse Madona Yssota quale parea que fosse lo melio de retornare al Re Marcho che andar en autra parte, e che tropo biassmo li ne parea avere. Alor disse Tristano que quello que plaçia a ley, si plaçea a luy. La nocte si possano anboro, e la nocte passano[422] con gran gioa.

Ala matina si leva Tristano e presse soe arme e monta a chavallo – e Yssota e Governale – e partite [fol. 167r] se de la torre e venonsene verso Titolin en Cornavalia. E chavalchano en tal manera che vegnonno ala corte de Re Marcho, e qui v'esmontoronno. E Tristano presse Madona Yssota per la mano, e foron venuti per la sala danançi alo Re onde era con li soy baroni. E Tristano disse, 'Re Marcho, un'altra[423] volta abi melior gardia que non àe avuto e non la dare ad altruy, qu'ello èi magior brigua d'aquistare que a donare'. E lo Re disse que non darea a nesuna persona neuno dono 'qué no[n] chave più mia donna'.

[75] A pogui giorni, viene una damissella enella corte del Re Marcho. Ella s'inamorò fortamente de Tristano, e disseli, 'Io volio che tu sey chavaliere de mi' amore'. E Tristano de queste parolle qu'ella li disse, Tristano si chorussava e dissia, 'Va' via, folle damissella, e queste parolle may non dire!' Sò que Tristano

---

420   Six full lines left blank; miniature never executed.
421   At this point, the scribe began abbreviating the queen's title. I expand these without comment.
422   MS *possano*.
423   Scribe wrote *autra*. The *u* is overwritten with an *l*.

Il Tristano Riccardiano *(Parodi's siglum 'F')*

[74] When Lady Yseut saw the knights fighting and saw their prowess, she said to herself, 'Whichever of these knights were to die, it would be a great shame'. Then Lady Yseut left her window and came to the door and had the drawbridge lowered and went between the knights. Governal said, 'My lady, make peace between the knights, so that one does not die in such fashion'. And Yseut said, 'I will do this gladly, if I am able'. ||| Then the queen commanded the knights and told them, 'Leave off this battle'; and the knights did as she commanded. Immediately the queen said to Palamides, 'Leave this battle, because I want you to carry a message for me, which I will tell you'. And Palamides replied and said, 'I will do [fol. 166v] as you command'. Then the queen said, 'I order you to go to the court of King Arthur and greet him on my behalf, and Queen Guenevere and all those of his court, and tell them that in the whole world, there are only two knights and two ladies'. Then Palamides said, 'I will do this willingly'. (But well he knew that the queen was sending him off more to remove him from her than for any other reason.) Then Palamides left the queen to carry the message as she had commanded.

And Lady Yseut took Tristan and Governal and brought them into the tower, and she looked at Tristan's wounds and found that he had no serious injury. Then Tristan said to Lady Yseut that it seemed that, at this point, they could leave together with less dishonor 'because you know the situation between you and me: how you couldn't keep yourself from me nor I from you'. Then Lady Yseut said that it seemed that it would be better to return to King Mark than to go somewhere else and that it seemed that they could have too much blame from it. Then Tristan said that whatever was pleasing to her, was pleasing to him. That night they could be together, and they passed the night with great joy.

In the morning Tristan arose and took his arms and mounted his horse – as did Yseut and Governal – and left [fol. 167r] the tower and went on their way toward Tintagel in Cornwall. And they rode in that fashion until they came to King Mark's court, and here they dismounted. Tristan took Lady Yseut by the hand, and they came through the hall before the king, where he was with his barons. And Tristan said, 'King Mark, another time take better care than you have and don't give her to others because it is more trouble to receive than to give'. And the king said that he would not grant any boon to anyone 'so that my lady would not be wrested from me again'.

[75] A few days later, a damsel came into King Mark's court. She fell deeply in love with Tristan, and she said to him, 'I want you to be the knight of my heart'. But Tristan was vexed about these words that she had said to him and said, 'Go away, foolish damsel, and never say such things!' What Tristan said

disse, si fo la Damissella Malastrugua[424] ed è fortamente choressata, e dissia enfra soe chore qu'ella non farae bene a Tristano, si ella potrà tanto fare.

A tanto la damissella se 'namorò de Guedis, e Guedis en chiama la damissella de soa amore.[425] A tanto s'avide la damissella que Tristano s'amava con Madona Yssota [fol. 167v] de follie amore, e tanto lo disse a Guedis (e Guedis era nepote del Re Marcho e chossino de Tristano.) E Guedis, per astio que avea de luy, achussòlo alo Re Marcho e disse, 'Messer lo Re, Tristano vagueçha vostra dama'. El Re Marcho disse che non potea essere. E Guedis disse que coysì era la veritate, 'e io lo farò a voy a chredere siché voy ne serete cierto'. A tanto Guedis pilloe due falçe remene[426] e messele entorno al lecto de Madonna Yssota. La sera quando Madonna Yssota era colchiata, apresso viene Tristano per una fenestra e pilió uno salto e saltoe en su el lecto de Madonna Yssota; e estete con ley la magior parte de la note. E quando si viene a partire, Tristano non si prende gardia de le fauçe e 'nchapoe ende le fauçe de le ganbe. Alor disse Tristano, 'Noy siamo morti, qué nostri opere si saprano'. E la Redina disse, 'Vae ne ala tua camera ||||[427] [fol. 168r] e queste cosse laysa fare a me ché io ne prenderò ben consilio'. Alor si parte Tristano e torna ala soa chamera. E Yssota si leva de soe leto e viene ale fauçe e ferite ne una de li ganbe. Encontenente gridoe e·ffes[s]e grande rumore siché tute le damisselle viegnono ala camera de la Redina; e rassonançi asay boni chavalieri, e dichono, 'Re Marcho, que è questo de Madonna Yssota?' Ed ello resposse que de queste cosse non sapia niente. May quilli que vegnono ende la camera d[en]no[428] essere o Tristano o Guedis encorpati de queste cosse. ||||[429]

E[430] Tristano disse, 'Io sonno aparechiato de provare a Guedis per forse d'arme ch'eli lì messe le fauçe entorno al lectto de Madonna, e non io'. Alor disse el Re Marcho, 'Or laysate estare queste cosse sopra me, e io ne daroe lo pentimento quello que sì co[fol. 168v][n]viene'. A tanto lo Re si parte – e li chavalieri e li baroni e le dame e damisselli – e torna chiascaduno a soa camera.

Ala matina si leva lo Re Marcho e viene en sala onde eranno li chavalieri con Tristano. Encontenente lo Re Marcho comandoe que sianno messe .v. pavalione ala marina. Fo facto soe comandamento. Encontenente montoe a chavallo la Redina e la soa gente e li baroni con grande conpagnia, e cominçono a far gran solaçio. May Tristano non chura d'altro solaçio si [non] da quello di Madona Yssota, e chominçanno enfra loro due a piè d'uno pavalione a giuchare a schachi. Estando en tal manera, echo venire .ii. chavalieri eranti, armati de tute arme sichome chavaliere erante. E vennonno ali pavalioni del Re Marcho, e salutano

---

[424] Form not in TR or TP, but is found in medieval texts in *comense* dialect: *malastruto* (*Spagna in rima*, ed. Rosiello, p. 544); *malastruda* (*Il 'Fierabraccia' comense: fra preziosità umanistiche e antico dialetto lombardo*, ed. Elio Melli, Biblioteca di Filologia Romanza della Facoltà di Lettere e Filosofia dell'Università di Bologna 10 [Bologna, 1996], p. 346).

[425] MS *Ghedis*. Emendation based on content and TR, p. 150; and TP, p. 230.

[426] Clear in MS, but superscripted *a* appears above the second *e*. Cf. TR, p. 150; and TP, p. 230: *falci fienaie*.

[427] Five full lines left blank at bottom of writing space; miniature never executed.

[428] Internal letters illegible.

[429] Six full lines left blank at mid-page; miniature never executed.

[430] A guide letter and red capital *E* indicate a new paragraph.

Il Tristano Riccardiano *(Parodi's siglum 'F')*

made the damsel wretched, and she was quite vexed and said in her heart that she would not treat Tristan well, if she could do as much.

Then the damsel fell in love with Ghedis, and Ghedis called her the damsel of his love. Meanwhile the damsel noticed that Tristan was loving Lady Yseut [fol. 167v] with a mad love, and she said as much to Ghedis (Ghedis was King Mark's nephew and Tristan's cousin). And Ghedis, because of the rancor that he felt toward him, accused him to King Mark and said, 'My Lord the King, Tristan is shaming you with your lady'; and King Mark said that couldn't be. And Ghedis said that such was the truth 'and I'll make you believe it so that you will be sure of it'. Then Ghedis took two mowing scythes and put them around Lady Yseut's bed. That evening when Lady Yseut was in bed, then Tristan came in by a window; and he made a leap and leapt into Lady Yseut's bed; and he stayed with her the greater part of the night. And when it came time to leave, Tristan did not take guard of the scythes and bumped into the scythes with his legs. Then Tristan said, 'We are dead because our deeds will be found out!' But the queen said, 'Go on to your chamber ||| [fol. 168r] and leave these things to me because I will surely think of what to do about them'. Then Tristan left and returned to his chamber; and Yseut arose from her bed and came to the scythes and wounded herself in one of her legs. Immediately she cried out and made a great noise so that all her damsels came to the queen's chamber – and a great many good knights gathered – and they were saying, 'King Mark, what's wrong with Lady Yseut?' And he replied that he didn't know anything about these things. But those men who came into the chamber said either Tristan or Ghedis must be guilty of these things. |||

And Tristan said, 'I'm prepared to prove to Ghedis by force of arms that he put the scythes there around My Lady's bed and not I'. Then King Mark said, 'Now leave these things to me, and I'll make whoever did it repent, as is fitting'. [fol. 168v] In that moment the king left – and the knights and the barons and the ladies and young men – and each one returned to his chamber.

In the morning King Mark arose and came to the hall where there were knights with Tristan. Immediately King Mark commanded that five pavilions be set up on the shore. His command was carried out. Immediately he mounted his horse, along with the queen and his people and barons, with a large company, and they began to amuse themselves greatly. But Tristan cared for no other pleasure if not Lady Yseut's, and the two of them began to play chess at the foot of one pavilion. While they were there in this manner, behold! – two errant knights coming along, fully armed as errant knights are. And they came to King Mark's pavilions, and

lo Re Marcho e tuti li baroni e chavalieri; e lo Re rende cortesamente lur saluto. E li chavalieri demandoron onde era la Redina Yssota. E lo Re resposse, 'Vedete ||| [431] [fol. 169r] la que giogua a squaçhi con Tristano'. E li chavalieri andorono en quella parte onde era la Redina Yssota. (May si alchuno me demandarae chi eranno li chavalieri, io diroe que·ll'uno era Lamorato di Gaules, e l'autro era so fratello.)

E Lamorato disse contra so fratello, 'Coysino, (sic) ell'è più bella la Redina d'Onguana[432] che Madonna Yssota'. E lo chuissino comiça a dire que più bella era Madonna Yssota que non è la Redina d'Ongana. E Lamorato disse, 'Per mia fé, si non fosse mio coysino, io provarea per forse d'arme que Madonna la Redina d'Onghana èi <l> più bella che non è Madonna Yssota'. E soe chussino resposse, 'Per mia fé, si tu non fosse mio chussino, ti mostrarea per força d'arme que Madona Yssota èi più bella que la Redina d'Oguana'. E tute queste cosse la Redina Yssota l'audia, e disse, 'Chavaliere, chi fillioli fosti voy?' Elo disse, 'Lo Re Pellinoro[433] fo mio patre'. Disse Yssota, 'Siete voy chavaliere erante?' Elli disse que sie. Alor disse Madona Yssota, 'Io non credo que tu fosse fillioll del Re Pelignoro perché lo Re fo cortese chavaliere. May tu non li retrae al soe lignaçio [fol. 169v] de cortesia, ché tu mi pare villanno chavaliere quando, denanchi da me, tu me disi villania'. Alor disse Lamoralto, 'Io ve preguo s'io voy abi decto villania, que mi perdonate, ché tuto al tenpo de mia vita non ve afalliroò[434] en tal manera'.

[76] Alor si partironno anboro li chavalieri e prendono cumiato da la Redina, e vieneno al'estrada a piede d'uno arbore e trovono una damissella que veniva ali pavalioni. E disseronno, 'Damissella, io ve preguo que voy me faciate uno meçagio alo Re Marcho, e dicate li que .ii. chavalieri errante sonno qua a piede d'uno arbore e demandano giostra'. |||[435] E la damissella disse, 'Questo farò io volonti[e]ri'. Alor si parte la damissella da li chavalieri e viene alo Re Marcho; e disse, 'Re Marcho, là giusso a piede d'uno arbore a .ii. chavalieri eranti[436] [fol. 170r] che ve dimandan giostra'. E lo Re resposse, 'Si de giostra me demandanno, io de giostra non li faliroe lorro'. Alor chomanda<no> lo Re Marcho que .ii. chavalieri montano[437] a chavallo e prendano l'arme per andar a conbatere con li chavalieri eranti le quali aspettano.

Encontenente fo facto; e [li chavalieri furono] armati e andoron a conbatere con li chavalieri erranti. E Lamorado disse – quando vidi li chavalieri – 'Ora vedremo chome la faranno li chavalieri de Cornavalia'. Alor abaysanno le lançe

---

[431] Four lines left blank at bottom of writing space; miniature never executed.

[432] Regarding these names, see TR, p. 152: *Lamorak, Orcania*; TP, p. 232: *Lamoratto, Organia*.

[433] Cf. TR, p. 154: *Pillinor*; TP, p. 232: *Pilione*.

[434] MS *asalliro*. Confusion of *s* / *f*. See below in this MS, fol. 170r: *faliroe*; and cf. TR, p. 154: *fagliero*.

[435] Seven full lines left blank at mid-page.

[436] Catchword at center bottom: *Che*. This crudely drawn cartouche was done in red and brown ink.

[437] MS *montana*.

Il Tristano Riccardiano *(Parodi's siglum 'F')*

they greeted King Mark and all the barons and knights; and the king returned their greeting courteously. And the knights asked where Queen Yseut was. And the king replied, 'See ||| [fol. 169r] her, playing chess with Tristan'. And the knights went over to the place where Queen Yseut was. (But if anyone were to ask me who the knights were, I would say that one was Lamorat of Gaul and the other was his brother.)

Lamorat said to his brother, 'Cousin, (sic)* the Queen of Orkney is more beautiful than Lady Yseut'; and his cousin began to say that Lady Yseut was more beautiful than the Queen of Orkney. And Lamorat said, 'By my faith, if you were not my cousin, I would prove by force of arms that My Lady the Queen of Orkney is more beautiful than Lady Yseut'; and his cousin replied, 'By my faith, if you were not my cousin, I would show you by force of arms that Lady Yseut is more beautiful than the Queen of Orkney'. And Queen Yseut heard all these things and said, 'Knight, whose son were you?' And he said, 'King Pellinor was my father'. Yseut said, 'Are you an errant knight?' He said yes. Then Lady Yseut said, 'I don't believe that you were the son of King Pellinor because the king was a courteous knight, but you do not reflect his courteous lineage [fol. 169v] because you seem to me a villainous knight when, in front of me, you speak villainously of me'. Then Lamorat said, 'I pray you, if I have spoken villainously to you, to pardon me because for the rest of my life I'll not fail you in such a way'.

[76] Then both the knights left and took leave of the queen, and they came to the road at the foot of a tree and found a damsel who was going to the pavilions. And they said, 'Damsel, I pray you to take a message for me to King Mark, and tell him that two errant knights are here at the foot of a tree, and they are demanding a joust'. ||| And the damsel said, 'I will do this willingly'. Then the damsel left the knights and came to King Mark; and she said, 'King Mark, down there at the foot of a tree are two errant knights [fol. 170r] who are demanding a joust of you'. And the king replied, 'If they demand a joust of me, I'll not fail to give them a joust'. Then King Mark commanded that two knights mount their horses and take their arms to go fight with the errant knights who were waiting.

Immediately it was done; and knights were armed and went to fight with the errant knights. And Lamorat said – when he saw the knights – 'Now we'll see how the knights of Cornwall do'. Then they lowered their lances and came to

---

*   The same change of familial terms occurs in TR, p. 152.

e vienon a ferire. E Lamorato li ferite de tuta soa forsa, e passòli l'eschudo e l'esbercho, e messe li la lançia ende le coste, e messe lo a terra del cavallo; ||||⁴³⁸ e lo so choissino abate lo so chavaliere semillantamente.

E lo Re, quando vidi li soy chavalieri a terra, comandoe ancho a due chavalieri que prendesseno l'arme e vadano a conbatere con li chavalieri. E li chavalieri encontenenti foron armati: .ii. chavalieri c'andoronno ala giostra. E li .ii. chavalieri erranti [fol. 170v] lur mostraron lur força e ferireno ali chavalieri de Cornavalia, e meteno li chavalieri e li chavalli en uno monte.

[77] E lo Re Marcho, quando vide queste venture, chomanda que pilion arme .x. chavalieri. Fo facto soe comandamento. E chomanda que vadan a conbatere ensieme coy li .ii. chavalieri erranti. Alor andoron a conbatere tuti. E Madonna Yssota questo ebe veduto, e disse a Tristano, 'Andiamo a vedere chome la farano li chavalieri de Cornavalia'.⁴³⁹ E Tristano encontenente andoe alo Re e disse, 'Re Marcho, tu vituperi oçi tuta Cornavalia quando tu mandi [.x. chavalieri] contra .ii. chavalieri si non .ii.' E lo Re disse que tanto ne manderà qué li chavalieri erranti s'eranno vinto.

Alor si achomínça la batalia, e li due chavalieri errante fieronno ali .x. chavalieri. En prima que ronpesseno le lançe çhiachaduno abatette .iii. chavalieri. Poy meteno mane al'espadi ||||⁴⁴⁰ [fol. 171r] e chomínçano ferire ali autri chavalieri e danno grandi colpi siché Tristano vide conbatere li due chavalieri. Disse al Re Marcho, 'Or pottette vedere due franchi chavalieri, e bene mostrano la lor prodessa – e franchamente – siché Lamorato e 'l soe choysino eberon vinti li chavalieri de Cornavalia'. Or si retornano a piede de l'arbore e anchor⁴⁴¹ demandano giostra alo Re Marcho. ||||⁴⁴²

Alor chomanda lo Re a Tristano, e disse, 'Tristano, prende l'arme per me, ché ti è mestieri'. Alor Tristano si ne vae ali pavalione molto airato, e chomínça se armare; e monta a chavallo e prende l[e] soa arme e sua lançia e suo eschudo. Alor .ii. chavalieri de Cornavalia avianno pressi d[e] le arme per andare e fare conpagnia a Tristano. Ello disse loro que la lor conpagnia non volia giae, [fol. 171v] may si volionno andare ala batalia sença luy, vadan en bon ora. Alor cavalcha Tristano tuto solo, e li chavalieri remasserono.

E quando Lamorato vidi venire lo chavaliere solo, disse, 'Questo è Tristano, nepote del Re Marcho! E si quostuy potemo vinçere, noy potemo dire que ogi avemo vinto Cornavalia'. Alor demanda Lamorato en prima la batalia a soe choisino; e lo chusino disse que de raysone en prima era soa, chioè perqué en prima fo facto chavaliere. Alor Tristano ferite alo chavaliere, e lo chavaliere a luy; e passòli l'eschudo e l'esbercho, e mèteli la lançia al costato e ronpe li la

---

438 Seven full lines left blank, mid-page; miniature never executed.
439 Omission in MS or its model. Cf. TR, p. 154: *Allora vegnono a la piazza, là dov'iera la battaglia de li cavalieri, e viderono ke diece kavalieri di Gornovaglia andavano a·ccombattere con due cavalieri erranti.*
440 Five full lines left blank at bottom of writing space; miniature never executed.
441 MS *anchoi*.
442 Six full lines left blank, mid-page; miniature never executed.

Il Tristano Riccardiano *(Parodi's siglum 'F')*

strike. And Lamorat struck him with all his might and passed through his shield and hauberk, and put his lance into his ribs, and knocked him to the ground from his horse; ||| and his cousin struck down his knight similarly.

And the king, when he saw his knights on the ground, commanded two more knights to take up arms and go fight with the knights. And immediately the knights were armed: two knights went there to the joust. And the two errant knights [fol. 170v] displayed their strength to them and struck the Cornish knights, and knocked down the knights and their horses in a heap.

[77] King Mark, when he saw this adventure, commanded that ten knights take up their arms. His commandment was obeyed. And he commanded that they go fight together with the two errant knights. Then they all went to fight. And Lady Yseut saw this, and she said to Tristan, 'Let's go see how the Cornish knights will do'. [...]* And Tristan immediately went to the king and said, 'King Mark, today you vituperate all of Cornwall since you are sending ten knights against two knights, instead of two'. But the king said that he was sending so many of them so that the errant knights would be defeated.

Then the battle began, and the two errant knights struck at the ten knights. Before they broke their lances, each one had unhorsed three knights. Then they put their hands to their swords ||| [fol. 171r] and began to strike at the other knights. And they were giving great blows so that when Tristan saw the two knights fighting, he said to King Mark, 'Now you'll be able to see two valiant knights, and they are displaying their prowess well – and valiantly – so that Lamorat and his cousin have defeated the knights of Cornwall'. Now they returned to the foot of the tree and again demanded a joust of King Mark. |||

Then the king commanded Tristan, and he said, 'Tristan, take up your arms for my sake, since it behooves you'. Then Tristan went over to the pavilions, very irate, and began to arm himself; and he mounted his horse and took up his arms and his lance and his shield. Then two Cornish knights had taken up their arms in order to go and accompany Tristan. He told them that he did not want their company at all, [fol. 171v] but if they wanted to go to battle without him, God speed. Then Tristan rode off all alone, and the knights remained behind.

And when Lamorat saw a lone knight coming, he said, 'This is Tristan, King Mark's nephew, and if we are able to defeat him, we'll be able to say that today we have defeated Cornwall!' Then Lamorat asked his cousin for the first battle; and his cousin said that by rights the first was his, that is to say, because he was made a knight first. Then Tristan struck at the knight, and the knight at him; and the elder knight passed through his shield and hauberk, and

---

*   Probable omission here.

lançia adosso. E Tristano fiere a luy e passa l'eschudo e l'esbercho, e mete li la lançia al costato, e mete lo a terra da cavallo. Al tirare que fesse de la lançia, espasmoe[443] lo chavaliere ||||[444] [fol. 172r] E Lamorato driça la testa del destrieri, e disse enfra soe chuore que bene lo vendicarae si 'l potrae.

Alor Lamorato vae enver Tristano, e Tristano enverso luy; e chiaschaduno abaysa la lançia. E Lamorato fiere a Tristano sobra l'eschudo e ronpe soa lança. E Tristano fiere luy e passa li l'eschudo e lo esberçho, e metelo a terra del chavallo. (E messe li la lança al costato dritto e ronpe soa lançia.) Poyché ebe facto questo colpi (sic), elli si retorna verso li pavalioni e smonta da chavallo e changiò[445] le arme. E lo Re Marcho molto si meravilia di li due colpi de Tristano que avea facto; e disse enfra soe chuore que 'perqué Tristano è choysì fellone verso da me? – ché si tu enverso da me tu non fosse choysì fellone, al mondo melior chavaliere non avea'.

Ad aqueste parolle viene Lamorato e disse, 'Io, Tristano, t'apello ala batalia de l'espade, que noy façiamo <vuno> uno asalto o .ii.; e si tu m'ày ma[n]dato a terra da cavallo, tu non m'ày rachate a fine'. Alor disse Tristano, 'Sire, non è tal odio tra noy .ii. che noy si debiamo arachare a fine'. 'Oltra Sire', disse Lamorato, 'donqua non sey choysì bono chavaliere chome altri ti tienon. Dapoy[fol. 172v] ché [cessi][446] la batalia tra noy doe al'espade, pare que tu tieme de conbatere con mecho al'espade'.

[78] Alor si parte Lamorato e torna a soe choysino, e montanno a cavallo e prendono lor camino lo più dritto andare alo desserto de Nirlantes ala Fontana Aventurossa. E si trovanno uno chavaliere e una damissella. E avianno uno corno al collo lo più bello que fosse may al mondo, ed era lo corno d'arento, tuto fornito a v[ergh]e[447] d'oro, e lo schaçiare ove estava apichato lo corno era tutto d'oro fino, ed era molto bello e bene fornito a modo de corno bene e realmente.

Quando Lamorato vide lo corno, demandoe lo chavaliere que corno era. E lo chavaliere que avea lo corno en gardia disse que non l'ausava dire. E Lamorato disse, 'Per mia fé, sì, diray! – o tue conbatray mecho'. E lo chavaliere disse que si farae. A tanto si desfidano li chavalieri e vegnonsi a ferire, l'uno con l'autro. ||||[448] [fol. 173r] E le lançe si ronponno, e metono mane al'espade e si si fieronno. May lo chavaliere non potte durare con Lamorato, e disse li, 'Or ti dirò que corno è questo, e qui lo manda'.

---

443   Clear in MS: *spalmoe*. Confusion of *s* / *l*. Correction based on TR, p. 156: *ispasimoe*.
444   Seven full lines left blank at bottom of writing space; miniature never executed.
445   MS *chanoçi*.
446   MS *selli*. Confusion of *s* / *l*. Correction from TR, p. 158: *cessi*.
447   MS *vguiie*. Probably misread or omitted *v(er)* abbreviation. See TR, p. 158: *a verche doro*. See Battaglia, *Grande dizionario*, vol. 21, p. 771, definition 7: 'lingotto di metallo, in partic. d'oro, pronto per essere fuso e lavorato' (thin bands, especially of gold, ready to be fused on and worked).
448   Six full lines left blank at bottom of writing space; miniature never executed.

put his lance into his side and broke his lance against him. And Tristan struck him and passed through his shield and hauberk, and put his lance into his side and knocked him to the ground from his horse. When he pulled his lance out, the knight writhed in pain. ||| [fol. 172r] And Lamorat directed his horse's head at Tristan and said in his heart that he would surely avenge him, if he could.

Then Lamorat came toward Tristan, and Tristan toward him; and each one lowered his lance. And Lamorat struck Tristan on his shield and broke his lance. And Tristan struck him and passed through his shield and hauberk, and knocked him to the ground from his horse. (And he put his lance into his right side and broke his lance.) After he had made this blow, he returned toward the pavilions and dismounted from his horse and changed his arms. King Mark marvelled greatly at the two blows that Tristan had made and said in his heart, 'Why is Tristan so perfidious toward me? Because if you were not so perfidious toward me, there would not be a better knight in the world'.

At these words Lamorat came and said, 'Tristan, I call you to battle with swords, so that we make one or two assaults. Even if you have sent me to the ground from my horse, you haven't brought things to a close'. Then Tristan said, 'Sir, there is not such hatred between us two that we must bring it to a close'. 'Most noble sir', said Lamorat, 'then you are not such a good knight as others hold you to be. Since [fol. 172v] you're avoiding the sword battle between us two, it appears that you're afraid to fight me with swords'.

[78] Then Lamorat left and returned to his cousin, and they mounted their horses and took the most direct route to go to the wilderness of Nerlantes, to the Fountain of Adventure, and they found a knight and a damsel. And he had a horn hung on his neck, the most beautiful that there ever was in the world; and the horn was made of silver, all decorated with thin bands of gold; and the strap on which the horn was hung was all of fine gold; and it was very beautiful and well-furnished in the manner of a fine, regal horn.

When Lamorat saw the horn, he asked the knight what horn it was; and the knight who had it in his care said that he did not dare tell. But Lamorat said, 'By my faith, yes, you will tell or you'll fight with me'; and the knight said that he would do so. In that moment the knights challenged each other and came to strike each other, the one against the other, ||| [fol. 173r] and their lances broke; and they put their hands to their swords and struck each other. But the knight could not withstand Lamorat, and he said to him, 'Now I'll tell you what horn this is and who is sending it'.

[79] A tanto remasse la batalia tra li .ii. chavalieri, e Lamorato disse, 'Or di', chavaliere, che aventura àe lo corno'. E lo chavaliere disse, 'Ello èi bonno da retenere le bone donne, e quello corno manda la Fada Morguana el realme de Gaules; e pote chonossere le bone donne da le malvagie: qué chalunque lo si pone a bocha, pieno de vino, s'illa à facta falimento a soe marito, no[n] ne[449] potte bevere; ançi si espargia tuto per lo petto'. Alor disse Lamorato, 'Questo corno manda la Fata Morgana en Gaules ala corte del Re Artù per destrugere la Redina Genevra. May per mia fé, tu non li portaray; ançi anderà là onde io ti diroe'. E lo chavaliere disse que 'non vi anderoe'. Alor disse Lamorato,[450] 'Donqua, venray tu ala batalia?' E lo chavaliere disse, 'Ançi vuolio conbatere que io non fassa lo messagio, che io non porti lo corno là onde elo èy mandato'.

A tanto prendeno li chavalieri l'arme e vanno ala batalia da capo.[451] E Lamorato diede uno colpo d'espada alo chavaliere molto forte que li mandoe l'ermo [fol. 173v] del capo. E quando lo chavaliere si sentì quasi dessarmato la testa,[452] disse, 'Chavaliere, io farò sò que tu volray'. E Lamorato disse, 'Tu portaray questo corno en Cornnavalia, al Re Marcho, e diray siqué Lamorato ve manda questo corno que voy debiate chonosscere le bone donne da le malvaçe'. E lo chavaliere disse, 'Questo messagio faroe io volontieri'.

Alor si parte la damissella e lo chavaliere con lo corno, e prendeno lur camino enver lo realme de Cornavalia. E tanto chavalchano que pervieno ala corte del Re Marcho. E vae lo chavaliere su en lo palagio del Re Marcho e saluta lo Re e la soa corte e li soy baroni. E lo Re li rende soe salute molto cortessamente. E lo chavaliere li apressenta lo corno e disse li, 'Questo corno ve manda Lamorato de Gaules per lo più meravillosso corno que sia ende 'l mondo. Per questo corno, potete chonoscere le bone donne da le rie'. E lo Re Marcho ne fo molto alegro de questa ventura. |||[453] [fol. 174r] E disse, 'Chome poterò io chonoscere le bone donne dale malvaçie?' E lo chavaliere disse, 'Prendete lo corno e inpiete lo de vino e date lo a bere ale donne. E quella que fie leale al soe marito berae con lo corno bene e cortessamente; e quella que averà facto falia al so marito non potrae bere con lo corno, ançi s'espargirae lo vino per lo petto tuto; e choissì si chonosseranno le bone donne dale malvaçie'.

Alor lo Re Marcho de quella ventura fo molto alegro, e tuti li baroni ne fanno gran festa. May Tristano que sape lo covenente de luy e de Madonna Yssota, n'è molto dolente de questa ventura. A tanto se ne vae uno vayleto ale donne, e disse, 'Io ve say dire novelle: che si è venuto una damissella e uno chavaliere, e ànno arechato del realme de Longres uno corno al Re Marcho, molto bello. Ed èy encantato en tal manera: que qualunqua donna à facto fallo a soe marito, non potte berre con lo corno; ançi s'espargi tuto pelo pecto lo

---

449   MS *Noue*. Resolution based on wording elsewhere in this text, such as fol. 174v below.
450   MS *lamoraro*.
451   MS *da clap*. Emendation based on TR, p. 158: *di capo*.
452   MS *vesta*. Emendation based on TR, p. 158, and TP, p. 236: *testa*.
453   Five full lines left blank at bottom of writing space; miniature never executed.

Il Tristano Riccardiano *(Parodi's siglum 'F')* 141

[79] In that moment the battle between the two knights was broken off, and Lamorat said, 'Now tell, knight, what adventure the horn has'. And the knight said, 'It's good when held by good women – and Morgan the Fay is sending that horn to the kingdom of Gaul – and one can know good ladies from wicked ones because whoever places it to her lips, full of wine, if she has betrayed her husband, she isn't able to drink from it; instead it will all spill on her breast'. Then Lamorat said, 'Morgan the Fay is sending this horn to Gaul, to King Arthur's court, in order to destroy Queen Guenevere. But by my faith, you'll not carry it to him; instead it will go where I tell you'. And the knight said that 'I won't go there'. Then Lamorat said, 'Well then, will you come to battle?' And the knight said, 'I do want to fight rather than to not deliver the message, rather than to not take the horn where it was sent'.

In that moment the knights took up their arms and began the battle once again. And Lamorat gave a sword blow to the knight, so powerful that he knocked his helmet [fol. 173v] from his head. And when the knight felt his head almost disarmed, he said, 'Knight, I will do what you wish'. And Lamorat said, 'You will carry this horn to Cornwall, to King Mark, and say "because Lamorat is sending you this horn, you must know good women from wicked ones"'. And the knight said, 'I will gladly deliver this message'.

Then the damsel and the knight with the horn departed, and they set out on their way toward the kingdom of Cornwall, and they rode so much that they came to King Mark's court. And the knight went up into King Mark's palace and greeted the king and his court and his barons; and the king returned his greeting very courteously. And the knight presented the horn to him and told him, 'This horn is being sent to you by Lamorat of Gaul, as the most marvellous horn that there is in the world. By means of this horn, you can know good women from wicked ones'. King Mark was very happy about this adventure ||| [fol. 174r] and said, 'How will I be able to know the good women from the wicked?' And the knight said, 'Take the horn and fill it with wine and give it to the women to drink, and she who is faithful to her husband will drink with the horn, well and courteously; but she who has failed her husband will not be able to drink with the horn; instead she will spill the wine all over her breast, and thus the good women will be known from the wicked'.

Then King Mark was very happy about that adventure, and all the barons rejoiced greatly about it. But Tristan, who knew how things stood between him and Lady Yseut, was very sorrowful about this adventure. In that moment a page went off to the ladies and said, 'I know some news to tell you: that a damsel and a knight have come; and they have brought to King Mark, from the kingdom of Logres, a very beautiful horn. And it is enchanted in this manner: that whichever lady has failed her husband, she cannot drink with the horn; instead she will spill

vino; e quella qu'è stata lealle al soe marito legieramente be[r]e[454] bene lo vino sensa nullo enpedemento'.

[80] [fol. 174v] A tanto manda lo Re per le donne che vegnanno danançi (ed era chonoschuto lo facto). E quando le donne foron danançi al Re, e lo Re fesse impire lo corno de bono vino e fesse lo porgere a Redina Yssota, e disse, 'Bevete'. Madonna Yssota disse, 'Per mia fé, io non beverò, ché si lo corno èy encantato o facto per malvaçitate o per me o per altruy, non volio que nosa[455] a me'. A tanto lo Re Marcho disse, 'Dama, non vale [già vostra][456] desdetta: or si pare vostra lealltade!' E la Redina prende lo corno per bere. Ela non lo si potte acostare ala bocha, e lo vino li si versò a tuto per lo pecto, e non ne pote bere. E diede bere ale altre donne qu'eranno alato de Madona Yssota, ed eranno bene .ccc.lii.[457] E non ve se n'atrovoe – si non doe – que potessano bere con lo corno.

A tanto disse lo R[e] Marcho, 'Io volio que tute queste donne sianno messe al fuocho, qué tute li ànno ben servito d'essere arçe; e volio que recordança ne sia'. ||||[458] [fol. 175r] A tanto si leva uno barone de Cornavalia qu'era allato del Re Marcho, e disse, 'Meser lo Re, si voy volete credere ale venture del realme de Longres e alo corno encantato, noy potreamo tra noy strugere le nostre donne que – noy teniamo – è tropo seria malfacto. May si voy avete animo ale nostre donne, fate ne lo vostre animo. Entendete que noy non volemo peroe strugere le nostre donne, qué noy tegniamo le nostre per belle e per bone'. E lo R[e] Marcho disse, 'Si voy non volete fare vendìta de le vosse donne e volete remanere con questo des<i>onore, nì io non vuolio fare vendìta de la mia. E [si] voy avete le vosse donne per belle e per bone e per leale, io atressie. E si voy [avete] le vostre donne per bone, e io la mia per meliore'. A tanto lo Re perdona a tute le donne e dà lor chumiato.

[81] Or disse lo conto que Tristano èi molto dolente quello non avea conbatuto con Lamorato que l'avia laysato per cortesia. E disse bene fra soe chuore che si lo trovarae, que li farae bene costare lo corno a Lamorato[459] que lo mandoe al Re Marcho.

[82] Ora torna lo conto a una damissella qu'era en corte del Re Marcho, la quale volea bene a Tristano (in qua derietro)[460] que Tristano non li volia dare soa amo[fol. 175v]re. Or si posse con Guedis, e la Malvagia Damissella disse a Ghedis sichome Tristano amava la Redina Yssota de folle amore. Alor lo disse Ghedis al Re, 'Or potemo noy bene choliere Tristano'.

---

454 MS *be[??]e*. Partially illegible due to uneven ink flow. Cf. TR, p. 160: *be ne sì bee*; TP, p. 238: *bera*.
455 Dialectal spelling. Cf. TR, p. 160: *noccia a mee*.
456 Omission in MS. Insertion based on TR, p. 160: *già vostra*.
457 The number of unfaithful wives differs. Cf. TR, p. 160: *.ccclxv.*; TP, p. 238: *.xlv.*
458 Six full lines left blank at bottom of writing space; miniature never executed.
459 MS *lamoraro*.
460 Allusion to an earlier portion of the narrative. Corresponds to TP, p. 240.

all the wine on her breast, but she who has been faithful to her husband will drink the wine easily without any impediment'.

[80] [fol. 174v] In that moment the king summoned the ladies to come before him (and the fact was known). And when the ladies were before the king, the king had the horn filled with good wine and had it handed to Queen Yseut and said, 'Drink!' Lady Yseut said, 'By my faith, I won't drink because if the horn is enchanted or made maliciously – whether for me or for others – I don't want it to harm me'. At that King Mark said, 'Lady, your refusal will avail you nothing: now your loyalty will be known'. And the queen took the horn to drink. She couldn't bring it near her mouth, and all the wine poured out on her breast, and she couldn't drink any of it. And the king gave drink to the other ladies who were alongside Lady Yseut – there must have been three hundred fifty-two – and he could not find any there, except for two, who were able to drink with the horn.

In that moment King Mark said, 'I want all these women to be sent to the flames, since all are well deserving of being burned; and I want this to be recorded'. ||| [fol. 175r] In that moment a baron of Cornwall who was at King Mark's side arose and said, 'My Lord the King, if you want to believe in the adventures of the kingdom of Logres and the enchanted horn, [and that] we could among us destroy our ladies, that we hold too great a misdeed! But if you have animosity toward [your lady], do about it as you desire. Hear that we do not want to destroy our ladies for this reason, because we hold ours to be fine and good'. And King Mark said, 'If you don't want to take vengeance on your ladies and want to remain with this dishonor, neither do I want to take vengeance on mine. And if you hold your ladies to be fine and good and loyal, I do as well. And if you consider your ladies to be good, I consider mine better'. In that moment the king pardoned all the ladies and gave them leave.

[81] Now the tale says that Tristan was very sorrowful that he had not fought with Lamorat whom he had released out of courtesy, but he swore in his heart that if he would find him, that he would make Lamorat pay dearly for the horn that he sent to King Mark.

[82] Now the tale turns to a damsel who was in King Mark's court, who cared deeply for Tristan (as was told a while back) to whom Tristan did not want to give his love. [fol. 175v] Now she had taken up with Ghedis, and the wicked damsel told Ghedis how Tristan loved Queen Yseut with a mad love. Then Ghedis said to the king, 'Now we'll surely be able to catch Tristan'.

Alor disse Guedis, 'Vedatili⁴⁶¹ la chamera que non v'intri, e choisè lo ve chollerette'. E lo Re Marcho disse que si faroe.

Alor comanda lo Re Marcho a Tristano e a Guedis che non debianno intrare ende la camera de la Redina sensa soa parolla. Elli dichono che bene lo faranno. Alor disse Tristano fra soe chuore que quello chomandamento non si disse si non per luy. Tristano alor ne foe più enfiamato de l'amore de la Redina. E demanda [a Branguina] chome potesse parlare ala Redina siché trovaron unde, si non per lo giardino, montare su en uno arbore e venire ala fenestra de la sala, e de la sala venire ende la camera.

E lo Re levassi (e Tristano gia- ||||⁴⁶² que con Yssota). Alor se | n'avide la Malvaçia | Damissella que stava | ala porta.⁴⁶³ E andò s|e ne al Re Marcho e | disse, 'Re, or èi Tristano con la Redina en[d]e la camera'. [fol. 176r] E lo Re fae chomandare ali soi baroni que si levano e vadano presto a luy, e prendano l'arme. Alor disse lo Re, 'Venite mecho'. E lo Re prende .i. espada e mete si ennançi ali soy baroni. E quando Branguina sentì venire lo Re e li soy baroni, si disse a Tristano, 'Leva encontenente! Echo lo Re Marcho con granda gente'. Alor Tristano non potte arechoverare a prendere altro que uno mantello, e volge si lo al braçio. E lo Re Marcho fo ala porta e vidi Tristano e disse, 'Ay, Tristano! Or non pote tu dire que tu non sey lo più deslealle e lo più falso homo del mondo'. E lo Re li diede uno colpo de l'espada molto grando, e Tristano lo rechevete en su el braçio onde ello avia volto lo mantello. E Tristano diede al Re uno colpo de l'espada e cholpoe lo [Re] su en la testa siché lo Re chade en terra e spasmato,⁴⁶⁴ e molto sangue de la testa li era issito.

E Tristano issì fora nella chamera e vae ende la sala. E li baroni fugian tuti – l'uno en qua e l'autro en là – ||||⁴⁶⁵ [fol. 176v] e Tristano vàsene alla fenestra e chade⁴⁶⁶ giusso da l'arbore, e vàsenne via ala soa casa. E disse ali soy conpagni – a Salvagio e a Sigris⁴⁶⁷ e a uno altro chavaliere⁴⁶⁸ e Governale – e disse lo facto que hera encontrato. Li quatre chavalieri eranno venuti per vedere Tristano – e qui per garire de le soe feritte, e chi chome aventura lo menava – e preson consilio de partirsi. E prendeno lor arme e vàsene via, tuti quatro ensieme,⁴⁶⁹ chome boni chavalieri che amavanno molto Tristano per la soa prodessa e bontade.

[83] Or torna lo conto al Re Marcho cho<i>m'elli⁴⁷⁰ tornò en sé del colpo de l'espada que ebe de Tristano. Si demandoe li soy baroni, 'Onde avete Tristano?'

---

⁴⁶¹ Cf. TP, p. 240: *Vietate a Tristano*.
⁴⁶² Eight partial lines left blank, flush right at gutter; miniature never executed.
⁴⁶³ MS *posta*. On next folio: *porta*.
⁴⁶⁴ MS *spalmato*. Confusion of *s* / *l*.
⁴⁶⁵ Five full lines left blank at bottom of writing space; miniature never executed.
⁴⁶⁶ MS *chide*. TR, p. 164: *discende*.
⁴⁶⁷ MS *figris*. Confusion of *s* / *f*.
⁴⁶⁸ Also in TR, p. 164: *un altro cavaliere*; and TP, p. 242: *Sigris et uno altro*. Probably an unusual name not recognizable to copyists; perhaps 'Gray' or 'Granor' as found in Florence, Biblioteca Nazionale Centrale, MS Pal. 556. See Heijkant, 'La tradizione', p. 91.
⁴⁶⁹ MS *en fieme*. Confusion of *s* / *f*.
⁴⁷⁰ Stray minim was written at the end of the line.

Then Ghedis said, 'Forbid him from entering Yseut's chamber, and so you will catch him'. And King Mark said that he would do it.

Then King Mark commanded both Tristan and Ghedis that they must not enter the Queen's chamber without his permission. They said that they would indeed obey. Then Tristan said in his heart that that commandment was not said except for him. Tristan was then even more enflamed with love for the queen, and he asked Brangain how he would be able to talk to the queen; therefore, they found no way there except through the garden, by climbing a tree and coming to the window of the hall, and from the hall coming into the chamber.

The king arose (and Tristan was lying with Yseut). Then he noticed the wicked damsel who was at the door. And she went to King Mark and said, 'King, now Tristan is with the queen in her chamber'. [fol. 176r] And the king had his barons ordered to get up and come to him quickly, and to bring weapons. Then the king said, 'Come with me!' And the king took a sword and placed himself in front of his barons. And when Brangain heard the king and his barons coming, she told Tristan, 'Get up at once! Here comes King Mark with a lot of people'. Then Tristan could not manage to grab anything but a mantle and wrapped it on his arm. And King Mark was at the door and saw Tristan and said, 'Ah ha, Tristan! Now you can't say that you aren't the most disloyal and the most false man in the world'. And the king gave him a very great sword blow, but Tristan received it on his arm where he had wrapped the mantle. And Tristan gave the king a sword blow, and he struck the king on his head so that the king fell to the floor in a faint and a lot of blood went out of his head.

And Tristan exited the chamber and went into the hall. All the barons were fleeing – some here and some there – ||| [fol. 176v] and Tristan went to the window and descended by means of the tree and went on his way to his own house. And he told his companions – Dodinel the Savage and Segris and another knight and Governal – and he told the affair that he had encountered. The four knights had come to see Tristan – this one to be healed of his wounds and that one as fortune was leading him – and they took counsel to leave. And they took their arms and went away, all four together, like good knights who loved Tristan very much for his prowess and goodness.

[83] Now the tale returns to King Mark, how he revived after the sword blow that he had had from Tristan. He asked his barons, 'Where do you have Tristan?'

E li baroni disseronno, 'Per mia fede, elli se n'andoe, que non si n'ebe neuno que li fossi sì ardito de parare li se danannçi'. Alor disse lo Re Marcho, 'Morto siemo, ché giuamay non s'era neuno homo tanto ardito que stia fora de Tittolin a quatro milia, qué li conpagni de Tristano s'eranno apiatati al desserto presso a Titolin e Tristano estarà armato en su l'estrada'.

A tanto vegnano .ii. chavalieri de Cornavalia a Titolin, armati a guisa de chavaliere. E Tristano parasi lor davançi e demanda lor giostra sichom'è l'ussato di li chavalieri erranti. E li chavalieri vienonno a ferire ala ba[fol. 177r] talia sense (sic) altre parolle a dire. E l'uno de li chavalieri fiere a Tristano siché li ronpe la lançia adosso. E Tristano fiere a luy siché lo manda a terra da chavallo. E quando Tristano ebe abattuto lo chavaliere, e' smontò a terra da cavallo e tallòli la testa alo chavaliere e possa monta a chavallo. (E questi .ii. chavalieri eranno fratelli carnali.) E Tristano fiere al'autro chavaliere siché non li valse nì targia nì asbercho que avesse, e passò li la lançia dal'autra parte. E·nnelo passare che fesse Tristano, si li ronpoe la lançia en corpo. ||| [471] E quando Tristano vidi quello colpo, disse, 'Chavaliere, arende ti a me'. E lo chavaliere disse que si farae.

[84] Alor li comandoe que prenda la testa del fratello en mano, e lo chavaliere la prende. E Tristano li disse, 'Vàtene alo Re Marcho e salutalo sichome mio mortale enemicho' – ed ello disse quello farà – 'e di' li chome [fol. 177v] l'ò facto de costoy, coysì farò de luy'. Alor lo chavaliere ne vae a Titolin, e giu[n]sse ala corte del Re Marcho e monta su en lo palagio. E saluta lo Re Marcho da parte de Tristano – sichome enemicho mortale – e disse che coisì farae de luy sichome à facto del fratello, 'e chome à facto de me que sonno presso ala morte, sichome enderietro vederete'. Alor lo chavaliere cade en terra, morto, con la testa del fratello en mano. ||| [472]

E quando lo Re Marcho vide quello, ebe granda paora. E chomandoe que fosse menato a sepelire, e la testa del soe fratello; e choisì fo facto. Alor disse Guedis, 'Re Marcho, dapoyqué avete casiate Tristano de la vostra corte, io non posso prendere[473] luy sichome io credea. Enfine a tanto que serae fora de vostra corte, voy non guassagnarete nulla con luy; però si voy lo volete destrugere – choma decto m'avete – mandate per luy; e farete fare le [fol. 178r] vostre letere sugillate de lo vostro sagello, e Branguina sia lo messagio de queste letere'. Alor disse lo Re a Guedis, 'Fàle fare a tuo senno, e io le faroe sugillare, e Branguina [sia] lo messagio'.

E quando foron fate, e Guedis le fesse sugillare del sugello del Re e alor manda per Braguina qué vuole que li facia uno serviçio. Alor andoe Branguina dinançi da luy, e lo Re li chomanda que vada a Tristano, 'e pòrtali queste letere, e di' li que io li perdono[474] *tuto lo mio maltalento, e qu'ello debia tornare seguramente'. E Branguina disse que lo farà volontieri. Alor si parte Branguina e torna*

---

471 Seven full lines left blank, at mid-page; miniature never executed.
472 Six full lines left blank, at mid-page; miniature never executed.
473 MS *credere de luy*. Emended based on TR, p. 166; and TP, p. 242: *prendere*.
474 MS *perdone*.

Il Tristano Riccardiano *(Parodi's siglum 'F')* 147

And the barons said, 'By my faith, he got away, because there was no one who was so bold as to appear before him'. Then King Mark said, 'We're dead, since there will never again be a man so bold who would venture four miles outside Tintagel, because Tristan's companions have hidden themselves in the wilderness near Tintagel and Tristan will be armed in the road'.

In that moment two knights of Cornwall came to Tintagel, armed in the fashion of knights; and Tristan appeared before them and demanded a joust of them as is the custom of errant knights. And the knights came to strike in the [fol. 177r] battle without saying anything else, and one of the knights struck Tristan such that he broke his lance upon him. And Tristan struck at him such that he sent him to the ground from his horse. And when Tristan had knocked down the knight, he dismounted from his horse and cut off the knight's head and then mounted his horse. (And these two knights were full brothers.) And Tristan struck the other knight such that neither targe nor hauberk that he had did him any good, and the lance passed through him to the other side. And as Tristan passed by, he broke off his lance in his body. ||| And when Tristan saw that blow, he said, 'Knight, surrender to me'; and the knight said that he would do so.

[84] Then Tristan commanded him to take his brother's head in his hand, and the knight took it. And Tristan told him, 'Go to King Mark and greet him as my mortal enemy' – and he said that he would do it – 'and tell him that [fol. 177v] as I have done unto this fellow, so I will do unto him'. Then the knight went on to Tintagel and reached King Mark's court and dismounted in the palace. And he greeted King Mark on Tristan's behalf – as a mortal enemy – and said that 'he will do unto him as he has done unto my brother, and as he has done unto me, who am near death as you will shortly see'. Then the knight fell to the ground, dead, with his brother's head in his hand. |||

When King Mark saw that, he was greatly afraid. And he commanded that the knight was taken to be buried, and his brother's head as well; and it was done. Then Ghedis said, 'King Mark, since you have chased Tristan from your court, I can't capture him as I once thought to do. Thus as long as he is outside your court, you'll not gain any advantage with him. For this reason, if you want to destroy him – as you have told me – send for him; and have [fol. 178r] your letters sealed with your seal, and let Brangain be the messenger for these letters'. Then the king said to Ghedis, 'Have them made as you think best, and I will seal them, and let Brangain be the messenger'.

And when they were ready, Ghedis had them sealed with the king's seal and then sent for Brangain because he wanted her to do him a service. Then Brangain went before him, and the king commanded her to go to Tristan 'and carry these letters to him and tell him that I pardon him all my ill will and that he must return safely'. And Brangain said that she would do it willingly.

a Yssota e còntale chome lo Re vuolie qu'ella vada a dire a Tristano qu'illo torna[475] sechuramente. Alor disse Yssota, 'Io credo que sia più per male que per bene questo messagio, cioè di Tristano. May tutavia mi saluta luy e tuti li soy conpagni per le mille volte da la mia parte'. E Branguina disse que lo farae volontieri.

A tanto si parte Branguina e monta a chavallo con conpagn[i]a de .ii. eschudieri; e partì si de la corte e vàssene a Tristano. E quando Tristano la vide, fesse ne gran festa e alegressa. E Branguina disse, 'La vostra [fol. 178v] pace è facta', e saluta luy e li soy conpagni da parte de Yssota per le cento[476] mille volte. E poy li diede la letera la[477] quale lo Re li avia date. |||[478]

[. . .][479]

[85] Ora disse lo conto que Tristano se ne vene en Cornavalia e viene alo castello de Dinas. E lo manischalcho viene, e quando Dinas vidi li duo chavalieri, si ne fo molto alegro de la lor venuta. E quando Madona Yssota sepe\<i\> qu'era venuto lo soe charo amicho en nel realme de Cornavalia, fo ne molta alegra, e fesse tanto que Tristano venne a ley.

[86] Uno giorno si era Tristano con Madona Yssota en chamera, e Yssota diçia una cançone ch'ella metesma l'avia enposta. Uno chavaliere que avia nome Durin[480] si la entesse; si l'andò a dire alo Re Marcho. E lo Re Marcho si lo ve trovoe, e scride lo e feritelo d'una lança atossichata che la Fata Morgana l'avia data – e Tristano era sensa arme nesuna – e ferite lo elo fiancho drito mortalmente. [fol. 179r] E quando lo re Marcho ebe sò facto, si s'en fugiò per paora de Tristano, che non ferisse lui. E Tristano, sentendo si coysì ferito, si chonove qu'era morto; però non pote venire derietro al Re Marcho nè giongerlo. E persò se n'andoe d'altra via e andò sene al castello di Pinogres[481] (tutto qu'altro li digua lo castello de Dinas).[482] E quie sene posse a giaçere, e disse qu'era morto (ed era, sensa nullo fallo), e nullo medicho li sapia dare consilio. |||[483]

[87] Or dichanno tute le persone chomunamente qu'ello era morto, ed ello metesmo lo sentia bene. E quando lo re Marcho sente que Tristano more, si n'àe granda gioa ché sape certanamentre qu'ello moye. E lo re mandava onni dì [per] sapere chome ello estava, |||[484] [fol. 179v] e onni dì n'avia tal novella che

475   MS *torne*.
476   MS *cente*.
477   MS *le*.
478   Six full lines left blank; miniature never executed.
479   For the contents of this lengthy ellipsis, see TP, pp. 244–711.
480   TP, p. 712: *Andret*; TV, p. 540: *Audret*.
481   See West, p. 258: 'Pynogre', a character from the Vulgate version.
482   Cf. TP, pp. 712, 715: *Dynas*; TV, pp. 540, p. 552: *castello de Dinas*; *Tav. Rit.*, pp. 497, 506: *Dinasso*.
483   Six and one half lines left blank at mid-page; miniature never executed.
484   Three full lines left blank at bottom of writing space; miniature never executed.

Il Tristano Riccardiano *(Parodi's siglum 'F')*

Then Brangain left the king and returned to Yseut and recounted to her how the king wanted her to go tell Tristan that he might return safely. Then Yseut said, 'I believe that this message is more for evil than for good, that is, for Tristan's good; but nonetheless, greet him for me – and all his companions – a thousand times on my behalf'; and Brangain said that she would do it willingly.

In that moment Brangain left and mounted her horse with a company of two squires; and she left the court and went off to Tristan. And when Tristan saw her, he had great joy and happiness because of it. And Brangain said, 'Your [fol. 178v] peace is made', and she greeted him and his companions on behalf of Yseut a hundred thousand times, and then she gave him the letter that the king had given to her. |||

[. . .]*

[85] Now the tale says that when Tristan came into Cornwall, he came to the castle of Dinas; and the stable master came out.** And when Dinas saw the two knights, he was very happy about their coming. And when Lady Yseut found out that her ami had come into the kingdom of Cornwall, she was very happy about it and did all she could so that Tristan came to her.

[86] One day Tristan was with Lady Yseut in her*** chamber, and Yseut was declaiming a song that she herself had composed. A knight who was called Durin heard her; he went off to tell King Mark about it. And King Mark found Tristan there and screamed at him and wounded him with a poisoned lance that Morgan the Fay had given him – and Tristan was completely unarmed – and fatally wounded him in his right flank. [fol. 179r] And when King Mark had done that, he fled for fear of Tristan, so that he wouldn't strike him. But Tristan, feeling himself wounded like that, knew that he was a dead man; for this reason he could not go after King Mark nor catch up with him. And for this reason he went away by another route and went off to the castle of Pinogres – although another one says it was the castle of Dinas – and here he lay himself down and said that he was dead (and he was, without any doubt); and no physician knew how to give him any advice. |||

[87] Now all the people were united in saying that he was dead, and he himself could well feel it; and when King Mark heard that Tristan was dying, he had great joy because of it, since he knew of a certainty that he was dying. The king would send every day to find out how he was doing, ||| [fol. 179v]

---

* MS contains a lengthy narrative ellipsis. See TR, pp. 167 ff.; and TP, pp. 245 ff.
** The final episode was lost from MS Ricc. 2543, but was conserved in TP, pp. 711 ff.
*** Possessive adjective choice based on TP, p. 712: *nella camera della reina*.

bene lo sastifano (sic). May tutto çioè que lo Re Marcho ne sia lietto, lo volria vedere, anche qu'ello morisse. Mai pur quando ello sentia qu'el pur moria e qu'era presso ala morte ed era sì canbiato que neuno non lo chonosia, <E> lo Re enchominçò a piangere e dissia, 'Certo gran danno èy de la morte de Tristano. Giamay sì bona lancia non si retroverà. May s'illo si fosse mantenuto lealmente enverso da me, l'omo non lo potrea tropo pregiare, sobre tuti li autri cavalieri del mondo'.

E la Redina Yssota non vole più vivere si Tristano more qué non vuollrie si non la morte – e de çiò non si cella dalo Rey Marcho – e volria que lo Re Marcho lo uçidisse qué·lla fosse fenita lo soe dolore; e vede bene que lo Re Marcho se ne pente de quello qu'àe facto a Tristano. E quanto Yssota ebe entesso chome Tristano non pote vivere si non tre dì<o>, ella disse, 'Moia, moia, qué io li farò conpagnia! E quello metesmo dì seray fenita lo mio dolore'. (E queste parolle disse Yssota de la morte de Tristano, e lo Re non è asay più chorossosse che non mostra per senbiante.)

[88] *E quando Tristano vide che non poe escanpare, elli disse a* [fol. 180r] *Sinogres, 'Manda queste novelle de la mia morte alo Re Marcho e dì li s'illo mi volie vedere vivo che ello vegna a vedere, per sò que io sonno presso ala morte. E direte que io non li sapio mal grado de la mia morte.*[485] *De sò direte dinançi da Yssota queste novelle e alo Re Marcho'.*

E quando lo Re Marcho sepe queste novelle, si chominçò a piangere. E disse, piangendo – sì alto ch'onni homo lo entesse – e' disse, 'Bene sapi, Idio, chome òe f<c>acto male, che i'ò mor<c>to lo mio caro nepote, c[i]oè[486] *lo melior chavaliere del mondo. E de sò èi onta a tuti li autri boni chavalieri'. E lo Re non remasse niente, qu'el montoe a chavallo e menoe secho tal conpagnia qu'elli fosse bene sechuro al castello de Pinogres.*

E quando vi fo dintro, si v'introe molto doloyrosso. E ven[n]e ende la sala onde era Tristano e giassia, ed era molto pegiorato ch'apena l'omo lo potia chonoscere. E quando Tristano vidi venire lo Re Marcho, si volle[487] *levare a sedere, may elo non podeo; si tornò a giasscere. May tuttavia fesse qua[n]to poteo, ciò en parlare. E chominço fortamente a piangere. E disse piangendo, 'Bello mio isio, bene en siate voy venuto, e siete alla mia fine che tanto l'avete bramata. Or è conpiuta vostra* [fol. 180v] *volontade e vostra gio[i]a, ché Tristano vederete ogi morto, e demane serà fenito. Io non posso più vivere si non que io aspetto la morte que tanto l'avete dessirata. E ancho ve ne pentirete: voy credette fare vostro prode de metere mi ala morte' – sò disse Tristano – 'e serà vostro danno, qué ancho venrae tempo que voy volleste avere dato meço lo*

---

[485]   TV, p. 542: *io non li·ssè cià sì mal grado dela mia morte como io faço de Audret.*
[486]   Scribe wrote *choe*, then lightly struck out the *h*.
[487]   MS *volse*. Confusion of *s* / *f*.

Il Tristano Riccardiano *(Parodi's siglum 'F')*

and every day he had such news that well satisfied him. But for all that King Mark was happy about, he wanted to see him, even to see him die. Yet when he heard that he really was dying and that he was near death and that he was so changed that no one would know him, then the king began to weep, and he said, 'Certainly, Tristan's death is a great misfortune. One will never again find such a good lance. Yet if he had maintained his loyalty toward me, one could not praise him too much, above all the other knights in the world'.

But Queen Yseut didn't want to live any longer if Tristan died, since she wanted nothing but death – and she didn't conceal that from King Mark – and she wanted King Mark to kill her so that her pain would be ended; and she clearly saw that King Mark was repenting for what he had done to Tristan. When Yseut heard that Tristan couldn't live more than three days, she said, 'Let me die, let me die, so that I will keep him company, and that same day my pain will be ended!' (And Yseut said these words about the death of Tristan, and the king was not very much more upset than his appearance showed.)

[88] And when Tristan saw that he could not escape, he said to [fol. 180r] Sinogres, 'Send this news of my death to King Mark, and tell him, if he wants to see me alive, that he must come and see, since I am close to death; and say that I don't begrudge him in spite of my death. This news you will tell King Mark in the presence of Yseut'.

When King Mark found out this news, he began to weep; and he said, weeping – so loudly that everyone heard him – he said, 'Lord God, well you know that I have done wrong, because I have killed my dear nephew, that is to say, the best knight in the world; and from that I have brought shame to all the other good knights'. And the king didn't wait at all before he mounted his horse, and he brought with him such company so that he would be very safe at the castle of Pinogres.

And when he was inside, he entered there, very sorrowful. And he came into the hall where Tristan was lying, and he was so much worse that one could hardly recognize him. And when Tristan saw King Mark coming, he wanted to rise up and sit, but he could not: he returned to lying down. But still he did as much as he could, that is, by talking. And he began to weep very hard and said, while weeping, 'My good uncle, you are most welcome here, and you are at my end that you have longed for so much. Now your wish is complete – [fol. 180v] and your joy – because today you will see Tristan dead, and tomorrow he will be finished. I cannot live any longer since I am awaiting the death that you have desired so much. But you will yet repent of it: you believed that you were acting for your benefit by putting me to death' – thus spoke Tristan – 'and it will be your downfall, because there will still come a time when you would like to have given half your realm if

vostro realme[488] [s]e voy non avesse morto Tristano. May quando io non posso fare altro, io ve perdeno<no>'. E poyqu'ebe decte queste parolle, <e> lo Re chominçoe fortamente a piançere.

E Tristano disse, 'Bello isio, non piangete qué 'l vostro pianto si parte de leticia. May, bello isio, tanto ve demando que questa fiata: que la Redina<roe ei la Rediera> que io vediroe che voy Yssota mi faciate venire ala mia fine, ché per certo morto sonno ogi o demane, qué io non posso più avere senno, ché io aspecto la morte'.

E lo Re disse, 'Bello nepotte, quando volray qu'ella vegna, si venrae'. E Tristano disse, 'Mandate me per ley'. Ello li mandoe, ed ella viene dolenta e trista, e may non dessiderò morte si non alora, poyqu'ella pure de' morire. Alor vuolria morire, nì d'altro Idio non pregua si non qu'ella moia con Tristano.

[fol. 181r] *E quando Tristano vide Madonna Yssota, que tanto amava e dessiderava, si seria riçacto volontire may non potìo (may ello ne fesse soe podere e soe forsse[489] de parlare). E disse, 'Madona Yssota, la vostra venuta <la uostra uenuta> èy tardi e non mi potete fare socorsso.' A tanto si levò enfra[490] le gente uno piante sì grande che non lo ve sapria dire nì contare nì dire la tenore.* |||[491] *'Or che ve diroe, chara mia donna? E' more Tristano que voy tanto amaste; non pote più vivere'.*

E Madonna Yssota disse, 'Bello mio amicho, morire ve cho[n]viene?' 'Madona', disse Tristano, *'cho[n]viene que Tristano moia, que già tanto ebe podere. Vedete braçia que queste sonno? Non sonno quilli que cotal colpi solianno dare; ançi sonno quelli[492] de uno morto. Sapiate que 'l mondo sarae[493] de mia* [fol. 181v] *fenita gran dapnagio; soè da choluy que al monndo tanto valse giae. E quello èy morto, tuto lo podere ch'elli solia avere'.* E decte queste parolle, <e> lo pianto vi si levò molto grande. Alor disse Tristano, 'Ay, lasso, quello colpo chome sì[494] doloyrosso alo mio corpo, ché tanto lo mondo ne serà abaysato!' E Tristano si lamenta molto forte chome quello che àe pietade de sí metesmo. (*May en chella sera v'àe grande luminere,[495] may Tristano no[n] vede niente: si è turbata la veduta.*)

[89] Ala matina que lo giorno èy chiaro, Tristano se sforça[496] de parlare. E disse sì forto che unn'omo l'entesse, e' disse, 'Ae, Siri Ydio, que potrae io fare, ché ogi è lo mio deretagno die – qué io debo morire – nì may altro giorno non aspecto. Sie serae Tristano ala fine de Idio perché sofrerà tanto que io fenischa choysì dessto'. E dapoyqué ebe decte queste parolle, lo pianto

---

[488] MS clearly *realmo*.
[489] MS *fesse*.
[490] MS *anfre*.
[491] Seven full lines left blank, mid-page; miniature never executed.
[492] MS *quello*.
[493] MS *farae*. Confusion of *s* / *f*.
[494] MS *fi*. Confusion of *s* / *f*.
[495] MS *lumere*, with a titulus over the first *e*.
[496] MS *sforda*.

Il Tristano Riccardiano *(Parodi's siglum 'F')*   153

you had not killed Tristan. But since I cannot do otherwise, I pardon you'. And after he had said these words, the king began to weep very hard.

And Tristan said, 'Good uncle, do not weep, because your weeping comes from happiness. But, good uncle, this much I ask at this time: that the queen – whom I would see – that you have Yseut come to me at my end, because I will surely die today or tomorrow, because I cannot have the ability to reason much longer, since I am awaiting death'.

And the king said, 'Good nephew, since you would like her to come, she will come'. And Tristan said, 'Send for her, for my sake'. He sent for her; and she came, sorrowful and sad, and never did she desire death if not now since she too seemed to be dying. Now she would like to die, nor did she pray to God for anything except that she might die with Tristan.

[fol. 181r] And when Tristan saw Lady Yseut whom he so loved and desired, he would willingly have stood up, but he could not (but he used all of his power and strength to speak). And he said, 'Lady Yseut, your coming is late, and you cannot give me succor'. In that moment, from the people there arose such a great lament that one could not begin to say or recount or tell its tenor. ||| 'Now what shall I tell you, my dear lady? Tristan is dying, whom you loved so much; he can no longer live'.

And Lady Yseut said, 'My fine ami, does it behoove you to die?' 'My lady', said Tristan, 'it behooves Tristan to die, who once had so much strength. Do you see what arms these are? They are not those which used to give such blows; instead they are those of a dead man. Know that in the world will be great harm from my [fol. 181v] end; it was from him who was once worth so very much to the world; and all the power that he used to have, that is dead'. And having said these words, a very great weeping arose there. Then Tristan said, 'Oh, alas! As dolorous as that blow was to my body, even so the world will be brought low by it!' And Tristan lamented very greatly, like someone who took pity on his very self. (That evening there was great illumination in the room, but Tristan saw nothing: his sight was dimmed.)

[89] In the morning when it was daybreak, Tristan forced himself to talk. And he said so loudly that everyone could hear him, he said, 'Ah, Lord God, what can I do? – since today is my last day – because I must die – nor do I ever expect another day. Yes, in the end Tristan will be with God because he will suffer so much, since I am finishing [my life] awake like this'. And after he had said these

li si levoe sì grande e sì meravilosso que magiore non si vide may, ed elli metesmo piangea.

E dissia a Sagremor, 'Dolçho amico, venete a me e arachate la mia spada e lo mio eschudo, qué io lo volio vedere';[497] [fol. 182r] ed ello lo fae encontenente. E <D>[498] Tristano prende l'espada e traysela fuora del frodo. Enchomença la abaysare e disse piangendo,[499] 'Ay, bella espada e schudo, que ve farete giuamay que ogi ve partrete del vostro segnore? E sò è perché la morte non àe de me piada'. E poych'ebe decte queste parolle, el chominçò a pi<n>angere più asay dolorossamente que da prima. E poych'ebe çoysì pianto grande pessa, elli esgarda ancho Sagremor e disseli, in pianto, 'Dir<m>e lo mi cho[n]viene,[500] bello amicho, e non lo posso più celare. Lasso, chome lo diroe? Serto, si diroe perché força lo mi fa dire'. E poy taçe uno grando pesso. E poy chominça uno pianto più grande che de prima.

E anchor disse, 'Sagremor, or sapiate che io ve dicho la più ontossa parolla che may dissese chavaliere. Ay, las[s]o, chome isserà de mia bocha? Certo, si farae que força lo me farae dire'. E anchor piançe da capo, e piançe per gran pessa. Ed elli esgarda Sagremor, e disse a Sagremor, 'Io non posso più celare che io non digua'. E chomiça a dire, 'Ay, Sagremor, io sonno vinto! – e rendere ve posso l'arme mie e mio eschudo [fol. 182v] e tuti mei fanti e mey cavalli; e mie prodesse mi cho[n]viene a laysare; e io li laiso mal mio grado. E io, Messer Sagremor, si ve preguo per cortesia o per vostra honore, que voy le mie arme portey ala Taula Retonta que sianno ala lor altessa; en lo loguo onde serà lo mio corpo, mando le mei arme, poyqué 'l corpo mandar non ve posso; e per sò deverianno fare honore ale mie arme. E diti loro que choisì m'aite Dio, que chome io vinite si prochaçiay lo loro honore. E però deveranno fare honore ale mie arme, e fate le ponere en luoguo che tuti li chavalieri erranti e tuti li autri chavalieri le possano vedere, ché tale chavaliere non me vidi may, che quando vederanno le mie arme, faranno per me molti regardi – e pessimi e mortali – e so fie que ventura encontrata mi viene de la ferita che Re Marcho mi diede, e tutta Cornavalia ne remarrà dessonrata. Or ve abo decto quello que dire ve vuolio nì dire ve volia'.

E dapoyqu'ebe decte queste parolle, ed ello si volse verso lo Re Marcho e chominçò lo a esgardare, piangendo. E disse, 'Bello issio, que ve pare de [fol. 183r] me? Sonno io quello chavaliere che soliate tanto donptare?'[501] Ed ello disse, 'Certa, none gamay'. E Tristano disse, 'Bello issio, ogi may èi falita la grande doptança che voy aviate de me. Ogi may è falita la grande dobitança qu'è stata entre voy e me. Neongcha de batalia non viene al de sotta che, si merçede mi chiamesse, non è neuno chavaliere que pietà non n'avesse. En questa batalia voy non aveste de me merchede' – disse Tristano al Re Marcho – 'e per uno soço colpo[502] que voy mi deste, sonno morto. May quando io non posso fare altro, io ve lo perdono' (e Dio li ne perdoni).

---

497   Catchword (no cartouche): *edelli*, however, the next words on *verso* are: *Ed ello*.
498   E D T, with spaces between, all trimmed with red slashes.
499   MS *pinagendo*, with scribal correction (horizontal S shape = invert symbol) underneath.
500   MS *Derme lo mi che viene*. Emendation based on TP, p. 718: *dire mi conviene*.
501   MS *doprare* with titulus over the *p*.
502   Cf. *Tav. Rit.*, p. 504: *per uno solo colpo*; TV, p. 548: *per un colpo, et d'uno colpo solamente*.

words, the weeping arose so great and so wondrously as one ever saw, and he himself was weeping.

And he said to Sagremor, 'Sweet friend, come to me and bring my sword and my shield because I want to see them'; [fol. 182r] and he did it at once. And Tristan took his sword and drew it out of the scabbard. He began to lower it and said, weeping, 'Ah, good sword and shield, what will you ever do, because today you will be parted from you lord? That is because death has no pity for me'. And after he had said these words, he began to weep very much more sorrowfully than before. After he had wept like that for a long while, he again looked at Sagremor and told him, in tears, 'It behooves me to speak, dear friend, and I can no longer conceal it. Alas, how can I say it? Certainly, I will speak because I am forced to say it'. And then he fell silent for a long while. And then he began a lament greater than before.

And again he said, 'Sagremor, now know that I am going to say to you the most shameful word that a knight ever said. Oh, alas! How will it come out of my mouth? Certainly, I must do what I am forced to say'. And yet again he wept, and he wept for a long while. And he looked at Sagremor and said to Sagremor, 'I can no longer conceal what I cannot say'. And he began to say, 'Ah, Sagremor, I am defeated! – and I can surrender my arms to you, and my shield [fol. 182v] and all my grooms and my horses; and it behooves me to leave my deeds of prowess; and I am leaving them behind in spite of myself. Sir Sagremor, I pray you for courtesy's sake and for your honor to carry my arms to the Round Table so that they may be hung on high; and in the stead of my body, I am sending my arms, since I cannot send my body there; and for this reason they must pay honor to my arms. And tell them that as God may help me so I endeavored to win honor for them. And for this reason they must pay honor to my arms and have them positioned in a place so that all the errant knights and all the other knights can see them, so that such knights who never saw me, when they see my arms, will have high thoughts about me – both grim and mortal – and that will be because of the adventure that came to meet me from the wound that King Mark gave me, and all Cornwall will remain dishonored by it. Now I have told you what I wanted to tell you and yet did not want to tell you'.

And after he had said these words, he turned toward King Mark and began to look at him, weeping. And he said, 'Good uncle, what do you think of [fol. 183r] me? Am I that knight whom you used to fear so much?' And he said, 'Surely not ever again'. And Tristan said, 'Good uncle, this very day the great fear that you had of me is ended. This very day the great fear is ended that has been between you and me. No one in battle ever went down who, if he asked me for mercy, there was not a single knight who did not have my compassion. In this battle, you did not have mercy for me' – said Tristan to King Mark – 'and by a dirty blow that you gave me, I am dead. But since I can do nothing else, I pardon you for it' (and may God pardon him for it).

E poych'ebe decte queste parolle, ed elli disse, 'Ay, che danno receve ogi la Taula Retonta de la morte d'uno solo chavaliere barone e cortesse e plieno de cortessia e de savere; ed è valente. E qui remane nostro dire – e giamae Tristano non ve darae colpo sopra voye nè[503] voy sopra me – e lo nostro estato; e lestridio è remasse a Yssota, bella e dolenta. Or sono io tuto canbiato, e Yssota v'era tuta canbiata'.

E dissia Tristano, 'Ay, Yssota, non serete voy ala mia fine? May sonno io certo che gran pianto ne farà Meser Lançoloto qua[n]do saprà la mia morte, almeno chostey ch'io v'òe contata. Voy [fol. 183v] li[504] salutarete molto da la mia parte, e direte li que seguramento doloyrosso moio que sì tosto remane nostra conpania. May la morte non àe de me pietade si ne fae remanere nostra conpagnia'. E dapoych'ebe fenito soe dire, ello si volle[505] [la conpagnia] enchaciata entorno, [e] disse, 'Segnori, io muori! ché la morte mi casçia, ché io non posso più vivere. Per çò che lo corpo me schopa di dolore'. Alor disse Tristano, 'A Dio fiate aconpagnati'.

E poy si volse verso Yssota e disse, 'Dame Yssota, io moio'. Ed ella disse, 'E io con voy volria, per mia fé, volria morire si se·nn'anderemo le nostre anime[506] ensieme'. E Tristano disse, 'Dame dolçe, volete voy mecho morire si n'anderemo le nosse anime ensieme?' Disse Yssota, 'Dolço amicho Tristano, noy siamo una anima e uno chuore'. [Tristano disse,] 'E dapoyché con mecho volete morire, or m'abraçiate – si voy piaçe – a çhò que fenischa e[n]de le vostre baçie'.[507]

[90] Ed ella si chinoe ende lo soe pecto, ed ello si la prende e si l'abraçia. E tanto la tiene stritta che disse sì alto che onni homo l'entesse, e [Tristano] disse, 'Vmay[508] non me ne enqualia si io moio. Lo perché èy questo: ché quando i'ò la mia donna en braçio con mecho'. Ed elli si lasi re[fol. 184r]cha al pecto e stringe la de tuta soa força chome ello àe, siché li fesse partir l'anima del corpo. Ed ello metessmo si morìo[509] con ley, e foron ensieme[510] morti ed abraciato en braçio, e bocha en bocha, e pecto a petto, morironno li due amanti. E demoranno coysì ensieme abraçati per grande pessa, morti. Tutta gente credea que fosseno vivi, ed elli sonno morti siché più non li fae mestieri. Morti sonno anboro per amore: en tal maniera morìo anboro li amanti, soè Yssota e Tristano, ch'era en quel tempo lo melior chavaliere del mondo afore di Meser Galiotto; e Yssota era la più bella donna del mondo a fora la Redina Genevra, la filliola del Re Pelis.[511] |||[512]

---

[503]   MS *Me*.
[504]   MS *me*.
[505]   MS *volse*. Possible confusion of *s* / *l*, but see the alternate reading in TP, p. 724: *Elli riguarda tucto intorno di sé e disse*.
[506]   MS *arme* with titulus.
[507]   Cf. TP, p. 724: *in vostre braccia*.
[508]   Thus in MS. Cf. TV, p. 549: *Oramai non me incuro quando io moro*; *Tav. Rit.*, p. 505: *Ora non curo io di mia morte*.
[509]   MS *moie* with line over the *i*.
[510]   MS *enseemi*.
[511]   Or perhaps *Pelus*. Written with a titulus over the *s*. Cf. TP, p. 726: *Pelles*.
[512]   Ten full lines blank at bottom of writing space; miniature never executed.

Il Tristano Riccardiano *(Parodi's siglum 'F')* 157

And after he had said these words, Tristan said, 'Ah, what harm the Round Table is receiving today due to the death of a lone baron knight, courtly and full of courtesy and wisdom; and he is valiant. And here our speaking breaks off – and never will Tristan strike a blow against you nor you against me. Our situation is ended; and the sobbing is left to Yseut, lovely and sorrowful. Now I am completely changed, and Yseut was completely changed toward you'.

And Tristan said, 'Ah, Yseut, won't you be at my end? But I'm sure that Sir Lancelot will make a great lament about it when he learns of my death, at least she whom I have recounted to you.* You [fol. 183v] will greet him a lot on my behalf and tell him that surely I die, sorrowful that our company must be broken up so soon. But death has no pity for me so that it is breaking up our company'. And after he had finished his speaking, he wanted his company gathered around; and he said, 'Lords, I am dying – because death is hunting me down, so that I can no longer live, because my body is bursting with pain'. Then Tristan said, 'May God go with you'.

And then he turned toward Yseut and said, 'Lady Yseut, I am dying'. And she said, 'And I would like – by my faith – I would like to die with you so that our souls go away together'. And Tristan said, 'Sweet lady, do you want to die with me so that our souls go away together?' Yseut said, 'Sweet *ami* Tristan, we are one spirit and one heart'. Tristan said, 'Since you want to die with me, now embrace me – if you please – so that I may end in your kisses'.

[90] And she bent over onto his chest, and he took her and embraced her. And he held her so tightly that he said so loudly that everyone could hear, Tristan said, 'Now it does not trouble me if I die. The reason is this: because I have my lady in my arms with me'. And he brought her [fol. 184r] to his chest and squeezed her with all the strength that he had left, so that he made her soul depart her body. And he himself died with her, and they died together; embraced in their arms, mouth to mouth and breast to breast, the two lovers died. And they remained together like that, embraced, for a long time – dead. All the people believed that they were alive, and yet they were dead so that they needed nothing else. They were both dead from love: in that fashion both the lovers died, that is to say, Yseut and Tristan, who was at that time the best knight in the world, except for Sir Galahad; and Yseut was the most beautiful woman in the world, except for Queen Guenevere, the daughter of King Pelles. |||

---

*   A noticeably corrupt reading here, translated literally.

[91] [fol. 184v] E quando lo Re vide morta Yssota – e Tristano – disse, 'Or [qu]e venture que queste sonno ché oncha may a Re non aviene sì grande esçaçhura! Melio me seria che io fosse morto ché dapoyché Tristano i'ò perdutto qu'era tuto mio honore, e tutta Cornavalia n'era enrada'. E[n] tal maniera piangeno li baroni de Cornavalia, cioè de la morte de Tristano; e l'uno piangea Tristano e l'autro Yssota; e non ve nì àe neuno nì picholi nè grandi che non fassano grandi pianti. E dissiano, 'Ay, Siri Tristano, chome noy averemo li nimissi tosto adosso, e specialmente qu'illi de Sansognia che çà recevenno molta onta e molto dessognore da noy. Or si vendicharanno de voy, Re Marcho, que credete fare suo bene, elli fesse soe danno de metere a morto Tristano perché anchor non è morto lo Re Arturo nì la soa gente, nì Lançeloto del Lac non è anchor morto que tanto v'amava. E non è anchora morto lo vostro lignaçio, e specialmente lo Re Gioni,[513] que tanto v'amava. E tuti quilli che odiran la novella – grandi e picholi – venrano al castello de Pinogres. [Disseno][514] che meravilia era, che anche [fol. 185r] fosse bene mosseranno che loro amore non era vanno; ançi era tanto puro e tanto leale che ne fie parlato de queste amore enfine que lo mondo bastarae, e dirà si chomunamente, 'Questo foe amor passo, cioè da Yssota e da Tristano'.

E qua[n]do lo Re Mar[ch]o entesse queste cosse, si disse, 'Io faroe anboro li corpi metere ensieme ende la grande giesa de Titolin, sichome esteron ad açio en lor vitta, choisì estaranno <d> ad açio en lor morte, ché non potiano vivere nì die nì nocte che non fossono ensieme. E si eranno con lor volontade perché tanto s'amavanno a lor vita'. Or li fesse metere ensieme lo Re Marcho, e·ffese lor fare una tonba sì bella e sì richa che non fo may veduta en Cornavalia sì bella nì sì richa, si non fo quella del Prinçe Galioto, lo filliolo de la bella giognante, lo sire d[e L]ontana Yssola que sapiate que quella tonba foe ed era sì bella e sì riche qu'era tuta lavorata ad orro e di pietre preçiosse – e de safay e de smiraldi e de carbonchi – e d'altre pietre preçiosse asay. E sapiate que quello prinçe fo segnore de .xxix. realmi, e amoe tanto Meser Lançeloto che ala fine ne morìo.

[fol. 185v] ||||[515] May noy layseremo ora<i> lo conto de parlare de lo possente[516] Galiotto, e torna de parlare de Cornavalia.

Ora disse lo conto del Re Marcho que fesse entalliare en quella sepultura due emagine que l'uno era en guissa de chavaliere e l'autro a guissa de donne. E quello del chavaliere era più richo entalio que quie l'esgardava, li paria vivo. E·ttenian si la manno alo pecto s[i]chome si tenisse la cordella del mantello; e l'autro si tenia verso la gente e tenia l'espada en mano con che osçisse L'Amoroldo d'Irlanda. E l'una [fol. 186r] emagine avia letere che dissianno, 'Meser Tristano'. E sapiate que [en] quello tempo non si trovavanno due sì belle esmagine.

---

[513] Clear in MS. Not found in analogous texts.
[514] Insertion based on TP, p. 728.
[515] Twelve full lines left blank at top of verso; miniature never executed. This is the largest intended image in the MS; also in an unusual position at the top of the folio.
[516] MS *pressente*, written *in extenso*.

Il Tristano Riccardiano *(Parodi's siglum 'F')*

[91] [fol. 184v] When the king saw Yseut dead, and Tristan, he said, 'Now what misfortunes these are, because never to any king did such a great calamity come! It would be better for me if I were dead since in losing Tristan, I have lost him who was all my honor, and all Cornwall was honored because of him'. And in this manner all the barons of Cornwall were weeping, that is about the death of Tristan; and one was weeping for Tristan and another for Yseut; and there was no one – neither small nor great – who wasn't weeping hard. And they said, 'Ah, Sir Tristan, now we will have enemies upon us very soon, and especially those of Saxony who have already received much humiliation and much dishonor from us. Now they'll avenge themselves upon us! King Mark, you believed you were acting for your good. You brought about your downfall by putting Tristan to death, because King Arthur is not yet dead nor his people, nor Lancelot of the Lake – he's not yet dead – who loved you so much. And your lineage is not yet dead, and especially King Gioni who loved you so much; and all those who hear the news – great and small – will come to the castle of Pinogres'. They said that it was a marvel that even [fol. 185r] showed clearly that their love was not vain; rather, that it was so very pure and so loyal that this love will be spoken of as long as the world will endure, and they all will say, 'This was a mad love, that is between Yseut and Tristan'.

And when King Mark heard these things, he said, 'I will have both their bodies placed together in the great church of Tintagel so that just as they were in life, so they will be at peace in death, because they could not live neither day nor night unless they were together; and so they were with all their will because they loved each other so much in their lives'. Now King Mark had them placed together, and he had made for them a tomb so beautiful and rich that there was never seen in Cornwall one so beautiful nor so rich, except for that of Prince Galehot, the son of the lovely giantess, lord of the Faraway Island. And know that that tomb was – and is – so beautiful and rich because it was worked all over with gold and precious stones, and with sapphires and emeralds and carbuncles and a great many other precious stones. And know that that prince was lord of twenty-nine kingdoms, and he loved Sir Lancelot so greatly that in the end, he died of it.

[fol. 185v] ||| But let us now leave the tale's speaking of the powerful Galehot: it returns to speak of Cornwall.

Now the tale says about King Mark that he had sculpted* on that sepulcher two images: the one was in the form of a knight and the other in the form of a lady. And the figure of the knight was so richly sculpted that it would have seemed alive to whomever looked at it. He was holding his hand against his breast, as though he were holding the cord of his mantle; and the other hand he was holding out toward the people and he was holding in that hand the sword with which he killed the Morholt of Ireland; and the one [fol. 186r] image had letters that said, 'Sir Tristan'. And know that at that time one could not find two such beautiful images.**

---

*   MS *entalliare*. This could be translated variously as to cut, to carve, to sculpt or to engrave. Since the figure of Tristan has one hand extended and holding a sword, the verb would seem to indicate a three-dimensional sculpture rather than a two-dimensional engraving or bas-relief.

**   This redaction completely elides the description of Yseut's funerary figure.

[92] E quanto Sagremor ebe <d> tanto demorato en Cornavalia dapoy la fine de Tristano, si si parte e portoe l'eschudo de Meser Tristano choberto d'uno bello drapo di çeta battuto ad oro e la espada soa avia al collo pendente, e nullo altro porta secho. E disse en giuamay si traerà enverso la Gran Bretagnia lo più tosto qu'illo poterò <pia(n)to>.[517]

Ora aviene que uno giorno che Messer Sagremor chavalchava per una foresta, tanto que perviene ala riva del mare. E alor trovoe uno chavaliere que veniva ala corte del Re Artù, e avia nome Meser Chiello lo Sinischalcho. E quando li due chavalieri vi fonno giunti ensieme, si salutò l'uno l'autro. E poy demandoe Sagremor que novelle eli avia a corte de lo Re Artù; e Meser Chiello resposse li, |||[518] [fol. 186v] *'Or sapiate che lo Re Arture piange choysì teneramente chome s'illo si vedesse morto dinançi a sé patre e matre e filli e fratelli: qué li viene novelle chome Messer Oregho*[519] *e Meser Bioberis erano morti, e Taulas lo Grande,*[520] *Serialbe*[521] *e Dainental*[522] *e Damaus;*[523] *e Messer Arpano de le Strette Montane*[524] *e Galiemonte*[525] *e Meser Palamides; e de tuti questi chavalieri piangea lo Re Arturo sì teneramente che nullo non lo pò rapagnare.*

[93] *'Certo', disse Messer Sacremor, 'echo uno grando danno; e anchor porto io pegior novelle'. E Messer Chielo disse, 'Or che novelle potrianno esse[re] pegiore che queste?' E Messer Sagremor chominça forto a piangere; e disse, piangendo <e disse>, 'Sapiate que i'ò qui la espada e l'eschudo que fo de Messer Tristano de Cornavalia, che foe sì bono chavaliere che non l'osso portare al costato, ançi le porto a collo per soa honore'.*

[94] *'Or chi fo questo coysie bonno chavaliere?' Ed elli recominçoe a piangere, e disse, 'Ora sapiate che foron de Meser Tristano de Leones, che morto è ora novellamente'. 'Certa', disse Messer Chiello, 'ora èi bene enpoverita la Taula Retonta dapoyché tuti* [fol. 187r] *li boni chavalieri sonno morti'. Encontenente*

---

[517]   Scribe added in red ink: *piato* with a titulus. Not found in analogous texts.

[518]   Five full lines left blank at bottom of writing space.

[519]   This spelling is also found in TV, p. 554, corresponds to *Erec.* Cf. *Tav. Rit.* p. 509, variant: *Arecho.*

[520]   This series of names is not found in TR, TP, TV, *Tav. Rit.* Instead, it would seem to allude to the later adventures of the Round Table knights (Lös. §339, §395a). *Taulas le Grand* 'hates Ban's kin, and, with Baridan, Damas, Damadas, and Senelas, he attacks Galaad and Bliob(l)eris'; all five attackers were mortally wounded (West, p. 287). See also Christopher W. Bruce, *Arthurian Name Dictionary*, Garland Reference Library of the Humanities 2063 (New York, 1999), p. 461: 'Taulat[4] the Great'.

[521]   All these names are clear in the MS, but likely had become corrupted due to the transmission and translation processes. 'Senelas' was brother or cousin of Taulas in the same adventure. See West, p. 278; Bruce, *Dictionary*, p. 445.

[522]   Probable corruption of 'Damatal', var. 'Damadas'. See West, p. 89; Bruce, *Dictionary*, p. 140.

[523]   Another of Taulus' cousins. See West, p. 89: Damas[2]; Bruce, *Dictionary*, p. 140: 'Damas of Desert'.

[524]   See Bruce, *Dictionary*, p. 34: 'Arpian[1] (Harpin) of the Narrow Mountains'.

[525]   I was unable to find this name in available reference sources.

[92] And when Sagremor had dwelt a long time in Cornwall after Tristan's death, he departed and carried Sir Tristan's shield – covered with a lovely silk drapery worked with gold – and he had his sword hung at his neck, and he brought nothing else with him; and he said that this very day he would cross toward Great Britain as quickly as he would be able to.

Now one day it happened that Sir Sagremor was riding through a forest, so far that he came to the seacoast. And then he found a knight who was coming from King Arthur's court, and his name was Sir Kay the Seneschal. And when the two knights had reached each other, one greeted the other. And then Sagremor asked what news he had of King Arthur's court; and Sir Kay answered him: ||| [fol. 186v] 'Now know that King Arthur is weeping so tenderly as though he had seen die before him father and mother and sons and brothers, because news came to him about how Sir Erec and Sir Blioberis were dead, and Taulas the Great, Senelas and Damatal and Damas; and Sir Harpin of the Narrow Mountains and Galiemonte and Sir Palamides; and for all these knights King Arthur is weeping so tenderly that nothing could pacify him'.

[93] 'Truly', said Sir Sagremor, 'here is a great loss and yet I bring worse news'. And Sir Kay said, 'Now what news can be worse than these?' Sir Sagremor began to weep very hard and said, weeping, 'Know that I have here the sword and the shield that belonged to Sir Tristan of Cornwall who was such a good knight that I don't dare to wear it [the sword] at my side; instead I am wearing it at my neck, to honor him'.

[94] Sir Kay asked: 'Now who was this knight, so very good?' And Sagremor began to weep again and said, 'Now know that these belonged to Sir Tristan of Leonis who has just recently died'. 'Truly', said Sir Kay, 'now the Round Table is indeed impoverished since all [fol. 187r] the good knights are dead'. At once

si partine l'uno da l'autro: e Meser Chiello lo Seneschalcho si ne vene verso la marina del mare, e Messer Sagremor se sen' andoe ala corte del Re Arturo.

 Ed elli vidi venire uno chavaliere lo quale avia nome Sagremor. Elli li fesse gran honore a Messer Sagremor perché eli sae ch'andoe ala conpagnia de Meser Tristano. E si li disse, 'Dìme, Sacremor, che novelli rechi tue de Cornavalia?' Ed elli resposse e disse, 'Certo, le novelle non sono tale chome io volria. May fate rassonare li conpangni vostri, e io ve lo diroe le novelle'. E lo[526] *Re Artù disse, 'Certo, io non potria ora fare più che .lx. chavalieri perché tuti li autri chavalieri sonno morti ala Enqu<i>esta del Sagradale'. Ed eli fesse encontenente montar uno [...]*[527] *su la torre, e fesse sonare uno corno que non sonava may, si non quando li conpagni de la Taula Retonta si divessano a rassonare.*

 E alora viene lo Re e li soy chavalieri, e Messer Lançeloto. E quando foron dintro ala corte, encontenente chominçano a piange[re] per amore de Palamides e per li autri boni chavalieri qu'eranno morti. E poy demandano Messer Sagremor che novelle avia en Cornavalia. Ello encontenente chominçò [fol. 187v] *a piangere, e disse, 'Certo, segnori conpagni, io vegnio de Cornavalia, e recho molte male novelle; e soè que Tristano – bello e cortesse e prode chavaliere – èi morto; de que èy gran danno ali conpagni de la Taula Retonta, cioè de la sua morte.* |||[528] *E ancora ve manda, pregando pietossamente, che voy debiate fare honore ale soe arme, e che per vostra honore le ve manda. Ancho me disse que mentre quello visce, prochaçhoe de vostra onore. E però disse que voy devereste fare honore ale soy arme, e dapoyqué per vostra honore ve le manda'. E dapoyché Sagremor ebe conpitto soe parlamento, elli chominçono fortamente a piangere. E disse, 'Bene deveria lo mondo fenire ogi may* [fol. 188r] *daché lo buono [chavaliere] de Tristano è morto'.*

[95] *Ora laysiamo tuti [en] lo dolore de Tristano que l'ànno messo en tristicia (sic), e tutto è per amore de Tristano. E lo Re Artù ne fesse uno lamento, e la Redina Genevera ne fesse uno altro, e Lançeloto ne-ffesse uno altro. E omni*[529] *dì enchominçanno uno grande piandto per quella dolore. E sapiate que lo lamento e 'l dolore de Meser Tristano fo per loro mantenuto uno anno e[n]de la maysone del Re Artù, e tuti si vestironno de roube nere. (E chò foe que primeramente viene lo vestire niero, per la dolore de Tristano.)*

 Ed èy fenito. *Deo gratias.*[530] *Amen.*

 Finito libro. *Referamus*[531] *gra[tiam] Cristo.*

 Qui sc[ri]psi[t] sc[ri]pba[t] senpre con damino viaiat.[532]

---

[526] MS *le*.
[527] Noun for 'herald' or 'trumpeter' was omitted in MS.
[528] Ten full lines left blank at mid-page; miniature never executed.
[529] MS *oi* with titulus on *i*.
[530] MS *gras* with a ~ above the *as*.
[531] Scribe used a final *-y* abbreviation to indicate *-us*.
[532] The final two lines, written in red, are a standard Latin blessing upon the scribe. It was written more accurately in an earlier segment of the MS (fol. 63r): '*Qui scripsit scribat senper con domino vivat / vivat in celis / Jhoannes nomine felix*' (abbreviations expanded by Balatresi, 'I codici', p. 38). Folios 188v, 189r–v, and 190r–v (original paper) are blank, but were numbered by the scribe on each *recto*. Fol. 192 has a modern machine number.

Il Tristano Riccardiano *(Parodi's siglum 'F')* 163

the one parted from the other: and Sir Kay the Seneschal went on his way toward the seacoast, and Sir Sagremor went on his way to King Arthur's court.

King Arthur saw a knight coming who was called Sagremor. He paid great honor to Sir Sagremor because he knew that he belonged to the company of Sir Tristan. And the king said to him, 'Tell me, Sagremor, what news do you bring from Cornwall?' And he replied and said, 'In truth, the news is not such as I would like; but have your companions assemble, and I will tell you the news'. And King Arthur said, 'In truth, I wouldn't be able to assemble more than sixty knights now because all the other knights have died on the Quest of the Holy Grail'. And at once he had a herald climb up the tower and had him blow a horn that was never blown except when the companions of the Round Table were supposed to reunite.

Then came the king and his knights, and Sir Lancelot. And when they were inside at court, immediately they began to weep for the sake of Palamides and for the other good knights who were dead. And then they asked Sir Sagremor what news he had about Cornwall. He immediately began [fol. 187v] to weep, and said, 'In truth, lord companions, I come from Cornwall and I bring very bad news, and that is that Tristan – handsome and courteous and valiant knight – is dead; such is a great loss to the companions of the Round Table, that is, due to his death; ||| but still he has sent to you, begging piteously, to pay honor to his arms, and for your honor he sent them. Also he told me that while he lived, he sought to bring you honor; and for this reason he said that you must pay honor to his arms, since for your honor he is sending them to you'. And after Sagremor had completed his speech, they began to weep very hard. And he said, 'The world must surely end this very day [fol. 188r] since the good knight Tristan is dead'.

[95] Now let us all leave off telling the sad news about Tristan that made them so sad, and all [the weeping] was for love of Tristan. And King Arthur made a song of lament about it, and Queen Guenevere made another about it, and Lancelot made another about it. And every day they began a great lamentation because of that sorrow. And know that the lamenting and the sorrow about Sir Tristan was kept up by them for a year in King Arthur's household, and all of them dressed themselves in black robes. (And that was the first time that dressing in black for mourning was done, for sorrow over Tristan.)

And it is finished. *Deo gratias. Amen.*
Having finished the book, let us give thanks to Christ.
May he who wrote [it] always write and live with the Lord.

BIBLIOGRAPHY

MANUSCRIPTS CITED

Florence, Biblioteca della Fondazione Ezio Franceschini, MS 1.
Florence, Biblioteca Nazionale Centrale, MS Cl. VIII, 1272.
—— MS Nuovi Acquisti 509.
—— MS Palatino 556.
Florence, Biblioteca Riccardiana, MS Ricc. 1729.
—— MS Ricc. 2543.
New York, The Morgan Library and Museum, MS M.41.
Paris, Bibliothèque de l'Arsenal, MS 5073.
Paris, Bibliothèque nationale de France, MS fr. 99.
—— MS fr. 757.
Venice, Biblioteca Marciana, MS Cl. IX, 175.

PRIMARY SOURCES

Attila flagellum Dei: poemetto in ottava rima riprodotto sulle antiche stampe. Ed. Alessandro D'Ancona. Collezione di antiche scritture italiane inedito o rare 3. Pisa, 1864.
Boccaccio, Giovanni. *Decameron.* Ed. Antonio Enzo Quaglio. I Garzanti, I Grandi Libri. 2 vols. Milan, 1980.
I cantari di Fiorabraccia e Ulivieri: Testo mediano inedito. Ed. Elio Melli. Biblioteca di Filologia Romanza della Facoltà di Lettere e Filosofia dell'Università di Bologna 3. Bologna, 1984.
Il Canzoniere di Nicolò de' Rossi. Ed. Furio Brugnolo. Medioevo e umanesimo 16. Padua, 1974. Vol. 1.
Il Canzoniere di Nicolò de' Rossi. Ed. Furio Brugnolo. Medioevo e umanesimo 30. Padua, 1977. Vol. 2.
Dante Alighieri. *De vulgari eloquentia.* Ed. and trans. Steven Botterill. Cambridge Medieval Classics 5. Cambridge, 1996.
Il 'Fierabraccia' comense: fra preziosità umanistiche e antico dialetto lombardo. Ed. Elio Melli. Biblioteca di Filologia Romanza della Facoltà di Lettere e Filosofia dell'Università di Bologna 10. Bologna, 1996.
La Geste Francor: Edition of the 'Chansons de geste' of MS. Marc. Fr. XIII (=256). Ed. Leslie Zarker Morgan. Medieval and Renaissance Texts and Studies 348. 2 vols. Tempe, Arizona, 2009.
La Inchiesta del San Gradale: Volgarizzamento toscano della 'Queste del Saint Graal'. Ed. Marco Infurna. Biblioteca della Rivista di Storia e Letteratura Religiosa, Testi e documenti 14. Florence, 1993.
Italian Literature I. Il Tristano Panciatichiano. Ed. and trans. Gloria Allaire. Arthurian Archives 8. Cambridge, 2002.

Italian Literature II. Il Tristano Riccardiano. Ed. A. Scolari. Trans. F. Regina Psaki. Arthurian Archives 12. Cambridge, 2006, at p. x n. 3.
Italian Literature III. Il Tristano Corsiniano. Ed. and trans. Gloria Allaire. Arthurian Archives 20. Cambridge, 2015.*Lancellotto: Versione italiana inedita del 'Lancelot en prose'*. Ed. Luca Cadioli. Archivio Romanzo 32. Florence, 2016.
La leggenda di Tristano. Ed. Luigi Di Benedetto. Scrittori d'Italia 189. Bari, 1942, at p. 372.
Il libro di messer Tristano ('Tristano Veneto'). Ed. Aulo Donadello. Medioevo Veneto. Venice, 1994, at p. 17.
Il Novellino: Libro di novelle e di bel parlar gentile. Ed. Giorgio Manganelli. Classici italiani BUR. Milan, 1989.
Le Roman de Tristan en prose. Ed. Renée L. Curtis. Vol. I. Munich, 1963; rpt. Arthurian Studies XII. Cambridge, 1985.
Le Roman de Tristan en prose. Ed. Renée L. Curtis. Vol. II. Leiden, 1976; rpt. Arthurian Studies XIII. Cambridge, 1985.
Il romanzo di Tristano. Ed. Antonio Scolari. Testi della cultura italiana 17. Genoa, 1990, at pp. 22–3.
La Spagna in rima del manoscritto comense. Ed. Giovanna Barbara Rosiello. Il cavaliere del leone 3. Turin, 2001.
La Tavola Ritonda o l'Istoria di Tristano: Testo di lingua. Ed. Filippo-Luigi Polidori. Collezione di opere inedite o rare dei primi tre secoli della lingua [8–9]. 2 vols. Bologna, 1864–6.
La Tavola Ritonda: Manoscritto Palatino 556, Firenze Biblioteca Nazionale Centrale. Ed. Roberto Cardini. I codici miniati. 2 vols. Rome, 2009, at pp. 10, 117.
Il Tristano Corsiniano: Edizione critica. Ed. Roberto Tagliani. Atti della Accademia Nazionale dei Lincei, Classe di scienze morali, storiche e filologiche, Memorie, anno CDVII (2010), ser. 9, vol. 28/1. Rome, 2011, at p. 20.
Il Tristano Riccardiano. Ed. E. G. Parodi. Collezione di opere inedite o rare di scrittori italiani dal XIII al XVI secolo, R. Commissione pe' testi di lingua nelle provincie dell'Emilia [74]. Bologna, 1896, at pp. xi–xix, liii–lv, lix–lxiv.

SECONDARY SOURCES

(Specific page indications refer to Ricc. MS 1729)

Allaire, Gloria. 'Arthurian Art in Italy'. In *Arthur of the Italians*. Eds Allaire and Psaki, pp. 205–32.
—— 'Literary Evidence for Multilingualism: The *Roman de Tristan* in its Italian Incarnations'. In *Medieval Multilingualism*. Eds Kleinhenz and Busby, pp. 145–53.
The Arthur of the Italians: The Arthurian Legend in Medieval Italian Literature and Culture. Eds Gloria Allaire and F. Regina Psaki. Arthurian Literature in the Middle Ages 7. Cardiff, 2014, at pp. 48, 52, 53, 56, 58, 59, 68 n. 146, 86 n. 68.
Balatresi, Rebecca. 'I codici 1729–1756 della Biblioteca Riccardiana di Firenze: Descrizione e storia'. Tesi di laurea in codicologia. Università degli Studi di Firenze, Facoltà di Lettere e Filosofia, 1996–97.

Balduino, Armando. *Manuale di filologia italiana*. Biblioteca Universale Sansoni. Florence, 1979, at p. 97 n. 77.
Battaglia, Salvatore. *Grande dizionario della lingua italiana*. 21 vols. Turin, 1961–2002. Online at: www.gdli.it.
Baumgartner, Emmanuèle. 'The Prose *Tristan*'. Trans. Sarah Singer. In *The Arthur of the French: The Arthurian Legend in Medieval French and Occitan Literature*. Eds Glyn S. Burgess and Karen Pratt. Arthurian Literature in the Middle Ages 4. Cardiff, 2006, pp. 325–41.
Baxter, Ron. *Bestiaries and their Users in the Middle Ages*. London, 1998.
Beasts and Birds of the Middle Ages: The Bestiary and Its Legacy. Eds Willene B. Clark and Meradith T. McMunn. University of Pennsylvania Press, Middle Ages Series. Philadelphia, 1989.
Bertoni, Giulio. *Poesie – leggende – costumanze del medio evo*. 2nd edn. Modena, 1927, at pp. 240, 249.
Bologna, Corrado. 'La letteratura dell'Italia settentrionale nel Trecento'. In *Letteratura italiana. Storia e geografia. I: L'età medievale*. Dir. Alberto Asor Rosa. Turin, 1987, pp. 511–600, at p. 532.
Briquet, C. M. *Les filigranes: Dictionnaire historique des marques du papier des leur apparition vèrs 1292 jusqu'en 1600. A Facsimile of the 1907 Edition* [...]. Ed. Allan Stevenson. 4 vols. Amsterdam, 1968.
Bruce, Christopher W. *The Arthurian Name Dictionary*. Garland Reference Library of the Humanities 2063. New York, 1999.
Cadioli, Luca. 'A New Arthurian Text: the Tuscan translation of the Lancelot en prose', *Journal of the International Arthurian Society* 2.1 (2014), 63–9, on 68.
Chiostrini Mannini, Anna. *I Davanzati: mercanti, banchieri, mecenati*. Florence, 1989.
Cigni, Fabrizio. Rev. of *Il romanzo di Tristano*, ed. A. Scolari; and *Tristano Riccardiano*, ed. E. G. Parodi, introduction and notes M.-J. Heijkant. *Rivista di letteratura italiana* 11.1–2 (1993), 323–37, at 323, 329.
—— 'La ricezione medievale della letteratura francese nella Toscana nord-occidentale'. In *Fra toscanità e italianità: Lingua e letteratura dagli inizi al Novecento*. Eds Edeltraud Werner and Sabine Schwarze. Kultur und Erkenntnis 22. Tübingen and Basel, 2000, pp. 71–108.
—— '*Roman de Tristan* in prosa e "compilazione" di Rustichello da Pisa in area veneta: A proposito di una recente edizione'. *Lettere Italiane* 47 (1995), 598–622, at 602, 622 n. 71.
Conseils pour l'édition des textes médiévaux. Fascicule I: conseils généraux. Eds Françoise Veillard and Olivier Guyotjeannin. École nationale des chartes, Groupe de recherches 'La civilisation de l'écrit au Moyen Âge'. Paris, 2001.
Cornagliotti, Anna. 'Un volgarizzamento del "Transitus Pseudo-Josephi de Arimathea" in dialetto veronese'. *Atti della Accademia delle scienze di Torino. Classe di scienze fisiche, matematiche e naturali*, tome I, vol. 113 (1979), 197–217.
Corti, Maria. 'Emiliano e veneto nella tradizione manoscritta del *Fiore di virtù*'. *Studi di filologia italiana* 18 (1960), 29–68: 29–68; rpt. in *Storia della lingua*

e storia dei testi. Eds Maria Corti and Rossana Saccani. Milan, 1989, pp. 177–216.
de Bofarull y Sans, F. *Animals in Watermarks*. Hilversum, 1959.
Delcorno Branca, Daniela. *Boccaccio e le storie di re Artù*. Il Mulino, Ricerca. Bologna, 1991, at pp. 46 n. 82, 155.
—— 'I cantari di Tristano'. *Lettere Italiane* 23 (1971), 289–305, at 293 n. 30.
—— 'Le carte piene di sogni'. Introduction to *La Tavola Ritonda, Palatino 556*. Ed. Cardini. Vol. 2, pp. 3–18, at p. 10.
—— 'Lecteurs et interprètes de romans arthuriens en Italie: un examen à partir des études récentes'. In *Medieval Multilingualism*. Eds Kleinhenz and Busby, pp. 155–86, at p. 163 n. 27.
—— 'Per la storia del *Roman de Tristan* in Italia'. *Cultura Neolatina* 40 (1980), 211–29, at 215 n. 23.
—— *I romanzi italiani di Tristano e la 'Tavola Ritonda'*. Università di Padova, Pubblicazioni della Facoltà di Lettere e Filosofia 45. Florence, 1968, at pp. 24, 45.
—— *Il romanzo cavalleresco medievale*. Scuola aperta, Lettere Italiane 45. Florence, 1974, at p. 9.
—— 'Sette anni di studi sulla letteratura arturiana in Italia: Rassegna (1985–92)'. *Lettere Italiane* 4.3 (1992), 465–97, at 480 n. 52, 482.
—— *Tristano e Lancillotto in Italia: Studi di letteratura arturiana*. Memoria del tempo 11. Ravenna, 1998, at pp. 60, 62, 68, 73, 75, 103–10, 112, 184, 235.
Dictionnaire du Moyen Français (1330—1500). Online at: zeus.atilf.fr/dmf/.
Di Domenico, Adriana. 'Un cavaliere sotto l'insegna del leone rampante: Una nuova ipotesi di committenza'. In *La Tavola Ritonda, Palatino 556*. Ed. Cardini. Vol. 2, pp. 113–22, at p. 117.
Dionisotti, Carlo. '*Entrèe d'Espagne, Spagna, Rotta di Roncisvalle*'. In *Studi in onore di Angelo Monteverdi*. Ed. G. G. Marcuzzo. 3 vols. Modena, 1959. Vol. I, pp. 207–41.
Giuliari, Giambattista Carlo. 'Proposta di una bibliografia de' dialetti italiani con un documento aneddoto in antico veronese'. *Il Propugnatore* 5 (1872), 305–39.
Grendler, Paul F. 'Form and Function in Italian Renaissance Popular Books'. *Renaissance Quarterly* 46 (1993), 451–85, at 456 n. 9.
—— 'Il libro popolare nel Cinquecento'. In *La Stampa in Italia nel Cinquecento: Atti del Convegno, Roma, 17–21 ottobre 1989*. Ed. Marco Santoro. Rome, 1992, pp. 211–44, at p. 216.
—— *Schooling in Renaissance Italy: Literacy and Learning, 1300–1600*. The Johns Hopkins University, Studies in Historical and Political Science, 107th Series 1. Baltimore, 1989.
Heijkant, Marie-José. 'From France to Italy: The Tristan Texts'. In *Arthur of the Italians*. Eds Allaire and Psaki, pp. 41–68, at pp. 48, 52, 53, 56, 58–9, 68 n.146.
—— Rev. of *Italian Literature I: Tristano Panciatichiano*, ed. Allaire. *Romance Philology* 58 (2004), 136–47, at 136.
—— 'La tradizione del *Tristan* in prosa in Italia e proposte di studio sul "Tristano Riccardiano"'. Catholic University, Nijmegen, 1989, at 9, 13, 38, 48, 135, 338.
Huot, Sylvia. *Outsiders: The Humanity and Inhumanity of Giants in Medieval*

French Prose Romance. The Conway Lectures in Medieval Studies 2012. Notre Dame, Indiana, 2016.

Infurna, Marco. 'La *Queste del Saint Graal* in Italia e il manoscritto udinese'. In *La grant Queste del Saint Graal / La grande Ricerca del Santo Graal: Versione inedita della fine del XIII secolo del ms. Udine, Biblioteca Arcivescovile, 177*. Udine, 1990, pp. 51–7, at p. 56 n. 25.

Iragui, Sebastian. 'The Southern Version of the Prose *Tristan*: The Italo-Iberian Translations and their French Source'. *Tristania* 17 (1996), 39–54, at 39.

Kibler, William W. *An Introduction to Old French*. Introductions to Older Languages 3. New York, 1984.

Löseth, Eilert. *Le Roman en prose de Tristan, le Roman de Palamède et la Compilation de Rusticien de Pise: Analyse critique d'après les manuscrits de Paris*. Bibliothèque de l'École des Hautes Études, Sciences Historiques et Philologiques 82. Paris, 1891; rpt. Burt Franklin Research and Source Works Series 426, Essays in Literature and Criticism 49. New York, 1970.

Medieval Multilingualism: The Francophone World and its Neighbours. Eds Christopher Kleinhenz and Keith Busby. Medieval Texts and Cultures of Northern Europe 20. Turnhout, 2010.

Migliorini, Bruno. *The Italian Language*. Rev. ed. T. Gwynfor Griffith. New York, 1966.

Monaci, Ernesto. *Facsimili di antichi manoscritti per uso delle scuole di filologia neolatina*. Rome, 1881–92.

Morosini, Roberta. '"Prose di romanzi" ... o novelle? A Note on the Adaptations of "franceschi romanzi". The Case of the *Tristano Riccardiano* and the *Novellino*'. *Tristania* 22 (2003), 23–48, at 42 n. 48.

Morpurgo, Salomone. *Le opere volgari a stampa dei secoli XIII e XIV indicate e descritte da F. Zambrini. Supplemento con gli indici generali* [...]. Bologna, 1929, at p. 274.

Mostra di codici romanzi delle biblioteche fiorentine. VIII Congresso Internazionale di Studi Romanzi (3–8 aprile 1956). Florence, 1957, at p. 176.

Paladini di carta: La cavalleria figurata. Firenze, Biblioteca Riccardiana, 8 maggio – 8 agosto 2003. Ed. Giovanna Lazzi. V settimana della cultura. Biblioteca Riccardiana 9. Florence, 2003, at pp. 14, 18.

Paradisi, Gioia, and Arianna Punzi. 'La tradizione del *Tristan en prose* in Italia e una nuova traduzione toscana'. In *Actes du XXe Congrès International de Linguistique et Philologie Romanes. Université de Zurich (6–11 avril 1992)*. Ed. Gerold Hilty. 5 vols. Tübingen and Basel, 1993. Vol. 5, pp. 323–37, at p. 332.

Piccard, Gerhard. *Wasserzeichen verschiedene Vierfüssler*. 3 vols. Stuttgart, 1987. Vol. 3.

La prosa del Duecento. Eds Cesare Segre and Mario Marti. Milan and Naples, 1959, at p. 1092.

Radaelli, Anna. 'Il testo del frammento Vb^2 del *Roman de Tristano en prose* (Biblioteca Apostolica Vaticana, Vat. lat. 14740)'. *Studi mediolatini e volgari* 50 (2004), 185–223, at 220.

Rajna, Pio. 'Tre studi per la storia del libro di Andrea Cappellano'. *Studi di filologia romanza* 5 (1890), 193–272, at 210.

Renzi, Lorenzo. 'Il francese come lingua letteraria e il franco-lombardo: L'epica carolingia nel Veneto'. In *Storia della cultura veneta, I: Dalle origini al Trecento*. Ed. Girolamo Arnaldi. Vicenza, 1976, pp. 563–89.

Riva, Franco. 'Lessico di antico veronese desunto da testi in versi (sec. XIII – sec. XVII)'. *Atti e memorie della Accademia di Agricoltura, Scienze e Lettere di Verona* 5 (1953–54), 171–237.

—— 'Storia dell'antico dialetto di Verona secondo i testi in versi (dal sec. XIII al sec. XVII)'. *Atti e memorie della Accademia di Agricoltura, Scienze e Lettere di Verona* 3 (1951–52), 305–53.

—— 'Storia dell'antico dialetto di Verona secondo i testi in versi: Morfologia e sintassi'. *Atti e memorie della Accademia di Agricoltura, Scienze e Lettere di Verona* 4 (1952–53), 65–88.

Rohlfs, Gerhard. *Grammatica storica della lingua italiana e dei suoi dialetti: Fonetica*. Trans. Salvatore Persichino. Piccola Biblioteca Einaudi 148. Turin, 1966. Vol. 1.

—— *Grammatica storica della lingua italiana e dei suoi dialetti: Morfologia*. Trans. Temistocle Franceschi. Piccola Biblioteca Einaudi 149. Turin, 1968. Vol. 2.

Ruggeri, Jole M. 'Versioni italiane della "Queste del Saint Graal"'. *Archivum Romanicum* 21 (1937), 471–86.

Salmi, Mario. *Italian Miniatures*. Trans. Elisabeth Borgese-Mann. New York, 1954.

Savino, Giancarlo. 'Ignoti frammenti di un *Tristano* dugentesco'. *Studi di filologia italiana* 37 (1979), 5–17, at 13; rpt. in *Dante e dintorni*. Ed. Marisa Boschi Rotiroti. Quaderni degli 'Studi Danteschi' 14. Florence, 2003, pp. 51–63, at p. 59.

Scanlon, Cesare. *Libri, scuole e cultura nel Friuli medievale: 'Membra disiecta' dell'Archivio di Stato di Udine*. Medioevo e umanesimo 65. Padua, 1987.

Segre, Vera. 'Illustrazioni cavalleresche fra manoscritti e carte dipinte nella Lombardia del Tre e Quattrocento'. In *Narrazioni e strategie dell'illustrazione: Codici e romanzi cavallereschi nell'Italia del Nord (secc. XIV–XVI)*. Eds Annalisa Izzo and Ilaria Molteni. I libri di Viella: Arte. Études lausannoises d'histoire de l'art 19, Studi lombardi 6. Rome, 2014, pp. 35–43 and fig. 16.

Shirt, David J. 'A Note on the Etymology of "Le Morholt"'. *Tristania* 1 (1975), 14–18.

Stussi, Alfredo. 'Esse, non effe!' *Italianistica* 23 (1994), 513–14.

Thomas L. Gravell Watermark Archive. *https://memoryofpaper.eu/gravell*.

Villoresi, Marco. *La letteratura cavalleresca. Dai cicli medievali all'Ariosto*. Università 219. Lingua e letteratura italiana. Rome, 2000, at p. 32.

Wessel, Jacqueline. '"Quirks and Twists": Looking over the Shoulder of the Middle Dutch *Ferguut* Scribe'. Paper read at the XXV Congress of the International Arthurian Society, Universität Würzburg, 25 July 2017.

West, G. D. *French Arthurian Prose Romances: An Index of Proper Names*. University of Toronto Romance Series 35. Toronto, 1978.

INDEX

Numbers refer to paragraphs.
Spellings reflect the norms of the manuscript and of this translation.

Acanor *see* Achan(n)o
Achan(n)o (king) 50, 52
L'Amor(r)ol(l)do / L'Omoroldo 7, 8, 16–17, 21, 30, 33–4, 45, 91 *see also* Ireland
Anguin *see* Languis
Arpano de le Strette Montane 92
Arthur *see* Arturo
Arturo / Arture / Artù / Artus(so) (king) 25, 34, 41, 48, 50, 63–4, 74, 79, 91–2, 94–5 *see also* Camelot, Round Table
Astor(e) da (de) Mare 25, 51
A(u)qua de l'Espina, Damaysella de 36–45

Ban of Benwick *see* Bando de Banucho
Bando de Banucho / Benichio / Benuçi (king) 48, 50
Bele Jaiande, la *see* Brunor's lady
Belide *see* Bellice(s)
Bellace *see* Bellice(s)
Bellice(s) / Belliçe (Faramont's daughter) 7–10, 12–14, 17
beverages 4, 6, 53, 79–80
Bendin (Beldin) *see* Ghedin
Bioberis / Broberis de Gaules 51, 92
Blanor (Lancelot's kin) *see* Bramor
Blioberis of Gaul *see* Bioberis de Gaules
boons 4, 7, 10, 27, 40, 49, 52
Bordo (Lancelot's kin) 25, 41–4, 51
Bordo (sic) *see* Bramor
Bors *see* Bordo
Bramor (Lancelot's kin) 48, 50–2

Branchina / Branghina / Branguina / Branquina 27, 30–1, 34, 53, 62, 65, 66–7, 69–71, 82, 84
Brando (sic) *see* Bordo
Brangain *see* Branchina
Branor (sic) *see* Brunor
Brescia *see* Presia
Breus 50
Brunor (lord of Island of Giants) 56–8
Brunor's daughter 58
Brunor's lady (giantess, mother of Galehot) 55–7, 91

Calvagno *see* G(u)alvagno
Camelot *see* Gamelletto; *see also* Arthur, Round Table
Caries *see* Gariet
Castello de Dinas 85–6
Castello de l'Encantatrisse 58
Castello de Pinogres 86, 88, 91
Castello de Plio 54–5, 57, 59, 61–3
Castello de Prodo *see* Castello de Plio
castle *see* Castello
Castle of the Enchantress *see* Castello de l'Encantatrisse
Castle of Weeping *see* Castello de Plio
Cento Chavalieri, re de 25–6, 50, 52, 58–9, 61–2
chess 53, 75
Chiel(l)o lo Seneschalcho / Sinischalco 92–4
Christ *see* Cristo
Chornavala *see* Cornaval(l)ia

Cornaval(l)ia / Cornavalla / Cornavalle   10, 12, 14–17, 20, 33–4, 43, 45–9, 51–3, 58–9, 61–2, 65, 67, 74, 76–7, 79–80, 83, 85, 89, 91–4   *see also* Tristan, Mark
Cornish knights   *see* Cornaval(l)ia
Cornwall   *see* Cornaval(l)ia
Cristo   55

Dainental   92
Damas   *see* Damaus
Damatal   *see* Dainental
Damaus   92
Danello Salvaçio / Salvagio   25, 82
Dei / Dey   *see* Dio
Delice   *see* Brunor's daughter
Dialices (giant)   55
Dinas   85
Dio   1–4, 7, 14, 16–17, 20, 50, 52, 54, 56–7, 62, 65–7, 89
Dodinel the Savage   *see* Danello Salvaçio
dogs   12–13, 53
Dolorossa G(u)ardia (castle)   31–2
Dolorous Guard   *see* Dolorossa G(u)ardia
Dominiidio   *see* Dio
drinking horn, enchanted   78–80
Durin (betrayer of Tristan)   86
dwarf   35, 37–9

Eliabel   *see* Eliabella
Eliabella (queen)   2–3
Erec   *see* Oregho
errant knights   21, 39, 40–4, 46–7, 58, 63, 67, 75–7, 83, 89
evil custom   55, 59–61, 63–4

Fada Morguana / Fata Morgana   79, 86
Faramont   *see* Fer(r)amonte
Faraway (Is)land(s)   *see* Lontana Yssola
Fer(r)amonte (king of Gaul)   6–14   *see also* Bellice(s)
Fontana Aventurossa   78

Fontana del Petrone   3
food   6–7, 19
fool at court   7
Fountain of Adventure   *see* Fontana Aventurossa
Fountain of the Stone   *see* Fontana del Petrone

Galahad   *see* Galieaçat
Galehot the Dark   *see* Galeoto lo Bruno
Galice (sic)   *see* Gariet
Galieaçat / Galiotto   3, 90
Galiemonte   92
Galeoto / Galioto lo Bruno (lord of Faraway Islands)   56, 58–64, 91
Gamelletto / Gamelloto / Gamelloti   47, 50–1
Gareth   *see* Gariet
Gariet   17, 25
Gaul   *see* Gaules
Gaules (kingdom)   2, 6–7, 12, 51, 62, 64, 79   *see also* Bioberis, Fer(r)amonte, Galeoto lo Bruno, G(u)overnal(l)e, Lamorato
Gawain   *see* G(u)alvagno
Genev(e)ra (queen)   25, 50, 63, 74, 79, 90, 95
Ghedin   41–2
Ghedis / Guedis (betrayer of Tristan)   75, 82, 84
Gioni (king)   91
Giossepe   *see* Josep
God   *see* Dio
Gospels, Holy   *see* Sancti Evvangeli
Governal   *see* G(u)overnale
Grail, Holy   *see* Sacradalle
Gran Bretagnia   92
Gray   *see* Granor
Granor   82
Great Britain   *see* Gran Bretagnia
G(u)alvagno   25, 32, 50
Guenevere   *see* Genev(e)ra
G(u)overnal(l)e   2–4, 6–10, 12, 14, 18–21, 34, 39, 42–5, 50, 53, 57, 61–2, 65, 72, 74, 82

Index

Harpin of the Narrow Mountains *see* Arpano de le Strette Montane
hawking 57
Hector of the Fens *see* Astor da (de) Mare
horses 2, 4, 6, 12–13, 17, 19, passim
Hundred Knights, King of *see* Cento Chavalieri, re de
hunting 2, 4, 15, 57

Idio / Ydio *see* Dio
inscriptions 3, 91
insignia, devices, armor colors 25, 28, 30–1, 52, 62 *see also* Knight of the Two Swords, split shield
Ireland *see* Landa
Irlanda *see* Landa
Island of Giants *see* Issola de (li) Giganti
Island without Adventure *see* Issola sensa Ventura
Issola de (li) Giganti 54, 58–9, 61–4
Issola sensa Ventura 17

Josep / Josseppe Abaçimaçia 55
Joseph of Arimathaea *see* Josep
jousting 7, 47, 72, 76–7

Kay the Seneschal *see* Chiel(l)o
Knight of the Two Swords *see* Palamides

Lambegues *see* Lambigues
Lambigues / Lanbigue(s) / Lanbique / Lanbis / Lanbugues 38–41
Lamorat *see* Lamorato
Lamorato / Lamorado / Lamoralto 75–9, 81
Lancelot of the Lake *see* Lancelot(t)o
Lancelot(t)o / Lançeloto / Lançoloto del Lac 3, 25, 44, 46, 48, 50–1, 54, 56, 59, 61–3, 89, 91, 94–5
Landa (Ireland) 7–8, 16, 21, 24, 27, 30–1, 33, 44–5, 48, 50, 52, 59, 65–6, 91 *see also* Anguin, L'Amoroldo, Ys(s)ota la Bronda

Languis (king) 21–2, 24–5, 27–31, 34, 44–5, 48, 50–2, 65 *see also* Ireland
Leonello 51
Leones / Leonis (kingdom) 2, 4, 6, 16–17, 94
letters 12–14, 63, 65, 84
Lionel *see* Leonello
Lo(n)gres / Long(r)ues / Longoes (kingdom) 7, 25, 31, 46–7, 60–1, 63, 79–80
Lontana Yssola / Lontana Is(s)ola / Lontane Issole / Lontane Payse 56, 58, 60–1, 63, 91
love potion 53

magical objects *see* drinking horn, love potion, split shield
Malvagia (Malastrugua) Damissella 75, 82
Marcho di Cornavalia (king) 10, 14–15, 16–20, 33–43, 45–6, 52–3, 59, 61–2, 65–6, 68–9, 74–7, 79–84, 86–9, 91
Maria (Mother of God) 1, 2, 4, 66–7
Mark *see* Marcho
Mary *see* Maria
Meliadus (king) 2–5, 10, 16–17, 52
Merlin *see* Merlino
Merlino (prophet) 2–3
messages, messengers 7, 12, 14, 35, 37–8, 58, 60, 65, 74, 76, 79, 84 *see also* letters
Milanda *see* Landa
monastery 67, 71
Morgan the Fay *see* Fada Morguana
Morholt, The *see* L'Amor(r)ol(l)do
music 19, 21, 86, 94

Naugales (kingdom) 58
Nerlantes *see* Nirlantes
Nirlantes 78
North Wales *see* Naugales

O(n)g(u)ana / Onghana (queen of) 75
Oregho 92

Orkney see O(n)g(u)ana

Palamides 25–9, 31–2, 44, 67–8, 70–4, 92, 94
pavilions 40–2, 46–8, 50, 52, 69, 75–7
Pelignoro see Pellinoro
Pelis (king) 90
Pelles see Pelis
Pellinor see Pellinoro
Pellinoro (king) 75
physicians 18, 39, 62, 86 see also Ys(s)ota la Bronda, skill as healer
poison 4, 17, 22, 86
Presia (city) 5

queen of Ireland (Yseut's mother) 33–4, 52–3

Round Table see Taula Retonda

Sacradalle / Sagradale 25, 94
Sacremor / Sagremor (Tristan's friend) 89, 92–4
sailors see seamen
Sancti Evvangeli 9, 49
Sansognia 91
Saromus see Sigris
Savia Donçella 2
Saxony see Sansognia
Sc(h)orçia / Scorcia, re de 24–5, 28–9, 31, 44
Scotland see Schorçia
seal, royal 84
seamen 46, 54, 59, 62
Segris see Sigris
Senelas see Serialbe
Serialbe 92
ships 16–17, 19–21, 34, 45–6, 48, 52–4, 58–60, 62
Sigris 25, 82
Sinogres (Tristan's friend) 88
split shield 50
squires 6, 12, 14, 24–5, 30–1, 34–5, 37, 39, 53, 59, 62, 65, 72, 84
swords 7, 10, 12, 17, 25, 33–4, 38, 52, 54, 56, 62, 73, 77, 79, 82–3, 89, 91, 93

Taula Retonda / Retonta 28, 43, 47, 89, 94
Taulas the Great see Taulas lo Grande
Taulas lo Grande 92
tempests 20, 46, 54
Thornwater, Damsel of see A(u)qua de l'Espina, Damaysella de
Tintagel see Titolin
Titolin (castle) 12, 14, 16, 18–19, 34, 45, 65, 67, 74, 83–4, 91
tribute of ten years 16–17
Tristan see Tristano
Trisstaino see Tristano
Tristano di Leonis,
  birth of 1, 2
  name 2, 3
  entrusted to Governal 3
  childhood and youth 4, 7, 15
  physical beauty 4, 7, 14, 17, 23, 37
  one of best knights 35, 44, 63, 90
  compared to Lancelot 3, 54, 63
  stepmother's hatred 4, 6
  avenges father's death 5
  flees to Gaul with Governal 6
  fool's prophecy 7
  mocked by the Morholt 7
  loved by Belide 8–10, 12–13
  letter and gifts from Belide 12–13, 17
  to Cornwall 10–11, 14
  combat with the Morholt 16–17
  poisoned wound 17–19
  leaves Cornwall 20–1
  cured by Yseut 22–3
  participates in tournament 24–5, 27–33
  queen discovers splintered sword 33–4
  returns to Cornwall 36, 65
  assignation with Damsel of Thornwater 37–40, 42
  fights Blanor 43–4
  sent to Ireland for Yseut 45–6
  champions Anguin against Blanor 48–9, 51–2
  meets damsel with split shield 50

Index

defeats Breus   50
returns to Cornwall with
    Yseut   52–3
plays chess with Yseut   53, 75
drinks love potion   53
on Island of Giants   54–8
combat with Galehot   59–62
lover of Yseut   66, 74–5, 79, 82
rescues Yseut from
    Palamides   72–4
jousts with Lamorat   77, 81
Mark's enemy   83–4
mortally wounded by Mark   86
dying of wound   87–9
visited by Mark   88
visited by Yseut   88
says farewells   89
dies with Yseut   90
mourned   91, 93–5
great love remembered   91
rich sepulchre   91
arms sent to Camelot   89, 93–4

Verlanda   see Landa

wet nurses   3–4
Wicked Damsel   see Malvagia
    Damissella
Wise Damsel   see Savia Donçella

wounds   17–18, 21–3, 39, 42, 61–2,
    64, 73–5, 82, 86, 89

Yseut   see Ys(s)ota la Bronda
Ys(s)ota la Bronda (Bionda) (daughter
    of Languis)   30, 63, 76–7, 84–5
great beauty   22, 27, 29, 37, 45,
    54, 56, 65, 75, 90
skill as healer   22–3, 33
loved by Palamides   27
betrothed to Mark   52
sails to Cornwall   53, 62, 65
on Island of Giants   54, 56–8, 61
watches Tristan in combats   56,
    62, 73–4
plays chess with Tristan   53, 75
drinks love potion   53
wedding night deception   65
orders Brangain's death   66,
    69–70
Tristan's nocturnal visits   75, 82
enchanted drinking horn   80
sings   86
despair at Tristan's wound   87
visits dying Tristan   88–9
dies with Tristan   90
mourned   91
great love remembered   91
rich sepulchre   91

ARTHURIAN ARCHIVES
ISSN 1463–6670

General Editor: Norris J. Lacy

ALREADY PUBLISHED

I, II. EARLY FRENCH TRISTAN POEMS
Edited by Norris J. Lacy

III. NORSE ROMANCE I: THE TRISTAN LEGEND
Edited by Marianne E. Kalinke

IV. NORSE ROMANCE II: THE KNIGHTS OF THE ROUND TABLE
Edited by Marianne E. Kalinke

V. NORSE ROMANCE III: *HÆRRA IVAN*
Edited by Marianne E. Kalinke, Henrik Williams and Karin Palmgren

VI. DUTCH ROMANCES I: *ROMAN VAN WALEWEIN*
Edited by David F. Johnson and Geert H.M. Claassens

VII. DUTCH ROMANCES II: *FERGUUT*
Edited by David F. Johnson and Geert H.M. Claassens

VIII. ITALIAN LITERATURE I: *TRISTANO PANCIATICHIANO*
Edited by Gloria Allaire

IX. GERMAN ROMANCE I: *DANIEL VON DEM BLÜHENDEN TAL*
DER STRICKER
Edited by Michael Resler

X. DUTCH ROMANCES III: FIVE INTERPOLATED
ROMANCES FROM THE *LANCELOT COMPILATION*
Edited by David F. Johnson and Geert H.M. Claassens

XI. LATIN ARTHURIAN LITERATURE
Edited by Mildred Leake Day

XII. ITALIAN LITERATURE II: *TRISTANO RICCARDIANO*
Edited by F. Regina Psaki

XIII. FRENCH ARTHURIAN ROMANCE III: *LE CHEVALIER AS DEUS ESPEES*
Edited by Paul Vincent Rockwell

XIV. FRENCH ARTHURIAN LITERATURE IV:
ELEVEN OLD FRENCH NARRATIVE LAYS
Edited by Glyn S. Burgess and Leslie C. Brook

XV. GERMAN ROMANCE II: *GAURIEL VON MUNTABEL*
Konrad von Stoffeln
Edited by Siegfried Christoph

XVI. GERMAN ROMANCE III: *IWEIN*, OR *THE KNIGHT WITH THE LION*
Hartmann von Aue
Edited by Cyril Edwards

XVII. GERMAN ROMANCE IV: *LANZELET*
Ulrich von Zatzikhoven
Edited and translated by Kathleen J. Meyer

XVIII. FRENCH ARTHURIAN LITERATURE V: THE LAY OF *MANTEL*
Edited by Glyn S. Burgess and Leslie C. Brook

XIX. GERMAN ROMANCE V: *EREC*
Hartmann von Aue
Edited and translated by Cyril Edwards

XX. ITALIAN LITERATURE III: *IL TRISTANO CORSINIANO*
Edited and translated by Gloria Allaire

XXI. GERMAN ROMANCE VI: *WIGAMUR*
Edited and translated by Joseph M. Sullivan

XXII. GERMAN ROMANCE VII: ULRICH FUETRER, *IBAN*
Edited and translated by Joseph M. Sullivan

Printed and bound by CPI Group (UK) Ltd, Croydon, CR0 4YY